D1167471

Peace and Security in the Asia Pacific Region

Peace and Security in the Asia Pacific Region

Post-Cold War Problems and Prospects

Edited by Kevin Clements
Secretary General
Asia Pacific Peace Research Association

United Nations University Press   The Dunmore Press

©1992 Kevin P. Clements
©1992 The Dunmore Press Limited
©1992 The United Nations University for the English edition
throughout the world except New Zealand and Australia

First Published in 1993
by
The United Nations University Press
The United Nations University
53-70, Jingumae 5-chome
Shibuya-ku, Tokyo 150
Japan

and

The Dunmore Press Limited
P.O.Box 5115
Palmertson North
New Zealand

Australian Supplier:
Nyroca Press
P.O. Box 90, Hawksburn
Victoria 3142

ISBN 086469 172 6

Text: New Century Schoolbook 10/12
Page Layout: Penny May
Printer: Brebner Print, Napier

Copyright. No part of this book may be reproduced in any manner
whatsoever without written permission except in the case of brief
quotations embodied in critical articles and reviews.

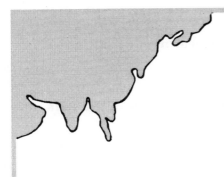

Contents

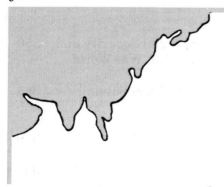

Acknowledgements

This book and the conference at which these papers were originally presented would not have been possible without the generous financial support of the John D. and Catherine T. MacArthur Foundation, the Indian Ocean Centre for Peace Studies, Westcroft Trust, the Public Advisory Committee on Disarmament and Arms Control (PACDAC), the Religious Society of Friends (Quakers), UNESCO, and the Sociology Department of the University of Canterbury. To all these organisations heartfelt thanks.

Leslie Livingston, APPRA Treasurer/Administrator has worked hard deciphering handwritten editorial comments, re-typing the edited manuscript in preparation for publication and helping compile the index. I thank her profusely for her commitment, enthusiasm, and dedication to this book.

Finally, I owe a special thanks to the editorial staff of the Dunmore Press, Murray Gatenby and Sharmian Firth who have been responsible for the final editing prior to publication.

Kevin P. Clements

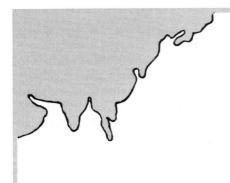

Introduction

Kevin P. Clements

The end of the Cold War has generated an unprecedented opportunity for new thinking about ways of resolving current economic, social and political problems and for thinking about what lies beyond the nation state. While there is little likelihood of the nation state losing its dominant role in international relations in the immediate future, there are many indications that its role is being dramatically modified by externally generated challenges. These external developments are challenging arbitrary and authoritarian conceptions of sovereignty based on an exclusive monopoly of force and coercion within a specific national territory.

There are dual processes at work here. On the one hand, despite the large number of secessionist movements aimed at establishing new independent nations, most states and peoples now acknowledge that there is no unilateral national action capable of reversing destruction of the biosphere, pre-empting or resolving international resource conflicts, ending global militarisation, gross violations of human rights, underdevelopment, or unfair international trading practices. The imposition of democratic norms on nations is a contradiction in terms and there is relatively little that individual nations can do on their own to

combat epidemic diseases, drug trafficking, and the homogenisa-
tion of global culture. There are, in other words, definite limits to
the power and significance of the modern nation state.

On the other hand, there is a very rapid expansion of official and
unofficial trans-national relationships which are transforming the
global order in both positive and negative ways. The world is no
longer as 'anarchic' as many international relations theorists used
to assert. On the contrary, most contemporary anarchy is occurring
within nation states rather than between them, and internationally there is a growing sense of order rather than disorder as
nations combine to meet common challenges. For example, there
are nearly 70,000 treaties binding nations in cooperative responses
to common problems.[1]

Similarly, there has been a dramatic increase in the number of
regional institutions that have developed over the past twenty years.
This regional activity has been accompanied by a more robust globalism as well. Since 1988, for example, the United Nations has
assumed a central role in world affairs which few imagined it would
ever have when it was paralysed by the Cold War. The United
Nations was responsible for 13 peace-keeping operations between
1947 and 1988 and has been involved in the same number in the last
four years. Demands on the United Nations are currently outstrip-
ping its ability to meet them. It is involved in the post-war recon-
struction/reconstitution of the state in El Salvador, and Cambodia,
and is being asked to resolve a wide variety of conflicts that were
unimagined by the founders of the United Nations.

Underlying and accompanying the development of these regional and global institutions has been a dramatic globalisation of
economic activity, with trans-national companies now dominat-
ing the world's major financial, manufacturing and commodity
sectors. Insofar as these generate employment, reduce the gap
between rich and poor, and facilitate the efficient sustainable
consumption of global resources, these developments must be considered positive. If they generate the opposite, then they must be
identified as a more problematic global tendency.

In addition to these developments there has been a radical expansion of regional and global non-governmental citizens' organisations. Boulding notes that in 1909 there were 176 international non-

governmental organisations, now there are a total of 18,000, about 25 per cent of which are 'universal' or global in scope and 74 per cent of which are regional (European, Latin American and Asian). These regional organisations often combine around specific issues when they want to make a specific global or national point.[2]

All these developments signify that some of the most dynamic economic, social and cultural activity is occurring in the spaces between nations, in the sub-regions and regions, and in the articulation of new conceptions of global interest and citizenship.

These developments were only dimly envisioned at the end of the second world war. The founders of the UN, for example, assumed the continued primacy and sovereignty of the nation state and only a limited transference of national power to international organisations. International relations theorists applied Adam Smith's 'invisible hand' metaphor to the nation state and assumed that states rationally pursuing their own national self- interest would (with a little fine tuning) eventually serve the interests of the whole globe. This rather naive conception of how to generate international well-being is well and truly challenged now by the intractable nature of most of the problems currently confronting the world. All states, the enlightened as well as the unenlightened, have discovered the limits of state power when confronted by puzzles and dilemmas that can only be unravelled through a systematic analysis of the interplay between external markets, nation states, and diverse cultures. Insofar as the answers to these problems are cooperative and trans-national, they have to be underwritten or guaranteed by regional and global institutions that state parties and peoples trust.

Thinking regionally means focusing on the diverse institutional/state mechanisms fostering regional identity and understanding the regional causes of and solutions for many national problems. Thinking globally means thinking about the ways in which the problems of both states and regions have global origins and demand global solutions. The distinctions between these levels of analysis are always somewhat artificial but they are heuristically important for problem solving since there is no point in applying regionalist or global solutions if a local one will do and vice versa.

One further complication is that the interests of states, markets and peoples do not necessarily coincide and what serves one set of interests may not serve another. Thus it is important to have some clear criteria for determining whether state centric, national, regional and global activities serve popular or élite interests primarily. Just as nation states are considered derelict in their duty if they do not serve all citizens equally – the weak as well as the strong – so too it could be argued that regional and global institutions which do not benefit all states and peoples equally are using internationalist rhetoric to advance essentially sectional élite interests. If the major outcome of regionalism and globalism is a perpetuation of the power of the strongest against the weakest - the élites against the mass of the people, then these processes must be adjudged defective.

The major criteria, therefore, for determining whether or not regionalism and globalism is positive and progressive is whether these processes result in all states having an equal voice (irrespective of their power), equal entitlements to safety, peace and security and equal access to the rights and privileges embodied in the Charters of the regional and global associations that govern their behaviour. Nothing will kill regional or global initiatives faster than selective rather than universal application of principles, especially when this selective application results in the perpetuation of international inequality. In the final analysis, however, the ultimate criteria for determining whether or not regional and global processes are positive or negative is whether or not they serve the interests of the weakest and the poorest in all countries or whether they are making their already bad condition worse. Multi-lateralism, as an organising principle (which is what regionalism and globalism is all about), is distinguished by three properties, 'indivisibility, generalised principles of conduct and diffuse reciprocity'.[3] Thus, these processes are exactly the opposite of anarchy; they represent an effort to develop norms and procedures for ensuring smooth and optimally just and peaceful relations between nations and peoples.

This book is concerned with analysing some of these questions in the context of the Asia Pacific region. In particular it identifies some of the major sources of conflict and violence (most of which seem to originate locally rather than regionally), and how these pose challenges to peace. It considers how these inter-state threats (see the Malik chapter), ethnic and sexist threats (see the chapters by Lawson and Kelkar) and human rights abuses (see the Robie chapter) challenge different organising principles. It then considers some conventional military/security responses and how they contradict the regional and common interest. It then concludes with some alternative ways of thinking about security and working towards the non-violent resolution of conflict. It is proposed in a number of chapters throughout the book that this last enterprise also involves a radical rethinking of traditional concepts of defence and security to include the environment, the satisfaction of basic human needs and confidence building within a common security framework. This is the task confronting peace researchers and policy makers in the region over the next ten years.

The first problem is how to conceptualise the region (i.e. which nations to include and which to exclude), and the second relates to a delineation of the role and significance of regional institutions in the co-ordination of transactions and relations between and within nations in the region. While there are no institutions in the Asia Pacific area to parallel those of the European Community (the quintessential model of regionalism) there is equally no doubt that arrangements such as the North American Free Trade Association (NAFTA), the Association of South East Asian Nations (ASEAN), the South Pacific Forum, the Asia Pacific Economic Cooperation Council (APEC) and so forth, are beginning to transform traditional conceptions of economic and political governance in the region and provide transitional steps beyond the nation state. These regional institutions are accustoming states and peoples to processes of trans-national dialogue and cooperative problem solving which is an important step towards global problem solving. Hopefully this trans-national process will also result in altered approaches to national problem solving as well.

Boundary Definition

For the purposes of this book the Asia Pacific region refers to all those nations and societies oriented towards or bordering the Pacific ocean (with the exception of Latin America) as well as South Asia (see chapters by Kelkar and Malik). There are cultural, geographical, economic and political reasons for this definition of the region. South Asia has made and continues to make a vital cultural contribution to those countries bordering the Asian section of the Pacific rim. Canada, the United States and Russia are significant economic and political actors in the region and have large and growing Asian populations. While they remain predominantly Atlanticist in their orientation they are beginning to acknowledge that their national destiny is tied to Asia as well as Europe.

Similarly, the Australian and New Zealand governments want to be acknowledged as fully fledged members of the Asia Pacific region. While Australia has a more developed Asian consciousness than New Zealand there is a general Australasian desire not to be treated as 'cultural misfits' in Asia and to ensure more consistency between geographical location, cultural preference and Asian awareness.

A former Australian Prime Minister, Gough Whitlam, argued in the 1970s that Australians should think of themselves as 'Euro-Asians' if they were to secure a place in the economic and political future of the region. While there remains an enormous gulf between this aspiration and the reality, there are powerful forces tying the Australian and New Zealand economies into Asia and there is a strong conviction in Australia and New Zealand that the future of both countries lies in the Asia Pacific region even though this sometimes generates anxiety about the compatibility of the Australasian and Asian cultural and political systems.

The Asia Pacific region, therefore, really consists of four distinct sub-regions. (1) The North Pacific comprising China, Japan, North and South Korea, Hong Kong and Taiwan – it is this sub-region which is of most interest to the United States, Canada and the Commonwealth of Independent States (CIS). (2) South East Asia which includes the six ASEAN nations, Indo-China and Burma. (3) The South West Pacific which consists of Australia, New Zealand, Papua New Guinea and the diverse states and territories of Micronesia, Melanesia and Polynesia. (4) South Asia – India, Bangladesh and Sri Lanka.

Demography

Excluding Russia, the Americas and South Asia, the Asia Pacific region more narrowly defined is still vast and complex. China,

Japan and Korea, for example, have a combined population of well over a billion. Southeast Asia and the Southwest Pacific have a combined population of over 442 million divisible into 40 different ethnic and cultural groupings, and 32 states and territories. The social, demographic and socio-political mix of the Asia Pacific region is mind boggling. With the exception of Burma, Mongolia and Laos the one common factor linking these disparate states and peoples is the Pacific Ocean – the world's water hemisphere. Communications and transport are profoundly conditioned by this ocean and many security analysts consider maritime rather than border disputes the most likely source of international conflict in the future. (See the chapters by Pugh, Bateman and Richards)

Since over half the world's population lives in the Asia Pacific area it is important to determine whether or not it is possible to move towards new ways of organising international relations in the region. If Asian states and peoples can make significant progress towards regular multilateral discussions, the non-violent resolution of dispute, democratisation, de-nuclearisation, demilitarisation, sustainable development, protection of the environment and human rights, this would provide an important model of trans-national cooperative problem solving for other regions and the world as a whole. An inability to move in this direction may result in a resurgence of nationalist and ethno-nationalist concerns that may impede movement towards regional and global community. Thus what happens in the Asia Pacific region is likely to have an important impact on the future of the world as a whole. This is why so much rests on whether it is possible to generate a genuine 'security community'[4] in such a disparate and diverse region.

Short and Long-Term Prospects

So what are the short and long term prospects for the emergence of an Asia Pacific economic and political community?

Unlike Europe – where the differences between the foundation states of the European Economic Community (EEC) were slight, where there is a common Judeo-Christian culture, and close geographic proximity – the differences between nations and peoples within the Asia Pacific region are considerable and the Pacific ocean provides tenuous geographic connections for many of the smaller entities. Economically, the region spans the most technologically advanced to the most underdeveloped systems. Politically the spectrum is equally wide. There are Westminister-style democracies, guided democracies, traditional autocracies, military juntas and three remnant communist regimes. Socially, there are peasant-based rural societies alongside advanced industrial urban societies. There is no immediate prospect of welding these disparate systems into a coherent community, yet the evidence suggests that the economic and political foundations for such a community are evolving.

In the first place, despite high levels of intra-regional trade, the Asia Pacific region is a significant exporter and accounts for 40 per cent of the rest of the world's imports. Economic growth rates have slowed a little in 1991 but remain higher than in most other parts of the world. The region is clearly positioning itself to become the biggest trading block in the world.

In 1990, for example, the total GDP/GNP of the North American Free Trade Association (NAFTA) was US$5,846 billion, Western Europe was US$5,354 billion and East Asia stood at US$3,916 billion, 66 per cent the size of NAFTA or 73 per cent that of Western Europe.[5] Asian commentators predict that there is every possibility that East Asia will overtake NAFTA before the year 2020 and Western Europe before 2010.[6] It is statistics such as these which generate concern about the division of the world into three highly competitive regions (Europe, North America, Asia Pacific) which will marginalise Africa, Latin America, South Asia and the non-oil producing countries of the Middle East thereby perpetuating what some call a 'global apartheid'.[7]

Although there is some unwillingness to develop free trade arrangements for the region as a whole (because of a desire for global liberalisation), there are significant moves in this direction within each of the sub-regions and if the 1992 GATT round fails it is highly likely that pressures will increase for the development of an Asian trading block with regional preference schemes. In any event, economics is in command throughout the region with the result that political and ideological differences are taking second place to economic development and interdependence.

The political implications of this economic interdependence are mixed. On the one hand it is difficult to maintain closed authoritarian systems while moving towards open market economies, so economic pressures are leading generally in the direction of pluralism and democracy. On the other hand while the international costs of negative political activity (e.g. political repression, bellicosity, corruption) are increasing, many Asian decision makers still sustain the illusion that good business requires strong and autocratic government. This generates slightly ambiguous signals about the role and purpose of government within the region. Increasingly (e.g. in Burma, Thailand, Indonesia, Malaysia and China) the argument for a strong (authoritarian and sometimes autocratic) state is coupled with a rejection of the socio-cultural decadence of the 'West' and by extension conceptions of individual human rights and liberties. Interestingly, Bruce Russett has hypothesised that minor and major powers, but especially major powers, are more likely to be involved in disputes and conflicts after increased levels of militarisation such as is occurring in the Asia Pacific region. But he also has some interesting theories concerning the connections between economic growth and dispute involvement. Basically he suggests that in democratically governed states dispute involvement and conflict tends to follow declines in per capita income with a two year time lag. In non-democratic states (most of those in the Asia Pacific region), involvement in international conflict and dispute tends to follow periods of economic advancement.[8] If Russett's hypothesis is correct then the Asia Pacific region, while currently peaceful, may become rather unpeaceful in the future. The authoritarian political and ideological preferences sometimes play themselves out with tragic consequences, (e.g. the recent violent suppression of pro-democracy movements in China, Burma and Thailand and the 1991 Indonesian massacre of demonstrators in East Timor). While Western governments have expressed outrage at such events, by and large their unaccustomed economic dependence on the Asia Pacific region means that these protests have been muted by the more compelling need to set aside both national and ideological differences in favour of economic growth and development. (See the chapter by King in relation to Papua New Guinea and Australia.)

Thus, although there are profound differences between Euro-Asia and Asian Asia on human rights questions (as the Australian government discovered when it tried to raise such questions with the Malaysian and Indonesian governments), the desire to deepen and consolidate economic relations stimulates a strong sense of political pragmatism, exploited by Asian states with a 'harder' more authoritarian conception of sovereignty.

The future development of institutions such as the Asia Pacific Economic Cooperation Council (APEC), for example, will not be affected much by political differences but more by external developments. If the GATT round fails for example, and there is a move towards regional protectionism, it is highly probable that APEC will become the vehicle for the development of an Asia Pacific trading block. If the GATT round is successful, however, it is more likely that existing sub-regional economic arrangements (such as Closer Economic Relations between Australia and New Zealand, ASEAN, etc.) will continue with more incremental moves towards regional trade harmonisation etc.

The Asia Pacific region provides a good illustration of the way in which economic rather than military power is becoming the critical determinant of political influence. The economic dynamism of the region is cited as a major justification for giving privilege to Asian political processes and culture in opposition to those of the West. This economic buoyancy (which sometimes verges on triumphalism) is being used as a justification for Asian nations playing a more active political role in regional and global arenas. While hegemonic pretensions are muted there is a clear jostling for leadership within the sub-regions and the region as a whole. It is a matter of some political importance, therefore, to determine which nations are 'core' and which 'peripheral' to the key economic, political and security discussions. To some extent, the answer to this hinges on whether or not the 'core' is defined primarily in economic or political terms. Economically, there is no doubt that Japan is the leading nation, but politically and militarily there are contenders. Structurally, each sub-region is dominated by certain core nations – Australia and New Zealand in the South West Pacific, ASEAN in South East Asia, and Japan, Taiwan and South Korea in the North Pacific. But the ways in which these nations unite/divide around different issue areas determines which will guide the region as a whole. (The United States, for example, is very keen to maintain the integrity of the Japan-United States security alliance not just to constrain Japan in the region but to ensure that it is not excluded from significant economic and political discussions.) It is in recognition of this that countries such as Malaysia (which have sub-regional leadership aspirations) proposed the East Asian Economic Caucus (EAEC). This proposal is an effort to develop a distinctive Asian-Asian caucus to harmonise and co-ordinate Asian economic activity under Japanese leadership. It would exclude North America and Australasia and, understandably, has generated some concern in Ottawa, Washington, Canberra and Wellington.

As long as each nation (irrespective of natural resource or population endowment) sees itself as more or less equal and willing to act cooperatively – which is the case within ASEAN – then sub-regional harmonisation of domestic and external policies works well. When the broader region is contemplated, however, especially in relation to the North Pacific, then much more vexed questions of political and economic leadership emerge.

This is one of the negative consequences of moving beyond a bipolar world. There are few alternative models to instruct nations on how to handle the transition from bipolarity to more multilateral arrangements. In the absence of such alternatives there is a reassertion of balance-of-power models which stress national competitiveness and leadership rather than a rigorous quest for more cooperative relations. Japan, China and the United States, for example, fall into this category. None of these states is preoccupied with the development of non-hegemonic models and all see themselves as leadership contenders in the Asia Pacific region. Indeed, many of their current actions tend to confirm the classical insight of Thucydides, that the strong do as they will while the weak do as they must.

Japan is casting around for a non-threatening political role commensurate with its economic strength but many sceptical commentators fear that Japanese decision makers might not be able to resist the domestic and external pressures to become a regional military superpower as well as the key economic player.[9] (See the chapter by Robinson.) China (see the chapter by Sichor) wishes to be seen as a major regional player and is positioning itself for military dominance in the South China Sea, and the United States still considers itself as a 'balancing wheel' for the whole region.[10]

The economic and political jostling between these different nations will undoubtedly have a significant impact on the security architecture in the region and more importantly on the prospects for short and long-term stable peace. If there is an imposition of now outmoded 'big power' politics on the region without any sensitivity to the more delicate links that are emerging between the smallest and largest entities, then it is probable that the region will be subject to a variety of regional and global hegemons seeking to impose their will on smaller powers. If there is a willingness to maintain momentum in favour of deepened economic integration however, it might be possible to moderate 'big power' demands in order to advance the functional relationships. If some parallel political and security institutions could be developed then it is possible that the region may fulfil its double promise of becoming the motor for the world economy in the 21st century while developing institutions to ensure the pre-emption of violent conflict in the future.

This task involves a switch from deterrent to problem oriented thinking (see the chapter by Burton) but it also requires a specific strengthening and expansion of existing institutions in order to deepen cooperative problem solving.

Thus far, the most successful institutional mechanism for harmonisation of regional interests and providing some counterweight to the big powers inside and outside the region is ASEAN. It has now acquired 25 years experience in building peace and stability in intra-regional relations. Its origins lay in a desire to prevent disputes such as the armed conflict between Indonesia and Malaysia (Konfrontasi) from erupting again and in laying down procedures for conflict management, control and resolution (enshrined in the 1976 Treaty of Amity and Cooperation).[11] These developments have been accompanied by efforts to harmonise economic policies and to develop a variety of bilateral/multilateral defence and security arrangements to reinforce the broader processes. These arrangements have been focused internally as well as externally but have not precluded extensive military and political involvement with states from outside the region (Thailand, Singapore, Malaysia and the Philippines, for example, have all maintained close connections with the United States and with Britain), while their support for ASEAN has deepened.

Regional institution building, therefore, need not be exclusive; it can be and normally is complemented by a variety of other relations. It also does not preclude the development of political and military preferences which stand in tension with some national/ bilateral policy positions. The promulgation of a Zone of Peace Freedom and Neutrality (ZOPFAN), for example, contradicts many national policies but represents an aspiration for regional neutralisation, denuclearisation and a withdrawal of all foreign military bases.

Perhaps the most useful development to flow out of ASEAN, however, is the post-ministerial meeting which facilitates political and security dialogues between the six member states, and Australia, New Zealand, Canada, the United States, China, Japan and Korea. This procedure now enables ASEAN nations to engage in dialogue with much larger powers on more or less equal terms to the mutual benefit of all groups. This post-ministerial meeting is an event which states look forward to each year as an opportunity to review what has happened in the region and to preview the future. It enables leaders and sectoral groups to air their regional concerns and to harmonise responses to common problems. Because the Treaty of Amity rigidly upholds the principle of non-interference, however, many of the most destabilising and violent internal conflicts are not placed on the agenda. Since internal rather than external violence is the most pressing, it suggests that there may be a need to reconsider the principle as proposed by the Secretary General of the United Nations since its rigid application often means that groups striving for recognition of their rights, or identity, are rendered voiceless in the very fora that might be able to help them. Modern communications make it exceedingly difficult for these so-called internal conflicts to remain that, and where these conflicts involve gross violations of human rights they generate regional tension and potential conflict as well. Whatever else may be said about them, they remain a major challenge to the more pluralistic security communities that are being developed and if they persist will eventually pose problems to regional and global institutions – as the Balkans tragedy vividly demonstrates.

While ASEAN is arguably the most important regional institution, the Pacific Economic Cooperation Conference (PECC) and

(APEC) are also important regional fora for ensuring that the political aspirations of the larger powers are mediated within a regional framework. None of these bodies has the power to directly determine outcomes for the larger powers. What they can do, however, is establish a regional normative framework within which to judge economic and political behaviour, and this is what they are doing. This occurs through the development of common codes of conduct, labour practices etc. and goes some way towards equalising both economic and political bargaining relations between small and larger powers.

The Prospects for a Common Security Regime in Asia

The dominant military power in the region remains the United States and while it is reducing its direct military involvement in Southeast Asia and in the North Pacific it does not wish to abandon its central military role since there is a perception in Washington that American economic influence is diminishing. The United States, therefore, along with Japan, is extremely reluctant to extend the principles facilitating economic integration to the military security realm in the Asia Pacific.

Both Japan and the United States continue, therefore, to negotiate military and security issues on a bilateral basis with other countries in the region and they have positively resisted efforts to establish regional/multilateral institutions which might circumscribe their behaviour. This is one of the major reasons why Japan and the United States remain so averse to the idea of developing a regional security framework equivalent to the CSCE framework in Europe. (See the chapter by Mason.) While the big powers, however, wish to discourage the emergence of a body equivalent to the Conference on Security and Cooperation in Europe (CSCE), it is in the interests of the small and medium-sized powers to move in the other direction to stimulate the development of 'habits of dialogue' and institutions within which both internal and external threats to peace (both positive and negative) can be addressed.

Intermediate powers (e.g. Australia and New Zealand at the foundation of the United Nations) have always been firm advocates of multilateral relationships since it is easier to minimise the impact of asymmetrical relations in the company of others than it is alone or in grossly unequal bilateral relations. The 'diffuse reciprocity' that flows from such multilateral relationships is a much better guarantee of incremental benefits through time than are the possible windfalls from single bilateral deals.

The Asia Pacific region is a rather complex mix in relation to peace and security issues. On the one hand, economic integration reduces the risk of violent international conflict considerably. On the other, levels of military expenditure, particularly in the North Pacific but also in South East Asia are high and are expanding in Japan, China and the two Koreas. Japan is now the third largest military spender in the world.[12]

These high levels of domestic military expenditure within the North Pacific in particular are resulting in a very active arms trade in and out of the region, with China being the most vigorous exporter of weapons followed by North and South Korea, Taiwan and Singapore. China supplies over 80 per cent of Burma's military equipment, for example, and it has dispatched missile technology to a large number of other nations as well.

Despite recent moves towards global denuclearisation, China remains committed to its nuclear option until the other nuclear powers drastically reduce their arsenals. China (in opposition to the testing moratoria of Russia, and France and a positive Senate vote from the United States) provocatively exploded a one megaton bomb in a 1992 underground test. While France has suspended its nuclear testing programme in the South Pacific in 1992 it has indicated that it will resume it if other nuclear testing states do not follow suit. If this happened it would reactivate a sub-regional irritant which has plagued Southwest Pacific relations since 1966.[13] There are also strong regional concerns about whether or not North Korea wishes to pursue a nuclear option. While there are no other regional powers that wish to go nuclear, Japan certainly has the means for doing so if it wishes to and there are other countries that are beginning to acquire the necessary nuclear capability for developing nuclear weapons sometime in the future. (See the chapter by Skubik.)

The reluctance of Japan and the United States to contemplate discussions about regional denuclearisation, arms control and disarmament, has meant that different nations and sub-regions have taken their own initiatives, e.g. New Zealand and Vanuatu

declared themselves unequivocally nuclear free, and at the instigation of Australia and New Zealand the Treaty of Raratonga
(August 6, 1985) established a Nuclear Weapon Free Zone in the
South Pacific which, when combined with the Latin American
nuclear free zone brought into existence by the Treaty of Tlatelolco,
ensures that a good proportion of the Southern hemisphere is
nominally nuclear free. (See the chapter by Richards.)

Similarly, the suggestion of ASEAN for a Zone of Peace Freedom
and Neutrality in South East Asia would, if implemented, result in
this becoming a nuclear free area as well. It is only in the North
Pacific that there is a widespread reluctance to contemplate sub-
regional denuclearisation but this may also turn out to be temporary
when there is an acknowledgement of the military uselessness of
nuclear weapons in generating political influence within the region.

In relation to broader questions of demilitarisation, and reduced military expenditure, there is a rather bizarre belief that
economic prosperity should manifest itself in the purchase of new
military technology. This has precipitated a round of military modernisation in the region which bears little or no connection to
defence needs or strategic circumstance. There is little national or
regional pressure for this conventional military expenditure to
decrease, although hopefully the new United Nations Register on
Arms Transfer may exercise a brake on it before it generates
vicious cycles and regional arms racing. Once again the tragic
events in the Balkans highlight the fact that most violent deaths
in war since 1945 have been caused by conventional rather than
nuclear, biological or chemical weapons. Thus any alternative
security regime in the region needs to address the levels and
quality of conventional arsenals alongside the weapons of mass
destruction.

Internal Conflicts

While the region is relatively free of international conflict there
are a number of internal conflicts that have significant regional
consequences, especially when they generate refugee populations
(see the chapter by Ferris). Leaving aside South Asia where there
is a bitter internal conflict in Sri Lanka, the Burmese government
is embroiled in violent conflict with its ethnic groups and pro-

democracy activists, the UN sponsored Cambodian settlement is tenuous and may still break down if the Khmer Rouge continue to play a spoiling role. Indonesia remains locked in conflict with the East Timorese. There is continuing insurgency in the Philippines, a long running but currently low key conflict between Papua New Guinea and Indonesia over Irian Jaya, as well as a new conflict between Papua New Guinea and Bougainvillean separatists (see the chapter by Lawson). The two Koreas still have some way to go before they are reunited and there are three significant international claims that have to be resolved if there is to be stable peace in the region: the Philippine claim to Sabah, the six nation claims to the Spratly/Nansha Islands, and the conflict between Japan and Russia over the Kuriles.

While ASEAN's post-ministerial conference provides a valuable opportunity for addressing some of these problems, and the Canadian government has supported Indonesian efforts to mediate discussion between claimants to the Spratly's and promoted unofficial and official efforts to build confidence in the North Pacific, it is clear that there is a need for some other kind of regional security framework to discuss these issues and devise ways of resolving them non-violently.

As mentioned above, there is implacable opposition to this proposal from the United States and Japan. And the ASEAN nations themselves (probably because they do not wish to address the question of internal conflicts directly) feel that the post-ministerial discussions are sufficient. Countries such as Australia,[14] Canada, and Mongolia, however, see a need for other institutions that might generate additional trust and confidence and also acquire a capability to prevent internal conflicts from generating external instability.

If the region cannot agree on the modalities for moving in this direction the United Nations might be able to assist. For example,the proposal of the former Secretary General of the United Nations, Javier Perez de Cuellar, to review the international principle of non-interference in the domestic affairs of other nations when this is used as a cover for the gross violations of human rights is something that such a regional institution might address. Obviously such a suggestion would arouse currently suppressed regional anxieties and it definitely should not be used to facilitate unilateral interference in the domestic affairs of other states. But under certain specified circumstances it is not impossible to conceive a regional mechanism for dealing with internal disputes that might be empowered to prevent slaughter or genocide. Proposed interference in the domestic affairs of another nation, however, should always be conducted under strict terms and conditions and under regional or preferably United Nations auspices.

Nations and regions should also make greater use of the International Court of Justice in relation to judgements about territorial disputes thereby bringing global instruments more directly into the resolution of regional affairs. The Spratly/Nansha dispute would be ideal for this body as would the Philippine claim to Sabah. The current Secretary General of the United Nations, Boutros Ghali, in his June 17 1992 *Agenda for Peace* outlines very precise procedures for utilising national, regional and United Nations' instruments to achieve the peace and security goals of the United Nations. This report establishes some important new means for alerting regional and global bodies to the possibility of violent dispute. Ghali proposes an expanded early-warning system, with preventive deployment where necessary, and more active approaches to mediation, negotiation and arbitration. All this will require the assistance of regional organisations if they are to prove successful. It seems desirable, therefore, for states and regional institutions to start addressing ways in which they can assist the preventive, diplomatic, peace-making, peace-keeping, peace-building and post-conflict reconstruction roles of the United Nations. There is no way that the United Nations acting alone will be able to deliver satisfactory outcomes in these areas without the very active support of states and regions.[15]

This brief *tour d'horizon* of the Asia Pacific region has only scratched the surface of some exceedingly complex economic, political and social processes. It is salutary to remember that behind these processes lie millions of individual actors who are both conditioned by and responding to the processes and who also make their own unique demands on decision makers.

There are many Asian non-governmental organisations trying to generate recognition for the principle that national, regional and international economic and political activities should serve the people and be oriented toward enhancing their quality of life and well-being. These groups actively and courageously promote human rights, community development, environmental causes and broader peace questions at a national level.

It seems vitally important to regionalise more of these groups and organisations so that they can coordinate action on rain forests, the trade in toxic chemicals, arms transfers, human rights, etc. The need for non-governmental organisations to develop a regional awareness to parallel that of government officials and politicians remains a challenge for all popular movements in Asia.

In all of these initiatives there is a need to develop what Karl Deutsch calls 'empathy' and 'responsiveness' if an Asia Pacific community is to be willed into existence. (See the chapter by Camilleri and specific proposals for maritime confidence building in the chapter by Pugh.) These qualities of empathy and responsiveness are as critical to international relations as they are to interpersonal relations. Without them state or non-governmental actors are unable to imagine themselves in someone else's situation and are therefore unable to respond constructively and creatively. Given the rich diversity of the Asia Pacific region there is an urgent need for considerable cross-cultural sensitivity/empathy, but there is also a need to follow up the functional economic links with political and social ones that mitigate if not eliminate the necessity for resort to violent settlement of regional disputes and conflicts. Only when this happens will there be a willingness to move towards alternative and more inclusive security policies based on reciprocity, sustainable development, de-nuclearisation, de-militarisation, and regional and global accountability.

Notes

1. Boulding, E., (1988), *Building a Global Civic Culture: Education for an Interdependent World,* NY: Teachers College Press, Columbia University, p. 19.
2. Ibid., pp. 35-36.
3. Caporaso, J., (1992), 'International Relations Theory and Multilateralism: the Search for Foundations', *International Organisation,* vol. 46, no. 3, p. 601.

4. See Deutsch, K.W, *et al.,* (1957), *Political Community and the North Atlantic Area,* Princeton NJ, Princeton University Press for an elaboration of this idea.
5. Sopie, N., (21-25 June 1992), 'The New World Order: Implications for the Asia Pacific', Unpublished MS presented to the 6th Asia Pacific Roundtable, ISIS Kuala Lumpur Malaysia, p. 18.
6. Ibid.
7. Falk, R., (1992), 'The Struggle to Shape Global Polity: A View from Civil Society' unpublished MS, p. 17.
8. See Bruce Russett, 'Peace Research, Complex Causation and the Causes of War' pp. 60-61 in Wallentseen, P. (ed.) 1988 *Peace Research: Achievements and Challenges,* London and Boulder: Westview Press.
9. Frampton, N.L., (21.08.92), 'Japan Could Become the Land of the Rising Sword', *The Dominion,* (Wellington).
10. Solomon, R., (6 August 1991), speech to American Chamber of Commerce, Auckland, New Zealand, p. 3.
11. For a detailed discussion on ASEAN see Acharya, Amitav, (1992), 'Regional Military-Security Cooperation in the Third World: A Conceptual Analysis of the Relevance and Limitations of ASEAN', *Journal of Peace Research,* vol. 29, no. 1, pp. 7-21.
12. Sipri Yearbook, *World Armaments and Disarmament,* Oxford: OUP, p. 159.
13. Clements, K.P., (1988), *Back from the Brink: The Creation of a Nuclear Free New Zealand,* London/Sydney: Allen and Unwin.
14. Evans, G., (6 December, 1989), *Australia's Regional Security: Australian Parliamentary Report,* p. 5.
15. Ghali, B.B., (1992), *An Agenda for Peace,* report of the Secretary General to the Security Council 17 June.

Part One

Sources of Conflict

1

Conflict Patterns and Security Environment in the Asia Pacific Region – The Post-Cold War Era

J. Mohan Malik

From Bipolarity to Regional Hegemonies?

Due to a shift in the world's economic centre of gravity, the 21st century has been described as belonging to the Asia Pacific region. In geo-strategic terms, it remains a volatile and conflict-prone region. The end of the Cold War and the demise of communism has changed the strategic landscape of Asia in a way that is marked by uncertainty and complexity. The post-World War II bipolar world order has come to an end. The most significant strategic development is the relative decline in the economic power and consequent reduction in the military presence and influence of the two superpowers: the United States and the former Soviet Union. The result is the transition from bipolarity to an undefined form of multipolarity.

The Soviet Union unwittingly contributed more to the change in security environment through its pursuit of an 'active disengagement' policy which has lowered its military profile in the region.[1] The reduction in land forces, withdrawal from Cam Ranh Bay in Vietnam, and declining naval activity in the Indian and Pacific Oceans are clear signs that the new Commonwealth of

Independent States is receding northward and the Pacific Fleet will be confined to home waters in the future. In the last decade of this century, this confederation of states will remain largely preoccupied with overcoming its own internal instabilities and with directing its efforts at rejuvenating its economy. It should not come as a surprise if the two former arch rivals become 'allies in the not-too-distant future'[2] and pool their resources to solve global problems.

With the Commonwealth of Independent States abdicating its role as a superpower abroad, American foreign policy faces an identity crisis and the Asia Pacific region is confronted with an entirely new strategic situation. There are many who believe that the world has become unipolar in the transitory stage from a bipolar to a truly multipolar world. Whether we are in a bipolar, unipolar or multipolar stage or in a phase that defies easy description is, of course, debatable. What is obvious is that even though the Commonwealth of Independent States still retains more than half of the world's strategic nuclear weapons, it has lost the political will and the economic capability to compete with the United States. This is, however, not the case with the United States which possesses significant military and economic capability, and above all, political desire to enforce its will – albeit in cooperation and consultation with other major powers. Not surprisingly, then, the United States has emerged as a cause for security concern for Asian states – though for entirely different reasons.

In large and relatively powerful states of Asia such as China, India, Pakistan, Indonesia and Malaysia, the prospect of a unipolar world dominated by an unchallenged United States or *Pax Americana,* even if in the interim period, is seen as an unwelcome development.[3] Some Asian countries regret the passing of the old order because 'to the non-aligned countries, bipolarity was not an unmixed curse [as] they were able to play off one against the other, had much room for manoeuvre and their support was avidly sought by both contenders'.[4] Apparently, the irrelevance of the Non-Aligned Movement (NAM) in the changed strategic environment and the disappearance of the Soviet bloc as a countervailing force (or restraining factor) in international politics make many Asian countries – especially NAM member-states no longer in a position to extract maximum security and economic advantages from either side – feel vulnerable and insecure.[5] The U.S. role in the recent Gulf crisis tends to reinforce these fears and apprehensions.

Whilst some Asian countries are apprehensive about a *Pax Americana* or a unipolar world, there are many others which are concerned with the impending reduction in the U.S. military presence in the Asia Pacific. Of particular concern is the timing and level of reduction given the uncertainties of the emerging world order. Thus with the break-up of the Soviet Union and reduction in the U.S. military presence, scenarios are being projected in which this 'vacuum' may be filled by regional heavyweights: Japan, China and India. The proponents of what might be called 'regional power hegemonism' (or multipolar world) theory argue that Saddam Hussein's misadventure in Kuwait was a cruel reminder to the world that the post-Cold War world might be more anarchic and more violence prone than it was in the preceding era. Conflicts that had been suppressed by the rivalry between East and West may now erupt, in much the same way that gangsters run rampant when the police lack the power to check them. In other words, whereas in the Cold War era regional powers were constrained to some extent by the risks of provoking a superpower confrontation, they might now feel freer to flex their muscles, aware of the decline in the ability of the superpowers to influence the outcome of regional conflicts. Hence, given their own security concerns *vis à vis* their large, powerful neighbours, most of the small and medium nations of the Asia Pacific see in a strong U.S. military presence a valuable counterweight to regional power hegemonism. Therefore, many small and medium nations – especially Singapore, Thailand, South Korea, and Australia – argue that 'there be no precipitous withdrawal of U.S. forward deployment'.[6] Singapore's offer to the United States of increased access to its base facilities in 1990 is indicative of the efforts to keep the U.S. engaged militarily in the region. As one Southeast Asian analyst has put it, 'the U.S. military presence is valued not so much for its actual use in combat but more as a [psychological] deterrent to an ambitious and unfriendly power'.[7]

Even after the end of the Cold War, the Asia Pacific remains important to the United States strategically as well as economically.

Strategically, the U.S. role is seen as that of a 'regional balancer, honest broker and ... security guarantor'.[8] What it means is that the United States will be seeking to maintain its bilateral alliance relationships with Asian countries (Japan, Australia, Singapore and South Korea) which are seen as providing the building blocks of Asian security, while shifting the burden for security commitment and expenditure from the U.S. to the region's nations. In other words, U.S. security interests in the post-Cold War era is in the prevention of conflict between alliance partners and other non-U.S. aligned states in the region and in the prevention of the domination of the region by regional powers hostile to U.S. national interests.

Economically, the Asia Pacific remains crucial for the sustained redevelopment of U.S. competitiveness and economic power, if the United States is to maintain its position as the paramount global power in both military and economic terms in the next century. It is the United States' largest export market and the maintenance of sea lines of communication for trade between the U.S. and the Middle East, Japan and Southeast Asia is of vital importance to U.S. economic interests. Therefore, we can expect the U.S. to retain its military presence to protect its national interests in the region – albeit at a much reduced level. Washington has already indicated a clear preference for maintaining the major principles of its Asia Pacific strategy which include 'forward deployment, overseas bases, and bilateral security arrangements, in order to maintain regional stability, deter aggression and preserve U.S. interests'.[9] It should be noted that the U.S. presence is intended to provide not merely a military but also an *economic and political* counterweight to the growing military and economic capabilities of Japan, China and India.

The Asia Pacific is a diverse and heterogeneous region, with countries at different stages of economic development, and with different types of political systems. In contrast to Europe, where NATO, the Conference of Security and Cooperation in Europe and even the European Community provide a structure for thinking about security issues in the region, Asia Pacific has failed to evolve regional security structures or forums. The geopolitical, economic, strategic, historical and cultural factors make the diverse and heterogeneous states of Asia take different paths to security. A major reason, of course, is that there has never been 'a common perception of threat or more particularly, an agreement on threat priorities'.[10] In the absence of regional security structures, a prominent Asian security analyst, Gerald Segal, believes that the Americans seem to be 'settling for an approach which 19th-century British strategists called "holding the ring" – the notion that one power could maintain stability by threatening to intervene in a conflict in the region and that this power had enough clout to deal with any possible hostile coalition. The advantage of such a strategy is that one can be vague about threats and capabilities'.[11] In short, continuing American military presence is intended to ensure that the U.S. is capable of adopting what may be described as an 'over the horizon posture' (OTHP) in the event of a conflict in Asia, as it did during the Gulf War.

Despite their differing perceptions of the nature of the present world order – unipolar or multipolar – all countries in the Asia Pacific share a common concern over the 'New World Disorder'. They all see dangerous trends manifested in racial tensions, religious differences, national rivalries, border disputes, struggles for territory and resources, the proliferation of high-tech weapons, and the rivalry for regional hegemony in many parts of the region at a time when the old world order has been destroyed but the new world order has not yet been established. The end of the Cold War, the disintegration of the Eastern bloc, the collapse of communism and the Soviet Union have called into question the basic premises and concepts underlying the foreign policies of many Asian states: for example, NAM, Third World Solidarity, North-South dialogue, South-South Cooperation, New International Economic Order and so on. The dramatic changes in the global and regional strategic environments have produced new challenges and opportunities. These changes have forced all countries in the region to formulate fresh policy responses and re-examine old premises of policies. There is a general agreement that the nature and the shape of world order in the 1990s and early 21st century will be very different from that of the post-World War II period.

In the last decade of the 20th century, many issues of regional stability and balance remain unresolved, with the potential to affect both the pace and direction of future events in the Asia Pacific. The major actual and potential post-Cold War conflict zones in the Asia Pacific are:

* The Korean peninsula where the two Koreas face each other in armed confrontation.
* The Russian-Japanese dispute over the Northern Territories or Kurile Islands.
* The Spratly Islands dispute in the South China Sea.
* The Indo-Chinese states, the Cambodian question and the intramember disputes among ASEAN states.
* Sea lines of communication (SLOCs) in the Southeast Asia which link the Pacific and Indian Oceans.
* Burma's internal instability with its potential to involve external powers such as China, India and ASEAN.
* The South Pacific island states' internal instability with the potential to involve extra-regional powers. (For example, the Bougainville dispute in Papua New Guinea, the Irian Jaya/Papua New Guinea border, the domestic conflicts in New Caledonia and Fiji.)
* Indian subcontinent: ethnic and religious conflicts in India, Sri Lanka, Nepal, India-Pakistan territorial dispute and the arms race in South Asia; and Sino-Indian conflict and competition in the Indian Ocean littoral and Southeast Asia.
* The threat of proliferation of nuclear and ballistic missile arms race on the Indian subcontinent and the Korean peninsula.

In addition, there is a need to monitor political and military developments in the Central Asian Islamic republics and Eastern Russia to ensure that the disintegration of the Soviet Union does not precipitate a threat to peace and stability in the wider Asia Pacific region. The spillover effects of the ex-Soviet Union's ethnic and democratic turmoil for the large, multi-religious and multi-cultural countries like China, India and Indonesia could be ominous. There is already concern that the separatist movements in Kashmir and Punjab in India and in Tibet and Xinjiang in China would get a boost from the developments across the border and much more international support. If the ethnic, religious and democratic aspirations of the various nationalities/minorities inhabiting these states are not realised, then the day is not far off when the centre will not be able to hold the union together.

The end of the Cold War may have removed the threat of a large-scale global conflict but the possibilities of small-scale regional conflicts abound in the region. Conflicts that are most difficult to resolve involve 'long-held suspicions with their historic roots, as well as religious and ethnic differences'[12]. In addition, old boundary questions may be opened up and new pressures to redraw colonial boundaries re-emerge. The bulk of the security problems the world is likely to face in the future will be region-specific. But unlike the Gulf crisis, many of these issues, for example, a South or Southeast Asian crisis, would not have an impact on the security and prosperity of states beyond the immediate region. Thus the Gulf conflict management model or the application of the collective security principle along similar lines can be ruled out, for the international response to Saddam Hussein's actions was the product of special circumstances that are unlikely to be repeated elsewhere. Moreover, the United Nations' utility in the region is doubtful given that it is 'still seen as built largely in the image of the West ... [and] lacking adequate regional representation. With Japan not being a member of the Security Council, and China likely to have conflicts of interest in any regional dispute, it could at best have a limited role'.[13] It should be noted that the United Nations' role during the first test of the so-called 'New World Order' came in for sharp criticism from many Asian countries.[14]

Emerging Trends

The pace of global and regional change is somewhat bewildering. Events are moving so fast that anything that one writes is almost certain to be out of date by the time that it is published in permanent form. Though the dramatic changes to the strategic environment are yet to settle into a manageable pattern, certain emerging trends and their implications can still be identified. Evidently, as the alliance structures of the Cold War dissolve into irrelevance, the term 'superpower' seems no longer appropriate. In the unfolding order of the 21st century, the United States will be one of several great powers – albeit the paramount or the dominant power of the international system. The other major trends or characteristics of the post-Cold War, post-U.S.S.R. strategic environment in the Asia Pacific are: (a) the role of regional powers; (b) military modernisation and the proliferation of weapons of mass destruction; (c) the changing concept of security with its emphasis on economic issues; (d) the changing character of conflicts; and (e) the growth of regionalism.

Role of Regional Powers

The demise of the bipolar power structure has brought into sharp focus the intentions, capabilities and role of major regional powers: Japan, China and India. Japan's strategic profile is a matter of continuing debate now, both within and outside Japan. The intentions and military capabilities of China and India are also a matter of concern in many Asian capitals. Even if the scenarios of China, Japan and India seeking to fill the 'vacuum' created by declining American and Soviet military presence are not realised in the short to medium term, the likelihood of such an eventuality in the longer term should not be dismissed. In the short to medium term, though, the dramatic increase in the number of key actors will undoubtedly make the security environment much more complex and intricate. What it means, argues strategic expert Robert O'Neill, is that 'like the managers of the Concert of Europe, all countries in the Asia Pacific will have to, first of all, keep track of several major and minor decision makers at any one time'[15] – for example, the United States, Russia, Japan, China, India, the ASEAN countries and Australia. However, keeping track of the activities of key regional actors alone will not lead us anywhere. All states in the region will have to (a) assess the implications of their actions simultaneously; (b) respond swiftly to any change in various combinations of partnership; and (c) manage their external relations in a manner that maintains the delicate balance of power. This is indeed a very challenging task for Asian diplomats who are used to examining issues in simplistic bipolar terms. But the failure to act swiftly and simultaneously on several fronts could lead to misperception. Wrong signals can make neighbouring countries hypersensitive to threats, and thus result in destabilising arms races. In short, the emerging multipolarity calls for a shift from the previously bipolar framework within which policy attitudes were largely set, and for a move towards flexible policy responses.

Now let us examine the role of the three major regional powers in the years ahead.

Japan

The question everybody seems to be asking is whether Japan's already predominant economic power will be translated into military power. Japan's defence expenditure is now the third highest in the world. Tokyo has already taken on the responsibility of protecting its sea lines of communications 1600 kms out to sea. This means that Japan's Self Defence Forces (SDF) can reach as far south as the Philippines. Tokyo undoubtedly has the economic and technological capability to become a military superpower.

During the Cold War era, common threat perception with regard to the Soviet Union cemented U.S.-Japanese security ties. It provided the rationale for the U.S.-Japanese Security Treaty which is also widely credited with restraining the growth of Japanese militarism. With the Soviet Union no longer posing a military threat to Japan and with the prospects of the resolution of the Northern Territories dispute with Moscow better than ever, Tokyo could become less dependent on Washington for security. Likewise, with the collapse of communism, the U.S. does not need Japan as a strategic bulwark against the 'evil' Soviet empire.

As a result, some analysts claim that 'Americans no longer see any need to endure the discomfort they have suffered from what many regard as Japan's manifestly unfair economic competition'.[16] Recent public opinion polls conducted in the United States reveal the American public sees Japan as a major threat to their nation's well-being. Thus, the argument goes that the U.S.-Japanese economic disputes, as manifested in the formation of trade blocs, protectionism and economic rivalry, could further erode the basis of U.S.-Japanese security and economic ties and lead to all-out trade war. Japan obviously fears the formation of trade blocs in the Americas and Europe because its prosperity hinges on its continued access to the big developed markets. In the absence of mutual security and economic bonds, it is feared that Japanese nationalism – as best expressed in Ishihara/Morita's *The Japan That Can Say No* – would respond to the aggressive economic offensive being pursued by the U.S. against Japan. As a worst case scenario, it has been suggested that U.S. economic interests will eventually force the U.S. to launch an economic embargo against Japan, resulting in *The Coming War with Japan.*[17]

These predictions are, to say the least, alarmist. They do not take into account the current interdependent nature of U.S.-Japanese economic and security relations. Whether Japan adopts an aggressive foreign policy or a higher military profile or not will be dependent upon several factors which include: one, a total rupture in the U.S.-Japanese alliance; two, a significant reduction in U.S. military presence in the region which would undermine the U.S. capability to respond effectively and decisively in crisis situations; three, the adoption of an aggressive foreign policy, especially towards Taiwan and Southeast Asia, by China;[18] four, the emergence of conditions which put Japanese economic growth and security at risk; five, the acquisition of nuclear weapons capability by either North Korea or both Koreas; and last but not least, a thaw in Russo-Japanese relations following the resolution of the Northern Territories dispute. Conceivably, the Russo-Japanese rapprochement could lead to increased Japanese access to oil and mineral resources from Siberia, thereby reducing Tokyo's resource vulnerability and dependence upon long, unprotected Sea Lines of Communication.

Though the possibility of Japan embarking on a militaristic path cannot be ruled out over the longer term, it remains highly unlikely, in the short to medium term, for a number of reasons. First, despite trade frictions, the U.S.-Japanese alliance is likely to survive because the two economies are now so interdependent that it is in the self-interest of both nations to overcome their differences. Second, the U.S. strategic and economic interests in Asia make a complete withdrawal of American forces highly unlikely. Third, the Soviet-Japanese dispute over Northern Territories still remains unresolved. And there is no guarantee that its resolution would lead to a thaw in Russo-Japanese relations given their historical suspicion of each other. Fourth, the instability on the Korean peninsula over the short term and the prospect of a unified Korea over the long term – with the potential to rival Japanese economic and political might – would remain a major security concern for the Japanese. In addition, the situation in and around China remains volatile and unpredictable. Fifth, Japan stands to gain nothing by developing and investing in the toys of death when it can dominate the whole world by building toys of life. The economic growth of a resource-poor nation like Japan is critically dependent on an uninterrupted supply of raw materials and oil. In other words, a military role would be highly counter-productive in economic terms. Sixth, the strong domestic aversion to militarism and constitutional restraints on defence policy will continue to apply brakes on Japan's ambitious plans to this effect. Not only that, Japanese policy makers cannot afford to ignore the concerns and apprehensions of Northeast and Southeast Asian nations about Japan's expanding military capability. And finally, the concern over a resurgence of Japanese racism-nationalism is also unwarranted. Even if it does stage a comeback, unlike in the past, it will have to contend and compete with Chinese racism, Korean brotherhood, Filipino or Indian nationalism.

The concern over Japan's future role can be attributed to the tendency among some analysts to confuse a greater diplomatic/political role by Japan with a military profile apparently because of historical reasons. The end of the Cold War, the expected reduction in U.S. military presence and Tokyo's response to the Gulf crisis or the lack of it is forcing Japan to reassess its strategic outlook and foreign policy approach. The Gulf War in particular, highlighted the need for a greater Japanese role in regional security affairs, collective security arrangements and in the United Nations peace-keeping operations. Many Southeast Asian countries and Australia have already indicated that they would welcome an active Japanese role in regional security issues, e.g. in seeking a peaceful resolution of the Cambodian and Spratly Islands conflicts.[19] During his visit to the ASEAN countries in May 1991, the Japanese Prime Minister announced that his country would become more *politically* engaged on the world stage. Therefore, Tokyo can be expected to pursue a more independent and assertive political/diplomatic role commensurate with its economic power and further develop its defence self-reliance to lessen U.S. leverage over its foreign and domestic policies. However, it is unlikely, in the near future, that Japan will abandon its defensive posture linked to the U.S.-Japanese alliance and embark upon an independent security role. As Australian Foreign Minister, Senator Gareth Evans, put it, '[t]here is no sign at present that Japan's military inclinations extend any further abroad than playing a role in UN peace-keeping operations'.[20] In fact, of the three regional powers, Japan is the most satisfied power and the greatest beneficiary of the existing distribution of global and regional power. Any dramatic change in the regional strategic environment would do more harm than good to Japan. However, this is not the case with China and India.

China

Geo-strategically, China is Asia's largest mainland state, it dominates the Pacific Ocean and shares common land and maritime borders – most of them disputed and unsettled – with many states in Northeast, Southeast, South Asia and Central Asia. It is the third largest nuclear weapon state in the world, not aligned with any superpower, enjoys an overwhelming military superiority in terms of men under arms and military hardware, and has a reputation of resorting to force to seize what it claims to be its own. In recent years, Beijing has also emerged as the leading supplier of conventional, nuclear and ballistic missile technology to the developing countries around the world. With the collapse of communism in the Soviet Union and Eastern Europe, it has acquired the dubious distinction of being the sole repository of conventional Marxist-Leninist thought. Above all, it remains a dissatisfied power as far as its place in the international system is concerned.[21] Their public protestations to the contrary notwithstanding, Chinese leaders, possessed of the 'Middle Kingdom' syndrome, have always seen their country as the superpower of the Asia Pacific region. Naturally, then, China has emerged as a cause for concern throughout the region. Its actions and proclamations are closely monitored and watched in all Asian capitals from Tokyo to New Delhi. 'Fears of expanding Chinese communism have virtually disappeared though fears of Chinese irredentism probably have not'.[22]

China's strategists are engaged in a debate over the broad contours and requirements of a national security policy into the early 21st century. The alleviation of the perceived threat from the north, i.e., the Soviet Union, the significance of open SLOCs for China's burgeoning trade and maritime interests, and Beijing's expanding geo-strategic horizons, extending into the Pacific and

Indian Oceans, have led Chinese military strategists to focus on their Southeast and Southwest borders. With the end of the Cold War and the reduction in the U.S.-Soviet forces in the Asia Pacific region, many Chinese defence analysts foresee a spiraling competition in Asia in which increasingly overlapping interests result in disputes and, ultimately, new 'hot spots'.[23]

Nonetheless, China's immediate strategic concerns remain centred around its relations with the new Commonwealth of Independent States, the Korean peninsula, Japan, Taiwan, its continued interests in Indo-China, its contested territorial claims in the South China Sea, and on the India-China border. The collapse of communism in the Soviet Union and moves towards greater autonomy and independence in the Soviet Central Asian Islamic republics bordering China's rebellious provinces – Xinjiang, Tibet and Inner Mongolia – have serious ideological and security implications for the Chinese. The situation on the Korean peninsula remains unsettled. Beijing also cannot remain oblivious to the threat of nuclear proliferation on the Korean peninsula. Though dependent upon Japanese economic and technological assistance for the realisation of its Four Modernisations (agriculture, industry, science and technology and defence) programme, China resents its eastern neighbour's role as a major player in global politics. Beijing is particularly concerned about the re-emergence of Japan as a military power following the end of the Cold War. The Sino-Japanese territorial dispute over the Diaoyutai (Senkaku) Islands in the East China Sea remains a potential flashpoint of conflict between the two giants. Though some analysts have talked about the prospect of a Sino-Japanese alliance taking shape towards the end of this century, the differences and historical contradictions between China and Japan should not be underestimated.

Despite expanding links with Taiwan, Beijing has not ruled out the use of force to reunify Taiwan and mainland China. Should there be instability surrounding the takeover of Hong Kong in 1997, it is likely that the independence movement would gain momentum in Taiwan. And the communist regime in China has made it clear that a declaration of Taiwanese independence would be grounds for war. A big question mark hangs over the future of communism in China. It is unlikely to survive the death of the aging communist leadership in Beijing. While a post-communist regime could be more accommodating on territorial disputes, such as the Spratly Islands, that bring China into conflict with Malaysia, Indonesia, the Philippines, Brunei and Vietnam, there is little likelihood of a peaceful resolution of the dispute in the foreseeable future. The steady growth of Chinese military capability and the withdrawal of the Soviet security umbrella from Beijing's regional rivals, India and Vietnam, might lead the Chinese to believe that time is on their side, and therefore, there is no hurry to seek peaceful solutions to territorial disputes which might dilute Beijing's claims. Surprisingly, in spite of their mutual hostility and ideological divide, both Taipei and Beijing have always adopted a similar posture on all territorial disputes whether they involve Russia, Japan, Vietnam, ASEAN states or India. In short, perception of China as a potentially destabilising force is reinforced by China's proclivity to interfere in its neighbourhood, its past readiness to use force in asserting its claims, its growing nuclear and blue-water naval capability, its internal political instability, and its unresolved border disputes.

However, in the short to medium term, China's role is likely to be constrained by its preoccupation with domestic economic and political issues, and its concern with finding itself a niche in the emerging world order. Since the Tiananmen massacre of June 1989, Beijing has been pursuing a non-confrontational and cooperative foreign policy primarily to win friends so as to end its isolation in the post-Cold War era of U.S.-Soviet detente which has greatly diminished China's status in the U.S.-P.R.C.-U.S.S.R. strategic triangle.[24] China's belated decision to sign the nuclear Non-Proliferation Treaty (NPT), announced in August 1991, which it had long denounced as a product of superpower hegemony, reflects Beijing's efforts to become a responsible and respectable member of the international community. In a major breakthrough in Southeast Asia, where fear and suspicion of China run deep, Beijing has managed to establish diplomatic relations with Indonesia and Singapore and normalised its relations with Vietnam. After much dillydallying, it cut off arms supplies to the Khmer Rouge and supported the UN Security Council framework for the resolution of the Cambodian conflict. Similarly, the allied efforts to evict Iraq from Kuwait would not have succeeded without

Chinese cooperation in the UN Security Council. Needless to say, China's attempts to project its image as that of a benign and stabilising force also owe a great deal to the exigencies of its externally oriented economy. It is safe to conclude that Beijing's pre-occupation with economic problems and political stability is likely to contribute to a more inward looking China for much of the rest of this decade. At the same time, the ongoing economic and military modernisation programmes would transform China into a superpower with the potential to undermine peace and stability if the region failed to evolve counterweights to balance and contain Chinese power.

India

India ranks as the third regional power in Asia behind Japan and China. India's geo-strategic location, its military interventions in Sri Lanka and the Maldives, its punitive action against Nepal for the latter's perceived tilt towards China, and above all, its growing military capability, especially naval power coupled with India's nuclear weapons and ballistic missile programmes, have become a matter of concern not only to its neighbours in South and Southeast Asia but even to countries as far away as Australia.

Apprehensions about India's intentions have been exacerbated by India's plans to develop its naval and air facilities on the Andaman and Nicobar Islands which are only 80 nautical miles from the north coast of Sumatra, and New Delhi's strong concern about the welfare of Indo-Fijians following the military coups in Fiji. Furthermore, Sino-Indian rivalry is expected to intensify as the world's two most populous nations seek to carve out bigger roles for themselves in Asia, especially as they step up their efforts to claim the mantle of the leadership of the orphaned South. The ongoing naval buildup programmes in both countries, in particular the emphasis on establishing large blue-water navies, are a signal of an emerging Sino-Indian competition in the Indian Ocean and the waterways of Southeast Asia.

India's attempts to develop a special security relationship with Vietnam to counter the Chinese security alliance with Pakistan indicate the spill-over effects of Sino-Indian conflict into South-east Asia.[25] Burma could prove to be the staging post for India-

China competition. China's growing influence in Burma through its massive arms transfers and the growing political and military links of Rangoon's military junta with Beijing has caused unease in New Delhi. India is concerned that Rangoon may offer port facilities to Chinese naval vessels.[26] There is little doubt that with the reduction in the superpower presence in the region, India is manoeuvering to place itself in a dominant position to meet the challenges thrown and the opportunities offered by the emerging multipolar world order.[27] As a result, India's conceptions of national security have expanded from a simple defence of borders to more complex notions of forward defence and regional influence, particularly in terms of maritime operations.

Nonetheless, for the rest of this decade, India's immediate security priorities remain the management of its relations with Pakistan and China, protection of its island territories and exclusive economic zone, the exclusion of extra-regional powers like China and the U.S. from South Asia and the resolution of its internal insurgency problems in the Punjab, Kashmir and India's northeast. Though India's capacity to project power into the Indian Ocean and Southeast Asia is considerable, '[it] should be seen against the need to protect a 7,500 kilometre coastline and 500 islands and to guard against possible threats from the north, rather than constituting a direct security threat to Australia or the countries of Southeast Asia'.[28] For one, India's amphibious force capability is considerably less than that required for power projection. Besides, there is neither any naval doctrine nor political will for employment of the Indian navy outside the Indian Ocean. Finally, India's economic crisis and the need to gain access to capital and technology would rule out any aggressive foreign policy behaviour on New Delhi's part.

In the short to medium term, at least, India's quest for regional great power status is likely to remain in a 'holding pattern' as defence expenditure is squeezed between the scarcity of foreign exchange and loss of cheap Soviet arms.[29] The collapse of its erstwhile superpower ally, the Soviet Union, has left India isolated and vulnerable. Throughout the Cold War, the Soviet Union was not only India's superpower ally in its conflicts with China and Pakistan but also its biggest trading partner and supplier of military hardware. India's close relations with the Soviet Union acted as a deterrent to China, while the Soviets viewed India as a bulwark against Chinese expansion and American domination of South Asia. Now this special cosy relationship with India could be a thing of the past. The end of the Kremlin's global ambition and the collapse of its centralised system will prove to be particularly problematic for trade and defence purchases. The Indo-Soviet Treaty, renewed for another 20 years in early August 1991, a few days before the abortive coup against Gorbachev, will remain a mere ceremonial document. According to *The Economist*, 'disruption in the Soviet Union has so affected supplies of spare parts that some bits of India's military machine are barely able to operate'.[30] Recent reports suggest that India's naval expansion has also been halted due to severe economic crisis, and that the 'Indian navy is likely to remain medium-sized for a decade or more, and well behind second-echelon powers like France and Japan ... a true bluewater capability to operate around the globe is unlikely in the first quarter of the next century'.[31]

Fears of Indian naval expansion into Southeast Asia and the South Pacific are, to some extent, exaggerated. In fact, alarm over India's military build up has been raised partly to justify increased defence spending by ASEAN states and partly to maintain the U.S. military presence in the area. India's geo-strategic location, size and its expanding military capability may give the impression of some hidden agenda, but the reality is that threat from Pakistan and China and 'internal security problems will continue to bedevil Indian military planners for some time to come and most of the military profile will be geared towards that'.[32]

Much as India would like to fill the vacuum created by the withdrawal of U.S.-Soviet fleets from the Indian Ocean, it lacks the economic capability, and above all, political will, to accomplish the task in the foreseeable future. India's military profile will have its locus of interest in the region of South Asia first, and then the waters of the Bay of Bengal that border Southeast Asia. At the same time, the Indian defence build up is likely to continue in the years ahead partly because of economic and technological imperatives and partly because of the new reality of defending the country against more than one enemy without the military and diplomatic support of any superpower. In short, India's military build up should be seen as largely the product of a nation seeking to resolve worrisome internal and regional crises whilst striving simultaneously to fulfil its perceived place as a major power in the region.

Military Modernisation and Proliferation of Weapons of Mass Destruction

Growing economic prosperity of the Asia Pacific states permits a greater allocation of resources to military modernisation and arms acquisition programmes. In Southeast Asia, all ASEAN countries are currently engaged in major arms acquisition programmes, involving the modernisation and enhancement of air and maritime capabilities.[33] Japan's Self Defence Forces (SDF) have an extensive and modern inventory of weapons and Japan's defence budget ranks it behind the superpowers. Most of the new funding for weapons in China is going towards the modernisation of the air force and navy, reflecting the changing focus of Chinese security interests. Despite resource constraints, India and Pakistan continue to increase their defence spending. The recent glut in the arms market has enabled 'the buyers to demand off-set manufacturing contracts, licensed production of equipment and greater access to technology through co-production and co-development of military hardware'.[34] This, in turn, has further facilitated the growth of domestic defence industries in Asian countries to fulfil their growing need for advanced weaponry.

A second factor seems to be the need to keep up with advanced technology. Acquisition of advanced technology has become the key determinant of a nation's economic and military power. The recent high-tech Gulf War also has the potential to re-kindle fresh arms races as armed forces and governments in the conflict-prone regions of the Asia Pacific draw their own conclusions from the Gulf War military operations. In a sense, the allied victory over Iraq may have undermined the fundamental premise of Chinese, Indian and Vietnamese security doctrines which are based on manpower and relatively low-tech weapon systems. For the developing countries of the region, one of the most important lessons of the Gulf War is that superiority in numbers matters very little against the quality of the weapons. This, in turn, is likely to strengthen the conviction in developing countries to acquire sophisticated, technologically-superior weaponry, especially ballistic and cruise missiles, thus rekindling new arms races. In short, the cost-effective utility of missile systems as demonstrated in the Gulf War might start a mad rush among many developing nations to acquire them, and thereby further undermine the global efforts to check the proliferation of short-range and long-range missiles.

Third, no longer sure of superpower security guarantees, many Asia Pacific countries are modernising their armed forces to meet new security challenges following the end of the Cold War. The fear of strategic abandonment by their former superpower allies figures prominently in the Indian, Pakistani, Vietnamese, Taiwanese and Korean calculus of deterrence. In short, the end of the East-West conflict has left many countries with no natural allies to bank upon in case of conflict with their neighbours. This, in turn, has given momentum to the efforts to stand on one's own feet.

Then there is the unfortunate Asian fallout from arms reductions in Europe. With the end of the East-West conflict, and the orientation of former Eastern bloc states shifting to economic issues, many European states are keen to get rid of superfluous weapons in their arsenals in return for hard currency. Thus, one unwelcome consequence of the European progress on arms control has been the search by arms traders for new markets in the Asia Pacific.

Finally, there is also some concern that amidst political and economic chaos in the country, some disgruntled Commonwealth of Independent States army officers or unemployed nuclear and missile scientists might be tempted to sell stolen nuclear weapons or their expertise for the right price to countries eager to 'go nuclear' just as their German counterparts did after World War II.[34] The U.S.-Soviet tactical nuclear arms cuts announced in the aftermath of the Moscow coup were motivated by the desire to minimise the risk of these weapons falling into wrong hands at a time of internal unrest and chaos.

Past experience shows that whenever a nation decides to acquire nuclear weapons, there is very little the world community can do to stop it. The global nuclear non-proliferation regime – the Nuclear Non-proliferation Treaty (or NPT signed in 1968), the Nuclear Suppliers Group (formed in 1975) and the Missile Technology Control Regime (or MTCR signed in 1987) – has sought primarily to apply a technical approach to proliferation. Nuclear weapons are essentially political weapons, and a technical approach alone is not effective. Technical constraints can buy time in the sense that they may slow down a nation's nuclear or missile programme but 'they cannot resolve the proliferation problem or contain the indigenous forces of technology in the Third World'.[36] There is no way of stopping the spread of industrial-military capability in the developing world. The risk of a nuclear and missile arms race is the greatest on the Indian subcontinent and the Korean peninsula which will impact on the security of adjoining regions.

Regardless of the progress in superpower nuclear arms control, nuclear weapons cannot be disinvented. 'Balance and deterrence', according to Robert O'Neill, are likely to remain 'integral elements of the security policies of all states which have nuclear weapons'.[37] The nuclear dimension of the post-Cold War world order will not only become more complex and potentially troublesome but also will be difficult to manage. It is feared that 'nuclear weapons may not remain in as few hands nor might all those hands be under as firm a discipline as they have been'.[38] The gradual diffusion of power and the proliferation of atomic bacterial and chemical (ABC), capabilities has the potential to upset the regional balances of power. Prospects of arms control and confidence-building measures do not look promising as there are several balances of power in the Asia Pacific region.

It is this realisation which has added momentum to the efforts to build anti-ballistic missile defences. Even after the collapse of the Soviet Union and drastic arms reductions, the United States remains committed to its Strategic Defence Initiative (SDI) programme which they see as the answer to the global proliferation of weapons of mass destruction. What does this mean for the Asia Pacific? Japan is already participating in the SDI project and China might seek to deploy its own version of Anti Ballistic Missile (ABM) defence and justify it in terms of the increasing threat from the Central Asian republics and the Indian subcontinent.

The Changing Notion of Security

The third major characteristic of the emerging strategic environment is the broadening of the concept of security. Security has traditionally been seen in military terms. However, the rise to prominence of new global issues has meant that traditional geostrategic considerations no longer dominate the foreign policy agenda. Today, the notion of security is assuming a more comprehensive, multi-dimensional character. The military dimension is decreasing in significance relative to economic and environmental concerns. Economic strength rather than military capability – a country's Gross National Product (GNP) and per capita income rather than the number of nuclear-armed missiles and men under arms – would be the dominant themes of international relations of the nineties and beyond. In other words, as economic strength becomes the single most important index of national power, the 'high politics' of diplomacy and security will give way to 'low politics' of economy and trade. After all, it was its total economic bankruptcy which led to the withdrawal of the Soviet Union from the superpower competition and the end of the Cold War.

This is not to say that conventional military forces are no longer important. On the contrary, traditional military concerns will remain on the agenda. But they 'will be increasingly supplemented by issues of economic and environmental security'.[39] Economic security essentially involves the maintenance of economic growth, open SLOCs, free and fair trade practices, access to finance, markets and natural resources. Environmental security issues are global warming, pollution, deforestation, acid rain, soil erosion, ozone depletion and the 'greenhouse' effect.

This broadening of the concept of security has come about as a result of the recognition that non-military threats to security – such as problems of maritime passage and seabed boundaries, refugee and population flows, terrorism and rising sea-levels – are as important as military threats.

The Changing Character of Conflicts

As a natural corollary of the changing concept of security, the character of conflicts between nations in the future will also change. Conflicts over natural resources, especially those offshore, will break out more frequently as 'economic security' takes a higher priority in nations' security calculations. There will be increasing competition among countries for resources and markets. 'As sustaining economic growth is seen to be more dependent on the exploitation of one's natural resources, there will be greater determination to protect such resources from external "predators".'[40] There are many 'contentious issues relating to economic security – such as the protection of trade links; protection of long and vulnerable sea lines of communication; rights of transit through straits and internal waterways; competing claims to offshore islands, reefs, and seabed and ocean areas; and the protection and exploitation of marine resources'.[41] The maritime dimension of national security is already receiving greater attention 'as a result of the extension of territorial waters and the 200-mile Exclusive Economic Zone (EEZ) provisions of the Third United Nations Conference on the Law of the Sea (UNCLOS III), the growing importance of off-shore resources, and the resulting overlapping claims from such extensions [as] in the South China Sea'.[42] These have already provided additional momentum to the arms acquisition plans of the ASEAN states.

Moreover, with the end of the East-West conflict, economic and technological aid to the developing world will dwindle as Western capital turns to the redevelopment of the former socialist countries. The growing economic disparities among nations are likely to create frictions and introduce stresses into inter-state relations. The growth of manufacturing in East Asian nations has led to an export-led growth relying on free markets. Collapse of such markets due to the formation of trading blocs, protectionism, principles of reciprocity which restrict market access and threaten freer global trade could pose significant threat to security and in some countries, political stability. Besides, in a world of ever-shrinking markets, the rush to exploit the economic potential of Indo-China, Central Asia and Russia could trigger conflicts of interest and tension among ASEAN states, South Korea and Japan. An eminent strategist, Edward Luttwak, believes that 'economic competition may become the modern equivalent of the old politico-military struggle for supremacy'.[43]

In short, future conflicts in the Asia Pacific would be regional rather than international, and focus on issues such as offshore territorial conflicts generated by a scramble to control energy resources, fisheries and raw materials. (In a sense, the Iraq-Kuwait conflict can be characterised as the first post-Cold War conflict over the control of natural resources motivated as it was by Saddam Hussein's desire to control 40 per cent of the world's total oil and petroleum resources and to salvage Iraq's economy from ruin.) Wars will no longer be fought to conquer countries or territories, because wars started with this purpose have completely failed to achieve their objective. The decade-long Iran-Iraq war is a case in point. Instead, outer space, oceans and sea-beds will become the targets of strategic contention. Efforts will be directed towards the control and exploitation of natural resources in these largely unexplored areas.

The Growth of Regionalism

The last major feature of the post-Cold War environment is the growth of regional organisations. The exigencies of the global economic system, combined with the move towards multipolarity, are forcing Asia Pacific states to interact more fully with each other. Economically, the countries have become more and more interdependent and integrated into the regional economy. Economic factors more than strategic considerations are turning former enemies – e.g., Indonesia and China, South Korea and China, Russia and Japan – into friends. Politically, they have developed regional structures for dialogue and consultations. The ASEAN and South Pacific Forum are the two successful examples of cohesive regional organisations. However, the regional organisation of South Asian nations, the South Asian Association for Regional Cooperation (SAARC), is yet to evolve into a cohesive regional structure for security and economic cooperation. In Northeast Asia, there is no regional organisation but bilateral dialogues have proliferated and they have contributed to the creation of an environment which is conducive to the promotion of political and economic cooperation. The Australian proposal for a regional economic body called the Asia Pacific Economic Cooperation (APEC) has won support from most of the countries and could serve to integrate Northeast with Southeast Asia and the South Pacific.

The future stability and growth of the region hinges to a significant degree on whether regional organisations like ASEAN, the South Pacific or APEC can help resolve intra-regional differences, stimulate credible economic cooperation among their members, and address emerging wider economic, political and security issues.

Conclusion

The emerging strategic environment represents a mixed picture. There is much to be welcomed and, at the same time, there is much to be feared. The threat of superpower confrontation has faded and old equations of superpower competition and conflict involving client states have become a thing of the past. The Asia Pacific region has emerged as a centre of economic growth and technological development. There is uncertainty regarding the role and behaviour of the emerging regional powers in the multipolar world of the 21st century. However, there are reasons to believe that the regional heavyweights will act with constraint and restraint at least for much of the rest of this decade.

The resurgence of ethno-nationalism around the world will have its impact on the large and heterogeneous, multi-lingual and multicultural Asian nations. The reduction in the superpower presence, the growth of major regional powers, the availability of economic resources, the quest for advanced technology, the withdrawal of superpower security guarantees, unresolved territorial and resource disputes are the factors pushing regional military expenditures upwards. Regional strategic trends indicate that the strategic environment is becoming more complex with the gradual diffusion of power and the proliferation of chemical, nuclear, ballistic missile and advanced conventional military capabilities. The world is seething with shifting alliances in a manner not seen since the decade before the First World War. In the process, established patterns of post-war trade are undergoing change. National security can no longer be looked at from the traditional geo-strategic perspective alone because of the broadening of the concept of security. Economic security and environmental security are as important as military security. The shape and character of future wars will be different from the previous conflicts. The control and exploitation of natural resources and colonisation of outer space and oceans will be the key objectives of future conflicts. The interdependent nature of world economy and the complexity of security issues will further facilitate the growth of regional organisations and bring about a change in the concept of the nation-state and national sovereignty.

Notes

1. Snitwongse, K., (1991), 'Strategic Developments in Southeast Asia', paper to the 25th anniversary conference on 'Strategic Studies in a Changing World', Strategic and Defence Studies Centre, The Australian National University, Canberra, 29 July-1 August 1991, p. 3.
2. *Newsweek,* (1991), 'How the West Can Win the New World Order', 10 September, p. 73.
3. Malik, J.M., (April, 1991), 'Asian Reactions to Australia's Role in the Gulf Crisis', *Current Affairs Bulletin,* vol. 67, no. 11, pp. 22-23, Richardson, M., (September, 1991), 'Mixed views on Pax Americana', pp. 33-34, *Asia Pacific 'Defence Reporter.*
4. Abraham, A.S., (29 January, 1991), 'Gulf War and the UN', *The Times of India.*
5. Malik, J.M., (September, 1991), 'Peking's Response to the Gulf Crisis', *Issues & Studies,* vol. 27, no. 9, pp. 123-128.
6. Snitwongse, K., (1991), (see note 1), p. 4.
7. Ahmad, Zakaria H., (1991), 'Images of American Power: Perspectives from Southeast Asia', *UPSK Occasional Paper,* Strategic and Security Studies Programme, University Kebangsaan Malaysia, p. 7; cited in Snitwongse, K., (1991), p. 4.
8. *Far Eastern Economic Review [FEER],* (1991), 'A shot across the bow', 19 July, pp. 10-11.
9. Snitwongse, K., (1991), (see note 1), p. 4.
10. Scalapino, R.A. *et al.,* (1988), *Asian Security Issues: Regional and Global,* Berkeley, Institute of East Asian Studies, University of California, p. 1.
11. Segal, G., (1991), 'Why Pacific Needs U.S. Punch', *The Australian,* 27 September, p. 11.
12. Snitwongse, K., (1991), (see Note 1), p. 16.
13. Harris, S., (1991), 'Security Issues in Northeast Asia', paper to the 25th anniversary conference on 'Strategic Studies in a Changing World', Strategic and Defence Studies Centre, The Australian National University, Canberra, 29 July-1 August 1991, p. 17.
14. Malik, J.M., (September, 1991), (see note 5).
15. O'Neill, R., (1991), 'World Order in the 1990s – Towards a New Global Security Structure?' paper to the 25th anniversary conference on

'Strategic Studies in a Changing World', Strategic and Defence Studies Centre, The Australian National University, Canberra, 29 July-l August 1991 pp. 4-5.

16. Stannard, B., (30 July, 1991), 'Meat in the Sandwich', *The Bulletin*, p. 32.

17. Friedman, G. and LeBard, M., (1991), *The Coming War With Japan,* St. Martin's Press.

18. Snitwongse, K., (1991), (see note 1), p. 6.

19. Evans, G., (May, 1991), 'Australia and Japan', *The Monthly Record,* Department of Foreign Affairs and Trade, vol. 62, no. 5, p. 222.

20. Evans, G., (1991), 'Australia's Regional Security Environment', paper to the 25th anniversary conference on 'Strategic Studies in a Changing World', Strategic and Defence Studies Centre, The Australian National University, Canberra, 29 July-1 August 1991, p. 4.

21. Malik, J.M., (September, 1991), (see note 5), pp. 125-126.

22. Harris, S., (1991), (see note 12), p. 9.

23. Malik, J.M., (1990), 'Chinese Debate on Military Strategy: Trends & Portents', *Journal of Northeast Asian Studies,* vol. ix, no. 2, Summer, pp. 14-15.

24. Malik, J.M., (September, 1991), (see note 5).

25. Garver, J.W., (November, 1987), 'Chinese-Indian Rivalry in Indo-China', *Asian Survey,* no. 11, pp. 1205-1219, Malik, J.M., (August, 1990), 'Missile Proliferation: China's Role', *Current Affairs Bulletin,* vol. 67, no. 3, pp. 4-11.

26. Subramanian, R.R. (1991), 'India's Military Profile: Implications for Asia Pacific', paper to the conference on 'Security in the Asia Pacific: The Challenge of a Changing Environment', Centre for the Study of Australia-Asia Relations, Griffith University, Brisbane, Queensland, 15-16 July 1991 p. 5.

27. Malik, J.M., (September, 1991), 'India's Response to the Gulf Crisis: Implications for Indian Foreign Policy', *Asian Survey,* vol. xxxi, no. 9, pp. 847-861.

28. Evans, G., (1991), (see note 19), p. 5.

29. Gordon, S., (1991), *India's Security Policy: Desire and Necessity in a Changing World,* Working Paper No. 236, Strategic and Defence Studies Centre, The Australian National University, Canberra.

30. *The Economist,* (14 September, 1991). p. 32.

31. McDonald, H., (10 October, 1991), 'India: Slow Speed Ahead', *FEER,* pp. 22.

32. Subramanian, R.R. (1991), (see note 25), p. 11.

33. Richardson, M., (9 July, 1991), 'In Asia Arms Sales Unbound', *International Herald Tribune [IHT],* p. 2, and Ball, D., (1991), 'The Changing

Asia/Pacific Security Environment and the South Pacific', in Henningham, S. and Ball, D. (eds), *South Pacific Security: Issues and Perspectives,* Canberra, Canberra Papers on Strategy and Defence No. 72, Strategic and Defence Studies Centre, The Australian National University, pp. 5-6.

34. Snitwongse, K., (1991), (see note 1), p. 15.
35. Waller, D., (10 September, 1991), 'A Nuclear Nightmare?' *Newsweek,* pp. 77.
36. Chellaney, B., (1991), 'South Asia's Passage to Nuclear Power', *International Security,* vol. 16, no. 1, Summer, p. 53.
37. O'Neill, R. (1991), (see note 14), p. 9.
38. *Ibid.,* p. 5.
39. Ball, D., (1991), (see note 32), p. 7.
40. Snitwongse, K., (1991), (see note 1), p. 16.
41. Ball, D., (1991), (see note 32), p. 7.
42. Snitwongse, K., (1991), (see note 1), p. 15.
43. *The Economist,* (28 September, 1991), p. 22.

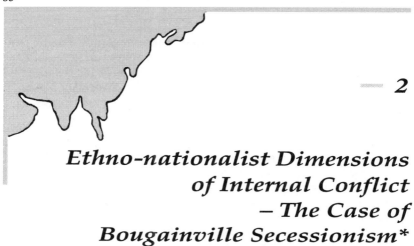

2

Ethno-nationalist Dimensions of Internal Conflict – The Case of Bougainville Secessionism*

Stephanie Lawson

Introduction

That the ideology of ethno-nationalism is a major factor in the current epidemic of secessionitis and similar maladies afflicting many of the world's 'nation-states' can scarcely escape even the most casual observation of world affairs. Indeed, the spectre of war and conflict is now much more likely to be associated with some kind of internal conflict in which ethno-nationalism is a prominent, if not exclusive, feature of the struggle. A survey conducted in 1988 gives some idea of the scope of the problem. It reported that out of a total of 111 states engaged in armed conflict, 63 of these conflicts were internal. A further 36 were categorised specifically as 'wars of state formation', in which the conflict centred on issues concerning autonomy or secession, many of which involved ethnically-related issues.[1] Since the publication of that report, the escalation of internal conflict in the Common-wealth of Independent States, Eastern Europe, the Middle East, Asia, and in the Pacific, projects an image of a world characterised increasingly by ethnically-driven political fragmentation. These developments invite more serious consideration of the role of ethnicity in shaping political movements, particularly of the secessionist kind, and the implications that these have for the *a priori* legitimacy of the state. More specifically, secessionist movements raise important questions about presumptions favouring the status quo with respect to state boundaries on the one hand, and the limits to the self-determination doctrine on the other.[2]

It is against this background that the case of Bougainvillean secessionism must be considered, for although the current struggle by Bougainvillean secessionists against the state of Papua New Guinea cannot be viewed simplistically as a conflict based exclusively on ethnic considerations, it nonetheless shares with many other secessionist movements a strongly ethno-nationalist character, and this needs to be analysed in conjunction with other relevant factors, such as the impact of resource exploitation, population growth, and social dislocation. It is certainly a prerequisite to considering the Bougainvillean secessionists' claim to be fighting a just cause against the authority of the state on the one hand, and in examining the position and legitimacy of the state *vis-a-vis* the rebels on the other. This is especially so when we consider that the state of Papua New Guinea contains over 700 different linguistic groups and, on these grounds alone, can be characterised as one of the most ethnically or culturally pluralistic nations in the world.[3] Papua New Guinea has also experienced a proliferation of 'micronationalist' movements which, although only weakly related to ethnicity in many cases, and often quite disparate in their origins, aims, and ultimate objectives, nonetheless share a 'common tendency towards disengagement or withdrawal ... from the larger, national community'.[4] Given these factors, the state of Papua New Guinea has good grounds for concern about fragmentation via the 'demonstration effect', for if there is one thing that a powerful separatist or secessionist movement does demonstrate, it is the vulnerability of the state's central government.[5]

Secessionism

Secession is a form of political opposition which is directed not merely against a particular government or a constitutional regime, but against the legitimacy and authority of the state itself.

In contrast, separatism is more limited in that it seeks a degree of autonomy which falls short of total independence from the existing state.[6] To this extent, separatists accord a qualified legitimacy to the central authority. Although many secessionists may be prepared to negotiate for, say, a grant of greater autonomy, devolution, or decentralisation, and therefore draw back to an implicit separatist position, its most extreme proponents reject any form of compromise, demanding complete sovereignty over the territory, its resources, and the people in question.[7] With the exception of external intervention by force, then, secession constitutes the most profound attack on the integrity of the state and therefore its identity and standing as an international actor.[8] At the same time, however, secessionist enterprises underscore the primacy of the state as the paramount form of political organisation. One need not endorse the realist perspective on international relations to recognise 'the assiduousness with which the status of statehood is sought by groups ... who do not enjoy it'.[9]

Some are prepared to identify secessionism almost exclusively as a species of ethnic conflict which is modified, at least in appearance, by the territorial character of the claims made on behalf of the secessionist cause.[10] At the same time, of course, nationalism in its broader, generic sense is itself a territorial ideology since it designates a particular geographic space as inextricably related to a particular 'people'.[11] The occupation of that space as a 'homeland' is therefore an imperative for the proper expression of the 'political will of nationalism'.[12] Territorial issues aside, the concept of 'a people' as constituting a nation is one of the most problematic in any discussion of ethnicity, nationalism, sovereignty, autonomy, and so forth. It is firmly grounded in a natural rights tradition of thought which grew with the rise of the nation in early modern Europe, and through which a unitary view of society was invoked. The essence of this society was expressed in the concept of the nation which was then taken as the legitimate basis of the modern state.[13] However analagous with earlier manifestations of 'imagined communities' it may seem, then, the distinctive character of nationalism is associated very closely with the principles of self-determination and popular sovereignty, and the particular currency accorded these in eighteenth-century Europe.

Contemporary ethno-nationalist secessionists derive an *a priori* justification for their challenge to the 'parent state' from the right to self-determination doctrine which has its modern origins in this tradition of thought. The doctrine has progressed through various stages and manifestations including the Wilsonian conception of the rights of minorities, and the anti-colonial version of 'racial' self-determination. The entrenchment of the self-determination doctrine as a natural right in the international moral order has been a significant factor in the genesis of many secessionist or separatist movements.[14] One of the most significant ideological achievements of ethno-nationalism, then, has been to link the normative concepts associated with the self-determination doctrine to the more specific categorisation of 'a people' as an ethnic group or *ethnie*. In turn, these *ethnies* have been endowed, as Smith suggests, with a self-conscious nationalism and legitimacy together with a fighting spirit and political direction – qualities which have turned ethnicity into an especially volatile issue, thereby aggravating existing tendencies to conflict.[15]

It is evident, then, that sympathy for the right to self-determination doctrine, especially insofar as it provides a basis for justifying ethno-nationalism, needs to be tempered with a critical regard for the ideas that underpin it. Gellner, amongst others, rejects the normative nationalist principle that homogeneous cultural units are the natural foundations of political life and that cultural unity between rulers and ruled is obligatory. This condition is not inscribed in the nature of things, nor is it a precondition of social life, and 'the contention that it is so inscribed is a falsehood which nationalist doctrine has succeeded in presenting as self-evident'.[16] Similarly, Smith says that there is nothing obvious in human nature or experience that insists on an ethnic division of humanity – much less that these divisions provide the only natural or legitimate basis for political units.[17]

There is certainly little empirical support for these ideas, and it is a commonplace observation that states are usually composed of more than one 'nation' or *ethnie,* and that the members of an *ethnie* are very often divided amongst a number of states. So despite the normative understanding borne by the nationalist conception that nation and state 'were destined for each other',[18] it is difficult to cite more than a handful of cases where nation and state are even approximately coterminous. Japan is sometimes offered as one example of a large modern country which closely approximates such a textbook polity,[19] and some of the tiny island states of the Pacific might also qualify. One investigator found that there are at least three times as many ethnic groups as states, and claimed that the only authentic example of a nation-state was Iceland.[20] Whatever the precise ratio is, it is quite clear that the so-called homogeneous state is not the norm. Throughout most of the world, then, states contain a plurality of ethnic groups each of which could well be characterised as 'nations' in their own right and which could therefore claim a right to self-determination.

This raises an obvious problem for conventional understandings of the international state system and the problem of world order, namely, the potential proliferation of states. After all, the *telos* of genuinely secessionist struggles is to create more sovereign states. Gellner argues, however, that although the number of potential nations in this world is very large, there is space for only a limited number of viable autonomous political units.[21] Whatever the merits of this argument, it is quite evident that the principle of self-determination promises much more than it can reasonably deliver, and that the matching of political and ethnic boundaries is virtually impossible.[22] This is one basis for the strong presumption in orthodox international relations theory against secession and in favour of retaining the sovereignty and territorial integrity of existing states.[23] It also underpins the reluctance of the United Nations to endorse an interpretation of the self-determination principle wider than that required for the emancipation of colonial people. But none of this should be taken to suggest that the imperatives of statehood should be accepted uncritically, nor that all ethnic particularism should be stamped out in the name of national unity as the modernisation school implied.[24] Further, the experience of Bangladesh provides one example of the relevance of the self-determination principle in a post-colonial context when dogmatic adherence to the principle of a state retaining its territorial integrity was clearly unwarranted.[25]

While traditional international relations theory promotes the preservation of the existing world order, political philosophy has also done so largely by default, since until very recently, there have been no serious attempts to work out a normative theory of secession.[26] Democratic theory has also been silent on such questions as why Bougainville should be part of Papua New Guinea rather than the Solomon Islands, or why it should or should not be an independent state. Rather, democratic principles take the existing boundaries of a state as given, 'and then urge political equality among the inhabitants of the state'.[27] The relationship between democracy and group freedom, however, is obviously an important one for democratic theory, and the call for greater self-determination on the part of minorities is, as Gastil points out, a justifiable concern for democrats.[28]

To the extent that secessionism is a manifestation of nationalist ideology, however, it can also be condemned in the terms that have described this ideology as 'an irrational curse, as moral insanity, as an atavistic phenomenon revealing human aggressiveness'.[29] Anderson's well-known treatment of nationalism is no less harsh in its ultimate judgement. According to Anderson, nations are 'imagined' political communities along several dimensions. First, they are imagined in the sense that members of even very small nations will never know most of their fellow members, 'yet in their minds lives the image of their communion'. They are also imagined as *limited* because they are recognised by their members as not being co-terminous with the whole of humankind, and *sovereign* because political autonomy is the nation's ontological dream. Finally, the idea of *community* makes possible a horizontal comradeship which transcends socio-economic class and it is this that has made it possible during the last two centuries for millions of people, 'not so much to kill, as willingly to die for such limited imaginings'.[30] That the Bougainville rebels are in the grip of such an imagining is beyond doubt, for they have declared their willingness 'to fight for our people until we all die'.[31]

There are several other aspects of the right to self-determination doctrine which bear at least cursory consideration here. First, the illusory nature of 'self-determination' as 'national autonomy' or 'sovereignty' must be recognised. This is well illustrated in Pettman's account of post-colonial Africa where she outlines clearly the extent to which external forces (of the diplomatic and market kind) have intervened and shaped internal political developments.[32] Another telling point concerns the conflict model of ethnic relations that has characterised South African politics for decades. Pettman notes that apartheid explicitly rejects both pluralist and assimilationist models, emphasising instead the notion that separate identities require strict separation so that 'different peoples' (which are defined as 'separate nations'), do not destroy each other.[33] Another equally important point is made by Gastil:

> Many an autocrat has come to power through his appeal as a defender or advocate of his group's right to self-determination. This has been a major part of the appeal of Hitler, Stalin, Mao and Castro to their respective peoples. Yet as the history of Haiti has shown repetitively, national independence has little to do with individual or even group freedom.[34]

Returning to normative theory on the issue of secession, it is with respect to this that Buchanan has canvassed various arguments which might plausibly be invoked to support a moral right to secede. He has done so within the general framework of liberal political philosophy which stresses, amongst other things, the notion of legitimate political authority as resting in some important respects on the consent of the governed (although this is tempered by the communitarian perspective).[35] But of the arguments considered by Buchanan, those associated with the 'right to self-determination' or 'normative nationalist' principle are given the least credence, although they are also acknowledged as amongst 'the most familiar and stirring justifications'.[36] Buchanan's analysis also underscores not only the difficulty (if not impossibility) of defining 'a people', but also the implications of the normative nationalist principle for the legitimacy of any state exhibiting cultural pluralism.[37]

Bougainville, Papua New Guinea: a Case Study

As suggested earlier, the normative nationalist principle poses particular problems for a state like Papua New Guinea which, amongst other things, is a classic example of an ex-colonial 'weak state'. It has an exceptionally diverse population, the component groups of which were brought together through the process of colonisation (and decolonisation), and which remain poorly integrated. Political identification remains highly localised and politicians are usually obliged to mobilise support through parochial appeals, thereby reinforcing the particularism of perceived interests as against any conception of national needs or the benefits that might flow from more effective integration at that level. As one commentator has pointed out, 'in Mount Hagen a Jiga is a Jiga and an Enga is an Enga. If they are in Port Moresby they regard themselves as Western Highlanders, perhaps even Highlanders. But only rarely do they regard themselves as Papua New Guineans'.[38] One consequence of this has been a history of separatist demands from Bougainville to Papua, the Gazelle Peninsula in East New Britain, and the Trobriand Islands which have emphasised, amongst other things, some kind of distinctive ethnic identity.[39]

Nationalism generally is a two-edged sword, and it has often been observed that it can serve as a force for disintegration as well as for unity.[40] This is especially well illustrated in the numerous ethno-nationalist movements in Papua New Guinea. In the specific case of Bougainville, May points out that the idea of ethnicity has worked as a unifying agent in bringing together the smaller groups in the province (Nasioi, Buka, Banoni, Siwai, etc.) into the larger group of Bougainvilleans.[41] This has been achieved by stereotypical labelling, best exemplified in the depiction of mainlanders as 'redskins' in contrast with Bougainvilleans who see themselves as 'blackskins'.[42] Similarly, the Papua Besena separatist movement has stimulated Papuan solidarity 'by invoking contrasting stereotypes held by Papuans of New Guineans who are regarded as barbaric and belligerent'.[43] At the same time these have worked against any emerging sense of a wider Papua New Guinean or Melanesian identity, a notion that has been pushed long and hard – but not very effectively – by Narokobi in his idealisation of the 'Melanesian Way'.[44]

The fact that the objective bases for ethnic distinction are in many cases quite spurious does little to mitigate the intensity of feeling that can be generated by the 'ethnic genie'. As May suggests, once let out of the bottle, this spirit has 'a powerful capacity to create its own history, boundaries, and sense of grievance against a larger society'.[45] This has been made easier for the Bougainvillean secessionists by several other factors which, taken together, form the basis of an argument that Bougainville is a 'special case'. These include the fact that the geographical location of the North Solomons province makes it more easily detachable from the rest of the country than any of the other regions which have spawned separatist movements.[46] Another major factor, of course, is the enormous copper mine at Panguna – operated by Bougainville Copper Limited (BCL) until its indefinite closure in May 1989.[47] But more on that shortly.

As with other parts of the country, Bougainville has a history of separatist activity and the present situation is often depicted as a continuation of a long struggle for independence from outside control.[48] In the period leading up to independence in 1975, separatist movements in Papua, the Gazelle Peninsula, the Trobriand Islands, and Bougainville, were especially active as each area sought to gain maximum advantage in the political restructuring entailed by the construction of the new state of Papua New Guinea. Added to this were various demands for greater local autonomy in many other areas. To placate these demands, the Constitutional Planning Committee had developed a proposal for a system of provincial government. But as the scheduled date for independence approached, further demands from Bougainville for relatively higher funding allocations, which were seen as a threat to an already fragile political unity, moved Chief Minister Somare to drop the provincial government provision from the constitution. Political leaders on Bougainville responded by issuing a unilateral declaration of independence on 1 September 1975 – two weeks before Papua New Guinea was to become a new independent state.[49] In subsequent negotiations, the Bougainvilleans were persuaded to drop their secessionist stance. The price for this was an especially favourable financial formula for Bougainville, and the adoption of the Organic Law on Provincial Government which provided for 19 provinces, including the North Solomons. This law has been described as 'almost a treaty' between the secessionist leaders and the national government.[50]

Despite these measures, which allowed the North Solomons substantial autonomy and contributed to a per capita income in the province of nearly four times the national average by 1984,[51] the leadership of the current secessionist movement has persistently claimed that the province has suffered exploitation and relative deprivation. More specifically, compensation and royalty payments to landowners in the Panguna area were seen as inadequate, especially in view of the large-scale environmental degradation caused by the mining operations, and it was this issue that precipitated the initial outbreak of violence in November 1988.[52] One of the major factors in the generation of the crisis, however, was a dispute within the landowning communities about the leadership of the Panguna Landowners Association (PLA), the management of the trust fund that it controlled, and the question of who should be regarded as the true titleholders to the land in question – the answer to which was decisive for the distribution of many of the financial benefits flowing from the mine.[53] Francis Ona, the current leader of the secessionist movement, is a former employee of BCL. He is also a member of the landowning community, but not a titleholder. The alleged Bougainville Revolutionary Army's (BRA) abduction and killing of Ona's uncle, Mathew Kove (who was accused of usurping a land title), in early 1989 illustrates the 'internal' nature of the initial dispute.

These particular issues have largely been lost sight of in the subsequent escalation of the crisis into one which now involves not just the Nasioi people from the mine area, but the whole of Bougainville Island (which is home to 17 other language groups). On this larger scale, the battlelines can now be depicted as 'blackskins versus redskins' in an ethnically-driven struggle for independence. On the occasion of Bougainville's first anniversary of 'independence', Joseph Kabui, the chairman of Bougainville's interim government (and also the last elected Premier of North Solomon's Province), delivered the following ethno-nationalist message to the people gathered in celebration of the occasion.

> Bougainville has reached the point of no return. There is no turning back. Bougainvilleans feel – and it is a feeling that is deep down in our hearts – that Bougainville is totally different from Papua New Guinea. Geographically, culturally, it's been a separate place since time immemorial. Ever since God created the universe, Bougainville has been separate, has been different.[54]

Francis Ona has also claimed that 'our diverse customs will not allow us to live peacefully together as Papua New Guineans'.[55] Ona, who signed one of his letters as 'Mi, Father of Nation, Francis Ona', has propounded the ethno-nationalist theme most explicitly in his 'Declaration of Independence: Republic of Bougainville', which reads in part:

> AND WHEREAS Bougainville is geographically apart and its people culturally distinct from Papua New Guinea....
> AND WHEREAS it has been a long standing wish and aspiration of the people of Bougainville to become a separate independent nation. ...
> AND WHEREAS it is the inalienable right of a people to be free and independent. ...[56]

The ethno-nationalist cause, however, has been given one of its biggest boosts by the behaviour of some members of the national security forces deployed in the province and the national government's poor handling of the situation. Gross human rights abuses by the security forces, including torture and summary executions, have now been well documented. In March 1990 all security forces were withdrawn from Bougainville, leaving the BRA in de facto control, and in the following month the Papua New Guinea government imposed a total blockade on the island with the intention of preventing even food and medical supplies from reaching the Bougainvilleans.[57] There is little doubt that the government's record in these respects has helped to consolidate ethno-nationalist sentiments on the island and mobilise stronger support for the secessionist cause.[58] On the other hand, the BRA has conducted its own campaigns against local people. Apart from political assassinations, it seems that the BRA has also been responsible for the intimidation, harassment, and assault of Bougainvilleans who express 'any opinion short of total support for independence'.[59] Under these circumstances, it is impossible to determine what most 'ordinary' Bougainvilleans really feel about the issue. It may be that 'ineradicable widespread secessionist sentiment'[60] pervades Bougainville and that 'Francis and the Supremes' are the leaders that the people there would choose, but these assumptions remain untested.[61]

Conclusion

In the resolution of the current situation, at least two major problems are posed for the national government of Papua New Guinea. One of these relates to the loss of a significant resource for the state in the Panguna mine. Since it began production in 1972 – and until its closure – proceeds from the mine contributed around 44 per cent of Papua New Guinea's exports (and 16 per cent of its internal revenue).[62] The problem of resources is one which is very frequently raised in debates over distributive justice when the issue of secession, or even greater autonomy, is raised. Buchanan, for example, explores the situation where a group of 'haves' seek to secede from the 'have nots' in order to 'end the burdensome sharing of their wealth'. He points out that in these circumstances secession may be resisted in order to prevent the violation of 'the worst off's right to a portion of wealth of the better off'.[63] Similarly, Walzer suggests that 'the will and capacity of the people for self-determination may not establish a right to secede if the secession would not only remove land but also vitally needed fuel and mineral resources from the larger political community'.[64] But these considerations are not conclusive, for arguments about distributive justice must also be mediated by considerations of discriminatory redistribution which Bougainvilleans can obviously appeal to. It should be pointed out, however, that these issues would not necessarily be resolved to the satisfaction of all Bougainvilleans if the island was to succeed in its quest for either complete independence or greater autonomy. As is evident from the original dispute within the PLA, arguments about distributive justice could easily remain the source of much strife within and between the various groups on Bougainville.

A second major problem for the state of Papua New Guinea concerns the more general question of political fragmentation. This has been canvassed by various commentators who have suggested that letting Bougainville go would start 'the unravelling of the nation' and lead to its eventual disintegration.[65] While it might be true that no other part of Papua New Guinea has as much potential to attempt a full-scale breakaway, mainly because of geographical factors,[66] the 'demonstration effect' referred to earlier can obviously serve as a powerful example to other regions, especially those with considerable mineral resources, to use the threat of secession if the terms of exploiting those resources are not entirely to their liking. One writer has argued that Bougainville's secessionist movement has set 'an unhealthy precedent for other regions to seek secession in an attempt to resolve their economic grievances', and that the present political climate contains 'symptoms of being further beset by similar claims by other P.N.G. regions should Bougainville succeed'.[67] With many other mining projects ready or in the planning stage, there is enormous scope for disputes over land, royalties, and compensation.[68] Prime Minister Namalui has also had the unenviable task of trying to assure potential investors that the national government is, in fact, in charge, and that mineral investment is safe.[69] Even if Bougainville does not become an independent nation, an alternative solution in the form of almost complete autonomy for the province would set the same sort of example. Again, this has important implications for the problem of distributory justice and the role of the state.

These issues are made more problematic by the depiction of various grievances as ethnically-based, and there is little doubt that if the ethnic factor on Bougainville is given any credence as a just cause for secession, it would provoke the escalation of similar claims in other regions. To the extent that ethnicity is invoked and mobilised as a political resource in such contexts, it takes on a clearly instrumental character. In the process of pursuing pragmatic political interests, however, there is little doubt that ethnic or cultural identity becomes more than a mere epiphenomenon. But while the intensity with which ethnic identity may be expressed in these circumstances might seem to lend support to the primordialist perspective, it is best depicted as an imperative categorical affiliation that emerges in response to a host of factors which together give form to perceptions of relative standing within the larger framework of the state.[70] No matter which way the phenomenon is viewed, however, the logic of extremism which attends the ethno-nationalist cause enables its leaders to systematically exploit their position as a strong bargaining tactic.[71] And this is a tactic that can be learned readily by other groups in Papua New Guinea – to the very great cost of the standing and authority of the state.

Given the way in which former colonial states like Papua New Guinea were formed, and the arbitrary and perhaps unjust manner in which their boundaries were drawn and imposed, current grievances may obviously have some objective historical bases. But re-drawing the boundaries now is not necessarily going to produce miracles of problem-solving, and it would almost certainly create new problems, which begs examination of the logic of ethno-nationalism. This logic proceeds from the premise that each and every *ethnie* is entitled to its own sovereign state, to the conclusion that once this has been achieved, greater justice and happiness for the members of that *ethnie* thereby follows. All the problems that attend the functioning of micro-states elsewhere, however, would undoubtedly descend on Bougainville. Despite its abundance of mineral resources, Bougainville would experience the same constraints on development that other island micro-states have experienced, including 'diseconomy of scale, distance from markets, narrow range of local skills, dependence on one or a few large companies, limited access to capital markets and heavy dependence on aid and external institutions'.[72] Furthermore, there is plenty of evidence from Africa and elsewhere to support the contention that freedom and prosperity does not follow automatically from political independence and that natural resources have often been pawned in the process.[73] Even the ability to pawn resources depends on finding a company willing to take the risk of dealing with a group that has already demonstrated considerable expertise in sabotage. Finally, and as suggested earlier, questions of distributive justice are unlikely to disappear in the event of either complete independence or greater autonomy. The disputes and problems will merely be transferred to a smaller arena in which the various groups within Bougainville will undoubtedly vie with each other for what they perceive to be their just portion of the goods, thereby demonstrating, amongst other things, the mythical nature of 'Bougainville nationalism'.[74] If their efforts to regain 'paradise lost' do succeed, then, those ethnic fundamentalists and their followers on Bougainville may well find that their pursuit of self-determination has led them instead to a fool's paradise.

Notes

1. Stavenhagen, R., (1991), 'Ethnic Conflicts and Their Impact on International Society', *International Social Science Journal,* vol. xliii, no. 1, p. 117.
2. At a more basic level, issues of this kind also raise questions as to the very nature of the state as a form of political organisation or community. These are beyond the scope of this paper, but for some fairly extensive analyses see Walker, R.B.J. and Mendlovitz, S.H. (eds), *Contending Sovereignties: Redefining Political Community* (Boulder, Co.: Lynne Rienner, 1990), and the special edition on 'Ethnicity in World Politics', *Third World Quarterly,* vol. 11, no. 4, October 1989.
3. That is, if ethnicity is understood in terms of the traditional (and simplistically deterministic) approach which takes 'objective' cultural structures such as language (or religion, or phenotype) as definitive of an 'ethnic group'. See Brown, D., (1989) 'Ethnic Revival: Perspectives on State and Society', *Third World Quarterly,* vol. 11, no. 4, pp. 5-6.
4. May, R.J., 'Micronationalism in Perspective' in May, R.J. (ed), *Micronationalist Movements in Papua New Guinea* (Canberra, Department of Political and Social Change, Research School of Pacific Studies, Australian National University, 1982), p. 2. May makes the point that this type of 'disengagement' is often anti-centrist only to the extent that it emphasises the attainment of development objectives via self-help projects rather than dependence on central government initiative. Even so, there is potential for movements of this kind to become vehicles for separatist sentiments and, as May points out, they can become 'a form of protest among groups who consider themselves relatively deprived, slighted or threatened', p. 448.
5. Horowitz, D.L., (1985), *Ethnic Groups in Conflict,* University of California Press, p. 281.
6. Samarasinghe, S.W.R. de A., (1990), 'Introduction' to Premdas, R.R., Samarasinghe, S.W.R. de A. and Anderson, A.B. (eds), *Secessionist Movements in Comparative Perspective,* London: Pinter Publishers, p. 2.
7. For definitions of the various kinds of nationalist movements, see Snyder, L.L., *Global Mini-Nationalisms: Autonomy or Independence,* Westport: Greenwood Press, 1982, pp. xv-xviii.
8. Suhrke, A. and Noble, L.G. (eds), (1977), 'Conclusion' in *Ethnic Conflict in International Relations,* New York: Praeger Publishers, p. 7.
9. Butler, P.F., (1978), 'Legitimacy in a States-System: Vattell's *Laws of Nature*' in Donelan, M. (ed), *The Reason of States: A Study in International Political Theory,* London: George Allen and Unwin, p. 61. It should be noted that phenomena such as ethnic conflicts, separatism,

secession, and so forth, are not explicable in the terms set by the realist paradigm for any conceptual framework that reduces these to traditional inter-state confrontations is obviously inadequate. See de Senarclens, P., (1991), 'The 'Realist' Paradigm and International Conflicts', *International Social Science Journal*, vol. xliii, no. 1, p. 17.

10. Horowitz, *Ethnic Groups in Conflict*, (see note 5), p. 230.

11. Murphy, A.B., (March 1991), 'Regions as Social Constructs: The Gap Between Theory and Practice', *Progress in Human Geography*, vol. 15, no. 1, p. 29.

12. Taylor, P.J., (1989), *Political Geography: World-Economy, Nation-State and Locality*, 2nd edn Harlow: Longman, p. 172.

13. Breuilly, J., (1982), *Nationalism and the State*, Manchester: Manchester University Press, p. 53.

14. Snyder, *Global Mini-Nationalisms*, p. 4, and Premdas, R.R., 'Secessionist Movements in Comparative Perspective' in Premdas, Samarasinghe and Anderson (eds), *Secessionist Movements*, p. 16.

15. Smith, A.D., (1981), *The Ethnic Revival* (Cambridge: Cambridge University Press,) p. 20.

16. Gellner, E., (1983), *Nations and Nationalism*, Oxford: Basil Blackwell, p. 125.

17. Smith, A.D., (1986), *The Ethnic Origins of Nations*, Oxford: Basil Blackwell, p. 211. It should be noted here that a reified notion of culture results in an overly deterministic view of the phenomenon. See Avruch, K. and Black, P.W., (January 1991), 'The Culture Question and Conflict Resolution', *Peace and Change*, vol. 16, no. 1, pp. 30-31. Another commentator has drawn attention to the reification of culture as a means of defining 'the contours of ethnic intolerance'. See Handler, R., (June 1990), Comment on Jonathan Spencer's, 'Writing Within: Anthropology, Nationalism, and Culture in Sri Lanka, *Current Anthropology*, vol. 31, no. 3, pp. 283-299.

18. Gellner, E., *Nations and Nationalism*, (see note 16), p. 6.

19. Henderson, G. and Lebow, R.N., 'Conclusions' in Henderson, G., Lebow, R.N. and Stoessinger, J.G. (eds), (1974), *Divided Nations in a Divided World*, New York: David McKay Co., p. 433.

20. Nielson, G., cited in Taylor, *Political Geography*, p. 188. The editorial on 'State, Sectarianism and Strife' in *Third World Quarterly*, vol. 11, no. 4, (1989), p. ix-x, gives the ratio of ethnic groups to states as four to one.

21. Gellner, E., *Nations and Nationalism*, (see note 16), p. 2.

22. Mulgan, R.G., 'Peoples of the South Pacific and their Rights' in Thakur, Ramesh (ed), (1991), *The South Pacific: Problems, Issues and Prospects*, London: Macmillan, p. 124.

23. This presumption is implicit in the realist paradigm, although it has

remained largely unexamined in international relations theory. Halliday notes, for example, that the legal-territorial conception of the state is the most deeply embedded yet at the same time neglected element in realism. See Halliday, F., (September 1990), 'The Pertinence of International Relations', *Political Studies,* vol. xxxviii, no. 3, p. 514. See also Jarvis, A., (1989), 'Societies, States and Geopolitics: Challenges from Historical Sociology, *Review of International Studies,* vol. 15, p. 281.

24. Brown, D., 'Ethnic Revival', (see note 3), p. 9.
25. Islam, M. Rafiq, (Fall, 1991), 'Secession Crisis in Papua New Guinea: The Proclaimed Republic of Bougainville in International Law', *University of Hawaii Law Review,* vol. 13, no. 2, p. 457.
26. Buchanan, A., (January 1991), 'Secession: The Morality of Political Divorce from Fort Sumter to Lithuania and Quebec, and his preliminary exploration: 'Toward a Theory of Secession', *Ethics,* vol. 101, no. 2, pp. 322-342.
27. Mulgan, R.G., 'Peoples of the South Pacific', (see note 22), p. 123.
28. Gastil, R.D., (Winter 1985), 'The Past, Present and Future of Democracy', *Journal of International Affairs,* vol. 38, no. 2, p. 162.
29. Snyder, *Global Mini-Nationalisms,* (see note 14), p. 254.
30. Anderson, B., (1983), *Imagined Communities: Reflections on the Origin and Spread of Nationalism,* London: Verso, pp. 15-16.
31. From a letter by Francis Ona reproduced in Polomka, P. (ed), (1990), *Bougainville: Perspectives on a Crisis,* Canberra: Strategic and Defence Studies Centre, Australian National University, pp. 10-12.
32. Pettman, J., in Pettman, R. (ed), (1979), *Moral Claims in World Affairs,* London: Croom Helm, esp. pp. 140-143. Issues of this kind have been canvassed extensively in the literature on trans-national relations, interdependence, and modernisation. For a succinct overview and commentary on this literature see Gourevitch, P., (1978), 'The Second Image Reversed: The International Sources of Domestic Politics', *International Organisation,* vol. 32, no. 4, pp. 881-912. For a more recent review of relevant literature which also deals with the notion of state autonomy see Jarvis, A., (1989), 'Societies, States and Geopolitics: Challenges from Historical Sociology, *Review of International Studies,* vol. 15, pp. 281-293.
33. *Ibid.,* p. 141.
34. Gastil, R.D., (Winter 1985), (see note 28), pp. 161-162.
35. Buchanan, 'Toward a Theory of Secession', pp. 322-342. Buchanan here draws on Beran who asserts that: 'Democratic liberalism is committed to the view that any territorially concentrated group within a state should be permitted to secede if it wants to and if it is morally

and practically possible'. See Beran, H., (1987),*The Consent Theory of Political Obligation,* London: Croom Helm, p. 41.

36. *Ibid.,* p. 328.

37. *Ibid.,* p. 329.

38. Woolford, D., (1976), *Papua New Guinea: Initiation and Independence,* St. Lucia: University of Queensland Press), p. 184.

39. May (ed), *Micronationalist Movements;* Lamour, P., (October 1990), 'Ethnicity and Decentralisation in Melanesia: A Review of the 1980s', *Pacific Viewpoint,* vol. 31, no. 2, pp. 10-27; and Premdas, R.R. and Steeves, J.S., 'Secessionists versus Central Authority: Papua Besena in the Elections' in Hegarty, D. (ed), (1983), *Electoral Politics in Papua New Guinea: Studies on the 1977 National Elections,* Port Moresby: University of Papua New Guinea Press.

40. Snyder, *Global Mini-Nationalisms,* (see note 14), p. 251.

41. May, R.J., (October 1990), 'The Ethnic Factor in Politics', *Pacific Viewpoint,* vol. 31, no. 2, p. 6.

42. Standish, B., (February 1990), 'Bougainville: Undermining the State in Papua New Guinea', Part II, *Pacific Research,* vol. 3, no.1, p. 5. This particular stereotype works both ways, that is 'blackskins ' will denigrate 'redskins' and vice-versa. It is also the most common stereotype referred to in the literature.

43. Premdas and Steeves, 'Secessionists versus Central Authority', p. 40.

44. Narokobi employs the essentialist technique of positing 'the other' and 'otherness' by way of providing a necessary contrast against which some uniformity for 'Melanesians' can be constructed: 'Though diverse in many cultural practices, including languages, still we are united, and are different from Asians and Europeans'. See Narokobi, B., (1983), *The Melanesian Way,* rev. ed, Boroko and Suva, Institute of Papua New Guinea Studies/Institute of Pacific Studies, p. 7. Of course, Bougainvillean ethno-nationalists can, and do, employ precisely the same technique in distinguishing Bougainvilleans from the rest of Papua New Guinea's people. The classic conceptualisation (and condemnation) of 'otherness' is to be found in Said, E., (1978), *Orientalism,* New York: Vintage Books.

45. May, 'The Ethnic Factor', p. 5. On a similar point, Smith argues that the demonstration of erroneous assumptions underscoring an 'ethno-history' is often largely irrelevant to ethnic identification and does little to mitigate the intensity of feeling that can be generated by it. See Smith, A.D., (1990), 'The Supersession of Nationalism?', *International Journal of Comparative Sociology,* vol. XXXI, nos. 1-2, p. 14.

46. In geographical terms, Bougainville (together with Buka Island which is part of the same land mass and is separated only by a shallow strait

of less than one kilometre) is usually described as part of the Solomon Island chain. But Spriggs points out that maps can be drawn in a number of ways and that much depends on presentation. Similarly, he draws attention to the various ways in which regional prehistories can be written according to which scales and boundaries are chosen. See Spriggs, M., 'Alternate Prehistories for Bougainville: Regional, Nationalist or Micronationalist' (forthcoming).

47. BCL is a subsidiary of Conzinc Riotinto of Australia (CRA) which began exploration in 1964. BCL was set up in 1967 and was granted leases from the colonial administration for mining, tailings disposal, and an access road. See Connell, J., 'The Panguna Mine Impact (1)' in Polomka (ed), *Bougainville*, p. 43.

48. Havani, M., 'Perspectives on a Crisis (3)', in Polomka (ed), *Bougainville*, pp. 17-27.

49. Bonney, N., (1986), *The Politics and Finance of Provincial Government in Papua New Guinea*, Canberra: Centre for Research on Federal Financial Relations, Australian National University, pp. 11-20.

50. Lamour, P., 'Ethnicity and Decentralization in Melanesia', p. 14.

51. *Ibid.*

52. Connell, J., 'Perspectives on a Crisis (4)', in Polomka (ed), *Bougainville*, pp. 28-29.

53. For details see Okole, H., 'The Politics of the Panguna Landowners' Organisation'; Filer, C., 'The Bougainville Rebellion, the Mining Industry and the Process of Social Disintegration in Papua New Guinea', both in May and Spriggs (eds), (1990), *The Bougainville Crisis;* and Dorney, S., *Papua New Guinea*, Sydney: Random House, esp. pp. 117-123.

54. Kabui, J., part of a speech recorded by the ABC's 'Four Corners' programme, 'Blood on the Bougainvillea', broadcast on ABC TV, Australia, (24 June 1991).

55. From a letter by Francis Ona published in *Times of Papua New Guinea*, (7-13 September 1989), quoted in Lamour, 'Ethnicity and Decentralisation', p. 15.

56. Reproduced in Polomka (ed.), *Bougainville*, (see note 31), pp.107-108.

57. Sasako, A., (February 1991), 'Inside Bougainville', *Pacific Islands Monthly*, p. 19, describes the grim realities of life, and death, on Bougainville without Western medicine, including penicillin, antibiotics, immunisation for children against preventable diseases such as measles, whooping cough, diptheria, polio, tetanus, mumps, and Hepatitis B, as well as treatment for diabetes and asthma.

58. Spriggs, Matthew, (23 August 1991), 'Bougainville Talks May Offer Chance for Peace', *Canberra Times*, p. 9.

59. Spriggs, M., (22 August 1991), 'The Long Haul to Compromise and

Consensus in Bougainville', *Canberra Times,* p. 9. ABC TV's 'Blood on the Bougainvillea' also reported that BRA rebels have not hesitated in taking revenge on people who previously worked for the national government.

60. Griffin, 'Bougainville is a Special Case', p. 14.
61. Callick, R., (August 1991), 'Forward to the Past?', *Australian Left Review,* no. 131, p. 25.
62. Connell, J., (see note 47), p. 43.
63. Buchanan, A., *Secession,* (see note 26), p. 115.
64. Walzer, M., (1978), *Just and Unjust Wars: A Moral Argument with Historical Illustrations,* London: Allen Lane, p. 93. Walzer adds that this also invites broader questions of distributive justice in international society.
65. ABC TV, 'Blood on the Bougainvillea', (see note 59).
66. See Griffin, 'Bougainville is a Special Case', p. 1, and May R.J., 'Political Implications of the Bougainville Crisis for Papua New Guinea' in May and Spriggs (eds), *The Bougainville Crisis,* p. 57.
67. Islam, M. Rafiq, 'Secession Crisis in Papua New Guinea',(see note 25), p. 465. One example of recent threats of this kind involves the rich Iagifu-Hedinia oil reserve in the Southern Highlands.
68. Alves, D., (1990), The Troubles on Bougainville', *The Round Table,* no. 316, p. 406.
69. North, D., (June 1990), 'Papua New Guinea: Taking the Battle to Washington', *Pacific Islands Monthly,* p. 18.
70. For discussion of the way in which ethnic or cultural identity is politicised in the contemporary Pacific see Linnekin, J. and Poyer, L. (eds), (1990), *Cultural Identity and Ethnicity in the Pacific,* Honolulu: University of Hawaii Press.
71. Agassi, J., 'The Logic of Consensus and of Extremes' in D'Agostino, F. and Jarvie, I.C. (eds), (1989), *Freedom and Rationality: Essays in Honour of John Watkins,* Dordrecht: Kluwer, p. 11.
72. Dolman, A.J., 'Paradise Lost?: The Past Performance and Future Prospects of Small Island Developing Countries' in Dommen, E. and Hein, P. (eds), (1985), *States, Microstates and Islands,* London: Croom Helm, p. 41.
73. Islam, M. Rafiq, 'Secession Crisis in Papua New Guinea', (see note 25), p. 472.
74. For a detailed critique of this myth see Filer, C., 'The Bougainville Rebellion'.

* I am very grateful to Ron May, Michael Goldsmith and Alistair Sands for their helpful comments and suggestions on an early draft of this paper.

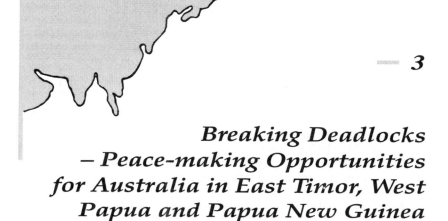

3

Breaking Deadlocks
– Peace-making Opportunities
for Australia in East Timor, West
Papua and Papua New Guinea

Peter King

Introduction

The most delicate challenges for Australian security policy lie in relations with Papua New Guinea (P.N.G.) and Indonesia. The conventional wisdom is that Australia must prop up the post-colonial state in P.N.G. against threats from within (such as Bougainville) and without (such as Indonesia), while simultane-ously building the best possible relationship with Jakarta.

This chapter argues that Canberra's P.N.G. policy arises out of a concept of security which is short-sighted, élite-centred, state-centric, militarised and 'law-and-order' driven. Having linked *a priori* the security of Australia with that of the P.N.G. state, Canberra seems to ignore the fact that the P.N.G. élite, and many of the foreign companies with which it cooperates, are becoming a major source of insecurity for the people of Papua New Guinea. It is P.N.G.'s politicians and bureaucrats who profit when foreign companies exploit P.N.G.'s forests for timber. It was the P.N.G. government which failed to make the required reviews of the 1974 Bougainville mine agreement, thus allowing grievances on the island to escalate until they exploded in 1989. It is the government's own 'security' forces which now loom as a threat to P.N.G.'s fragile and much abused constitutional order. Yet Canberra continues to offer remarkably uncritical economic and military support to this government. In response to threats from secessionists and 'raskol' gangs, Canberra augments police as well as military aid, thus ignoring Bougainville's profound grievances about the behaviour of the security forces, and accepting a definition of 'law and order' which largely ignores élite corruption and misbehaviour.

Canberra's 'befriend Indonesia' policy is likewise focused on a friendship between states rather than peoples. Like the P.N.G. state, the Suharto regime is a significant source of insecurity for its people: notably for the East Timorese and West Papuans – neither of whom accept rule from Jakarta – but also for the many other groups who have suffered from repressive, corrupt and authoritarian rule. In the interests of *realpolitik*, commercial advantage and short-run tranquillity Australia has turned a blind eye to these problems. Yet they will not go away, and have the potential to wreck the 'befriend Indonesia' policy entirely.

Australia's defence policy aimed at defending Australia's north against a campaign of harassment coming 'from or through the archipelago'[1] also raises a question about bilateral relations with Indonesia. The policy has been coupled with an unprecedented peace-time build-up of Australian naval and air strike capacity, and an ongoing transfer of military assets to the north and west. Although Australian reassurances appear to have largely quelled Indonesian concern over a possible 'threat from the South', the policies which have been called 'the new Australian militarism' also jeopardise the 'befriend Indonesia' policy.

There is a need to rethink the security dimension of Australia's relations with both Indonesia and Papua New Guinea. This chapter provides some background for such a debate.

Australia and Indonesia

There are two principal kinds of conflict resolution applicable to the vexed relationship between Australia and Indonesia over the past 40 years. First there are diplomatic settlements of state-to-state disputes which avert trouble by applying principles of *realpolitik* to conflicts involving the suppression of self-determination and the denial of human rights. Examples of this would be Australian acquiescence in the Indonesian annexations of West Papua in 1969, and, especially, of East Timor in 1976. In December 1989 Australia's recognition of Indonesia's annexation of East Timor was carried a stage further with the conclusion of the Timor Gap Zone of Cooperation Treaty, which drew a new maritime boundary of 250 kms with Indonesia and included an agreement on joint resource (largely oil and gas) exploitation in the Timor Sea. The other kind of conflict resolution – of which there are no examples yet – would address the aspirations and rights of minority peoples in Eastern Indonesia, whose suppression and denial by governments in Jakarta has troubled Indonesia's bilateral relationship with Australia since the 1960s.

Unless the profound commitment of the peoples of East Timor and West Papua to self-determination and independence is respected by Australia and accommodated by Indonesia, there is a long-term danger, not only of perpetual trouble in the Australia-Indonesia bilateral relationship, but of upheavals in Timor, West Papua and Papua New Guinea itself, which may damage the relationship further. Australian preventive diplomacy aimed at addressing human rights issues would be useful. Although this is unfamiliar territory for government, Australia should try and relate to Indonesia in ways which build a sound long-term relationship between peoples as well as states. Because the Suharto regime will not last indefinitely, Australia must strive also to avoid over-identification with any particular ruling clique, pending the democratisation of Indonesia's political system.

In the government's view, however, since the unfortunate Jenkins affair in 1986 (in which a front-page article in the *Sydney Morning Herald* likened the Suharto family's corruptly acquired corporate and financial empire to that of the recently deposed Marcos family in the Philippines, and precipitated a stormy patch between Canberra and Jakarta lasting for many months),[2] the bilateral relationship with Jakarta has become more substantial than ever. According to Canberra, this is because of the diligence and determination of Australian diplomacy and the influence of moderate Indonesian Foreign Ministers, Mochtar Kusumaatmadja and Ali Alatas. Apart from the Timor Gap Treaty (ten years in the making) there has been collaboration rather than competition in efforts to move the Cambodian civil war towards a settlement;[3] the Labor government's regional economic initiative, Asian Pacific Economic Cooperation (APEC), has met with approval among ASEAN countries, including Indonesia,[4] and an Australian media presence has been restored in Jakarta. An Australia-Indonesia Institute, launched in 1989, has placed high priority on promoting journalistic exchanges and training programs between the two countries.[5] (The new Institute has been set up inside the Department of Foreign Affairs and Trade with an initial budget of $700,000, and a brief to support, subsidise and facilitate cultural, business and academic activities and exchanges. A counterpart institution is to be established in Jakarta eventually.[6])

Treaties: Australia-P.N.G. and P.N.G.-Indonesia

The Australian government points to new developments in both P.N.G.-Indonesia relations and P.N.G.-Australia relations which seem to stabilise the two P.N.G. legs of the much discussed Australia-Indonesia-P.N.G. triangle, which have often shown signs of shakiness in the past. The Joint Declaration of Principles (JDP) signed by Canberra and Port Moresby in 1987 replaced a much less formal and onerous Australian security commitment of 1977 with a new agreement that the two sides will consult and consider action together in the event of aggression against either.[7]

This ANZUS-like undertaking to P.N.G. was adopted against opposition from the Department of Foreign Affairs and Trade (DFAT) and its then Minister, Bill Hayden. DFAT has traditionally contended that a formal security guarantee of P.N.G. might offend Indonesia or over-encourage Port Moresby and lead to trouble in the handling of sensitive Irian border issues. But in fact the security provisions of the JDP seem to have had little influence one way or the other up to now, although they may have marginally reassured disgruntled nationalists among P.N.G.'s élite who have long argued that Australia cannot be trusted.[8]

The JDP may also symbolise Australia's commitment to P.N.G. unity at any price, made manifest in the Hawke government's seemingly open-ended military and financial support for P.N.G.'s disastrous 'security' operation against the secessionist rebels of Bougainville.

The other item of triangular reinforcement was Port Moresby's new agreement with Jakarta – the Treaty for Mutual Respect, Friendship and Cooperation, initiated at Port Moresby's request and signed in 1986. This treaty foreshadowed a more intense effort at avoiding a repetition of the border and refugee problems which followed the *Organisasi Papua Merdeka* (OPM) West Papuan liberation movement) uprising in Irian Jaya during 1984. Through a commitment to more cross-border trade and more social and political interaction in the northern border towns of Jayapura (in Irian Jaya) and Vanimo (capital of P.N.G.'s West Sepik province), and a new determination to achieve more intimate understanding between military and political élites in the two countries, P.N.G. also hoped to solidify its ASEAN relationships free of Australian tutelage as far as possible.

Australia applauded the new 'maturity' of P.N.G. relations with Jakarta – and P.N.G.'s policy has indeed toughened against the West Papuan liberation movement, which is something Canberra has been urging on Port Moresby for nearly 20 years. It is noteworthy that Canberra's own policy towards East Timor has also recently shown a new level of toughness at the expense of the Timorese people. In all of this the current Australian government believes that since 1986 a positive balance in the Australia-Indonesia relationship has been achieved. None of these developments, however, has solved or even salved any of the deep problems in the bilateral relationship – especially not the conflicts, injustices and incompatibilities at the base of these problems.

East Timor

In East Timor the Fretilin resistance to Jakarta's occupation survives all attempts by Defence Minister General Benny Murdani to talk and repress it out of existence.[9] Indeed, since 1989 there has been an upsurge of nationalism among the students of Dili, with strong support from the local Catholic hierarchy. The former colonial power, Portugal, remains adamant that the Timor Gap Treaty is illegal and denies the right of the Timorese people to dispose of their own resources. Portugal is determined to take

Australia to the International Court of Justice.[10]

Australian official spokespersons, from the foreign minister down, have been forced into erroneous, self-contradictory discourse on the Timor issue, and Australian opinion remains inflamed 17 years after the unexplained killing by the Indonesian army of four Australian journalists who witnessed the takeover of Bacau. Gareth Evans, for example, was arguing right up until the massacre that while there were abuses in Timor, they were moderating[11] – partly under the influence of Australia, which now funds direct development programs and encourages the Timorese to accept their fate. Canberra still ostensibly accepts Benny Murdani's line that Fretilin is an insignificant force in decline, and that its struggle is hopeless.[12]

For Richard Woolcott, former head of Foreign Affairs and Trade and Ambassador to Indonesia (1975-8), exonerating Indonesia over Timor is an important sub-plot in the larger drama of celebrating President Suharto's 'New Order' for giving Indonesians '22 years of relative calm':

> It was only that he [Suharto] was concerned that a chaotic situation was developing [in Timor] – a civil war starting, and Fretilin's connection with Cuba and the Soviet Union. They [*sic*] simply took the decision that they were not prepared to allow .. Indonesia to be threatened by, a weak, unstable ministate in East Timor.[13]

This tendentious historiography and identification with a regime which began with a bloodbath (for Dick Woolcott, 'a massive upheaval')[14], and which has, at times, had the worst democratic and human rights credentials in Southeast Asia, is an indictment of Australian foreign policy. This is especially so in Timor where there have been approximately 200,000 deaths as a result of invasion, occupation, resistance, repression, dislocation, famine and avoidable disease.

The Dili massacre of 12 November 1991 – when security forces fired on unarmed mourner-demonstrators without any direct provocation – merely confirmed what close observers of the scene had long known: that thousands of Timorese are prepared to die for independence and that the key players in Indonesia's military leadership (Murdani, Sutrisno) are prepared to condone killing in order to block the resistance.[15] This clearly undermines Indonesia's legitimacy to rule Timor, and the events of November 12, 1991, have generated another opportunity for international action to bring about self-determination for the Timorese.

Irian Jaya/West Papua

Timor is one conflict that will not go away; the 'forgotten war' in the former Dutch colony of West Papua (Irian Jaya) is another. Indonesia occupied West Papua in 1963 and annexed it after the so-called Act of Free Choice in 1969. Following P.N.G.'s independence in 1975, Canberra's fundamental attitude has been one of neutrality on border and related issues between Jakarta and Port Moresby. Australia has discouraged P.N.G. from showing Melanesian solidarity with West Papuans, on the one hand, and urged an avoidance of conflict with Indonesia at almost any cost, on the other. Despite the 1987 Joint Declaration of Principles which seemed to undercut this traditional line, the P.N.G. government has (since 1988) negotiated a rapprochement with Jakarta on border and refugee issues.

There has been a P.N.G. consulate in Jayapura since 1989, and an Indonesian consulate is planned for Vanimo. In August 1990 P.N.G. Foreign Minister, Michael Somare, announced that the Defence Force would destroy OPM camps on the P.N.G. side of the border, while Defence Minister Ben Sabumei promised coordinated joint patrols with Indonesia's armed forces (ABRI) in the border region.[16] During the previous 15 years the P.N.G. government had prided itself on avoiding or rejecting these sorts of actions.[17]

What is also strange is that these commitments were undertaken in the same week that Michael Somare made a formal protest to Jakarta about Indonesian military incursions into P.N.G. and the killing of P.N.G. citizens.[18] They also followed an episode in which P.N.G. and Australia acted together to squash a fresh upheaval in Jayapura. A planned OPM flag-raising demonstration was foiled by police and red beret commandos arresting hundreds of people and detaining a number of Cenderawasih University students. Four Irianese who sought asylum inside the

P.N.G. consulate in Jayapura were handed over to the Indonesians, apparently after the Australian embassy in Jakarta moved against them.[19] (They 'left on their own volition', according to Gareth Evans.)[20]

In July 1990 P.N.G. deported OPM deputy leader Melky Salosa to Jayapura, after criminal charges had been dropped. The government did not consider deportation to a third country which they had often used in similar situations in the past. The Australian Foreign Affairs Minister condoned the deportation on the grounds that Salosa did not have refugee status. Salosa was subsequently sentenced to life imprisonment. In mid-1991 his body was found on the P.N.G.-West Papua border. The Indonesian authorities claim he died from hunger one week after escaping from prison, but according to West Papuan sources, the Indonesian military executed him and fabricated the escape as an excuse.[21]

Indonesia and 'Stability' in P.N.G.

Australian-Indonesian convergence on Melanesian issues took another turn in early 1990. During a visit to Jakarta Australian Federal Opposition Leader John Hewson was told by Benny Murdani that P.N.G. lacked the troops required to crush the Bougainville rebellion, and that Australia should give more help. 'It would not be healthy for the region if Bougainville was allowed to secede', said the Indonesian Defence Minister.[22] (Such a development would be particularly unhealthy for Indonesian control over East Timor and West Papua). The Australian Government, which had delivered military helicopters to the P.N.G. Defence Force in 1989, had no disagreement with Murdani, as a DFAT spokesperson made clear.[23] Whether attempts to devise a political solution based on constitutional autonomy for Bougainville will meet with Indonesian (or Australian) disapproval remains to be seen, but the Australian government does not seem prepared to promote this kind of solution for Bougainville, let alone West Papua or East Timor.

Benny Murdani apparently believes that Jakarta has a responsibility for stability in P.N.G. if Australia is reluctant to intervene, and there is a worrying pattern in P.N.G.-Indonesia relations, which makes Indonesian intervention plausible. Senior P.N.G. military officers – both serving and retired – have been a conduit for subversive pressures from Indonesia in recent years. In 1987 Tony Huai, Defence Force Commander in the Paias Wingti government, admitted accepting gifts from the then Indonesian Armed Forces Commander, Benny Murdani, during an unauthorised trip to Jakarta. On this trip, Huai leaked confidential details of Australian negotiations with P.N.G. over the Joint Declaration of Principles, and he has been an outspoken opponent of the OPM as well.[24]

Former Defence Force Commander Ted Diro was also on Benny Murdani's gift list during his fund-raising efforts as People's Action Party leader before the 1987 national elections. Murdani's contribution, during Diro's visit to Jakarta for the signing of the new P.N.G./Indonesia cooperation treaty in 1986, was US $139,400. In 1987 Diro was charged with perjury over evidence he gave concerning this gift before the Barnett Inquiry into forestry corruption, but he escaped punishment on a legal technicality.

During the Namaliu government (1988-92), Defence Minister Sabumei and Foreign Minister Somare also enjoyed very close relations with the Indonesians. In the course of the visit by ABRI Commander-in-Chief General Tri Sutrisno to P.N.G. in December 1990 – the first by an Indonesian army leader since 1975 – Ben Sabumei called for joint military exercises with Jakarta, and made a remark which puzzled some observers, but which simply reflects a history of close contact (often at the expense of the OPM) between the two military services: 'Our two armed forces must be seen as an instrument or catalyst to bring about change in the attitudes and preconceived view that exist between the people of our two countries', said Ben Sabumei.[25] How better to bring about such change than through Jakarta-style military predominance in P.N.G. politics?

The new Jakarta/Jayapura-Vanimo/Port Moresby honeymoon is one that Canberra ostensibly favours: it certainly represents a substantial diversification in P.N.G.'s foreign relations as well as some potential for reduced dependence on Australia. But the long-term implications are troubling not only for P.N.G. itself but for Australia and regional peace as well. Ethno-nationalism in Irian, in

Timor and in Bougainville cannot be repressed in the long run, not even by a grand triangular collusion of the Big Three of the Western South Pacific. And in any case the human rights implications of such collusion could be intolerable, not least inside P.N.G. itself.

Papua New Guinea and Security

New concepts of security, particularly in a fragile society like P.N.G., have ecological, social, political and economic as well as military dimensions. Threats to security can develop internally as well as externally. Such threats are becoming more influential in the post-Cold War world. Even if they originate externally, they may readily leapfrog the conventional defences of the state and society: military forces, customs regulations, investment and taxation regimes, labour and immigration laws, resource protection measures, laws against foreign political funding of elections and so forth.

The most vital external security issues facing P.N.G. arise out of Jakarta's control of Irian Jaya/West Papua. These have an important military dimension as to whether security is pursued through cooperation with Indonesia to crush the West Papuan liberation movement (as at present), or by a P.N.G. effort (ideally backed by Australia) to uphold the rights of West Papuan nationalist refugees and to encourage a negotiated settlement between the OPM and Jakarta. General Murdani's corrupt gifts to P.N.G. leaders suggest that one kind of Indonesian threat has already leapfrogged P.N.G.'s conventional defences and subverted state policy.

There are two other major threats to P.N.G. at present: resource destruction and social and environmental degradation on the one hand, and political decay and political disintegration on the other. The two threats are in fact becoming closely linked, and they are being driven by international forces. Large international companies, hungry for resources, especially timber, are negotiating corrupt deals with local political, business and bureaucratic élites. The corporations are Australian, Japanese, South Korean, Taiwanese, Singaporean and Malaysian. The list of past and prospective damage is lengthy: from irreversible destruction of forests and fauna to massive avoidance of tax and royalty payments; from the debauching of political and administrative processes to the contamination of village water supplies. Even where corruption is not significantly present, as in the mining industries, the multinational assault on national resources involves a close bond with the local modernising parliamentary and public service élite which fuels a popular hunger for 'development' at almost any cost. When local industry is unprofitable, and external aid is declining, the short cut to a balanced and expanding budget – with sustainable salaries for demanding bureaucrats, and schools, clean water and aid posts for the people – is a big mine. Papua New Guinea will soon have (or have had) five: Bougainville in the North Solomons province and Ok Tedi in Western province (copper and gold), and Missima in Milne Bay province, Lihir in New Ireland province and Porgera in Enga province (gold). The downside of mining dependence, of course, is that a mine leaves a nasty hole in more than one sense if shut down. In the North Solomons the Bougainville Revolutionary Army has dug a 17 per cent hole in the P.N.G. budget.[26]

The other large problem of mining is ecological damage, which can result in a loss of livelihood for the people, unemployment, urban drift, social division and political turmoil. On Bougainville the end result of large-scale mining in a closely knit traditional community has been rebellion, civil war and *de facto* secession. No one knows whether the secession can be overcome and the mine reopened. At Ok Tedi in the Western province the bills are just starting to come in. The mine, which is in very remote, wet and rugged country, has only recently turned a profit after almost ten years of production. The mining company management has forced the P.N.G. government, as 20 per cent owner of the company, to waive the expensive but ecologically essential requirement of a permanent tailings dam. The result will probably be massive chemical pollution and poisoning of the Fly River and devastation of the livelihood of tens of thousands of river dwellers who have had nothing but vague promises of compensation from the government. The Ok Tedi mine, with its near-total dependence on the Fly for supplies and for export of copper, is as vulnerable to blockage as Bougainville was to rebellion. In January 1992 a clear indication that the Bougainville problem is not 'one-off' emerged with the closing of the small Mt. Kare gold mine in Enga province, following a destructive assault by an organised gang apparently representing dissatisfied landowners. The huge Porgera mine nearby was immediately perceived to be under threat.

In Papua New Guinea forestry is the resource industry with the biggest potential for causing ecological and social breakdown. It has become an essential case study in the business of resources plunder, ecological devastation and political and administrative corruption. What is ultimately at issue in the light of such gross (and still unchecked) exploitation, destruction and abuse of office is the survival of democratic political processes. According to the findings of Judge Barnett's Commission of Inquiry into forestry (1987-9), P.N.G.'s forest industry is totally out of control.[27]

A magnificent resource is being devastated by foreign interests in corrupt collusion with political notables, senior civil servants and comprador businessmen. This process jeopardises the livelihood and well-being of entire communities of traditional landowners. The foreign companies (the worst offenders are Malaysian companies which have already devastated the forests of Sarawak and Sabah) employ divisive tactics and make fraudulent promises to local landholders, and then set up landowner front companies to pressure the national government into granting timber leases. Foreign companies employ the following tactics to achieve and maintain leases.

1. Promise the earth in the logging agreements – sawmills, wharves, permanent roads, schools, housing, reforestation – but actually deliver nothing or next to nothing. Licences are never fully withdrawn in practice for failure to fulfil the terms of a logging agreement.

2. When logging is in progress maintain bribes to politicians, civil servants and other 'élites' through concealed shareholdings in the landowner companies. Play off landowners against each other, and defraud 'friendly' landholders by illegally charging royalty payments to their share of profits, which will normally be grossly understated. (Only one of the companies investigated by Judge Barnett had ever declared a profit in P.N.G.)

3. Plunder, rather than protect, the resource – and as rapidly as

possible, in case the political wind changes. Log near waterways and on steep slopes, clear fell where possible and do not
hesitate to let valuable logs rot if they fail to meet the exacting
standards of Japanese importers. (Rip out and rip off practices
are particularly prominent where grossly undercapitalised companies meet their initial capital requirements by rapid plunder
of the most valuable timbers.)

4. Mis-state the quality (species) and quantity of logs exported in
   order to minimise royalty payments, and then sell the logs to
   yourself off-shore at around 20 per cent below the world market price, which minimises earned revenue and lowers taxation. (Only one company – Australian – in the history of the
   P.N.G. timber industry has *not* undertaken transfer pricing,
   and the Barnett report made little difference to the practice,
   apart from the payment of a few million kina in back taxes by
   major offenders.)

Thus in P.N.G. an industry which earns a modest 70 million
kina (US$70 m.) in export revenue has totally devastated the
timber resources and greatly damaged the ecology and agricultural prospects of one province (New Ireland), and bids fair – or
did until the P.N.G. government announced a U-turn in 1989[28] – to
do the same for the whole country. At the same time the foreign
companies involved have flagrantly corrupted leading members of
two national governments and brought government itself into
deep disrepute. The attempt to discipline Minister of Forests, Ted
Diro, local sponsor and secret shareholder in the P.N.G. subsidiary of a Singapore logging company, led to the downfall of the
Paias Wingti government in July 1988.[29]

Despite damning criticism of him in the Barnett report, Diro
was made Deputy Prime Minister by Wingti's successor, Rabbie
Namaliu, in May 1990. Diro had the second largest following – of
Papuans – in the Namaliu government after the Pangu Party, and
he clung to office until, in September 1991, a leadership tribunal
finally found against him on 70 out of 81 changes of official
misconduct. On 20 October Diro finally resigned in the midst of a
constitutional crisis brought about by the refusal of the (Papuan)
Governor General, Sir Serai Eri, to dismiss him from office.[30]

Political Decay in P.N.G.

Corrupt businessmen and politicians operating in league with unscrupulous foreign interests to exploit resources, revenues and local people undermine social and political stability. Politicians frequently claim that their clan, tribal, regional or party followers expect them to flourish by fair means or (by Westminster standards) foul, but the end result – traditional group prosperity in particular – is held to justify the means. This is a thoroughly disingenuous claim. Diro himself was found culpable by the leadership tribunal for 'representing' landowner groups in dealings with a logging company in which he had a concealed interest.[31]

Social resentment is growing rapidly in P.N.G. Students at the University of P.N.G. defend the redistributive effects of rascal gangs and praise the Bougainville rebellion as a legitimate protest against a corrupt and self-serving élite in Port Moresby whose unscrupulous pursuit of power and personal profit needs to be checked.

Similarly, some responsible members of the P.N.G. élite are now showing alarm at the paralysis of government brought about by the never-ending parliamentary votes of no-confidence based on the curse of party and side-swapping. These votes lower the political time horizons from years to months, weeks and even days. One success of the Namaliu government was to change the Independence Constitution in order to give incoming governments 18 months grace (previously six) before they must face no-confidence motions in Parliament. The 18 month interval would also apply to any government formed after a successful no-confidence motion.[32]

This move may forestall what one observer has called 'extra-constitutional ways' for remedying social and economic ills, such as political and social rebellion by urban and rural rascal gangs). The gangs, having mastered the gentle art of turning a profit from car theft and break-and-enter, have now begun to make political connections, as unruly and irresponsible politicians find their services indispensable for spoiling a rival's campaign or for payback after its success, and for intimidating officials or purloining evidence of criminal behaviour.

'Law and order' problems generally are now a source of profound social tension and malaise: they are a great and growing cost burden for business, government and the individual (including poor Melanesians), and a greater threat to sound 'development' than persistently low commodity prices. In P.N.G. as elsewhere in the Pacific (notably Fiji), the forces of law and order (in P.N.G. parlance, 'the disciplined forces', meaning the police as well as the military) have, in fact, become prime elements of instability and insecurity for governments and people alike. The Defence Force leadership itself has defied the government openly on several occasions since the 'coup that never was' in 1977: troops have rioted and vandalised Parliament on pay issues (in 1989), and at least one former P.N.G. Defence Force Commander (Ted Diro) has talked about a military coup as a legitimate response to the country's present malaise. The Police Commissioner who made a chaotic coup attempt after the government ordered the withdrawal of all police and military forces from Bougainville in March 1990, still enjoyed sufficient support among the police to make his trial for felonious treason the occasion for yet more coup talk than ever. (He became Minister of Defence in the new Wingti government of Argun 1992!) In mid-1991 the government was forced to dismiss the Defence Force Commander on Bougainville, Colonel Leo Nuia, when he boasted to the ABC TV programme, *Four Corners*, of his unauthorised efforts to reconquer Bougainville Island for the P.N.G. government in defiance of the peace accords of the Honiara Declaration which had been reached between the Bougainville secessionist leaders and the P.N.G. government in January 1991.[33]

The 'disciplined forces' are part of Australia's post-colonial legacy. They are nurtured by growing project aid to the police and by Australian military aid totalling $52m. in 1990-91, including a substantial emergency supplement spurred by the Bougainville crisis.[34]

This supplement included:

* Helicopters, grenade launchers, heavy machine guns, small arms and ammunition.
* A Special Air Service counter-insurgency training team.

* Training and equipment to expand the PNGDF by 450 soldiers.

Total Australian aid to P.N.G.'s military in 1990, including this supplement and the portion of Australian budgetary aid which P.N.G. directs to defence, was around A$70m, more than P.N.G.'s own defence budget.

P.N.G.'s biggest law and order problem is the secession movement on Bougainville, and here again the 'disciplined forces' performed poorly in a counter-insurgency role. Both police and military forces were involved in gross abuses of human rights in late 1989, and especially during the attempt to crush the rebels in January and February of 1990. Colonel Nuia admitted to *Four Corners* that Australian-supplied helicopters were used as gunships, and to dump the bodies of executed Bougainvilleans at sea. The helicopters were also used to strafe 'suspect' villages.

The depredations of the military and the police and the suffering imposed on Bougainvilleans by the military-enforced blockade of the island were supposed to end with the Honiara Declaration of January 1991, but they have in fact continued.[35] On the other hand the BRA rebels are not ecologically inclined, as outside supporters have assumed, and they show keen interest in reopening the mine on suitable terms – without Bougainville Copper Limited and its parent, Conzinc Rio Tinto Australia. CRA and, even more, the Australian colonial government and the independent government of P.N.G. have a lot to answer for in failing to protect the economic and ecological well-being of the Bougainville people.

A Policy for Australia

The above examination of key security issues confronting Australia and its former colony reveals the inadequacy of current policies. What follows is a more adequate agenda for the future. Its implementation will not be easy; it has pitfalls of its own, and there is no guarantee of success, but it is important to think of new ways of solving security problems if P.N.G. militarisation and disintegration, and Indonesian repression and expansionism, are to be avoided or prevented.

1. Australia should dedicate itself to regional self-determination and support for democratic, non-corrupt and civilian forces in Indonesia and P.N.G. in the years ahead. In particular Australia should:

   (a) Formulate and promote proposals for imaginative resolution of the conflicts in East Timor, West Papua and Bougainville. In each of these cases, creative use of multilateral forums, and/or a 'quasi-state' solution, could be useful. Rather than actively condoning Jakarta's effort to repress the OPM and coopt the P.N.G. state into doing likewise, Australia should encourage P.N.G.'s involvement in efforts at resolving conflict in West Papua.
   (b) Suspend the provisions of the Timor Gap Treaty providing for joint development in the zone of cooperation, pending an acceptable settlement of the Timor problem.
   (c) Phase out military aid to Indonesia.

2. Australia should pursue a two-track form of preventive diplomacy toward Indonesia, with much more emphasis on the non-state track (person-to-person, non-governmental organisation (NGO)-to-NGO). In this way controversial issues such as human rights, self-determination and the environment might be addressed more directly.

3. If necessary Australia should commit itself to back P.N.G. militarily over the border with Irian Jaya/West Papua – something which is already implied by the 1987 Joint Declaration of Principles, and will be required during the period of diplomatic manoeuvre recommended here.

4. Notwithstanding any commitment to P.N.G., Australia should forestall an arms race with Indonesia by unilaterally curbing its naval and air strike capacity, and by seeking arms control understandings with Indonesia.

5. Australia should use what influence it has over Port Moresby (for example through the leverage of its $300m. aid programme) to preserve P.N.G. from the two major (and interwoven) non-military security threats it now faces: resource destruction and environmental degradation on the one hand, and political decay and disintegration on the other. In particular, Australia should:

(a) Make clear that current aid levels cannot continue under conditions of parliamentary paralysis and gross corruption.

(b) Phase out Bougainville-related military aid to P.N.G., and make police ('law and order') aid conditional on a serious attack upon élite illegality and disorder.

(c) Redirect Australia's aid, if necessary by channelling it through non-government organisations, so that more of it goes to the empowerment of the people rather than the aggrandisement of the state.

(d) Press for a process of reconciliation, devolution and reconstruction on Bougainville. Given the Australian stake in the Panguna mine, these efforts could perhaps most usefully be pursued through multilateral agencies such as the South Pacific Forum, or through steps to revive the Multi-national Supervisory Force envisaged in the Honiara Declaration.

(e) Encourage and resource an effort by the South Pacific Forum to monitor, document and police the activities of resource-plundering companies at work in the region.

6. Contribute to an international fund for establishing a conflict mediation service run by the South Pacific Forum: a clearing house for professional help to governments where local resources for conflict-avoidance or resolution are demonstrably inadequate or perceived (by the parties) as biased. One argument in favour of this is to contrast the abject failure of P.N.G.'s effort to resolve the Bougainville crisis by force with the partial successes achieved by ad hoc efforts at conflict resolution – first by a Swedish expert, and later courtesy of third parties such as New Zealand and the Solomon Islands (respectively the Endeavour Accords of August 1990 and the Honiara Declaration of January 1991, discussed above).

What the Australian approach to the Indonesian relationship lacks at present – under the influence of the still-ascendant Indonesia Lobby (with strong roots not only in the government bureaucracy, but in federal politics, the academy and the media) – is a long-term, principled strategy to cope with issues of human rights and political upheaval, not only in Melanesia but in Indonesia itself – issues which are likely to reassert themselves decisively before long. A clear commitment by Australia to self-determination in the region could have averted the tragedy and nightmare of Timor, and would lead the Australian government to seek a peaceful resolution of the protracted conflicts in Timor and West Papua instead of constantly averting its gaze. As a high priority, Australian and international NGOs[36] need to be given more space and resources to reshape the Australia-Indonesia relationship.

There is no need for Canberra to carry the full burden of human rights and ecological concern in its bilateral relationship with Jakarta; there is room instead for a two track diplomacy, both official and non-governmental. But it is disheartening, and certainly counterproductive in the long run, for the government to adopt a knee-jerk adversarial attitude towards activist groups and concerned advocates who point out the dangers and abuses of Indonesia's policy towards its regained (but cruelly exploited and deeply alienated) province, Irian Jaya, and its 'first colony', East Timor.

If peace on Bougainville Island needs to be negotiated, so does peace in East Timor (negotiation was tried briefly in 1983) and also in West Papua, whether the UN continues to recognise Indonesia's annexation or not.[37] No third party is in a stronger position than Australia to promote these three exercises in peacemaking – or the devising of (at least) federal, confederal or other new constitutional arrangements to guarantee local autonomy in vital areas like resource management, immigration and cultural and linguistic survival. If Portugal's rights in the East Timor dispute could be acknowledged in order to roll back Indonesia's occupation, so should P.N.G.'s rights in relation to Irian Jaya. West Papua was annexed to Indonesia before P.N.G. had a say, internationally – and the Irian conflict has been a source of profound insecurity (military, political and cultural) for P.N.G. since 1975.

By supporting such initiatives and new policy departures which seek systematic protection and support for the victims of Indonesian-style 'development', Australia can begin to rebuild its international reputation (and its credibility with the Suharto regime), so gravely damaged by the events of 1974-75.[38] That is why the provisions of the Timor Gap Treaty providing for joint development in the zone of cooperation should be suspended, and why military aid to Indonesia should be phased out, as a discreet signal that authoritarian military regimes practising various forms of neo-colonial exploitation and repression are not ultimately acceptable in a region which should be democratic and tolerant of social and cultural diversity as well as economically vibrant.

As for economic aid, the voluntary aid organisations dedicated to basic human need should be funded generously and supported diplomatically to play a much larger role in aid disbursement, in the human rights area and in the overall Australia-Indonesia relationship. In fact the Australian Council for Overseas Aid (ACFOA) has complained that the subsidy extended by the Australian International Development Assistance Bureau (AIDAB) for NGO aid programmes has been in decline while the government has increased contributions for 'aid' disbursed by the World Bank and the Asian Development Bank.[39]

The pursuit of the above agenda will inevitably offend the ruling Indonesian generals, just as it is likely to offend ruling commercial and political élites in Papua New Guinea. Fear of élite displeasure, however, is no reason for avoiding policies which are essential for long-term peace and justice in the region.

Notes

1. Dibb, P., (1986), *Review of Australia's Defence Capabilities*, Canberra: Australian Government Publishing Service.
2. Robinson, R., (3 December 1986), 'Explaining Indonesia's Response to the Jenkins Article: Implications for Australia-Indonesia Relations', *Australian Outlook*, 40.
3. In 1984-5 Foreign Minister Bill Hayden's efforts to sponsor negotiations for a Cambodian settlement were viewed with suspicion in the ASEAN capitals – even in Jakarta, which feels more affinity with Hanoi than the ASEAN mainstream for reasons to do with suspicion of China and a shared nationalist revolutionary experience.
4. Evans, G., 'Australia and Indonesia: a Developing Relationship', Address to a conference on Indonesia's New Order – Past, Present and Future, Australian National University, December 4, 1989 in *Australian Foreign Affairs and Trade: the Monthly Record* (AFAT), 60, 12 December 1989.
5. Australian Associated Press has an office in Jakarta; but no Australian newspaper has a resident correspondent. Persistent efforts by the

Australian Broadcasting Corporation to establish a presence in Jakarta were rewarded in 1991.

6. Evans, 'Australia and Indonesia', p. 706. On the new institute, see Australia-Indonesia Institute, *Annual Report, 1989-90*, Australian Government Publishing Service (AGPS), Canberra, 1990, and Van Langenberg, M., 'Cooperation is the Name of the Game: Introducing the new Australia-Indonesia Institute', *Inside Indonesia*, No. 20. October 1989.

7. Joint Declaration of Principles Guiding Relations between Papua New Guinea and Australia, reproduced (with zoological art work) in *Australian Foreign Affairs Record* (AFAR), 10, 58, November-December 1987.

8. When asked by the members of a Sydney University study tour in 1985 why a formal defence treaty had not been offered to P.N.G. at independence, Australia's then High Commissioner, Michael Wilson, responded that it was important to keep the P.N.G. government in a 'constant state of uncertainty' about Australia's protective intentions. A treaty could 'encourage imprudence and recklessness' in relations with Indonesia. (*Interview*, Port Moresby, May 16, 1985.)

9. *Background Briefing* (ABC Radio National, April 15, 1990. Reporter: Mark Aarons; transcript published by the Commonwealth Parliamentary Library's Media Information, Current Awareness and Hansard Service) *Background Briefing* also reported these words from an informal address by General Murdani to a closed meeting of civil servants, Dilli, February 3, 1990: 'Don't dream there will be a nation called Irian or Ambon, or a nation called East Timor – there won't be. In the past there were small nations which wanted to be independent but, without a moment's thought [*sic*], the Indonesian Government prevented this from happening' (*ibid*). See also 'Don't Dream, or Else', *Inside Indonesia*, No. 23, June 1990.

10. 'Portugal Protests at Timor Treaty', *Sydney Morning Herald*, 13 February 1991.

11. ... 'overall, over the passage of time [in East Timor], things ["crook" things – Evans] have been generally improving ... under the kind of pressure that we, among other countries, are putting on the Indonesians' (Gareth Evans quoted in *Background Briefing*, April 15, 1990. See Note 9 above.) Mark Aarons's report casts grave doubt on the Minister's claim of improvement, and one wonders how the pressure which Australia supposedly exerts might be distinguished from support. For example: 'there are many claims of abuse which are made, which prove not to be well founded' (Evans, *ibid.*) Now East Timor was a closed province until 1989, and the military pressure inhibiting investigation of anything going on there remains as heavy as ever.

12. 'Timor Rebel Leader Asks Hawke to Step In', *Sydney Morning Herald* (citing AAP), 11 February 1991. When an Australian parliamentary delegation visited East Timor in February 1991 the Fretilin leader Xanana Gusmao appealed by letter (passed to the parliamentarians) for Prime Minister Bob Hawke to pressure Indonesia into seeking a peaceful settlement of the Timor conflict. Gareth Evans replied that Fretilin ('some group that is still contesting ... the incorporation of East Timor into Indonesia') should 'accept the reality of the situation', take up Indonesia's amnesty offer and surrender.

13. Interview with Richard Woolcott: 'Moralising is Out of Place', *The Bulletin*, 21 February, 1989.

14. Woolcott calls the massacre a 'traumatic experience' (*ibid*) for Indonesia. Traumatic for the Indonesian people, perhaps; but, there is no doubt that the Suharto regime set about destroying the Indonesian Left after September 30, 1965.

15. Parkinson, T., (30 November 1991) 'Indonesia's Secret War of Secession', *The Australian*. General Sutrisno upholds the Army's right to shoot 'agitators'.

16. *The Age*, (20 August 1990).

17. See King, P., (1985), 'The Foreign Policy White Paper of 1981: a Critique', in King, *et al.* (eds), *From Rhetoric to Reality? Papua New Guinea's Eight Point Plan and National Goals After a Decade*, University of Papua New Guinea Press, Port Moresby, p. 277. Defence Minister Sabumei has also promised to share intelligence with the Indonesians about OPM operations in the border region (*The Australian*, 29 October 1990), and, during a visit to Port Moresby, ABRI (Armed Forces) Commander-in-Chief Sutrisno proposed 'joint military land and maritime exercises with P.N.G. AAP Report by Chris Falray, (11 December 1990) – reproduced in *West Papua Update* (Australia West Papua Association, P.O. Box 1148, Collingwood, Victoria, 3066), No. 10, (December 1990). A closer military relationship was finally given the formal imprimatur of a Status of Forces Agreement signed by Rabbie Namaliu and Benny Murdani in Jakarta. 'Namaliu hails Jakarta Border Pact', *The Australian*, (15 January 1992).

18. Agence France Presse report, 14 August 1990, quoted in *West Papua Update*, No. 9, (October 1990), p.2.

19. *West Papua Update* (citing *Tapol Bulletin*), No. 8, (June 1990), pp.1-2.

20. See Evans letter of February 6, 1990 to Russell Rollason, Executive Director, Australian Council for Overseas Aid. Quoted in *ibid.*, p. 2.

21. *West Papua Update*, No. 9, (October 1990), p. 5; *Pacific New Bulletin*, (September 1991).

22. *The Age*, (Lindsay Murdoch), (July 26, 1990). In a conversation with

Foreign Minister Bill Hayden in 1984 I learned that Murdani (then ABRI Commander-in-Chief) had told Hayden in several official encounters that Indonesia (or at least Murdani himself) regarded the political and social stability of P.N.G. as Australia's strategic responsibility.

23. *The Age,* (26 July 1990).

24. Dorney, S., (1990), *Papua New Guinea: People, Politics and History since 1975,* Sydney: Random House, p. 204.

25. *West Papua Update,* No. 10, (December 1990).

26. On P.N.G.'s prospects for a mining (and oil and gas) boom in the mid-1990s see David Parsons and David Vincent, (1991), *High Stakes: mineral and petroleum development in Papua New Guinea,* National Centre for Development Studies, Australian National University. Parsons and Vincent warn of the 'downside' of a mining boom – domestic inflation and the squandering of fiscal windfalls.

27. Commission of Inquiry into Aspects of the Forestry Industry, *Final Report,* Port Moresby, (1989). The full collection of Justice Barnett's reports is fast becoming a collector's item. The government has only printed a few of the more than 20 volumes tabled in Parliament and there are no plans to print more. Barnett himself now works in Western Australia after his term on P.N.G.'s National Court. He was assaulted and seriously injured in Port Moresby during the Commission of Inquiry – by persons so far unknown.

28. *Kundu News Bulletin,* Consulate General for P.N.G., Sydney, (June 1990).

29. On Diro's activity as Forests Minister see Commission of Inquiry, *Interim Report No. 2: the Gadaisu Timber Permit - Angus (P.N.G.) Pty. Limited,* (January 1988).

30. Sir Serei also resigned under pressure from the Namaliu government. *Sydney Morning Herald,* (28 September and 30 October 1991).

31. *Sydney Morning Herald,* (28 September 1991). According to the Barnett Inquiry, Diro was 'party to a plan to systematically cheat [the Magi Wopten people of his own Central Province] of their rightful profits'. See, *A Summary of the Commission of Inquiry into Aspects of the Timber Industry in Papua New Guinea,* New Guinea Island Campaign, PO Box 368, Lismore, NSW, p. 19.

32. *Sydney Morning Herald,* (19 July 1991).

33. The *Four Corners* programme, 'Blood on the Bougainvillea', reported by Deborah Snow, went to air in June 1991.

34. 'Government to focus on Highland Security', *Sydney Morning Herald,* (13 August 1991). Project aid for the police force was $8m. in 1990-91. 'P.N.G. Security Treaty Refused', *Sydney Morning Herald,* (12 August 1991).

35. *Bougainville Information Service*, (Gabriel Lafitte), *Annual Report*, (May 1991) and *Situation Report*, (May 1991).

36. Such as: the Australian Council for Overseas Aid (ACFOA) which includes the Indonesia-Australia Programme for Cooperation, sponsored by ACFOA since 1987 as a bilateral NGO forum; Amnesty International; the International Commission of Jurists; the Australia-West Papua Association; the various Timor support groups, and the Rainforest Information Centre, Lismore.

37. Bell, I., Feith, H. and Hatley, R., 5, (May 1986), 'The West Papuan Challenge to Indonesian Authority in Irian Jaya: Old Problems, New Prospects', *Asian Survey*, XXVI.

38. Mr Hawke's brave and vociferous stand in favour of resisting aggression in the Persian Gulf during recent times has brought into sharp relief an earlier – much closer to home – Australian failure to act on this salutary principle.

39. ACFOA, *Briefing Notes on Cuts to the Australian Aid Program, 1990-91*. ACFOA explains how the Hawke government contrived to represent a $100m. cut in the aid budget as a 1.6 per cent increase in real terms.

4

Violence Against Women in India – Perspectives and Strategies

Govind Kelkar

Introduction

For more than a decade, feminist scholars and activists in the women's movement in India have been engaged in a debate with the state and in society over the forms and nature of violence against women. They have concentrated on intra- and extra-family/household gender relations and on the role of the state in reinforcing patriarchal oppression. Out of these studies a reconceptualisation of the issue of violence against women has emerged. This chapter provides an overview of the approach of the women's movements in India to the problem of violence against women, considers the mechanisms that perpetuate such violence and focuses on major strategies formulated to combat it.

The resurgence of the Indian women's movement has undermined the assumption that women are 'apolitical' and 'naturally backwards' who nurture their domesticity and subordination. Feminist theorists have argued, that women's political issues require a confrontation with class, caste and patriarchal relations. Women's struggles for the basic needs of food, water, fuel, and health care and environmental integrity are very political.

These struggles radically question the existing patterns of re-source allocation. Campaigns against rape and familial violence, while linked to the struggles of poor women against the class-caste hierarchy of landlords and the coercive power of the state (ex-pressed through police rapes, lax patriarchal attitudes on the part of the judiciary, and discriminatory laws against women), reso-nate with more broad-based women's actions against male vio-lence and cultural control within the family. In many ways, the women's liberation movement has not only linked women-specific violence with class and caste issues, but also radically challenged other forms of power, privilege and discrimination in society.

Defining Violence Against Women

Violence against women, must be seen in the context of particular sets of power relations. It is produced within class, caste and family relations in which male power dominates. A narrow view of violence may suggest an act of illegal, criminal use of physical force. But this is incomplete. Violence also includes exploitation, dis-crimination, unequal economic and social structures, the creation of an atmosphere of terror, threat, or reprisal, as well as religious cultural and political violence. Specific violence against women flows from control and coercion exercised through hierarchical and patriarchal gender relationships in the family and society.

Women-specific violence has the function of keeping women in the house in powerless positions.'Women become instruments through which the social system reproduces itself and through which systemic inequality is maintained'.[1] This is achieved through women's economic and emotional dependence and resourcelessness. Women are considered men's property, their sexuality, fertility and labour are systematically controlled. Violence against women and their consequent submission and subordination is reinforced by the socialisation process. Familial structures embody hierar-chic gender relations which give women little or no independent social existence. These tend to establish 'possessional rights over women which men have as husbands, fathers or older male rela-tions'.[2] Such possessional rights are expressed as an exchange of a promise of protection (whether actually fulfilled or not in reality) in return for submission and exclusive use.

In order to change this situation, women's access to resources is crucial. The state, however, overlooks familial violence against women and perpetuates it in order to uphold 'cultural legitimacy', and 'law and order'. Moreover, the coercive arms of the state (police and army) often use sexual violence against women in caste and communal clashes and against women in police custody. There are all kinds of discriminatory laws which women find very difficult to fight. Agricultural labourers, poor peasants, *Dalit* (the oppressed castes) and *Adivasi* (indigenous) women have repeatedly questioned the Indian state for working in close alliance with patriarchal, fundamentalist forces. Such women at the Nari Mukti Sangharsh Sammelan (Struggle for Women's Liberation Meeting) in February 1988, passed the following resolution.

> Women face specific forms of violence: rape and other forms of sexual abuse, female foeticide, witch-hunting, sati, dowry murders, wife-beating. Such violence and the continued sense of insecurity that is instilled in women as a result keeps them bound to the home, economically exploited and socially suppressed. In the on-going struggles against violence in the family, society and the state, we recognise that the state is one of the main sources of violence and stands behind the violence committed by men against women in the family, the work place and the neighbourhood. For these reasons, a mass women's movement should focus on the struggle against them in the home or out of it.[3]

At a Women's Conference in Calicut, Kerala in December 1990, over 300 participants raised important feminist issues about sexual attacks and other forms of violence against women in the family, state and society, and also about appropriate strategies to counter such violence. The Conference noted:

> A woman faces violence from the time she is conceived in the womb. Amniocentesis is the latest technical way of murdering female children before they can fight back and the implications are far worse because the mother is coerced through all the available social and psychological pressure on her and

values which are anti-women. Her home is the main area of attack, drunken husbands, dowry hungry in-laws, financial problems and young female children deprived of nutrition exemplify the force with which a woman is attacked within the four walls of her social haven.[4]

Equally important were the concluding consensus and the questions which emerged in the conference's workshop on violence.

> ... Only a systematic process of empowerment of the individual woman by women's awareness building and solidarity groups can protect her against all forms of violence and it is only through these networks that the political and legal strategies can be made effective. But when will the law be made accessible to us? How do we protect women activists from attacks by patriarchal forces?
> Why do we choose to remain quiet when we face violence personally?
> How do we stop women from becoming the active and passive instrument of patriarchal oppression?[5]

These questions indicate not merely that the law is inadequate, but that the social position of women, far from improving with the years, is actually falling. Since the early eighties there has been an obvious contradiction between growing patriarchy and the social neglect of women on the one hand, and the protest and resistance of the women's liberation movement, on the other. In the last decade government has formulated a series of supposedly pro-women policies and enacted laws to halt crimes against women. There has been a growth in media reporting and a rise in consciousness of sexism. Women-specific violence has been acknowledged as a human rights matter. The women's movement has also grown and spread. At the same time, however, there has been an increase in violence against women, rapes and dowry murders, and sexual and murderous attacks on young and pregnant women of religious minorities, ethnic groups and of agricultural labourers in communal and caste clashes.

The Indian government has not attempted to outlaw the subordination of women to men or to change the relations of dependence within the family; on the contrary, the state legitimises patriarchal dominance.

Increasing Violence Against Women

In July 1991, serious concern was expressed in Parliament by the release of government statistics of 11,259 dowry-related murders during the last three years. The official dowry murder toll has risen steadily from 2,209 in 1988 to 4,835 in 1990.[6] In August 1990, the Minister of State for Home Affairs admitted in Rajya Sabha that despite two amendments to the Dowry Prohibition Act, there was a rise in dowry deaths. In Delhi in 1983, on average two women died of burns every day.[7] In Bombay, a survey of two police stations indicated that in a period of eight months in 1984, one woman was burnt to death every five days. In Bangalore, suicides and 'dowry deaths' nearly doubled in 1984 as compared to the previous years. According to police reports, an average of two women committed suicide every day in 1984. In Madhya Pradesh, records from the biggest hospital showed that one woman died of burn injuries every five days. According to various women's organisations an equal number of burning/suicide cases go unreported, mostly on account of the refusal of police to register cases, or when they do register a case, to minimise the offence. For example, over 90 per cent of the cases of women burnt in Delhi were registered as accidents, only five per cent were noted as murders and five per cent as suicides.[8]

The dowry witch-hunt takes its heaviest toll in middle-class urban areas, but the burning of women for more money and domestic goods in the form of dowry is quite widespread in the slums and rural areas. Although woman-burning is prevalent all over the country, it is most acute in Delhi, Haryana, Punjab, Western Uttar Pradesh and the Saurashtra region in Gujarat.

Police officials admitted to the press in August 1990 that changes in the laws relating to rape have not checked the incidence of rapes. Official statistics gave the following figures: the number of reported rapes in 1976 was 3,893; 1978, 4,558; 1980 5,023; 1984 6,203; 1985 6,356; and by 1988, 6,888. The Bureau of

Police, in 1985 estimated that roughly 20,000 rapes were committed in India every year. This itself seems a very conservative estimate. The police themselves state that only one quarter of the total number of rapes that take place are actually reported by rape survivors or their families. Furthermore, the majority or rapists in India are set free for want of adequate evidence.

Mass rapes are used by upper cast, large-landowning men for the repression of poor peasant, agricultural labourers (*Dalits* and *Adivasis*) whenever they get organised and demonstrate for higher wages or the implementation of land reforms. In a seminar on custodial rape in New Delhi in 1982, it was noted that 42.5 per cent of rapes committed in rural and tribal areas were by policemen, army personnel and forest guards. In February 1988, for instance, a group of 14 policemen assisted by homeguards and securitymen, plunged the Pasaria village in Bihar into a terror of looting, destruction and mass rape. This was done in order to avenge an earlier assault on two of their colleagues. However, a far greater example of patriarchal crippling of the women took place a year later in March 1989, when Justice O.P. Sinha acquitted the policemen, accepting the Defence Counsel's argument that these women could not be equated with 'such ladies who hail from decent and respectable society' as they were engaged in 'menial work' and were of 'questionable character'. The judgement read, 'It cannot be ruled out that these ladies might speak out of falsehood to get a sum of Rs. 1,000, which was a huge sum for them'.[9] There was a social silence after the judgement; the only exceptions were women's organisations, but they were unable to launch a movement against it.

Another escalating form of violence against women is the killing of women as witches, particularly in the indigenous (tribal) communities. In Singhbhum district of Bihar, 200 women are killed every year because they are thought to be witches.[10] There is an economics of witch-hunting, an economics related to the development of male control over privatised land and the destruction of women's traditional land rights – the usufruct right or real life-interest in land. In a recent study of 'Women, Land, and Forests'[11] in the Jharkhand region of Bihar, over a period of 30 years, in 95 cases of Santhals killed by Santhals, 46 were cases of witch-killing in which 42 of the killed were women and most of them were widows with land. The women accused of being witches were closely related to the accusers (as step-mothers, old women, young and old widows). Witch-hunting, like other forms of violence against women, however, cannot be explained in economic terms alone. Traditionally it was often used by men of dominant lineages against potential threats. It was also used to get rid of unwanted females – chiefly widows but also pregnant women whom the men concerned do not want to marry. In sum, witch-hunting has helped establish the socio-political authority of men in a culture in which this authority was formerly shared.

Recently, women's organisations, social analysts and feminist activists have been concerned by the results of the 1991 Census. Official data indicated that women are being killed in large numbers. In 1901, there were 1,072 women for every 1,000 men. Since then the ratio of females to males has steadily declined (with the exception of some increase in 1981) and at present there are merely 929 women for every 1,000 men. Importantly, time and again over the last fifteen years, it has been pointed out that the declining number of women is not a biological phenomenon. It is the cumulative effect of social practices, particularly the allocation of family resources in favour of men, i.e. preference for males in the distribution of nutritious food, health care, education and economic resources.

Amniocentesis is popular in various parts of India. From 1978 to 1983, 78,000 female foetuses were reported to have been aborted after amniocentesis tests.[12] Advertisement for amniocentesis, or the commonly called sex-determination test, crudely pose the choice between female foeticide and dowry saying, 'Better pay Rs. 500 now than Rs. 500,000 later'.

There is much more to it than just crass advertisements. Crimes against women are manifestations of a political malaise in India and of a malady in the organisation of the socio-economic system. Atrocities committed against women within families/ households have often been hidden from the public eye by a social attitude which is a mix of apathy towards women and an inexplicable sense of privacy. The taken-for-granted nature of the unequal distribution of the patriarchal social system and the secrecy of oppression of women within the family is maintained. Foucault maintains:

Power is tolerable only when a good deal of its workings are concealed. Its efficacy is proportional to the degree of that concealment. For power, secrecy is not an abuse but a necessity; and this is not only for its greater efficiency but also for its acceptance.[13]

The general unwillingness on the part of women to speak about unequal gender relations in society and violence within the family, therefore, is not surprising. Given women's unequal, resourceless position in society and family, it would be in their interest to concentrate on positive aspects of cooperation, outside the marriage as well as within it. Nonetheless, women and feminist theorists have questioned the normal assumption of development planning and mainstream economics in which the family/household is an undifferentiated unit and its members equally share power and resources.

To understand the nature of violence against women in India today, it is necessary to look at women's subordination in the structure of material production.

The well-known economist, Amartya Sen, suggests that 'there has to be a clear analysis of the existence of both cooperative and conflicting elements in family relations'.[14] According to Sen, while there are many 'cooperative outcomes' that are beneficial for all the members concerned, the different members however, have 'strictly conflicting interests in the set of cooperative arrangements'. The respective bargaining power of men and women within the 'cooperative conflict' existence, depends very much on their resources and power outside the family/household. The family/household members who are socially powerless and resourceless (usually women) are likely to remain within that situation, even when the outcomes of cooperative conflict are quite unsatisfactory for them. In the existing social situation of resourcelessness and powerlessness of women, it would be less favourable for them to leave the household. In case of the breakdown of cooperative arrangements, the fallback position of women (i.e. outside the family/household) is much worse. Women's 'breakdown response' is, therefore, reflected in their lack of entitlements to resources, consumption and decision-making outside the family/household as well as within it.

The dowry witch-hunt in India stems from women's subordination in the structure of material production, the organisation of marriage and family and the sexual division of labour. These create gender-specific personalities – men tend to value their role as 'bread winners' and 'supporters' of the family as the principal one in the national economy, while women are excessively undervalued because of their dependence, greater ignorance of the outside world and preoccupation with household chores.

Women's Movement: Strategies for Combatting Violence

1. Campaign Against Rape

Notwithstanding women's social position in India it would be wrong to assume that women have been passively groaning under ever-increasing oppression within and outside the family. Violence of rape and dowry related women-burning emerged as major issues in the women's movement in the early 1980s. The judgment of the Supreme Court in the Mathura case in 1979 drew country-wide attention to the ineffectiveness of rape laws and women's organisations mobilised to address rape as an example of a more general level of women's oppression. The campaign around the Mathura case argued, for the first time, that 'rape is violation of a human right of a woman to have control over her own body'.[15] And, 'rape was seen as the most brutal expression of patriarchal power associated with the economic and political power in society'.

In the Mathura case, the High Court of Bombay convicted two policemen of raping a minor, tribal girl called Mathura, from Chandrapur in Maharashtra. Mathura had complained that she was raped in the police station in the middle of the night. The Supreme Court revised the judgment of the Bombay High Court and acquitted the policemen. It dismissed Mathura's testimony as a 'tissue of lies', arguing that, while there was no clear evidence that she had actively resisted intercourse with the two men, there was proof that she was not a virgin. According to the Court, since Mathura was a tribal girl, there was no question of her being 'violated' or of her right to say no. And that because of her past sexual conduct, she could not possibly have wanted to resist the sexual act.

The upper-class, patriarchal judgement of the Supreme Court triggered strong reactions from activists and lawyers. An open letter from four legal experts – Upendra Baxi, Vashuda Dhagamwar, Raghunath Kelkar and Lotika Sarkar – asked the Supreme Court to reopen the case. At the same time, there were meetings and rallies by women's organisations, lawyers' collectives, and forums against rape in several parts of India. For instance in Bombay, the 'Forum Against Rape' was formed. The Forum collected 10,000 signatures and submitted a petition to parliament for reopening the Mathura Case and amending the rape laws. Equally active were the 'Stree Sangharsh Sangatana' (Women's Struggle) in Delhi, National Federation of Indian Women, national student wing of the Communist Party of India (Marxist) and the Coordination Committee for Women's Organisations in Pune. For the first time, 8th March was celebrated as Women's Struggle Day, with several thousand women participating in demonstrations. Poster exhibitions on women's oppression, small meetings in schools, colleges, in offices and factories all played an important role in focusing on defects in the law.

The demand for a review of the Mathura case was accompanied by demands that a new offence of custodial rape be recognised in order to combat sexual aggression in police stations, jails, remand homes, hospitals, schools or by government employees. The women's movement proposed reform of the Criminal Procedure Code for conducting rape proceedings in camera; and of the Evidence Act in order to presume the absence of consent in prosecution for custodial rape, rape of pregnant women, or gang rape, where sexual intercourse by the accused is proved and the rape survivor states in her evidence that she did not consent. The enactment on the presumption of absence of consent while not easy was eventually passed into law.[16]

There were, however, failures too. Feminists were unable to gather enough strength to demand legislation in cases of marital rapes and 'power rape', where a man abuses his dominant position to force sexual relations. Some of the welfare-oriented women's organisations. which generally do not question patriarchy or the fundamental aspects of women's subordination within and outside the family opposed raising the question of marital rape on the ground that it would 'endanger the family as a going institution'[17] and women would lose further support. Not surprisingly, these women's organisations did not join the feminist organisations and individuals in critiquing the family and the state, nor saw rape for what it is, a crime of annihilation by man of the woman as a human being'.[18]

II. Protest Against Dowry Murders

The initial protest against harassment and killing/burning of women because of inadequate dowry was in June 1979. Ever since, women's organisations have been demanding more stringent, deterrent measures to check crimes against women. For the past few years in Delhi and other major cities in the country, women's organisations and housewives have held sporadic demonstrations against husbands, in-laws, lawyers, and police officers involved in cases of woman-burning or killing by other means. In early 1982, thirty women's organisations in Delhi, under the name of 'Dahej Virodhi Chetna Manch' (Anti-Dowry Consciousness Raising Forum) jointly organised a protest march against dowry, and they were joined by several hundred ordinary women and men, including the 'parents of dowry victims'. They questioned police inaction and highlighted government lethargy towards the problem. They demanded ostracism of bride-burners and killers and pleaded with legal pundits and legislators to suggest some system of summary trials for such crimes against women.

These demonstrations acted as checks on the husbands and in-laws by exposing the real nature of violence, i.e. protracted harassment and battering of a woman, followed by killing and/or burning her, thereby preventing an easy escape through a facade of suicide or accidental death. They also pressed for effective change in and implementation of laws, for tightening of the loopholes in legal procedures and for more consideration of women's unspoken experiences of harassment, torture and molestation in police inquiries. Moreover, there emerged a number of neighbourhood action committees, and crisis centres/support centres and women's centres, where women in distress (e.g. rape survivors, harassed daughters-in-law/young married women, battered wives, etc.) could be helped and could get moral, and emotional support, physical relief and shelter as well as legal aid.

This resulted in a social awakening leading to increased attention being paid to the question of violence against women by the media, progressive political parties, trade unions, professional groups and non-government organisations. Conscious women activists organised *Padyatras* (long-marches), performed skits and plays, and made movies on dowry murders and the oppression of women. Women newspaper reporters, who were also members of feminist networks, magazines like *Manushi* (Delhi) and *Baija* (Pune) and various feminist network bulletins, reported on both the problems of women and their attempts at resistance. Feminist academics, who had been involved in studies on women's roles in mass movements and their participation in nation-building, questioned the limitations of male-biased social sciences in the study of demographic patterns and female roles in economic production. These studies further pointed out inequalities in the socio-economic, political system and the national neglect of some in the fields of employment, health and education.

Women's organised efforts could no longer be ignored and the government responded by amending laws on dowry and setting up 'anti-dowry cells' and mobile police squads for women in Delhi and other cities. It is mandatory for these cells to investigate cases of dowry-related harassments and any 'unnatural death' of women within seven years of marriage. While these measures sought to improve the existing legal situation related to women, they failed to question women's subordination and dependence on men within the institution of marriage and family. The state still continued to create structures and legislate for the subordination of women. The construction of socio-economic dependence of one partner on the other is at the core of legal treatments of husband and wife statuses.

III. *Extra-legal Strategies: Public Shaming and Community Action*

Women have started employing a variety of extra-legal tactics in their cause. There were several cases of dowry murders for example, which women brought into the community arena to punish the offenders and/or to publicly humiliate them. This happened particularly in cases where the police and judiciary had failed to take action. For instance, in 1982 in a skillfully organised dowry murder case, a husband was set free by the court for want of adequate evidence. Subsequently, enraged women activists marched to his house, manhandled and stripped him and paraded him naked in the crowded market area of Lajpat Nagar, New Delhi, thus publicly shaming him for the murder of his wife.

On the 13 December 1990, Suparna Sengupta, (mother of a three year old) was burnt to death in Chittaranjan Park of New Delhi. This murder triggered off a unique movement of community action against the crime and general harassment of women. There was no arrest or investigation on the following day; the local police officer was allegedly bribed. On hearing the news, five women of *Purbosree Mahila Samiti* (Eastern Women's Organisation) of the area immediately went to the dowry-death house. They were joined by members of the local community who protested outside the house, so that by late evening police conceded protesters demands and arrested all six members of the family. Because of community opposition the family was not allowed to re-enter the house or live elsewhere in the area. Importantly, the younger women of the area were very active in mobilising for the action and organising the demonstration.

IV. *Towards Breaking Women's Silence in the Family*

Women's protest through demonstrations and studies has made the violent crime of burning women visible as a serious social problem. It has drawn attention to the oppression, conflict and violence hidden behind the superficial portrait of love, support and nurturance in the family. Further, these demonstrations have opened the areas of female subordination and domestic violence to public attention, bringing in a culture of 'speak bitterness' enabling harassed wives, and rape survivors to speak out. Women's new ability to describe their plight has merged with the resurgence of feminist consciousness-raising efforts and led to its consideration by others. Moreover, these groups have particularly suggested a critical scrutiny of the family and the role of the state is reinforcing the familial structure of domination.

There is a need to look at familial authority relations according to which dowry violence is organised and at the property relations which this authority structure realises and maintains. Socio-economic arrangements of gender-based disparity, e.g. lower wages for women, their under-reporting in the labour force, and their disadvantaged position in health and education, have been justified on the assumption that women's employment is secondary to that of men. There is, therefore, a close connection between the family and the organisation of the politico-economic system. In other words, the family approach legitimises the subordination of women in policy making and organisation of the economy.

The Constitution of India declared the equality of sexes as an egalitarian guiding principle, and acknowledged that a family should basically be an egalitarian unit, founded on equal rights and willing choice by the individuals who form a family. In practice, however, the subordination of women to men and of junior to senior pervades family life in all classes and castes of India. The ideology of subordination is required by the material structure of production. Women are subordinate to men (and thereby dependent too) because men may own land and hold tenancies, while women, by and large, do not. Customary practices preclude women from inheriting land as daughters, except in the absence of male heirs. This is wrongly justified by arguing that women receive their share of the patrimony at the time of marriage in the form of dowry.

Hindu laws of property and ownership of the means of production give women negligible rights in relation to family income assets and property. The Hindu Succession Act which put daughters on an equal footing with sons in regard to succession to parental property, and the Dowry Prohibition Act are not unimportant, but they can be appealed to only in certain circumstances in cases of disputes among families or where legal land ceiling provisions make it expedient for large land holdings to be divided 'on paper'. In most cases, daughters waive their land rights in favour of their brothers. Otherwise, they are denounced as 'selfish' sisters and risk alienation from or severance of ties with their natal families. Women's effective exclusion from the possession and control of land is largely the basis of their subordination and dependence on men in rural India.

In recent years, however, the family has emerged as a political issue in India. While the government has formulated policies to further strengthen the family, the women's movement has raised questions about the confining nature of the family and women's organisations have raised questions about the role of women in Indian planning. As a result of pressure from women activists and scholars, a chapter on 'Women and Development' was incorporated in the Sixth Five Year Plan. The chapter admits that women are 'the most vulnerable members of the family' and will continue to be so 'for some time in future'. It further promises to give 'special attention' to the interests of the 'vulnerable members'. Nevertheless, the Sixth Five Year Plan insists that 'the family is the unit for programmes for poverty eradication'. The problem of the oppression of women in the family was acknowledged, but the family was retained as the basic unit of economic development, thereby preventing a constructive analysis of the problem of women.

V. *Women's Rights to Land, Property and Inheritance*

Women-specific violence can be combatted only if fundamental change is made to the existing propertylessness and resourcelessness of women,[19] so that women have inalienable rights to land, property, and inheritance, and the existing wage system (where women workers are paid less than men) is rectified. Grassroots women's organisations, who are concerned with the political and ideological oppression of women and their links with male inheritance of land and other property and the economic subordination of women in earning power, do not, however, take up feminist issues in their work. Like the gender division of labour, the gender division of private property is also regarded as natural and, therefore, not to be questioned.[20]

A woman's relation to productive property/land is always mediated through her relation to her husband, father, or brother. Discussing the Women's Conference in Patna (1988) and the Shetkari Mahila Aghadi (Peasant Women's Alliance) meeting in November 1989, Gail Omvedt underlines the link between violence against women and their propertylessness and resourcelessness.

> Brutal suppression in fact keeps women in their propertyless and resourceless state... On the other hand, the basic eco-

nomic dependence of women, their propertylessness and resourcelessness, renders them fearfully weak in standing up and challenging the violence and power that is used against them in society. In the workforce, women are overwhelmingly relegated to the unorganised sector (as agricultural labourers, unorganised sector wage workers, peasant gatherers and sellers of forest produce and unpaid subsistence producers) and are economically weak; the Hindu patrilineal and patrilocal family system cuts them off from access to property except through men; and their resources in terms of education, skills, socialised self-confidence, etc. are much lower than those of men.[21]

Poor peasant women of the people's movement in Bihar in northern India have demanded changes in the gender division of socio-political work (invariably the preserve of men) and the sharing of housework and child care.[22] These women critically questioned the existing sexual division of work in politics and the present-day responsibility of the 'wholetimers' (fully engaged in political work) in maintaining themselves and putting the entire burden of the household on the wife. The women resented their husbands doing political work at their expense and as a corrective measure suggested that a whole-timer should 1) share equally and fully the responsibilities and burden of household work and child care; 2) participate in agricultural work or other production in order to support himself as well as the dependants of the family; e.g. wife, sister mother, daughter so that they might participate in mass politics and assist the process of social transformation.

Recent studies in India indicate that planned changes for rural development and agrarian transformation through land reforms did not succeed. In a case study of Palghat district in Kerala, for instance, there was conclusive evidence that changes in land relations from the 1920s on affected women adversely.[23]

In the early seventies, the Committee on the Status of Women in India received many representations from women of different states regarding the discriminatory features of some of the new land laws. In a camp of women agricultural labourers in May, 1980, in Bankura district in West Bengal, similar home truths were pointed out by a number of poor peasant women.[24] During field work in 1984-85 in the villages of Etawah district in Uttar Pradesh, Devi, a bhangi (scavenger caste) woman sharply remarked: 'No women ever control any assets, not even the children they bear, who are known as their father's children. This has been going on for generations.' Raj Kumari, a chamar woman, added:

> Land is passed on from father to son. Even the jewellery that is a gift to woman on her marriage is not given to her, it is kept by her parents-in-law. If a man dies or remarries, the woman is completely dependent on others for her survival. A man can gamble or drink away his land but a woman is always concerned about her children. She can never see them starve, she would do all in her power to raise them to the best of her ability. So land should be owned jointly by both the husband and wife.[25]

Similar reports came from the rural areas of Bihar where women have been struggling against the prejudices of state officials as well as those of their men towards women having independent land rights. In the eighties the government was reported to have worked out a new policy thrust for land reforms to make them more progressive and result-oriented. In December 1988, the Ministry of Agriculture proposed that at least 40 per cent of *pattas* (land title deeds) be issued exclusively for women in future allotments of government surplus lands as well as homestead units. The remaining *pattas* should be issued jointly in the names of husband and wife.[26] These provisions, however, did not travel beyond the proposed plan statements. It was noticed that only in a few pockets of Bihar and Tamil Nadu were some land *pattas* (about 10 per cent of the total distributed land) given to women.

A woman's access to land means a significant reduction in her household's risk of absolute poverty and provides security in facilitating credit from institutional sources. It further means a substantial rise in the woman's social position and less vulnerability to violence in the family. It has been observed by some grassroots workers in Maharashtra, Uttar Pradesh and Bihar that single women – widowed, divorced, deserted or abandoned – are working as agricultural labourers on the farms of their brothers, uncles and brothers-in-law. Separate land deeds in women's names, therefore, would help ensure that they would not be left destitute. The Bodhgaya women who got land were reported to have asserted: 'We had tongues but could not speak, we had feet but could not walk. Now that we have land, we have the strength to speak and walk.'[27]

VI. *Women's Critique of the State*

The state of India never set out to fundamentally restructure relations of hierarchy and power within the family or to enable women to have independent access to property and other resources. Through its construction of family-centered development programmes, and assignment of productive and reproductive functions, and above all of land/property holding and technology control functions, to the (male) heads of households, the state seems to be further eroding the rights which women earlier enjoyed.

There is an illusion of improvement in women's position, created largely by the enactment of some violence-shield laws. But they have not empowered women to halt the increasing violence and destruction of their lives. The women's movement has repeatedly criticised the state for policies that reinforce patriarchy and the male-headed private family as well as the perpetuation of class and caste. It has held that the state has done nothing to delegitimise processes which are in agreement with the advocacy and interests of patriarchy and class, caste-based social structures, nor has it made substantive policies for the development and liberation of women. Besides, social practices and legal norms giving possessional rights over women to men, rules of legitimacy of off-spring, etc., continue to denigrate and restrict women to being sexual, sub-human objects.

While a number of legislative measures were carried out to provide relief from domestic and social violence, in practice, however, the patriarchal assumption of women's subordination and dependence on men continues to inform law and socio-political processes. The increasing number of dowry murders and rapes, as noted in the second section of the study, demonstrate that the state has done nothing in substantial terms to ensure that women are protected against the experience of familial and social violence. Despite state pretensions of enacting progressive laws regarding custodial rape, the courts, police and lawyers continue to judge women from a male perspective, and worse, from the perspective of rapist men.

More recently, some critical feminist analysts have not only questioned the movement's efforts for women's rights, but have also suggested a limited use of progressive laws.[28] The demand for legal change can play an important role in defining the goals of a mass movement, particularly during the early years of the movement, and dialogues related to legal enactments do lay bare certain complex aspects of inequalities in the social structure and the patriarchal nature of the polity. Nonetheless, this can lead to the state taking over and defining the goals of the movement. Consequently, the women's movement's dependence on the state for constitutional equality and non-discrimination can be politically debilitating. There is always a risk that the movement will be so fixed on women's legal rights that it will not move on to other equally pressing women's issues.

In the light of this self-criticism and caution in dealing with the state, some feminist analysts critically question state management and control of women's studies in various universities and colleges throughout the country. Such a sponsorship of women's studies has the definite purpose of preventing serious analysis of the patriarchal state and of further promoting the growing alienation of women's studies from the movement. Dorothy Smith describes the ruling apparatus,

> [as], the familiar complex of management, government, administration, profession and intelligentsia, as well as the textually mediated discourses that coordinate and interpenetrate it. Its special capacity is the organisation of particular places, persons and events into generalised and abstracted modes vested in categorial systems, rules, laws and conceptual practices. The former thereby become subject to an abstracted and universalised system of ruling mediated by texts.[29]

Dorothy Smith's concept provides a way of linking the question of the state with the politics of everyday life in the women's movement. The question is: if feminist analysis is critical of the state, then why would women, in certain circumstances, prefer dependence on the state to dependence on individual men or families? Carol Pateman says, 'Since women do not live with the state' as they do with men, they, therefore, are able to collectively struggle against the state for their entitlements.[30] There is also a need to realise that women are not only divided by class, caste ethnicity and other differences, but may enter into actual conflicts of interest with other women, over the nature of and relations with the state. There is, for instance, a marked difference between the All-India Women's Conference and poor peasant women's organisations over the analysis of the state and welfare policies. Unlike the former, poor peasant women involved in the liberation movement have increasingly realised that the phenomenon of violence against women will not be challenged without a struggle to end the subordination of women, and the transformation of unequal social relations based on oppression and exploitation.

Notes

1 This was discussed in a three-day meeting on 'Women and Violence', in Surat in January 1985. The responsibility of summing up the discussion was given to Maethreyi Krishna Raj and Govind Kelkar. For a full report, see, 'Women and Violence', *Economic and Political Weekly*, vol. xx, no. 12, March 1985.

2. *Ibid.*

3. Omvedt, G., Gala, C. and Kelkar, G., (1988), *Women and Struggle, A Report of the Nari Mukti Sangharh Sammelan*, Patna, p. 80.

4. Purewal, J., Kapoor, N., and Ozha, P., (1990), 'Report on the Women and Violence Session at the Calicut Conference', (unpublished).

5. *Ibid.*

6. *The Bangkok Post*, (1 August 1991), Bangkok, Sharma, K., (September 10, 1990), 'Rise in Rapes, Dowry Death' *Times of India*, also, Vohra, S., (August 20, 1990), 'The Galloping Monster of Rape', *Times of India*.

7. Kelkar, G., (1987), 'Violence Against Women: An Understanding of Responsibility for their Lives' in *Third World, Second Sex*, Davis, M. (ed) Zed Books. Also, Kelkar, G., 'Women and Structural Violence in India'.

8. *Indian Express*, (27 April, 1984), Editorial.

9. Rajadhyaksha, R., (January 28, 1990), 'Rape', *Illustrated Weekly of India*.

10. Manimala, (January 28, 1990), 'Witch-hunt', *Illustrated Weekly of*

India, x.

11. Kelkar, G. and Dev, N. (1991), *Gender and Tribe: Women, Land and Forests in Jharkhand,* New Delhi, Kali for Women, and London: Zed Books. See chapter on 'Land Rights and Witches.'

12. Gokhale, S., (10 May, 1990), 'Female Foeticide: Census Pointers', in *Times of India.*

13. Sheridan, A., (1980), *Michel Foucault: The Will to Truth,* London: Tavistock Publications, p. 181.

14. Sen, A., (1984), *Resources, Values, and Development,* Oxford: Blackwell, pp. 374-375. Also, *Women, Technology and Sexual Divisions,* (April 1984), Oxford: typescript.

15. Datar, C., *Anti-Rape Campaign in Bombay,* typescript, n.d.

16. Baxi, U., (1990), Violence Against Women in the Labyrinth of Law: Notes Towards Career of Symbolic Politics within the Institutions of Bore-Dom, (typescript), paper presented at a workshop in Nehru Memorial Museum and Library, New Delhi, p. 11.

17. *Ibid,*

18. Griffin, S., (1979), *Rape: The Power of Consciousness,* San Fransisco: Harper and Row, p. 39.

19. See Omvedt, G., (1990), *Violence Against Women, New Movements and New Theories in India,* New Delhi, Kali for Women; Madhu Kishwar, (April 9, 1989), 'Dowry Deaths – the Real Murders', *Indian Express*; Kelkar, G., (1989), 'Peasant Movements and Women in Two Bihar Districts', Occasional Paper No. IX, Nehru Memorial Museum and Library.

20. See Jayawardana, K., and Kelkar, G., (September 23, 1989), 'The Left and Feminism', *Economic and Political Weekly,* Bombay.

21. Omvedt, G., *Violence Against Women,* (see note 19)., p.5.

22. Kelkar, G., (July 1989), 'Peasant Movements and Women in Two Bihar Districts', Occasional Papers on Perspectives in Indian Development, Nehru Memorial Museum and Library, New Delhi, No. IX.

23. Sardamoni, K., (1983), 'Changing Land Relations and Women: A Case Study of Palghat District, Kerala', in Mazumdar, V. (ed), *Women and Rural Transformation, Two Studies,* (ICSSR and CWDS), New Delhi: Concept Publishing Company.

24. *Ibid,* Editor's Note p. x.

25. Kelkar, G., *et al., Rural Women, and Consciousness in India,* New Delhi: Manohar Publications, forthcoming.

26. *The Times of India,* (December 21, 1988), New Delhi.

27. Alka and Chetna, (1987), 'When Women Get Land - A Report From Bodhgaya', *Manushi,* New Delhi, no. 40, p. 26.

28. Kapoor, R., (1991), 'Feminism, Fundamentalism and Rights Rhetoric',

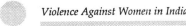

(unpublished). Cossman, B. and Kapoor, R., (1991), 'Women and Poverty in India: Law, Legal Literacy and Social Change', (draft). Also my discussions with women activists during Calicut Conference, December 1990.

29. Smith, D., (1987), *The Everyday World as Problematic: A Feminist Sociology*, Boston: Northeastern University Press, p.108.

30. Pateman, C., (1988), *The Sexual Contract,* Stanford: Stanford University Press.

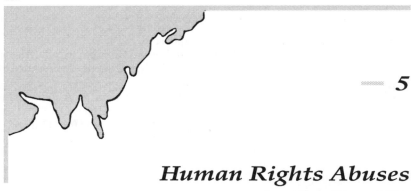

5

Human Rights Abuses
in the Pacific
– A Source of Regional Insecurity

*David Robie ***

Introduction

Until the mid-1980s, international human rights organisations gave Pacific Islands states a clean bill of health. Apart, that is, from colonised East Timor and Irian Jaya, which figured regularly in the annual Amnesty International Report through documentation of Indonesian violations. Now human rights violations are becoming a growing concern in the region and are an issue Pacific political leaders have been reluctant to face. Papua New Guinea Justice Minister Bernard Narokobi, for example, branded Amnesty International a 'criminal, illegal and immoral organisation' in an extraordinary outburst in August 1990 after it had made public a damning report about violations on Bougainville Island.[1] Narokobi was once an outspoken champion of human rights.

The Amnesty International Report for 1990 and 1991 detailed violations in East Timor, Fiji, Kanaky/New Caledonia and Irian Jaya as well as Bougainville.[2] The partial lifting of the ten-month economic (including medical) and communications blockade of Bougainville in January 1991 enabled journalists and researchers to investigate allegations that up to 3,000 islanders had died through lack of medicines or treatment. Papua New Guinea withdrew troops and riot police in March 1990 after it failed to quell a rebellion that left more than 150 people dead and devastated the copper-producing island's economy. Port Moresby imposed the blockade two months later – a policy alleged by some to be 'bordering on genocide'. Already there had been mounting evidence of extra-judicial killings, torture and beatings by the military, and the Bougainville Revolutionary Army (BRA) had also carried out assassinations and ill-treatment of its opponents.

According to an Amnesty International document made public in November 1990, at least 19 people had died in extra-judicial executions, or after being tortured in police or military custody.[3] More than 50 people were reported as ill-treated or tortured by members of the security forces. Forms of ill-treatment included beatings at roadblocks, death threats, sexual abuse and the deliberate torture of detainees. The victims were suspected members or sympathisers of the BRA and included political leaders, journalists, medical professionals, government workers and ordinary villagers. Most of the violations were said to have happened within the legal framework of the state of emergency, which gave security forces sweeping powers of arrest, detention and seizure. Amnesty also received other reports of alleged extra-judicial executions and other ill-treatment that so far it has been unable to confirm.

But it was allegations about the involvement of Australian military aid in what became dubbed the St Valentine's Day massacre that provoked most controversy. On 14 February 1990, United Church pastor Raumo Benito and five of his congregation were savagely beaten by Papua New Guinea Defence Force soldiers and then shot dead. An eyewitness to the macabre killings escaped, but the bodies were never recovered. Amnesty International reported that one of the four former Royal Australian Air Force Iroquois helicopters handed to Papua New Guinea as aid during the Bougainville rebellion was used to dump the bodies in the Pacific Ocean. The pilot was an Australian, although New Zealand pilots were also hired to fly the helicopters. The case was among several human rights violations investigated by Australia's Joint Parliamentary Foreign Affairs and Defence Inquiry which visited Papua New Guinea in February 1991.

Amnesty described the institutional, legal and constitutional provisions for protecting human rights in Papua New Guinea as vulnerable when confronted with a serious political crisis. It blamed the breakdown of safeguards on two major factors. First, judicial and quasi-judicial institutions that were responsible for enforcing constitutionally guaranteed rights failed to operate in practice. 'Second, the government and Parliament failed to act decisively when confronted with serious allegations of human rights abuse', Amnesty said. 'As a consequence few, if any, of the alleged perpetrators have been brought to justice and the vast majority of victims have been left without redress.'[4]

What follows are the case studies of Fiji, Papua New Guinea and East Timor. These case studies illustrate some of the ways in which human rights abuse, in the form of torture and extrajudicial executions, stimulate profound personal insecurity and undermine the process of democracy. Each of these domestic cases has negative consequences for regional peace and stability. Each one highlights a need for a regional body to monitor such abuses of power to hold the violators of human rights accountable for their actions.

Fiji: The Case of the Constitution Ten

While the situation in Papua New Guinea is arguably the worst in the South Pacific, civil and human rights have been fragile in Fiji since the military coups in 1987. The case of a kidnapping and torture of an academic by five soldiers during October 1990 was a blatant example of human rights violations with the apparent tacit support, if not actual instigation, of some authorities.

Fijian human rights campaigners believe an abduction case exposed a sinister side to the post-coup regime which could eventually lead to 'salvagings' or disappearances of dissidents such as in the Philippines or El Salvador. Political fallout from the case continued after the academic, Dr Anirudh Singh, a 40-year-old senior lecturer in physics at the University of the South Pacific, visited Australia and New Zealand for medical treatment during November-December 1990. When the lecturer publicly spoke out against the torture, Fiji Information Minister Ratu Inoke Kubuabola issued a press statement that implied threats against Singh.[5] Kubuabola said that by making statements about a pending case in Fiji during his trip abroad, Singh had 'openly flouted' due process of the law to 'discredit the Fiji government and judiciary'. At a human rights meeting in Auckland addressed by Dr Singh, his right arm still bound in a splint as a result of the torture, two Maori activists purporting to be from the separatist Te Ahi Kaa (Keepers of the Fire) movement disrupted the gathering to read out the minister's statement.[6] Two members of the militant Taukei movement also threatened Singh with further physical ill-treatment.

But Singh refused to be intimidated by the threats and flew back to Fiji in early January to face charges of sedition and unlawful assembly. Six other Indo-Fijians were also charged – economics lecturer Ganeshwar Chand, education lecturer Dr Sudesh Raj Mishra, physics lecturer Dr Surendra Prasad, lecturer Trilochna Reddy, physician Dr Ram Krishna Reddy and former schoolteacher Ram Sumeshwar Yadav. The charges followed a peaceful protest at a prayer meeting during which a copy of the racially discriminatory republican constitution was symbolically burned.

Three journalists also faced charges of 'maliciously fabricating' a report about further protests against the constitution. Their newspaper, the *Daily Post*, reported a plan by University of the South Pacific-based protest groups to burn further copies of the constitution. This is believed to be the first time any prosecutions have been brought under the vaguely worded Section 15(a) of Fiji's Public Order Act 1976, which declares: 'Any person who ... fabricates or knowingly spreads abroad or publishes, whether by writing or by word of mouth or any false news or false report tending to create or foster public alarm, public anxiety or disaffection or to result in the detriment of the public ... shall be guilty of an offence'.[7] The three *Post* journalists – publisher Taniela Bolea, chief subeditor Robert Wendt and reporter Subash Verma – would have faced a maximum penalty of one year in prison or a fine of $F1,000 if found guilty. However, the charges against them were dropped ten months later, in August 1991. Media sources in Suva said the arrests could have been part of a campaign by the interim government to close down the indigenous Fijian-owned newspaper because its outspokenness had become an 'irritant' to the regime. After the paper stopped publication for a month, it resumed again in February 1991 with Nemani Delaibatiki, former editor of the crusading *Fiji Sun*, which closed in 1987 after the coups rather than publish under self-censorship, at the helm. Delaibatiki, not popular with the regime, returned from New Zealand to take up the position.[8]

A report from Amnesty International warned that the accused activists and journalists would be considered 'prisoners of conscience' if they were found guilty and jailed.[9] 'We are certainly keen to protect human rights on our doorstep', said Amnesty's New Zealand executive director Colin Chiles. Amnesty considered the so-called Constitution Ten had been charged over the non-violent exercise of their constitutionally guaranteed rights of freedom of expression, assembly and association.

Singh said he had no regrets about the symbolic burning of the new republican Fiji constitution at a protest rally on 18 October 1990, during the Hindu festival of Diwali: 'It won't even burn', one of about 200 protesters shouted at the time amid cries of 'Azadi!' (Freedom!). The burning incident sparked off the brutal kidnapping that followed. 'It was a spontaneous event, but we're not apologising for it', said Singh. 'We have a right to freely express our views against the racial discrimination of the constitution.' He rejected a *Daily Post* editorial declaring that such a 'provocative' act as the burning was bound to attract reaction from extremists.

'It wouldn't have been provocative at all if it hadn't been used by the propagandists and mischief-makers of the regime to stir up trouble', Singh said. 'This is how the regime always deals with any public criticism or opposition. It claims that indigenous culture and tradition are under threat ... or the chiefs are being insulted ... or their land is being taken away. The mischief-makers provoke hostile and racist feelings'.[10]

After the burning of the constitution, Kubuabola called the incident 'despicable and treasonous' and police were ordered to investigate and identify the protesters. The public prosecutions director described the burning as a seditious act intended to 'raise the discontent or disaffection among the inhabitants of Fiji'. The demonstration itself was said to be illegal.

Four days after the burning, Singh, chairperson of the Group Against Racial Discrimination (GARD), was among several academics and students briefly detained by police for questioning. On

24 October, four soldiers in plain clothes abducted Singh in daylight near his Suva home as he walked towards suburban Flagstaff to work. They bundled him into a car with the number plate D8654, which was later traced to an officer in the Fiji Military Forces. The abductors drove Singh to the Colo-i-Suva rainforest area on the outskirts of the capital, where they held him prisoner for 11 hours. He was tortured by three of the soldiers while they interrogated him about his political activities. Describing his ordeal to the *Fiji Times* the next day, Singh said:

> I saw two men walking towards me. They looked supicious but I didn't pay much attention. Then suddenly one of them hit me ... and then the other. I fell down. [A car arrived]. I struggled and tried to make as much noise as possible, but they managed to drag me to the car. They covered my eyes with some sort of padding and then pulled a balaclava over my head. The balaclava was tied around my neck. I found it difficult to breathe normally and had to use my mouth ... One of [my abductors] tied my hands together, the other my feet while another put a noose around my neck. Then they punched and questioned me repeatedly, asking the whereabouts of certain people. [He was beaten in three spells before one man went away.] The two others then went to sleep ... They woke up about 6 pm and started hitting me on my eyes and face. They then laid my hands against a root [of a tree] and smashed my hands repeatedly with a steel pipe. They also chopped off my hair and burned strands with cigarettes.[11]

Amnesty twice wrote to the interim Prime Minister, Ratu Sir Kamisese Mara, on 24 and 29 October, expressing concern about the kidnapping and torture of Singh. However, the regime replied there was 'no evidence to suggest the involvement of police or military personnel'. But Kubuabola issued a statement condemning the kidnapping: 'It's not the responsibility and right of any citizen to take the law into its own hands'. In its second response, on 30 October, the regime confirmed that a police investigation had been launched immediately after the abduction. But it made no mention of the arrest of five soldiers – a captain, a sergeant and three corporals – on the same day.

The soldiers, including Captain Sotia Ponijiase, who had served with the British and New Zealand Special Air Services, pleading guilted to abduction and grievious bodily harm charges. On 22 November they were given one-year suspended jail sentences and fined $F170 on each count. Sentenced along with the former SAS captain were Sergeant Waqa Vakaloloma, Corporals Iliesa Raiqiso and Vate Qualo, and Lance-Corporal Samueli Keni.

Adi Kuini Bavadra, at the time leader of the Fiji Labour Party-led Coalition, accused the Fiji military's shadowy Counter-Revolutionary Warfare Unit of having organised the abduction. The new Fiji Intelligence Service has wide-ranging powers to search people and property, open mail and tap telephones. (It is not yet certain how extensively these powers are being used, although people believed to represent a 'security threat' are clearly under surveillance. Many political dissidents believe that telephones and mail are monitored, but hard evidence is lacking.)[12] Lawyers and human rights campaigners also condemned the court hearing as having been 'arranged' to prevent much of the truth becoming public and to legitimise the torture. Singh was not even called as a witness to identify the soldiers.

Defence lawyer Vijaya Parmanandan told the court that the statement by Captain Ponijiase, who claimed to police he had organised the abduction, was not entirely true: 'In fact, it was a valiant effort by [Ponijiase] to take all the blame himself. The fact is that the accused, on the request of the four other men, helped work out a plan for the abduction and questioning of Dr Singh'.[13] Parmanandan also said Singh's hand injuries were not inflicted while he was being questioned by the soldiers, but when 'he caught his hands in the door while being bundled into the vehicle used to abduct him'. This statement was not challenged by the prosecutor even though a Canadian doctor at Suva's Colonial War Memorial Hospital had independently signed a medical certificate saying Singh's injuries had been caused by beating from a metal object – the pipe. Singh, suffering from broken bones in his hands and multiple wounds, burns and bruises on other parts of his body, was treated in hospital for two weeks.

Coup leader Major-General Sitiveni Rabuka's personnel staff officer, Major Sakiusa Raivoce, told the court the accused were all 'men of impeccable character and were loyal soldiers'.[14] He said

Ponijiase had served with the élite British and New Zealand SAS; Vakaloloma had been abducted for three days by Lebanese militia while serving with the United Nations Interim Forces in Lebanon. (In April 1991, Ponijiase was ordered home to Fiji by the UN following international protests against his inclusion in the UN observer team in Kuwait, United Nations Iraq-Kuwait Observation Mission (UNIKOM). UN officials revoked Captain Ponijiase's commission after his conviction for torture had been revealed.)

Singh believes he is among the first victims of a growing circle of repression. Fiji is 'experiencing a paralysis of fear – people are not fighting for their rights' and he warns of police state methods in future.

> People know that what is happening is wrong, but they will not go against the regime. This is how a police state operates. Think of Nazi Germany. Think of Stalin's Russia. People are afraid to speak out and suspect each other. This is Fiji today. This cycle [of repression] is characterised by a degradation of moral standards to justify atrocities committed by or on behalf of the regime, and the use of litigation and propaganda to further supress civil and human rights by referring to the 'legitimacy' of such actions. The regime began [in September 1990] when it attempted to stifle academic freedom at the University of the South Pacific by threatening to cut off funds.[15]

Although the threat was not immediately carried out, since then Dr Tupeni Baba, an indigenous Fijian cabinet minister in the deposed Bavadra government, was forced to resign from his post as head of humanities (although he remained on the academic staff). Also a secret fallback plan for the closure of the university was revealed.[16]

Condemning the abduction and torture of Singh, the *Daily Post* has also protested over the arrest of its journalists involved in the affair. The paper said the arrests seriously challenged the freedom of the press: 'The worrying thought that emerges here is if the police action is a possible start of suppression of this freedom ... While the *Post* men were in custody, the real culprits (burners of the constitution and Dr Singh's basher) were still at large. Someone appears to be barking up the wrong tree'[17].

Singh was under no illusions. He believes he was provoked into making the constitution protest because freedom of speech in Fiji has been stifled under the regime and the news media operates under conditions of strict self-censorship. 'The *Daily Post* has been the bravest of the media and the consequences are upon it now', he said. 'We have been totally frustrated by our lack of freedom of expression.' Since the constitution burning and abduction, the regime has clamped down even harder.

A U.S. Congress human rights report on Fiji has pointed out that the constitution includes a detailed bill of rights but gives the Parliament wide powers to overrule guarantees of basic freedoms in the event of a 'perceived threat to national security'. It cited details of the Constitution Ten case, and it also noted:

> The principal human rights concerns in 1990 included ques-
> tions, in view of the new constitution's unequal representa-
> tion features, about the right of citizens peacefully to change
> their government; discrimination against ethnic Indians
> and women; inhibitions on freedom of speech and press; and
> indications the government is attempting to dicourage po-
> litical activity by university faculty members. On the plus
> side, the government dropped previous plans to introduce
> annual media licensing requirements, opposition views were
> widely reported in the press, and unions were able to exer-
> cise vigorously their legal rights to organise and bargain
> collectively for their members.[18]

Papua New Guinea: Executions and Torture

However, more severe condemnation has been reserved for the Papua New Guinea government over its human rights record on Bougainville. Many human rights commentators regard the Port Moresby government and senior ministers as having been evasive over the issue. When the Australian SBS *Dateline* television team broadcast a documentary on Bougainville in February 1991 show- ing chilling pictures of the humiliation and torture of a farmer and environmental activist, Aloysius Minitong, and other evidence of human rights abuses,[19] the Papua New Guinea government would not be drawn. Instead, the government banned the team for having gone to Bougainville 'illegally', while Foreign Minister Sir Michael Somare pledged cases would be investigated when 'order was restored' on the island.[20]

In June 1991 the PNG Government sacked Colonel Leo Nuia as military commander responsible for Bougainville following his admission on Australian television that atrocities had happened on the island under his command.[21] The ABC *Four Corners* programme confirmed that the Australian-donated helicopters had been used to dump bodies at sea after the St Valentine's Day massacre. The government ordered an inquiry and Somare accused Nuia of earlier telling 'lies to the government that these atrocities did not take place'.

Ill-treatment by government security forces has not been limited to Bougainville. The patterns of human rights violations and abuse of authority have been evident in other parts of the country for several years. According to Amnesty International: 'Members of police riot squads (Mobile Squads) have been singled out for abusive behaviour, but regular duty officers, prison warders and members of the Papua New Guinea Defence Force engaged in controlling civil unrest have also been accused of the ill-treatment and in some cases unlawful killing of civilians'.[22] The history of aggressive and abusive behaviour by members of police riot squads is revealing because they were deployed to restore order in the first months of the Bougainville crisis, and previously had a reputation for repression on the island. Many of the most disturbing features of riot squad behaviour on Bougainville appear to be part of well-established patterns. Primarily used to quell civil unrest, the squads were first used to counter rioting on Buka Island in North Solomons Province in 1962. Seven years later, a permanent riot squad depot was established on Bougainville to deal with unrest. By 1973, riot squads were being used to crush tribal fighting in the Highlands. With considerable autonomy from the normal chain of command within the Royal Papua New Guinea Constabulary, the squads have developed serious problems of accountability and discipline.

During the so-called 'Operation Lomet' in the Highlands, for example, several civilians were beaten and one man, Inake Umia, of Tosoempa village, disappeared after being detained by police on 22 October 1988. Riot squad members denied any knowledge of the man when relatives and friends asked about him – his body was found in the Ramu River nine days after his arrest. He had a broken neck and two bullet holes in his head. In June 1989, a university student, Joeman Mel, was killed and six others wounded when riot police stormed an 'illegal drinking club' at the university in Lae with teargas, shotguns and rubber bullets. Following an inquiry by the Ombudsman, a police officer was later found guilty of manslaughter and was jailed. Among the Bougainville 'execution' case histories:[23]

* *Vincent Amora*. A 20-year-old maintenance worker at the Australian-owned Bougainville Copper Ltd's Panguna mine, Amora was detained along with another man on suspicion of being a BRA militant by security forces on 24 November 1989. They were beaten before being taken to Army Camp 10 at Panguna. Eyewitness reports said Amora was then thrown semi-conscious out of a military vehicle onto the ground outside the army camp, kicked and beaten with rifle butts. He was shot in the head and his body delivered to Arawa General Hospital. A postmortem report said: 'This person was tortured to death then shot ... The scalp was wet with blood and covered ... by brain tissue. The entire body bore multiple bruises and lacerations ... [He was shot in the head] with a high-velocity bullet from close range'. No charge.

* *Pastor Raumo Benito, Sira Devatavi, Lazarus Geman, Joe Siravia, Allan Mateavi, Moiva Sivanai and Kurangik*. On 14 February 1990, United Church pastor Raumo Benito and six members from his congregation from Teanana village in north Bougainville were beaten and all but one of them shot by security forces. The survivor provided an eyewitness account and then went into hiding. Pastor Benito and his companions were loading household goods onto a truck to take them to another village when they were stopped by security forces, who accused them of being BRA militants. The detainees were beaten with gun butts, driven to Tinputz village and then flown by helicopter to military headquarters in Arawa. After further beatings they were driven to a bridge just past Aropa airport.

Ordered out of the truck, they were beaten again, told to strip naked, forced to walk to an isolated spot off the road and then shot. The man who escaped was rescued, naked, by nearby villagers. The bodies of those killed were not recovered. They were dumped into the sea from an Iroquois helicopter – Australian supplied and piloted. No security force personnel were charged over the murders.

* *Ambrose Leo.* His body was delivered by security forces to Arawa Hospital on 18 July 1989, with a note attached that read: 'This is your first billion of your 10 billion'. (A reference to the BRA's original demand for 10 billion kina – about $N.Z.19 billion – in compensation for land and environmental damage.) A postmortem report concluded that Leo had been beaten, kicked and stabbed in the ear before being shot twice at close range. He was still alive after the first shot; the cause of death was brain damage from the second shot. No charge.

* *Alosius Minitong.* A farmer in his mid-40s and an opponent of environmental destruction around Panguna mine, died in police custody on 28 December 1989 after having been detained for three weeks without charge. He was reportedly tortured after being arrested on 7 December on suspicion of being a BRA member.Although his precise cause of death has not been determined, one medical professional said that it was probably pneumonia. The SBS *Dateline* programme showed disturbing pictures of Minitong's torture. The pictures were taken by his captors, who naively had them developed through a local chemist shop on Bougainville. The staff, realising the importance of the pictures, made duplicate copies.

* *Peter Tarapiu and John Tuka.* Tarapiu, a university student, died about 16 August 1989, after being beaten by security forces. His parents, who witnessed his death, said soldiers beat Tarapiu repeatedly with their rifle butts and a piece of wood. The autopsy report said he was killed by damage to the spinal column 'consistent with a heavy blow' to the back of the neck. Tuka, whose body arrived at Arawa Hospital the same time as Tarapiu, was said to have been killed by a gun shot at close range. He had a large hole in his left cheek which exposed dislocated fragments of his cervical spine; his right cheek was hanging loose. No charges.

East Timor: The Santa Cruz Massacre

When Indonesian troops opened fire on Timorese mourners at
Santa Cruz cemetery, Dili, on 12 November 1991, killing many
people, including a 20-year-old Malaysian-New Zealand student,
Indonesian human rights violations and East Timor self-determination became international issues. The preliminary report by the
Indonesian investigating commission, headed by Supreme Court
Judge Djaelani (a former military officer), was welcomed by Australian Prime Minister Paul Keating and Foreign Minister Senator Gareth Evans.[24] They described it as 'credible and encouraging'. The United States said the investigating commission appeared to have taken a 'serious and responsible approach'.

New Zealand also welcomed the report but was reluctant to
comment directly until the release of the final document, expected
in March. Although the N.Z. Government suggested a cautious
UN involvement by sending an official to Jakarta to discuss the
massacre, it was not prepared to support the pleas by human
rights groups and the N.Z. victim's mother, Helen Todd, for a full
inquiry.[25] The N.Z. Government's response to the massacre, and
ongoing human rights abuses in East Timor – and in the other
Melanesian colony, Irian Jaya – and the Djaelani report, have led
to allegations of hypocrisy. A visiting representative of the Fretilin
resistance movement, Francisco Pang, who was snubbed by two
N.Z. cabinet ministers, accused the Bolger Government of appeas-
ing Indonesia.

The preliminary Djaelani Report put only partial blame on the
military to alleviate international pressure on Indonesia, and the
reshuffle of the military command in East Timor was only window
dressing. When compared with detailed reports prepared by human rights groups such as Amnesty International, Asia Watch
and Jakarta's Legal Aid Institute and the credible accounts by
foreign eyewitnesses, the Indonesian commission's version was
deeply flawed. The Djaelani Report found 50 people had died
when soldiers opened fire on the crowd of more than 3,500 mourners –rejecting the military's claim that only 19 were killed yet far
short of the independent estimates of 100 or more victims. The
report also found another 90 people were still missing and may be
dead, injured or in hiding.

In an unprecedented move, President Suharto ordered the report to be publicly released and expressed condolences to the victim's families. However, the report claimed that the soldiers acted in self-defence and blamed Fretilin as the catalyst for the massacre. The report said that on the morning of the massacre demonstrators, some carrying Fretilin banners and pictures of the national resistance leader, Xanana Gusmao, moved towards the Santa Cruz cemetery. Foreigners were involved in the demonstration and the tension soon reached 'boiling point'. Finally, the shootings were said to have been triggered after a 'disorderly, wild and unruly atmosphere' deteriorated into the stabbing of intelligence officer Major Gerhan Lantara and an East Timorese conscript, an alleged stray gunshot, and the lobbing of a hand grenade that did not explode into the crowd.

However, an Asia Watch dossier exposed many of the flaws in the Djaelani report.[26] The human rights agency's report also called on all countries which had expressed concern over the killings to join forces and press for a 'genuinely independent inquiry'. To pressure for a proper, thorough investigation, it demanded that all suppliers of military aid and training to Indonesia – including New Zealand – should suspend the assistance until all those in the military chain of command responsible for the killings were prosecuted. Noting that there were no independent eyewitness accounts of the stabbing of Major Gerhan, Asia Watch said:

> Even if the Indonesian account is accurate, these knifings took place almost an hour before the troops opened fire and in a very different part of Dili. (The Indonesian report says the stabbing occurred at 7.20 a.m. the shootings at 8.10 am) The troops present when the firing started were from different military units than Major Gerhan, and it is not clear that they knew about the stabbing. If they did not, then the knifing cannot have 'provoked' them to shoot; if they did know and they deliberately opened fire in retaliation, then shooting on the crowd is not so much responding to provocation as wreaking vengeance, and the deaths are still wholly inexcusable.[27]

Asia Watch also rejected the claim that the military was convinced it was under attack after the alleged stray shot.

First, if the army command knew its troops would be confronting thousands of people they wished to disperse, they should have been equipped with tear gas not guns. There have been enough demonstrations in East Timor in recent years, and enough expectation of a major one during the Portuguese parliamentary visit, that a supply of non-lethal methods of crowd control should have been an elementary precaution. Since the Indonesian report acknowledges that officials believed such a mass demonstration was planned, the fact that they sent troops with guns shows either a deliberate decision to use force or incompetence of the highest order.

Second, none of the eyewitnesses can recall hearing a single shot before the volley of gunfire started. If there were such a shot, it is far more likely to have come from one of the hundreds of armed soldiers than from the crowd at the cemetery whom eyewitnesses attest had no firearms of any kind. The same Indonesian report, indeed, which mentions the shot, notes that it was impossible to tell where it came from or who fired it.[28]

The report of the hand grenade was also claimed to be misleading. Bishop Ximenes Belo, the apostolic administrator in the predominantly Roman Catholic territory, has been quoted as saying that the grenade was lobbed at a Dili police station, not among the troops in the cemetery. 'There have been no other reports to substantiate the grenade-throwing at all', says Asia Watch. 'Certainly the Indonesian version does not justify the army's plea of self-defence'. Bishop Belo estimated that 180 people were killed in the massacre. Some human rights agencies have put the figure as high as 200, but most estimates range between 75 and 100. The preliminary Djaelani Report appeared to have been drawn heavily on a single, detailed military dossier prepared shortly after the massacre took place. The military account appeared to be a summary of information gathered from officers – it was not an eyewitness account.

Need for a Pacific Human Rights Agency

Fijian, Indonesian and Papua New Guinean authorities need reminding of two United Nations declarations. The first, Declaration 3452, is on 'the protection of all persons from being subjected to torture and other cruel, inhuman or degrading treatment or punishment'. When allegations are made, the state has a responsibility to 'promptly proceed to an impartial investigation'. If it is established that an act of torture has taken place, then Article 10 criminal proceedings should be be instituted.

Although court hearings cannot at present be carried out on Bougainville, this does not absolve the PNG Government from its responsibilities. This is clear from UN Resolution 44/162 of December 1989: 'Principles on the effective prevention and investigation of extra-legal, arbitrary and summary execution'. This resolution calls for governments to set up an independent commission of inquiry (Article 11) in cases where there is an apparent pattern of abuse and /or where the 'established investigative procedures are inadequate because of lack of expertise or impartiality'. The article describes the principles:

> Members of such a commission shall be chosen for their recognised impartiality, competence and independence as individuals. In particular they should be independent of any institution, agency or person that may be the subject of the inquiry. The commission shall have the authority to obtain all information necessary to the inquiry and shall conduct the inquiry as provided for under these principles.[29]

These conditions clearly apply to Bougainville. Such an independent commission should be established immediately in Papua New Guinea. According to Australian National University researcher Matthew Spriggs, co-editor of *The Bougainville Crisis,* high on the agenda of such a commission must be the identification and questioning of the members of the Papua New Guinea Defence Force clearly visible in the photographs of Aloysius Minitong's torture: 'Papua New Guinea's army is not too big that identification would be difficult'.[30] The Australian pilot who flew the helicopter that dumped the bodies of Pastor Benito and his parishioners should be interviewed; his identity is known to Australian and Papua New Guinea authorities. 'The international standing of Papua New Guinea can only be further damaged', Matthew Spriggs says, 'if it continues to pass the buck on human rights by effectively doing nothing'. Clearly the South Pacific needs an independent agency to monitor human rights in the region and to exert pressure on governments accused of abuses.

Notes

1. Robie, D., (4 September 1990), 'Amnesty accusations draw fire,' *Dominion*, Wellington.
2. *Amnesty International Report 1990*, London: Amnesty International Publications.
3. 'P.N.G.: Human rights Violations on Bougainville, 1989-90,' (November 1990), Amnesty International Report, London, p. 1.
4. *Ibid.*, p. 2.
5. Fiji Ministry of Information press statement, (17 December 1990), Suva.
6. Public meeting addressed by Dr Anirudh Singh, Auckland, 18 December 1990; see 'Maoris interrupt academic', (27 December 1990), *Press*, Christchurch.
7. Robie, D., (17 December 1990), 'They put a noose around my neck', *Auckland Star*.
8. See Robie, D., (1989), *Blood on their Banner: Nationalist Struggles in the South Pacific*, pp. 240-242, Sydney: Pluto Press; Delaibatiki became the first journalist charged under Fiji's 66-year-old Official Secrets Act because of an expose about the Fiji military, but he was acquitted.
9. 'Fiji Civil Rights Activists and Journalists Arrested', (November 1990), Amnesty International Report, London.
10. Writer's interview with Dr Singh, (12 December 1990), Canberra.
11. *Fiji Times*, (25 October 1990).
12. 'U.S. Congress Human Rights Report on Fiji 1990', (December 1990), p. 4.
13. *Fiji Times*, (8 November 1990).
14. *Ibid.*
15. Writer's interview with Dr Singh, (7 January 1991) Auckland.
16. Fiji Independent News Service dispatch, (20 December 1990).
17. *Fiji Daily Post*, (29 October 1990).
18. 'U.S. Congress Report', *op. cit.*, p. 2.
19. *SBS Dateline*, (23 February 1991); rebroadcast on TVNZ's *Foreign Correspondent*, (28 February 1991).
20. *Canberra Times*, (27 February 1991).

21. ABC *Four Corners* documentary, (24 June 1991), 'Blood on the Bougainvillea'.

22. Amnesty International, 'P.N.G.: Human Rights', report, *op. cit.*

23. See case details, Amnesty report, *op. cit.*, pp. 22-27.

24. 'Advance Report of the National Commission of Inquiry into 12 November 1991 Incident in Dili', (6 January 1992), unofficial translation by Indonesian Embassy, Wellington.

25. Open letter by Helen Todd to N.Z. Prime Minister Jim Bolger, (9 December 1991); see full text of letter, Robie, D., 'Terror in Timor', *NZ Monthly Review* (March 1992), pp. 14-18.

26. 'East Timor: The November 12 Massacre and its Aftermath,' (12 December 1991), *Asia Watch*, New York, vol. 3, no. 26.

27. *Ibid.*, p. 6.

28. *Ibid.*, p. 7.

29. Amnesty International Report 'P.N.G.: Human Rights', pp. 16-17.

30. Spriggs, M., (27 February 1991), 'P.N.G. still is not taking human rights seriously', *Canberra Times*.

* An earlier version of this chapter appeared in D. Robie (ed) *Tu Galala* (1992), Wellington.

6

Peace, Security and the Movement of People in the Post-Cold War Era

Elizabeth G. Ferris

Introduction

Three years after the Soviet withdrawal of troops from Afghanistan, the fighting goes on and most of the 3.5 million Afghan refugees in Pakistan remain in camps.

Vietnamese are forced onto planes in Hong Kong for deportation to Vietnam. They have been found not to be refugees under the UN Convention. But a few years ago, Vietnamese leaving for the same reasons in the same conditions were almost guaranteed a ticket to a resettlement country.

350,000 Cambodians wait on the Thai border for eventual repatriation to Cambodia. For a decade, they have been pawns in a power struggle in and outside Cambodia. Unlike the Afghans, they will probably return. But the peace process is a fragile one and there are many mines.

A million Sri Lankans have been displaced within their country by the violence and another 200,000 are in India, waiting for an end to the fighting.

Malaysian pushbacks of Vietnamese boats, Japanese policies toward illegal migrants, treatment of tribal people in the Chittagong hill tracts, East Timorese refugees.... The examples go on and on. This chapter considers the forced migration of people as a *security* issue for Asian governments in the post-Cold War era. The *forced* movement of people generates intense political debate throughout Asia and the world. This discussion outlines a global context for understanding the political impact of population movements and illustrates how developments in Asia influence and are influenced by external events and by changes in the international system of assisting refugees and migrants. This is followed by a brief survey of specific cases of forced migration in Asia and some comparisons about the causes of population displacement and the policies of host governments. The conclusion connects peace, security and the movement of people in regional and global terms.

The Global Context

The forced migration of people – though certainly not a new phenomenon in human history – has acquired increased political significance in today's interdependent international system. Contemporary refugee migrations involve millions of people on all continents and affect political processes in diverse regimes. Governments of industrialised and developing countries alike struggle to formulate coherent policies toward refugees, migrants and displaced people. Both democratic and authoritarian regimes seek to contain the political fallout resulting from the arrival of masses of displaced people. Refugees have become both a symbol of social change and a human reminder of the political violence which pervades the contemporary world.

Political scientists and peace researchers have traditionally paid little attention to refugees and displaced people, largely interpreting such migrations as marginal to the central processes of international politics. In the great debates over the causes of war and the conditions for peace, refugees are usually seen as the tragic but politically irrelevant by-products of conflict. This discussion begins with a different premise: refugees and other uprooted people have a significant political impact in many ways, and the study of forced migration is essential to a broad understanding of the complexity of international and national political phenomena.

In surveying the literature on theoretical approaches to forced migration, a number of different paradigms can be identified: refugees as a humanitarian/emergency issue, as a foreign policy issue, as a development issue, as a human rights issue, and as an international systemic issue.[1] Indeed the evolution of scholarly thinking about refugees reflects the dominant intellectual and policy oriented paradigms in the field.

During the 1970s and 1980s, scholars began to analyse the situation of uprooted people from the perspective of national foreign policy and/or national immigration policy. This paradigm explains the ways in which governments respond to a specific situation of forced displacement in terms of the government's foreign policy objectives. This approach is based on the realisation that while there exists a substantial body of international law and norms, it is national governments that decide whom to admit to their territories. Control of national borders remains the essence of national sovereignty and national sovereignty remains the linchpin of the international political system. While a government may abuse, repress and even slaughter its own citizens with relative impunity, the flood of refugees which results from such actions quickly becomes the 'business' of other nations. The way in which a government responds to refugees from a neighbouring, or even a distant, country will be affected by relations between the governments and will in turn greatly influence future relations between those countries. At the same time, policies toward refugees of other nations reflect the domestic economic and political tensions of the host country. Thus, Malaysia's reaction to Vietnamese asylum-seekers has less to do with Malaysian-Vietnamese relations than with Malaysian political concerns over upsetting a delicate national ethnic balance. Or as Loescher and Scanlan[2] persuasively demonstrate, U.S. policy toward refugees was determined largely by U.S. foreign policy. Over 90 per cent of refugees admitted to the U.S. between 1950 and 1985 came from countries with communist or leftist governments.

Today, as the Cold War dissipates and more comprehensive approaches to security are evolving, scholars are looking at refugee issues as security concerns. Thus the International Institute of Strategic Studies in London has embarked on a project to look at the security issues involved in the displacement of people. As Gil Loescher (1991) argues, there is growing awareness that mass migrations are the result of the breakdown of national security and, at the same time, that they pose fundamental challenges to the security of nations.[3] Myron Weiner considers the types of international movements generated by factors related to national security and stability in contrast to those uprooted by economic pressures. He goes on to analyse the circumstances in which such migrants are seen as security threats and the different ways that states behave when they regard refugees as a threat to their international security and internal stability.[4]

The changes occurring in patterns of international migration are challenging the behaviour and paradigms of states. But the fact is that these changes are primarily affecting the way that *Western* governments see these issues. When a million Ethiopian/ Eritrean refugees went to the Sudan, scholars didn't jump to the conclusion that this was a security issue. But when half a million asylum-seekers arrived in Europe in 1990, governments and scholars began to see their arrival in terms of security. In other words, the change in paradigmatic emphasis is not just the result of changing objective conditions – but changes in perceptions. And these changes have their origins in the demise of the Cold War.

Specifically, Western governments need to find new enemies and new scapegoats to replace Communism and the Soviet empire. Legitimate fears about the cultural impact of the arrival of large numbers of people from culturally-distinct places has led to widespread backlash and violence in many European countries. But the concern with security comes less from the present situation than from fears that these numbers will be far greater in the future.

More cynically, the sudden concern with refugees and migration issues as security issues reflects the need for researchers in the field of international relations to look at issues other than the arms race and potential nuclear war. Thus there is more concern today with a broad range of issues, such as environmental security, than was the case 10 years ago – reflecting perhaps growing awareness of environmental issues, but also reflecting perhaps a reduced salience of traditional issues associated with security and war.

Thus, scholars are increasingly looking at migrations of people in terms of security. The growth of this paradigm reflects real security concerns, diminishing traditional threats to national security to Western powers, the logical outcome of a focus on national foreign policies, and the need by researchers to find other issues to study in a world where traditional enemies have become somewhat elusive.

Definitions

Discussion of migration questions always brings up the thorny question of definitions. Forced migration refers to people who are compelled to leave their countries. Those who leave because of economic reasons – because they cannot support themselves or their families in their own countries – are considered to be economic migrants. These economic migrants may come to a foreign country legally – that is, with the permission of the government of the receiving country – or illegally, without that permission. Current estimates are that there are 45-70 million migrants in the world, of whom half are considered 'irregular migrants', that is, those living in a country without the approval of the host. In addition, there are far larger numbers of people who have left their rural communities for urban areas in search of work. The United Nations estimates that some 300-400 million internal migrants are expected in the decade of the 1990s.

Refugees are those who are forced to leave their countries because of fear of persecution or because of the generalised conditions of war. The definition of refugees as formulated in the 1951 UN Convention includes those who are outside their countries of origin and who fear persecution because of their race, ethnic origin, membership in a social group, religion, or political opinions. This definition was developed in the aftermath of World War II to respond to the needs of those displaced as a consequence of that conflict. Although the definition was formally expanded in 1967 to all geographic regions and although the definition has been expanded in practice, serious shortcomings remain. Distinctions between economic and political motivations for flight are breaking down. The protection and assistance needs of internally displaced people may be as severe as those facing refugees, but they remain outside the scope of the definition. The United Nations High Commissioner for Refugees (UNHCR) estimates that there are about 18 million recognised refugees in the world today.[5]

Adding to this definitional ambiguity is growing recognition of a third category of forced migrants – those who must leave their homes because of environmental factors, such as famine, desertification, de-forestation, toxic waste dumping, nuclear tests and accidents. Many of these environmental conditions are the result of political decisions. Current estimates are that some 10 million people have been displaced because of environmental factors, but estimates of future numbers are as high as 60 million in the next two decades.[6]

Discussion of definitions is important in that the way people are defined affects the kind of assistance they will receive from the international community. It shapes the way the international community perceives the individuals – as helpless victims to whom the international community has a particular responsibility or as potential security threats.

Internally Displaced People

While refugees are those who have crossed an international border because of persecution or war, a larger number of people have fled their communities for the same reasons as refugees, but remain within their countries of origin. These internally displaced people are usually more vulnerable to violence as they remain closer to the conflict which displaced them. Moreover, provision of assistance to internally displaced people is usually more difficult than to refugees, as the on-going violence creates logistical and political problems for relief agencies. Frequently, internally displaced people are not anxious to be identified because of fear. In many countries, governments or other armed forces view displaced people with suspicion; in those cases displaced people do not want to call attention to themselves not even to get material assistance.

While refugees have access to an international system of protection and assistance (although that system is often inadequate), there is no such system for responding to the needs of internally displaced people. UNHCR's mandate only applies to those who have crossed an international border. Those who remain within their countries' borders are more vulnerable because they have no such international agency or body of international law to which they can appeal (although the International Committee of the Red Cross is able to help in some specific instances).

This issue of internally displaced people received a great deal of media and political attention in the aftermath of the Gulf War as governments argued that the humanitarian needs of Iraqi Kurds outweighed traditional respect for national sovereignty. But the intervention of Western forces raised more questions than it answered – particularly about the suitability of such intervention in the many other situations of internally displaced people.

New Challenges on the Global Level

These past few years have been a time of unprecedented change in the global refugee system and there are now indications that the international system of refugee protection – a system built up so carefully in the post World War II period – is breaking down.

A few trends illustrate this point:

* The number of refugees and internally displaced people is increasing. In 1990, there were one million more refugees than there were in 1989. In 1991, there were two million more than in 1990. They flee wars and ethnic conflicts, death squads and persecution.

* Solutions for refugees are becoming more elusive. While the repatriation of 40,000 Namibians was a joyous event, return of refugees in other areas is more problematic.

* As wars drag on, sometimes for generations and often supported by outside powers, solutions become less likely for those displaced by the violence. Refugee camps have become a semi-permanent fixture in many regions. At the same time, new outbreaks of violence in countries such as Yugoslavia and Peru, to name but two of many examples, also raise fears of further large-scale population displacements.

* Increasingly, for a number of reasons, refugees are coming to countries in the North in search of safety and asylum. In the United States, for example, up to a million Central American refugees have entered the country over the past decade seeking

security from the on-going political violence in El Salvador and Guatemala. Most live without any legal status whatsoever. In 1975, the Federal Republic of Germany had 9,627 asylum-seekers. By 1985 that number had increased to 110,000 and by 1989 to 350,000 (most of whom were Central Europeans). Many European governments have experienced a 300 or 400 per cent increase in the number of asylum-seekers over a three-year period. Improved transportation and communication coupled with deteriorating conditions in countries of first arrival seem to be the major reasons for this flow.

* This has led to increasingly restrictive policies by Northern governments. Governments are making it more difficult for asylum-seekers to receive asylum or to remain in their countries, even as they use ever-more sophisticated methods to limit the number of asylum-seekers reaching their territory. Along with increasingly restrictive governmental policies has come a rise in expressions of racism and xenophobia. From Sweden to Switzerland, expressions of hatred and fear of foreigners is becoming more evident. Most recently, outbreaks of violence against foreigners in former East Germany raise questions about the political impact of migration and popular response in the context of rapid political change in central Europe.

These factors are leading to a breakdown of the international system of refugee protection - a system characterised by a consensus that it was the responsibility of the international community to provide protection and assistance to refugees. Specifically, there is evidence of:

1. A more restrictive application by national governments of the classic definition of refugees embodied in the 1951 UN Convention and the 1967 Protocol.
2. Increasing questions about the suitability of the definition in an age where most refugees are displaced by war and violence, not by individual persecution, and where the line between economic and political motivations for flight are blurred.
3. A weakening of the United Nations High Commissioner for Refugee's (UNHCR's) leadership role in refugee protection and

assistance. Most obviously, UNHCR has experienced serious shortfalls in the last three years. Budgets and programmes have been cut with major consequences for refugees and for non-governmental organisations (NGOs). Member governments are urging UNHCR to tailor its programmes to fit the resources available – not to shape its programmes in response to the needs of refugees.

The stakes in such an erosion of the international system are high. Ninety per cent of the world's refugees come from countries in the south and ninety per cent of them remain in the south. Governments of countries far poorer than those of Western Europe or North America – countries which host far larger numbers of refugees – are questioning why they should be expected to provide for refugees when richer countries are closing their doors.

Asian Complexities

These trends on the global level are reflected in developments in Asia, and yet Asian refugee issues are also shaped by unique political and economic forces. This survey of Asian refugee situations focuses on several very different situations, where the causes of displacement, the treatment of refugee groups by host countries, and the influence of foreign powers and future prospects are all different.

The Afghan refugees in Pakistan who fled in the aftermath of the Soviet invasion of 1979 are the first group described here. A second group comprises those who were uprooted as a result of the war in Indochina. Although the war formally ended in 1975, the human consequences of that war have displaced millions of Vietnamese, Cambodians, and Laotians. Some of these uprooted people have been considered refugees by the international community and have been resettled in distant countries. Many still languish in camps waiting for an end to the violence; their repatriation is linked to questions of peace and economic stability in their countries of origin. A third group of uprooted people includes those displaced because of internal violence – violence which often has ethnic components. The specific groups considered here are the situation of Burmese refugees, Sri Lankan displaced people and refugees, and Filipino displaced people.

The causes in these three cases are quite different, but they share certain characteristics. It is also important to note that there are many other situations of uprooted people in Asia. The treatment of tribal hill-people in the Chittagong tracts in India, displaced Bangladesh people, the vast trans-migration schemes in Indonesia, the treatment of illegal immigrants in Japan, the whole question of sex tourism and forced prostitution, the impact of migration on culture and identity in the Pacific Islands – these are all issues which are related to peace and security in the region.

Afghan Refugees: Victims of the Cold War?

The Afghan refugees constitute the world's largest refugee population, with about three and a half million living in camps in Pakistan and another two million in Iran. In addition, an estimated two million Afghans are internally displaced within their own country. Thus, almost half of Afghanistan's pre-war population of 15.5 million has been uprooted. Some Afghan refugees left in 1978 following the coup in Kabul. Most fled after the Soviet invasion of 1979. The repressive anti-Islamic policies of the government led to armed uprisings throughout the country which in turn led to harsh Soviet counter-insurgency campaigns. The ensuing war, with widespread bombings of rural areas, led to the flight of millions of Afghans from their homes.

In April 1988, the United Nations facilitated an agreement providing for the withdrawal of the Soviet troops, and the prohibition of intervention in Afghan and Pakistani affairs, including the continued arming of resistance groups. The Soviet troops began their withdrawal in May 1988 and completed their pull-out, as foreseen in the agreement, by February 1989.

But more than four years after the agreement and three years after the Soviet troop withdrawal, the vast majority of refugees remain in exile. Political instability and violence continue in Afghanistan and the legacy of the war will live on for decades, most concretely in the presence of millions of mines which make re-settlement of agricultural communities difficult. About 75 per cent of the refugees in Pakistan live in camps throughout the North West Frontier Province; an additional 20 per cent of them live in Baluchistan. While the refugees come from many different ethnic groups, the majority are Pathans – as is most of the population on the Pakistan side of the border. Almost half of the refugees are children; a little more than half of the adults are women. Many of the men were killed or remained behind to continue the struggle, and many of the male refugees left the camps periodically to fight inside Afghanistan.

The conflict in Afghanistan illustrates the human costs of the Cold War. U.S. military aid to the Mujahidin between 1980 and 1987 was estimated at well over $2 billion – the largest undeclared U.S. military action since Vietnam.[7] Additional arms came from China and Saudi Arabia. The war dragged on for over a decade in large part because of the superpowers' involvement.

Pakistan's involvement with the refugees also had a security component – with global implications. By allowing the refugees to live in Pakistan and by allowing the Mujahidin to carry out military operations inside Afghanistan from Pakistani territory, Pakistan increased its importance to the United States as a 'holding line against Soviet expansion'. U.S. support for Pakistan has been manifest in many ways. The current six-year aid package, approved in early 1987, is for more than U.S.$4 billion. U.S. concerns about nuclear non-proliferation and evidence of Pakistan's nuclear progress were overshadowed by the need to continue the war in Afghanistan. Within Pakistan, the military has become stronger.[8]

The creation of *armed* refugee camps on the border of Afghanistan was a major obstacle to the establishment of peace in the country. As in the case of the Cambodian refugees on the Thai-Cambodian border; the Afghan refugees pose an obvious security risk to the government of their country of origin.

This raises many contradictions. Although armed groups or individual combatants are not considered under international law to be refugees, in practice such distinctions are difficult in the Afghan case. Many of the Afghan men were away from the camps for long periods of time as they continued the armed struggle back home. The Mujahidin and the Islamic religious leaders made virtually all decisions in the camps, limiting the role of the UN High Commissioner for Refugees (UNHCR) and the 20 or so international NGOs providing services in the camp. In comparison with most other refugee situations, the Afghan refugee situation is one where the armed groups have significant control over camp life. Before refugees are eligible to be registered for assistance, the Pakistan government requires that they belong to one of the Mujahidin parties.

But the security considerations of the Afghan refugees go beyond the actions of the armed groups. The vast majority of the refugees come from rural backgrounds (like the vast majority of Afghans), but they have been living in urban or semi-urban settings and in the artificial life of camps for more than ten years. Most of them have not been involved in farming for the past decade and there is fear that they are losing their knowledge and experience in the area where they will have to make their future livelihoods.

The provision of food rations and the availability of basic services within the camps has led refugees to become dependent on relief. Although training programmes and income-generating projects have been initiated, they are not a substitute for the agricultural work to which most of the refugees will return. On the other hand, access to medical care and other health services has resulted in improved material conditions for the refugees. For example, the mortality rate for refugee children under the age of five is 130 per 1,000 – high by standards of developed countries - but low in comparison to the corresponding 300/1000 rate in Afghanistan.[9] Since 1979, UNHCR has spent over $600 million in aid to the Afghan refugees in Pakistan alone – and the costs of repatriation will be substantial.

The vast majority of the Afghan refugees are eager to return to their country and their lands. With the signing of the peace accord, hopes were raised that repatriation to Afghanistan would occur on a large scale.

In July 1990, the UNHCR initiated a pilot project to provide incentives for up to 250,000 refugees to return home. Opposed by most Mujahidin factions, the programme had only limited success. While UN Operation Salaam estimated that more than 200,000 would return to Afghanistan in 1990, ration cards for only about 78,000 people were turned in. As in other situations, it is estimated that larger numbers returned spontaneously, without international assistance. And it appears that another 36,000 - 60,000 Afghan refugees returned from Iran.[10] Questions about repatriation and about the prospects of future large-scale return of the refugees inevitably raise questions about the conditions to which they are returning.

One of the lessons learned from the Afghan case is that peace is more than a negotiated agreement; it must be carefully nurtured and sustained in order to allow for the return of displaced populations. Although the Cold War is over, in Asia it is still evident in the fact that over 5 million Afghan refugees are not yet able to return home. Improved relations between the U.S. and the Soviet Union and even the withdrawal of Soviet troops from Afghanistan are not sufficient to permit the establishment of peace in the country. The presence of millions of mines throughout the country is a formidable obstacle – not just to the return of the refugees and other displaced populations, but to the country's potential to become self-sustaining in the future. The presence of hundreds of thousands of guerrilla forces who for at least a decade have learned that the way to resolve conflicts and to stand up for one's nationalist aspirations is through violence, is bound to be a de-stabilising force for Afghanistan – even after the refugees return home.

Indo-Chinese Refugees: the Consequences of War, Fifteen Years Later

The war in Southeast Asia produced a whirlwind of movements of people – people torn from their lands, forced into exile, setting off for other countries by boat and on foot. The human consequences of the war are still being felt throughout the region. Vietnamese boat people, Cambodian refugees living as political pawns on the Thai-Cambodian border, Laotian refugees – each pose a somewhat different set of problems for host governments. But like the Afghan refugees, Indo-Chinese refugees are a lasting consequence of the Cold War and any durable solution to their plight will most likely be long and painful.

The Vietnamese

The exodus of boat people from Vietnam reached its peak in 1979 when as many as 50,000 people were fleeing by sea each month.[11] At the same time, the violence of the Khmer Rouge and the aftermath of the Vietnamese occupation of Cambodia uprooted millions from their home communities. Many poured across the border into Thailand. As the numbers escalated, the Thai government felt abandoned by the international community. It did not want the refugees and although it was being pressed by the international community, particularly the United States, to adopt generous policies towards the new arrivals, the government felt that it could no longer cope.

In mid-1979, the Thai government began towing Vietnamese vessels back out to sea. Similarly the Malaysian government began pushing Vietnamese boats out to sea; by one estimate some 40,000 Vietnamese were pushed away from Malaysia in 1979 alone.[12] In June 1979, the Thais rounded up 40,000 Cambodian refugees and forced them at gunpoint to return to their country, via a deep escarpment into a heavily mined field. 10,000 people died in this exercise, either from exploding mines or from Thai gunfire when they tried to turn back. The cruelty and inhumanity of the actions were roundly condemned. The international community responded; a special United Nations session was convened in Geneva in July 1979 on the plight of the Indo-Chinese refugees.

At that meeting the basic outlines of the policy toward Indo-Chinese refugees were worked out – a policy which lasted almost a decade. Thailand and other countries would admit refugees in return for a promise by the international community that the refugees would be re-settled outside the region. Thailand – like Malaysia, Indonesia, Hong Kong and others[13] – was unwilling to accept the refugees for permanent settlement and argued, with considerable justification, that the refugee situation was the product of the Indo-China war – which it did not create. So a *quid pro quo* was reached – countries in the region would preserve the right of first asylum, in return for assurances that the refugees would be quickly moved from the region.

One of the most interesting options instituted by the 1979 conference to deal with the Indo-Chinese refugees was the creation of the Orderly Departure Programme (ODP) – a programme without parallel in the world. Under this programme, Vietnamese are allowed to depart legally from Vietnam for Western countries as refugees, without recourse to flimsy boats or through uncertain first asylum countries.

For two years this new policy seemed to work, with large numbers of refugees resettled by Western countries, principally the United States, Canada, Australia and Western Europe. But growing fears that the resettlement option in itself was serving as a pull factor – and increasing evidence of 'compassion fatigue' in the West – created pressures for other actions. For example, in 1980, the U.S. resettled more than 166,000 Indo-Chinese refugees and more than 132,000 in 1981. But by 1982, U.S. interest was waning (as a result in part of the spontaneous arrival of 125,000 Cubans and growing concern about the numbers of Lao and Cambodian arrivals). In late 1981, the U.S. resettlement rejection rate of Vietnamese boat-people in Hong Kong was 20 per cent; this figure rose to more than 65 per cent in late 1982. The buildup of rejected cases increased the defensiveness of both the Thai and Hong Kong governments.[14]

In 1981 Thailand instituted a policy of 'humane deterrence' – a policy echoed the following year in Hong Kong. The rationale of the policy was to make life in exile more difficult as a way of deterring further arrivals. So resettlement options were curtailed, the camps were made less comfortable, and refugee freedom of movement was limited. In Hong Kong, people arriving after 2 July 1982 were detained in special closed camps. Camp populations in Southeast Asia and Hong Kong dropped from 130,000 in 1979 to 52,000 in 1981. Between 1982 and 1986, boat-people continued to arrive at a slightly decreasing rate, but resettlement opportunities declined and the number of long-stayers increased. Since 1987, many Vietnamese had travelled overland through Cambodia and then by a short boat trip to Thailand. By January 1989, the number of Vietnamese entering Thailand reached 2,500 per month and reports of piracy on the South China Sea reached alarming proportions. Thailand, like Malaysia, again began towing Vietnamese boats back out to sea.

Since 1979, over a million Vietnamese, Cambodians, and Laotians have been resettled in the U.S., Canada and Australia and another 150,000 or so in West European countries. But in spite of the active resettlement programmes, Thailand still has nearly 100,000 'residual refugees', (refugees that no resettlement country wants – Vietnamese army deserters, North Vietnamese who cannot prove they have been persecuted at home, criminals, etc).

'The idea that the rest of the world will default on promises to empty the camps through resettlement is a recurring political nightmare for Thailand.'[15]

The increasing numbers of Vietnamese arriving in Thailand were paralleled in Hong Kong as well. Nearly 35,000 Vietnamese arrived in Hong Kong in 1989 – bringing the total number there to 57,000. From 1975-1989, some 140,000 refugees arrived in Hong Kong from Vietnam, of whom some 115,000 were resettled, half in the U.S. In spite of the policies of humane deterrence, and prison-like conditions in detention centres, the Vietnamese continued to arrive, with an increase in social tensions and violence in the camps. Most of the new arrivals were from North Vietnam, raising questions as well about their claim to refugee status.

A similar dynamic was evident in the case of Malaysia which for over a decade granted temporary asylum to more than 250,000 boat-people, all but 20,000 of whom were resettled. But in 1989, nearly 2,000 Vietnamese were arriving each month and in May of that year, the Malaysian government began turning back the boats.

In response to these developments, in June 1989, another international conference was held in Geneva and a Comprehensive Plan of Action (CPA) was adopted by the international community.

The CPA was seen as another international response to protect the right of first asylum in the region by making it clear that it was the responsibility of the international community – and not just that of the country in which the refugees happened to arrive – to provide for their future. But unlike the case a decade earlier, the CPA made it clear that the West's commitment to resettlement was not open-ended. Only those individuals found to be refugees under the Convention would be resettled. While this policy was deplored by many U.S. politicians and by a number of NGOs, in fact it was hard to argue against it.

In both Vietnam and Hong Kong, screening procedures were instituted. Although criticised on procedural grounds by Amnesty International and other human rights groups, the screening procedures in themselves were greatly improved over time. In December 1989 the first group of Vietnamese were forcibly returned, followed almost two years later by a second group of returns with prospects of further forced repatriations to come.

Nonetheless, people continue to flee Vietnam – in spite of the often desperate conditions of exile and in spite of the lack of present-day resettlement opportunities. The debate over the reasons for their flight is crucial to understanding what will happen to them. Some argue that they are fleeing poverty and economic suffering which are the result of the international isolation of the country. Others, particularly in the United States, see those who leave as individuals fleeing the persecution of a communist regime. The latter group wants to prevent forced repatriation; the former see such returns as necessary for the survival of asylum for those few who do have legitimate fears of persecution.

In comparison with other countries in the region, there is no question that Vietnam is a poor country. For the majority of people in Vietnam, life is a matter of survival, a struggle to make ends meet by pursuing a variety of both traditional and creative sources of income. There are some informal economic changes aimed at stimulating growth, but Vietnam is still economically isolated by the trade embargo of the U.S. and other Western countries. It is also prevented from access to development assistance from international bodies like the International Monetary Fund, the World Bank and the Asia Development Bank. Political reforms can only be successful if they are accompanied by an improvement in the standard of living.[16] In recent years, inflation has averaged about 700 per cent per year and unemployment is over 20 per cent in urban areas.

But perhaps because of the high emotional feelings resulting from the Vietnam war, the situation of the Vietnamese asylum-seekers, refugees or economic migrants continue to provoke international interest and concern. It has become a security issue for many governments. The fact that resettlement was developed as the most likely option for most of the Vietnamese undoubtedly acted as a 'pull factor'. In other words, Vietnamese were not only leaving their country because conditions were so bad, but also because there was an option (until the various cut-off dates) to leave the country.

Presently the situation in Hong Kong appears to have reached an impasse as the Hong Kong and British officials are determined to deport Vietnamese found not to be refugees back to Vietnam.

But such deportations are highly charged events. The Vietnamese in Hong Kong's closed camps are adamantly refusing to go quietly. Demonstrations, hunger strikes and violence have increased. Opposition by the U.S. to such deportations has given way to a grudging acceptance that there are no other feasible alternatives. Moreover, the number of Vietnamese arriving in Hong Kong continues to increase. 14,000 arrived in Hong Kong in the first half of 1991 – a 300 per cent increase over the same period in 1990.[17] While Hong Kong receives the most media attention, the situation is the same in other Southeast Asian countries where, sooner or later, such deportations will also have to take place.[18]

Following relatively low numbers in the early years, by 1989, a record 39,000 Vietnamese had left via the Orderly Departure Programme (ODP) (with 29,000 of those cases going to the U.S.). Bilateral agreements between the U.S. and Vietnam provided for the regular departure of family members (including Amerasian children) and former re-education camp prisoners. But these programmes have not stopped Vietnamese from leaving. And some estimates place the number of people on the ODP waiting list at close to one million!

Lao Refugees

Policies toward the Vietnamese boat-people were shaped by the presence of hundreds of thousands of other Indo-Chinese refugees – the Lao and the Cambodians – who fled to Thailand. Events in those two countries were profoundly altered by the Indo-Chinese war, and like the Vietnamese, the Lao and the Cambodian refugees were victims of political developments and conflicts. In Laos, the Pathet Lao proclaimed the Lao People's Democratic Republic on 2 December 1975. In all three countries, changes of regime took place in 1975 and in all cases, these changes were accompanied by the massive displacement of people. First those who had worked with the former regime took flight, followed by a broader range of people.

In Laos, a policy of national unification was carried out by the government with the guidance of Vietnam. The rapid socialist transformation of the Lao economy and society was carried out and a climate of fear and suspicion combined to lead many to flee to neighbouring Thailand.

From 1975 to 1986 approximately 325,000 Lao left their country for Thailand – a figure representing 10 per cent of that nation's population. The Lao refugees represent two different ethnic groupings: the lowland Lao and the hill-tribe Lao. The Thai government's policy was to place the lowland Lao into camps, but as the stream of lowland Lao continued, the Thai government adopted a number of measures designed to curb the influx. Informally, there were many reports of 'push-backs' occurring along the Thai-Lao border in which would-be refugees were prevented from entering. Also in 1980, an agreement was reached between the UN High Commissioner for Refugees (UNHCR) and the Lao government providing for voluntary repatriation.

As in the case of the Vietnamese, the Thai government instituted a policy of 'humane deterrence' in 1981, which represented the government's efforts to reduce the influx of refugees. Humane deterrence included several policies. Most significantly, no Lao entering the country after a specific date (August 1981) was considered a refugee or eligible for resettlement. Rather, they were considered to be illegal immigrants and were transferred to less attractive closed camps in which services were restricted to an essential minimum. Moreover, foreigners were generally denied access to the camps as the government felt that the refugees might associate their presence with resettlement possibilities.

These measures led to an immediate drop in the number of Lao refugees entering the country in 1982. During 1983, the Thai government began relaxing its restrictions, allowing processing of resettlement cases – first the difficult cases (e.g., handicapped refugees) and then individuals by order of arrival date. This precipitated another surge in new arrivals during 1984 and the first half of 1985. In July 1985, the Thai government in collaboration with UNHCR instituted a screening procedure for new Lao arrivals. Following interviews with the newly arrived Lao, decisions were reached to accept some and to reject others. The screening procedure was designed to reduce the number of people leaving Laos for economic reasons while granting asylum only to people with genuine fears of persecution. But then the question arose of what to do with the 'screened-out' Lao. Following long negotiations, the Lao government finally agreed to accept the returnees. In the last ten years, over 3,000 Lao returned to Laos

(1,700 in 1989 alone) under UNHCR auspices; reports also indicate that over 17,000 Lao have returned unofficially without
international assistance. The Comprehensive Plan of Action (CPA)
also provided for full access by all Laotian asylum-seekers to the
Laotian border screening programme which was established in
July 1985. About 90 per cent of the lowland Lao who were interviewed in 1989 were screened in and allowed to enter a camp
where they would be eligible to apply for resettlement.

The situation of the hill-tribe Lao has been quite different. The
first arrivals in Thailand were those individuals who had fought
for the U.S. Central Intelligence Agency (CIA) before the change
of government. The majority of the hill-tribe Lao arrived in 1975
and there was virtually no resettlement of this group until 1979-
1980. Between 1975 and July 1986, about 125,000 more hill-tribe
Lao arrived; over half of those were resettled. The Thai government has always treated the hill-tribe Lao more leniently than
other groups. Because of their closer identification with the U.S.
government and the fact that their resettlement outside the
region is not a realistic option, the highland Lao have been
considered to be more 'bona fide' refugees than the lowland Lao.
But in spite of the fact that large numbers of highland Lao have
been resettled, the future is difficult in that cultural adjustment of
these people in resettlement countries has been enormously difficult.

Cambodians

Cambodia's involvement in the Indo-China war produced tragic
consequences for its people – consequences still felt today even as
the peace agreement is being implemented. From 1970-73 intensive U.S. bombing devastated the countryside. By early 1972, two
million Cambodians were homeless. By one estimate the war had
claimed some 450,000 Cambodian lives by the time the Khmer
Rouge came to power in April 1975. At least one million of
Cambodia's total population of seven million died of starvation,
disease, punishment or murder during the Khmer Rouge regime.
The December 1978 invasion by Vietnamese forces led the following year to an outpouring of refugees. During the Khmer Rouge
regime few could get out of the country (from April 1975 –

December 1978 only 34,000 Cambodians crossed into Thailand though some 320,000, mostly ethnic Vietnamese, went to Vietnam). The flight of so many Cambodians in 1979 was the result of fear of the policies of the new Vietnam-backed regime, food shortages and likelihood of famine and perhaps the built-up suffering produced during the years of Khmer Rouge rule. Well over 500,000 Cambodians had arrived on the Thai border by October 1979. Khao I Dang camp was opened for them, but was closed in 1980 when the numbers increased. People were confined to the border, for the most part to the Cambodian side of the border. Relief assistance, food and medical care were provided under the auspices of the joint International Committee of the Red Cross (ICRC)-UNICEF mission which coordinated the work of some 95 NGOs. But the joint mission could not control the growing militarisation of the area and by the end of 1980 both UNICEF and ICRC decided to withdraw from the Joint Mission exercise.

The growing presence of the refugees along the border led to the Thai governments determination that the Cambodians would not be a permanent presence in the country. The Thai government not only tried to force some 10,000 to return to Cambodia, as mentioned above, but refused to consider them as refugees. Instead they were classified as 'displaced persons'; the UNHCR was not permitted to work with them and in 1982 a new United Nations agency was created, the UN Border Relief Organisation (UNBRO), to provide assistance. But unlike UNHCR, the UN Border Relief Organisation had no mandate to provide for protection along the border. ICRC was supposed to provide that protection, but there were many limits on its operations. In particular the Thai government forbad international personnel to stay in the camps after 5 p.m. And there have been cases where ICRC personnel have stood as helpless witnesses while refugees were killed before their eyes.[19]

The creation of UNBRO coincided with the formation of the Coalition Government of Democratic Kampuchea, composed of the different political and military groupings which dominated the camps. From the beginning the camps were dominated by the military forces; this was recognised and each camp was openly controlled by one of the three main guerrilla forces.

Thailand saw the refugees as a buffer from Vietnam – a buffer which was necessary now that Cambodia no longer filled that role. The U.S. Lawyers Committee for Human Rights said, 'Encouraged by China and with U.S. acquiescence, Thailand adopted the policy of encouraging the growth of guerrilla groups opposed to the Vietnamese-backed government in Phnom Penh along the border it shares with Cambodia'.[20] At the same time, Thailand wanted to ensure that the refugees would not remain in the country – hence their efforts to prevent the Cambodians from establishing a recognised presence in Thai territory. The border was thus a fluid one. The refugees' or displaced persons' camps were on the Cambodian side of the border but the people would flee into Thailand during the frequent military offensives. But in late 1984/85, Vietnamese troops launched their biggest offensive ever, forcing the refugees into Thailand proper and building fortifications right up to the international border in an effort to stop the guerrillas.

The situation of the Cambodian refugees along the border was unique in that it was the population base of a 'government in exile' recognised by the United Nations. The UN recognised the unlikely Coalition Government of Democratic Kampuchea (CGDK) as the legitimate Cambodian government and the Thai authorities maintained that the CGDK had jurisdiction over the people in the camps. In practice, the military guerrilla groups controlled the camps. Although material supplies and technical support were provided through UNBRO and the NGOs, the camps were administered by the different military factions of the CGDK. 'These factions find it relatively easy to manipulate information and relief goods to their advantage; assistance intended for beneficiaries is routinely diverted for political and military purposes', Niland recorded.[21] In August 1989, for example, it was reported that one of the military factions was regularly sending UN rations adequate for about 25,000 soldiers to its military bases.[22]

The camps along the border are violent places, subject to shelling and frequent artillery fire from troops as close as one kilometre away. Forced conscription and forced portering of the refugees by the military forces were commonplace. Given the heavy incidence of mines in the border areas, casualties were high. Abuses and violence by the Thai Rangers (Thai military forces charged with providing security in the border area) were also commonplace and have been well-documented.[23] The guerrilla forces controlled the camps and forced the refugees – many of whom were there because they have no choice – to go to fight inside Cambodia. 'Relief officials generally use a figure of 90 per cent when quantifying the number of people who have no desire to be part of DK-controlled areas' (Democratic Kampuchea, Pol Pot's forces).[24]

A particular human rights abuse was the existence of so-called 'satellite' or hidden border camps which were physically close to the UN-administered camps and served as military bases for the guerrillas. Perhaps 100,000 civilians lived in those camps, with no access to relief supplies and services, and vulnerable to forced combat. Periodically people would be forced from the UN-administered camps into the hidden camps, in spite of NGO protests and reports from human rights groups.

Thailand's ambivalence toward the refugees is clear. While the Thai government wished to provide support to the guerrillas opposing Vietnam, it didn't want to be permanently burdened with the Cambodians and refused to allow the camps to be moved to safer positions within Thailand further from the border. Before 1984/85, Thailand refused to allow Cambodians to stay on Thai soil, except for brief periods following military offensives.

Like the Afghan refugees, the Cambodian refugee population included a sizeable military component which posed a security threat to the existing government in Cambodia.

The question of the return of the refugees has become a hot political issue and is linked to developments inside Cambodia and to the status of negotiations taking place. Since 1979, UNHCR, in cooperation with the Cambodian Red Cross, has facilitated the reintegration of 400,000 Cambodians returning from Thailand, Laos and Vietnam. Most of these returned between 1979 and 1983 before the fighting in the country escalated. But most of the repatriations themselves have not involved the UN as they have been either spontaneous or forced, as in the case of returns to the hidden border.

In November 1991, there were 350,000 Cambodian refugees along the border (and perhaps 150,000-200,000 displaced within Cambodia). The signing of a peace agreement for Cambodia in October 1991, although it had been in process for years, came very suddenly and there are many concerns about the safety of the refugees to be repatriated. In particular the situation inside Cambodia is far from calm. 'Buried land mines, malaria, shortages of food and medicine, renegade soldiers, bandits and rivalries over land and power all risk derailing the peace', reported Gallagher.[25]

Peace in Cambodia depends in part on the return and reintegration of the refugees. Repatriation is now underway although the operations have been marred by delays and security concerns. UNHCR has been given responsibility for coordinating the repatriation; ironically, after years of being denied a protection role in the border camps, UNHCR has been asked to assume that function – now that it is time for the refugees to leave.

Violence and Displacement

Internal conflicts are a major source of population displacement in Asia, as in the rest of the world. The causes of the conflicts differ of course, reflecting the particular ethnic and political forces in the country. But while the causes differ, the results are distressingly similar. People are displaced, first within their own country, and then, in some cases to other countries.

Burma

Although recent statistics are lacking (the last ethnic census was in 1931) the Karens are estimated to number approximately three million out of a total Burmese population of 35 million. The history of the Karens, and the other ethnic minorities in Burma, is one of tension and conflict. The Karen rebellion began in fact in January 1949, one year after the country's independence. Since the early 1950s the Burmese government has gradually reduced the Karen-held territory. Part of the traditional homeland of the Karens lies near the Burma-Thai border and until recently the Karens controlled much of the black market trade between the two countries. From 1975 until about 1984 small numbers of Karen refugees would cross into Thailand during government dry season offensives. When the rainy season began, the Burmese troops would be withdrawn and the Karens would return to their homes. However, in 1984 the situation changed as the Burmese committed many more resources against the Karens. They attacked in greater force and on a much wider front and were able to maintain their basic supply lines. The Burmese have constructed roads into the area and give no signs of withdrawing – in fact, the offensives against the Karens, the Karenis and the Mons have increased in the last five years. In addition to these groups, there are other displaced groups such as the Kachin, the Shan, and the Wa. Recent agreements between the Burmese and Thai governments to increase production of lumber from the border regions have added to the displacement of people – and paradoxically increased international pressure on the two governments. (As one NGO representative sardonically commented, when it was just refugees along the border, there wasn't much concern, but now that the teak forests are threatened, there is an outpouring of interest.)

In 1987-88 the popular uprising against the Ne Win government resulted in virtual anarchy for several weeks and finally a military coup in September. The repression which followed led to an estimated 10,000 deaths and the flight of thousands of students, with as many as 7,000-10,000 arriving on the Thai-Burmese border. Many of the students began military training with the minority armies on the border, but after a couple of years, they reportedly left the border area and found their way back to Burma. Presently, about 2,000 students live in the border regions while another 1,500 are in Bangkok. On several occasions in the past three years, students have been sent back to Burma. A recent Amnesty International report (August 1991) highlighted the human rights concerns of the students. In September 1991, the Thai government announced its intention to create a 'safe camp' in a former police camp near the Burmese border and to transfer all the students there where they would be screened; students found not to fear persecution in Burma would face appropriate legal action. This move is opposed by the students who fear repercussions to their families back in Burma and who worry that international guarantees would not apply to the camp.[26]

Today, about 40,000 Karen refugees live inside the Thai border. Politically it is unlikely that the Karen guerillas will succeed in their struggle for autonomy but so far the guerrillas have given no indication that they are willing to compromise. So the struggle drags on and the Karen refugees remain in camps. While the camps are for the most part in areas inhabited by Thai Karens, relatively little integration has taken place. They are not recognised as refugees and UNHCR does not assist them (although it does provide some assistance to Burmese students living in Bangkok where they are recognised as refugees). The Thai government does not wish to make an issue of the Karens as the Burmese-Thai relationship is important to both governments. The Saw Maung regime has moved closer to the Thai government. In opening Burma to more investment and economic agreements, Thailand has reportedly won 75 per cent of these agreements, particularly in teak, fishing and gem production. Many of the logging concessions granted by Saw Maung are in Karen territory and there is growing cooperation between Thai and Burmese military forces.[27] While the Thai government has allowed them to stay temporarily, it refuses to allow them to construct any permanent facilities (such as schools or hospitals) or to develop long-term programmes. Rather, the Thai government wants them to return to Burma at the earliest possible opportunity.[28]

The Philippines

Around 500,000 Filipino people have been forced to leave their homes and communities because of violence. Within the Philippines they are known as internal refugees. Like refugees in other parts of the world, they flee because of military actions and human rights violations. But unlike refugees who have crossed an international border, those displaced by the violence in the Philippines, like those displaced by the violence in Sri Lanka have no recourse to international conventions or to UN bodies created to protect and assist refugees.

Why do they flee? As Sister Constance M. Pacis explains:

> Displacement in the Philippines has traditionally come in two forms: forced evacuation and strategic hamletting. Forced evacuation includes those who leave because of armed activities, unexplained killings, fights between warring groups, bombings, etc. Strategic hamletting is a military programme designed to counter local insurgency where civilians in villages are relocated to centres called hamlets or population

resource centres. While strategic hamletting was used extensively in the past, presently most of those displaced are
uprooted because of the generalised violence.[29]

One study of 37,000 displaced families in 1988 cites a number
of reasons for displacement. While various armed groups were
responsible for these actions, 85 per cent of the victims stated that
the perpetrators of the violence were either the army, the Philippine Constabulary or the Police. Indeed, the whole issue of displacement in the Philippines has to be understood in the context
of the government's efforts to counter the growing insurgency in
the country.[30]

But the armed insurgency itself has to be understood in the
context of the extreme and increasing inequality between rich and
poor. Presently about 70 per cent of the Filipino population lives
in extreme poverty. Coupled with the economic situation, the
disillusionment with the Aquino government's ability to institute
fundamental reforms has created despair and a drive for change.
This situation – intolerable for a majority of the Filipino people –
has given rise to an armed insurgent movement in which the New
People's Army (NPA) is the major, but not the only actor. The NPA
is the armed wing of the Communist Party of the Philippines and
the number of members is estimated at 25,000 about half of whom
are armed.

In response to the violence of the NPA and in an effort to stamp
out dissent, the government has instituted a massive counter-
insurgency campaign which uses aerial bombardment and shelling as well as raids and arrests to try to root out the insurgents.
Special Operations Teams have been created to carry out the
'ideological war'. Composed of élite soldiers, they are trained to go
into a community to identify the insurgents and their supporters.
The methods used to obtain this information are usually violent.

In addition to the army and police, civilian volunteer groups have
been created. These groups are defended as necessary for internal
security and are recruited from the 70 per cent of the population that
is desperately poor. But the groups often function independently, as
paramilitary vigilante gangs, much like the infamous death squads
in Latin America. The raids and repression are the most immediate
causes of the displacement, although there are many cases where
civilians get caught in the crossfire between warring groups.

The displaced seek shelter in nearby villages, sometimes walking and hiding in the bush for days to reach a safe place. The health consequences are serious. People live in crowded conditions and suffer the psychological effects of the disruption of family life and family separation.

Sri Lanka

Within Sri Lanka's population of 16.5 million, 74 per cent are Sinhalese (mainly Buddhist), 18 per cent are Tamils (mainly Hindu) while Muslims number about 7 per cent. The violence in Sri Lanka is often seen as an ethnic conflict, with its roots in the colonial period (when Britain imported Tamils to work on the plantations and provided them with favours in comparison to the dominant Sinhalese population).[31] Policies of discrimination against the Tamils in the 1960s and 1970s and the failure of traditional political mechanisms to respond to Tamil grievances led to the creation of a Tamil liberation movement dedicated to achieving the establishment of an autonomous state. In July 1983 ethnic tensions escalated with anti-Tamil riots in Colombo and elsewhere. Many Tamils moved north to predominantly Tamil areas of the country. As violence intensified after 1983, escalating into civil war, growing numbers of Tamils fled to the Tamil Nadu state in India where there were about 50 million Tamils with close links to the Sri Lankan Tamil minority. By 1987, the war had gone on for almost five years and an estimated 135,000 refugees were living in and outside camps in India. In addition, many others were displaced within Sri Lanka.

Following various peace initiatives, a peace accord was signed between the Indian and Sri Lankan governments in July 1987 in an effort to end the five-year civil war. The Indian Peace Keeping Force (IPKF) arrived to replace the Sinhalese-dominated Sri Lankan army in the northern and eastern provinces. While the IPKF was initially seen as an ally by the Tamil population, its efforts to destroy the leading Tamil militant group, the Liberation Tigers of Tamil Eelam (LTTE, or Tigers) led to an escalation of conflict. In fact, the IPKF became a part of the conflict and the levels of violence increased. The death toll in the Northeast section of the country reached 10,000 in the 1983-89 period.

But in the expectation that peace would permit the repatriation of refugees from India, UNHCR opened offices in Colombo in November 1987 and at four other sites in the country. In 1988 and 1989, some 43,000 Sri Lankans were returned to their homes and by 1990, UNHCR's programme of re-integration was being phased out and UNHCR field offices were being closed. This repatriation from India was paralleled by small-scale deportation of some Tamils from Europe in 1988-89.

But in mid-June 1990, violence again broke out. The last contingent of the IPKF left in March 1990, three years after its arrival. As the IPKF left, it turned over control of the Tamil-majority areas to either elected Tamil authorities or to the Tigers. Over 1,000 members of the IPKF were killed during the war and with their departure, violence intensified within the country. Internal disputes between various Tamil liberation movements increased as the LTTE fought not only the Indian forces, but the more moderate Eelam People's Revolutionary Front which had allied itself with the IPKF. Within 10 days in June, the LTTE guerrillas attacked police stations and the Sri Lankan military retaliated, with the result that 1,000 people were left dead and more than 100,000 were internally displaced.

Even as UNHCR was winding up its programme to facilitate the return of refugees from India, new refugee flows were being created. From June to September 1990, some 140,000 Sri Lankans left the country through Mannar Island.[32] In India, the Tamil Nadu government began re-opening camps that had been closed in 1987 and cyclone shelters were used to house the new arrivals. In Sri Lanka, the government set up camps for the internally displaced; by late June there were 300,000 displaced in more than 100 camps. By late July the number had increased to over 880,000 internally displaced, of whom 355,000 were in 350 camps in Jaffna district. By September more than one million were displaced in the northeast province, half of them in Jaffna.

While UNHCR was present in Sri Lanka, the escalating violence and large numbers of internally displaced, who were often in desperate conditions, created a fundamentally different situation for UNHCR. The UNHCR began to provide assistance to internally displaced people – although it had no mandate to do so. UNHCR's actions were explained by the fact that the High

Commissioner has a mandate to take 'ad hoc humanitarian measures as may be deemed necessary'. Its intervention was also justified on the grounds that internal displacement was fuelling an exodus of asylum-seekers to other countries, principally to India. 'Reducing the pressure to leave Sri Lanka in such circumstances could therefore be said legitimately to address some of the immediate causes of the refugee outflow', wrote Clarance.[33] UNHCR's response in this situation was to create Open Relief Centres (ORCs) as temporary places where displaced persons on the move could freely enter and leave and where they could obtain essential relief assistance. These ORCs were established in several areas of the country and are estimated to have provided assistance to 30,000 people between September 1990 and June 1991.[34]

In addition to the internally displaced Tamils and those who fled to India, conflicts between the government and the Janatha Vimukthi Peramuna (JVP) and outbreaks of Sinhalese nationalism led to perhaps 30,000 deaths in the south of the country in 1988 and 1989. An estimated 96,000 Tamil-speaking Muslims and ethnic Sinhalese have also fled the violence in the eastern province since 1987.

Within the past year the situations of Sri Lankan refugees and internally displaced alike, have worsened. After Rajiv Gandhi's assassination, there was a crackdown on Tamils living in the state of Tamil Nadu. All Sri Lankans living outside the camps were ordered by the state government in June 1991 to register themselves at the nearest police station. Some 26,000 people were arrested for failure to register (including a number of persons who had become Indian citizens.)[35] Following the order, there were reports of Tamil refugees losing their jobs, being evicted from their accommodation and being denied admittance to public schools. However, the Tamil Nadu government officials have said that the refugees would not be forcibly returned to Sri Lanka until the situation there is returned to normal.

In addition to this, there were an estimated 100,000 Sri Lankans in Iraq and Kuwait before August 1990. The forced return of so many Sri Lankans back to the country increased both the economic and political pressures on the government. (Some 60,000 returned in the September-October 1991 period alone.)

In September 1991, Amnesty International issued a report on Sri Lanka which detailed human rights violations by both the government and the Liberation Tigers. The report found that the Sri Lankan government forces have arbitrarily detained and deliberately killed thousands of people. Most of the killings in the east are attributed to paramilitary death squads operating in plain clothes and unmarked vehicles. Over 3,000 people have disappeared while in army custody in the east since June 1990. In a series of 32 recommendations, the Amnesty International report urges the Sri Lankan government to admit responsibility for thousands of disappearances and extra-judicial executions in the last seven years and to create a climate that protects human rights. But Amnesty International also condemns the Tamil Tigers for the same range of human rights abuses. Since the June war, the LTTE has massacred Sinhalese and Muslim villagers, tortured and killed Tamil dissidents and expelled 50,000 Muslims from the north. Hundreds of Sri Lankan police who surrendered to the LTTE on the outbreak of war are believed to have been murdered.[36]

Connections: Peace, Security and the Movement of People

Violence produces refugees. Wars, ethnic conflicts, foreign invasion, and the uncertainty they create force people to leave their communities and often, their countries. Although circumstances vary, the pattern seems to be that people are often displaced in stages: first fleeing to another part of the country (as in Sri Lanka and Cambodia) and then, when security still is not found, to another country.

At the same time, the presence of refugees can be an obstacle to peace. Obviously exile warrior groups create political and military pressure which must be taken into account in working out agreements to end the conflict. Certainly in both Cambodia and Afghanistan, the presence of large armed groups on the borders, was and is, a political force which must be dealt with in negotiations to bring peace and stability to the country. But refugees not only complicate the actual crafting of a ceasefire or peace agreement; their presence and the prospect of their return raise larger questions which will affect the durability of the peace. If and when the refugees return to Cambodia or to Sri Lanka, for example, they must be able to survive economically and not become a destabilising force in a country recovering from war. They must also be reincorporated into the political process. The longer refugees have been away from their country of origin, the more difficult their integration when they return. Their lands may have been taken by others, there may be resentment among the population that remained (and suffered from the violence) about perceived preferential treatment for returnees, or they may have lost the skills necessary for survival back home. Although most Asian refugees are women and children civilians, the return of armed warrior communities poses a special risk similar to that of dealing with de-mobilised soldiers. Forces which are accustomed to resolving conflicts by violence, which are trained in violence, and which have access to arms are a de-stabilising force in any setting. When those individuals have been out of the country and away from their community's social norms and mores, the danger may increase.

Refugees are clearly perceived as security concerns in Asian countries by their host governments. The government of Thailand, for example, sought to keep the Cambodian refugees out of the country even while recognising their potential role as a buffer with Vietnam. Pakistan, as noted above, has been able to use the presence of the refugees as a way of increasing its importance to other countries, particularly the United States. But such security concerns are not equally perceived for different refugee groups. Thus, although the Thai government was concerned about the impact of large numbers of Laotian refugees, there does not seem to be the same security concerns associated with their presence as for the Cambodians.

Connections: Peace, Economic Stability and the Movement of People

A survey of Asian refugee situations demonstrates the close relationship between peace and economic stability. In Vietnam, people leave for both political and economic reasons; most of the asylum-seekers claim a combination of factors led to their decision to leave. As long as Vietnam's diplomatic isolation continues and the government's ability to provide economically for its citizens remains limited, people will continue to leave. In the Philippines, economic pressures have been a major factor in the growth of insurgent movements which in turn have led to brutal counter-insurgency policies – policies which kill and displace people. Without economic justice, violence is likely to escalate as will the displacement of people.

This chapter has not dealt with the broader question of trends in Asian migration, but analysis of those trends reveals that people throughout Asia are leaving for economic reasons. Migrant workers, legal or otherwise, are leaving the poorer, less-developed countries to work in countries where jobs are available. Since the mid-1970s oil boom, there are over three million Asian workers in the Middle East. Within the Asia Pacific region, intra-regional migration is increasing dramatically. This is happening in spite of governmental restrictions on immigration. Thus Japan has at least 100,000 undocumented migrant workers in spite of tough new laws and employer sanctions. Malaysia exports skilled workers to Singapore and imports large numbers of unskilled workers from the Philippines, Indonesia and Thailand. The Malaysian government estimates that there are 350,000 Indonesians working illegally on the Malay peninsula, but the trades union congress estimates that the number could be a million. The Pacific Islands has a history of migration; some 20 per cent of Palau's work force resides abroad.[37] This labour migration in Asia is supported, if not encouraged, by the governments of sending countries because of the economic impact of the remittances transferred by workers. The Philippines, for example, has been very 'successful' in promoting overseas employment for its citizens, although the human costs have been very high.[38]

In this context, where millions of Asians are moving to other countries in search of work and economic survival, the question of the motivation of migrants and refugees comes to the fore. Although the 1951 UN Convention makes a clear distinction between those who leave their countries because of persecution and those who leave for other reasons (including economic reasons), in fact the distinction is not so clear. People leave their countries for a variety of reasons. Many of the Cambodians arriving in Thailand in 1979 and 1980 talked of the famine and lack of food – rather than the Vietnamese invasion or even the destruction by the Pol Pot regime – as a prime reason for leaving. Similarly, Sri Lankan asylum-seekers in Europe speak of an economy devastated by war and the difficulties of finding a job or economic survival.

Violence not only kills and displaces people directly, but it also disrupts and destroys the economic infrastructure of a country. In those circumstances, the distinction between economic migrants and refugees fleeing persecution loses meaning. The clarity of the UN definition simply does not match the ambiguity of the human needs of people forced to flee their communities. Given both economic and political trends in Asia and the world, this ambiguity is likely to increase in the future. Governments which try to apply a strict interpretation of the UN Convention on Refugees risk excluding people whose lives are at risk if they are returned home. But governments which adopt a more liberal interpretation risk higher numbers of people arriving on their borders asking for asylum.

Connections: International and Regional Developments

Events in Asia shape and are shaped by developments at the international level. In terms of the forced movement of people, for example, the end of the Cold War has made the negotiation of a political settlement in Cambodia possible. Although peace in Afghanistan remains elusive, it is certainly more likely today than in an era characterised by 'proxy wars'. The normalisation of diplomatic and economic relations with Vietnam by the U.S. and other Western powers is certainly more likely in the post-Cold War era than in the past 15 years. All of these are positive signs and indications that developments at the international level can positively affect the situation of refugees in Asia.

And yet, not all conflicts and not all refugees are the product of superpower politics. Ethnic conflicts and the struggle for democracy in Burma are the prime reasons for the presence of 40,000 Karen refugees on the Thai-Burmese border. The violence in Sri Lanka is the result of a complex mixture of ethnic, political and economic forces which will not be resolved by the passing away of the Cold War. While the international community has been able to mobilise pressure for peace in the case of Cambodia, such a solution is less likely (for a number of reasons) in Burma, Sri Lanka, and the Philippines.

With respect to the relationship between the international sys-

tem for refugee protection and developments in Asia, it is important
to note that the system evolved in response to needs of European
displaced people. The fledgling efforts of the League of Nations and
the first High Commissioner for Refugees, followed by the United
Nations Relief and Rehabilitation Agency (UNRRA), and finally
UNHCR were all developed in the context of Europe and its wars.
Even while these efforts were underway and the international
community was working to find the appropriate formula for responding to refugees, they were not seen as being applicable in other
regions. In August 1947 the partition of India led to half a million
deaths and to the flight of about 14 million people across what had
now become international borders to what they considered to be
their homeland. But there was no organised humanitarian response
from the international community – although the numbers and the
needs of those displaced people were probably greater than that of
the displaced Europeans being helped by the predecessors of UNHCR.

Although the international refugee system has been broadened
in theory and in practice over the past forty years, there are still
some anomalies. For example, 107 countries have signed the 1951
UN Convention and/or the 1967 Protocol relating to the Status of
Refugees. Among those who have not signed either international
convention are Afghanistan, Bangladesh, India, Indonesia, Malaysia, Pakistan, Singapore and Thailand which together are host
to a large share of the world's refugees. Although UNHCR is active
in all of those countries (except India), governments in the region
have retained the right to decide under what circumstances and for
which groups UNHCR will be allowed to work. Thus Thailand allows
UNHCR to work with Vietnamese, Laotian and a small percentage
of the Cambodian refugees in the country while not permitting it to
operate with the large Cambodian border population or with the
Burmese refugees on the border.

Of the Asian refugee situations examined here, the Indo-Chinese
case stands out for the degree of interest and responsibility assumed
by the international community. While Sri Lankan, Burmese, and
Afghan refugees have been largely cared for in countries of first
asylum (although international funds have been provided, particularly for the Afghans), solutions for the Indo-Chinese refugees have
been sought from abroad. This is perhaps logical given the international involvement in the war in Indo-China – a war which was the

prime cause of displacement. Both the 1979 and 1989 UN conferences on Indo-Chinese Refugees saw resettlement outside the region
as a vital component to resolving the problem of Indo-Chinese
refugees. But since the mid-1980s there has been growing concern
that resettlement has contributed to the problem rather than providing a definitive solution. The existence of resettlement opportunities, particularly given economic conditions in Vietnam, has undoubtedly encouraged Vietnamese to leave their country. This was
recognised at a very early stage by governments of Southeast Asia,
as evidenced by the 1981-82 implementation of humane deterrence
policies which limited resettlement opportunities for new arrivals.
Even when the international community later sought to close the
door on further resettlement, the expectations and the hope for
resettlement led tens of thousands of Vietnamese to sell all their
goods and to risk travel on the high seas in hopes that the 'rules of the
game' would change (as they have changed so many times). While
the individual Vietnamese asylum-seekers may not be refugees
under the terms of the 1951 UN Convention, they are certainly
victims of false expectations raised by earlier, well-meaning policies.

The coming years will undoubtedly bring new challenges to Asian
governments struggling to develop policies toward refugees and
migrants arriving on their borders. Most of all, governments and
other concerned groups face the challenge of reaching and implementing solutions to the violence in Sri Lanka, Afghanistan and
Cambodia, of resolving ethnic conflicts throughout the region and of
meeting the economic needs of their people. The way in which Asian
governments respond to the needs of foreigners arriving at their
borders will depend in large part on national political and economic
factors. But ultimately the fate of the refugees and displaced people
in Asia depends on progress in reaching the goals of 'Peace and
Security in the Post-Cold War Era'.

Notes

1. See, for example, Ferris, E., (1992), *Beyond Borders*, (forthcoming), or
   Ferris, E., (ed), (1985), *Refugees and World Politics,* New York: Praeger.
2. Loescher, G. and Scanlan, J.A., (1986), *Calculated Kindness*, New York:
   Free Press.
3. Loescher, G., (1991), 'Mass Migration as a Global Security Problem',

World Refugee Survey - 1991, Washington: U.S. Committee for Refugees, pp. 7-14.

4. Weiner, M., (1991), 'Security, Stability and International Migration', Mimeo.

5. Refugee statistics are notoriously difficult to obtain, particularly for those individuals who may meet the criteria for refugee but who are not recognised by the governments of the host country as refugees. The most comprehensive statistics are those published by the U.S. Committee for Refugees in its annual *World Refugee Survey*, (1991), Washington, DC: U.S. Committee for Refugees.

6. Jacobsen, J.L., (1988), *Environmental Refugees: A Yardstick of Habitability*, Washington, DC: Worldwatch Institute.

7. Task Force on Militarisation in Asia and the Pacific, (1988), *The Afghan Crisis*, New York.

8. Feith, D., (1988), *Stalemate: Refugees in Asia*, Parkville, Victoria, Australia: Asia Bureau Australia.

9. *World Refugee Survey 1989*, (1989), New York: U.S. Committee for Refugees.

10. *World Refugee Survey 1991*, (1991), New York: U.S. Committee for Refugees.

11. Although Vietnamese had left the country earlier – an estimated 135,000 were evacuated with the last U.S. troops in 1975 – the outflow increased in the 1977-79 period because of the imposition of North Vietnamese authority over the South, increased persecution of ethnic Chinese, the establishment of new economic zones and the incarceration of thousands of political prisoners. Moreover, Vietnam reversed its policy of discouraging deportations in 1978-79 and began realising some concrete economic benefits by impounding refugees' goods and making them pay in gold for their departure. (See Feith, *op. cit.*)

12. Cerquone, J., (1987), *Uncertain Harbors: The Plight of Vietnamese Boat People*, USCR Issue Paper. He also asserts, as do others, that a modest estimate is that 100,000 Vietnamese died at sea from 1979-1987.

13. Because they fled by boat, Vietnamese refugees are the most far-flung of the Asian refugees. They landed in Thailand, Malaysia, Singapore, Indonesia, Australia, the Philippines, Brunei, Macau, Taiwan, Hong Kong, Korea and were picked up at sea even further away. Following China's invasion of Vietnam in 1979, about 230,000 mostly ethnic Chinese Vietnamese fled to China where most have become fairly self-sufficient and well-integrated into Chinese life.

14. Cerquone, J., (see note 12).

15. 'No Place Called Home', (1989), *Chicago Tribune Magazine*, special supplement on refugees.

16. These observations are taken from Imalia Komalo, 'Vietnam and Hong Kong', (June 1990), *Refugees*, no. 108E.

17. Muncy, S., (1991), 'Assessment of Needs in Indonesia', *Impact*, Issue no. 3.

18. From 1975-1988, over 100,000 Vietnamese landed in Indonesia, 99,000 of whom were resettled in third countries. More began to come in 1979 when Malaysia began pushing back Vietnamese boats (arrivals in Indonesia jumped from 7000 to 31,500 in 1989) Feith, D., (see note 8), p. 21. Similar pressure is now building up. Galang camp in Indonesia now has 20,559 persons, about 70 per cent (14,000) of whom arrived in 1990. Like their counterparts in Vietnam, screening is a major issue and refugees are traumatised and angry about the procedures. Singapore has followed a much more restrictive policy that an asylum-seeker is not allowed to enter unless there is a firm guarantee that another country will accept him or her. And since early 1979, Singapore has firmly adhered to a policy that no more than 1,000 refugees will be allowed in the country at any one time. About 35,000 refugees have been given temporary asylum in Singapore and resettled elsewhere. Feith, (1988), p. 24. For those refugees from Hong Kong and the Philippines who have been 'screened in' and are awaiting resettlement, plans are underway for a Regional Resettlement Transit Centre in the Philippines. (The Centre was formally opened on 4 June 1991, but the volcanic eruption in the Philippines has delayed its operations.)

19. See for example the account in 'No Place Called Home', (1989), *Chicago Tribune Magazine.*

20. Lawyers Committee for Human Rights, (1987), *Seeking Shelter: Cambodians in Thailand*, New York: Lawyers Committee, p. 26.

21. Niland, N., (August 1990), 'Report from the Border', Briefing Paper prepared for the Asia-Pacific Task Force.

22. Raper, M., (August 1990), 'Research and Teaching in the Service of Refugees', Paper prepared for the Institute of Social Studies, The Hague, The Netherlands.

23. Niland, N., (see note 21), p. 1. See also Reynell, J., (1989), *Political Pawns: Refugees on the Thai-Kampuchean Border*, Oxford UK: Refugee Studies Programme. Jackson, T., (1987), *Just Waiting to Die: Camho-dian Refugees in Thailand*, Oxford: Oxfam.

24. Niland, N., (see note 21), p. 9.

25. Gallagher, D., (22.10.91), 'Cambodia: The UN Needs the Means to do its Job', *International Herald Tribune.*

26. Jesuit Refugee Service, (October 1991), *Diakonia.*

27. Dunford, J., 'Burmese refugees in Thailand', in *Asian Refugees: A Role for the Churches?* Report of the CCA/WCC/CICARWS Asian Refugee

Working Group Meeting, Bangkok, May 17-19, 1989.

28. In addition to these two well-known groups of Burmese refugees, the ethnic minorities and the students, more than 250,000 Burmese refugees, mainly Muslims of mixed Burman and Indian ancestry, fled to Bangladesh in late 1978. This flight followed the large-scale Burmese army persecution of Muslims in Arakan State. Although some were repatriated shortly thereafter, an undetermined number remain in Bangladesh. *World Refugee Survey 1989*, (1990), Washington, DC: U.S. Committee for Refugees.

29. See 'Internally Displaced: The cry from the Philippines', (September 1990), *Refugees*, WCC, no. 110E.

30. See 'Internal Refugees in the Philippines', (1988), Citizen's Disaster Rehabilitation Center, Inc.

31. In fact, the ethnic situation is more complicated than that. Sri Lankan Tamil 'repatriates' are Tamils born in Sri Lanka but never granted citizenship. Their ancestors came from India in the nineteenth century to provide labor for the British estates. These 'repatriates' have always been separate from the indigenous Sri Lankan Tamils. In 1949, this group of nearly a million people, known as Indian or plantation Tamils, were disenfranchised by the Sri Lankan government. In 1964 an agreement for the return of some 525,000 plantation Tamils to go to India and some 300,000 to remain in Sri Lanka and become citizens was worked out. There are still some 350,000 stateless Tamils in Sri Lanka. It has been particularly difficult for those who have gone to India as they have always lived in Sri Lanka. Feith, D., (see note 8), p. 37.

32. These figures and the description of UNHCR activity are based largely on Clarance, W.D., (1991), 'Open Relief Centres: A Pragmatic Approach to Emergency Relief and Monitoring during Conflict in a Country of Origin', *International Journal of Refugee Law*, vol. 3, no. 2, pp. 320-328.

33. *Ibid.*, p. 324.

34. Tamil Information, (September 1991), no. 2.

35. *Ibid.*

36. Amnesty International, (September 1991), 'Human Rights Violations in a Context of Armed Conflict'. See also reports of University Teachers for Human Rights, the only independent Tamil human rights group collecting information on human rights in the northeast of the country, for further confirmation.

37. Figures taken from Stahl, C.W., (June 1991), 'South-North Migration in the Asia-Pacific Region', pp. 163-193 in *International Migration*, vol. xxix, no. 2.

38. Sarmiento, J.N., (June 1991), 'The Asian Experience in International Migration', *International Migration*, vol. xxix, no. 2, p. 199.

Part Two

Arms, Defence and Insecurity in the Asia Pacific Region

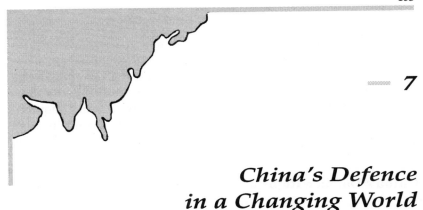

China's Defence in a Changing World

Yitzhak Shichor

Introduction

As in most countries, the development of China's defence system has always been determined by the interaction between domestic politics and the perception of the international situation. Over time, the relative weight of each of these elements has changed. In the 1950s, exogenous inputs (primarily the wars in Korea and Indo-China, the U.S. global containment policy and the Sino-Soviet alliance), combined to launch China's first military modernisation drive. It underscored professionalism and regularisation – in line with the overall institutionalisation process adopted by the newly established People's Republic of China (P.R.C.), but it was out of line with Mao's revolutionary doctrines and experience.[1] This 'rightist' deviation was corrected in the 1960s and 1970s. Despite China's growing isolation from the world community and the increasing threats to its security (the Vietnam War and the Soviet military build-up along its periphery), its conventional military system was at a virtual standstill. Cut off from its Soviet supply sources, China kept a huge army equipped with antiquated weapons constantly ready to deal with a major emergency using the two ends of the strategic spectrum: the most advanced (nuclear deterrence), and the most backward (People's War). By the late 1970s, however, following the changes in the domestic and international situations and, particularly, the abortive Chinese invasion of Vietnam, those strategies that required constant military preparedness against an overall confrontation while underrating other forms of conflict, had apparently become rather superfluous.

China's Defence Reforms

From the early 1980s, therefore, China's post-Mao leaders, led by Deng Xiaoping, have launched a series of defence reforms as part of a comprehensive Four Modernisations programme. These reforms, the lowest in the programme's priority list, had taken final shape by 1985, following extensive debates. Reflecting an ostensible accord between officers and officials, as well as among themselves, these military reforms included a number of components: the size of the People's Liberation Army (PLA) was cut by 25 per cent, with one million soldiers discharged, and a growing part of the military industrial potential diverted to civilian production; China's eleven military regions were reorganised into seven, thus reducing the number of regional headquarters; political and ideological indoctrination was almost completely discarded, as emphasis was placed on professionalism, upgrading outdated weapons and military equipment and improving command, control and communication. At the same time, initial formulations of new military doctrines (such as Comprehensive National Strength, Active Defence, People's War Under Modern Conditions, and the Three Dimensional Strategic Boundaries) appeared, implicitly – though not explicitly – at the expense of Mao Zedong's military thought.[2]

These reforms were motivated by a combination of domestic and international considerations. Domestically, China's leaders seemed to agree that military power could not be built on weak economic foundations. Consequently, first priority was given to modernisation and development as the cornerstone of 'comprehensive national strength'. In this strategy military power was a dependent rather than an independent variable. Thus, domestic constraints such as the lack of capital, backward technologies, quantity production, low-level manpower, etc., dictated a slow, gradual and selective military modernisation. What made such a policy possible was China's perception of the international situation.

By 1985 Beijing's defence policy was firmly grounded on the assumption that there was no major immediate threat to Chinese security. The primary source of such a threat had been removed by the conspicuous improvement in Sino-Soviet relations. Furthermore, China's leaders believed that the prospects of another world war, or superpower confrontation, had diminished. This relaxation of international tension thus provided China with the breathing space needed for pursuing its overall modernisation, without having to allocate too much of its limited resources for defence.

These defence policies – and the assumptions on which they had been based – were undermined by the June 1989 Tiananmen Square demonstrations, by the reluctant performance of the People's Liberation Army (PLA) in the early phase of the crisis, and the U.S.-led negative reactions from the West. These developments provided China's conservative leaders with the evidence they had been looking for – that, perhaps, the primary threat to P.R.C. security came from inside rather than outside the country. Believed to be exacerbated by foreigners, this kind of threat (termed 'peaceful evolution'), had to be dealt with by a modified defence policy. Indeed, as soon as the student demonstrations in May-June 1989 were brutally suppressed, the advocates of professional military modernisation became silent, and published discussions of defence reform were suspended. Instead, China's reinstated conservative leaders launched a series of campaigns aimed at reinforcing the PLA's political and ideological consciousness. These campaigns (including the 'two supports' and the resuscitated 'learn from Lei Feng'), revived Mao Zedong's military doctrines as well as methods similar to the radical policies used in the 1960s and 1970s.[3]

In fact, for a while it appeared as if China was backtracking into its traditional seclusion and isolation, advocated by those who underscore political and ideological considerations in the reform of China's military system. Reportedly headed by Yang Baibing, Secretary General of the Chinese Communist Party (CCP), the highest defence policy-making group, the Central

Military Commission (CMC), as well as director of the PLA General Political Department), they have apparently won the battle over those in favour of technological and professional considerations in the reform of China's military system. But the war was far from over.[4]

The Gulf War Challenge

Triggered by Iraq's invasion of Kuwait in early August 1990, the Gulf War epitomised, at one stroke, the extensive changes that had been taking place in the international balance of power since the late 1980s, forcing the Chinese to reconsider their defence policy and its underlying assumptions. The Gulf War mirrored, among other things, the incredible weakness of the Soviet Union, the emergence of the United States as the only real superpower, the astonishing performance of superior military technology, the intimidation of countries whose defence is based on inferior military technology, the higher probability of regional and local conflicts, and, last but not least, embryonic signs of Japan's readiness for greater political and military involvement in international affairs. Undoubtedly aware of some of these changes in the world situation even before the Gulf War, China's decision-makers felt a new concern.

Indeed, initial hints of a modified attitude towards military modernisation appeared on August 1, 1990 (one day before the Iraqi invasion of Kuwait) on the occasion of the 63rd anniversary of the founding of the Chinese Red Army. P.R.C. Defence Minister Qin Jiwei, considered an advocate of military professionalism, emphasised the PLA's determination 'to make new contributions' in defending the country.[5] In a speech commemorating the Army Day, Jiang Zemin, the Chinese Communist Party Secretary General, went a good deal further:

> To ensure a stable environment for socialist modernisation we must maintain a strong force and build up strong national defence... If we have a military force whose strength corresponds to our country's status, we will easily deal with whatever contingency that may occur and will remain invincible.[6]

Understated in China's strategic analysis in the mid-1980s by the assumed lack of imminent threats, the need to 'deal with whatever contingency' has suddenly become more real following the Gulf War. For some Chinese leaders, the conflict offered further proof that, whereas the danger of a global confrontation has indeed diminished, international relations are far from stable. In fact, the Chinese have become more convinced than before that multipolarity, the weakness of the Soviet Union, and the related breakdown of the world bipolar system, have bred regional tensions leading to instability and to local wars. This has been one of the main lessons drawn by China's leaders, both military and civilian, who carefully studied reports and documentary films on Iraq's invasion of Kuwait and, later, on the allied counter-offensive.[7]

Recent Military Reforms

In late 1990, long before this sophisticated counter-offensive was launched, the Chinese had already resumed their interest in professional military reform. Suppressed for a year and a half, a series of articles, commentaries and interviews were published, primarily in the PLA organ *Jiefangjun Bao* (Liberation Army Daily). Also, a number of high-level meetings were held to discuss, among other things, the implications of the Iraqi invasion for China's defence modernisation.

For example, a conference of the PLA General Staff Department, held in November-December 1990, upheld the criteria of management work, training, combat power and fighting skills. These clearly professional criteria, that completely ignored the need to promote political education and ideological indoctrination in the PLA, were nevertheless praised and later circulated by the Central Military Commission (CMC).

On January 11, 1991, the CMC itself reportedly held a secret enlarged meeting in Beijing to discuss Middle East events and their significance for Chinese security. The meeting finalised the future plans of the PLA, calling for air force and naval modernisation, a further cut in manpower and, most important, an increase in defence expenditure.[8] Reached before the amazing display of Western military technology in the Gulf, these decisions reflected a revised Chinese prognosis of international affairs in the 1990s. Earlier the

Chinese had insisted that economic development is, and would be, the main feature of international relations, while military power would play a subordinate role. Now, following the Gulf War, the weakening of the Soviet Union and, consequently, a higher probability of regional conflicts, the Chinese maintain that military power will still play a crucial and indispensable role in what they call 'the comprehensive national strength'.[9] Valid universally, this modified outlook also applied to China's particular case.

As mentioned above, economic modernisation had been considered an essential precondition for defence modernisation by P.R.C. leaders (civilian and military), since the early 1980s. Now, international developments have led the advocates of professional military reforms to reassert themselves, suggesting that, perhaps, it is the other way around: 'Without a strong national defence, there will be neither security nor development to speak of'.[10] Senior Colonel Liu Yichang, an associate research fellow at the P.R.C. Academy of Military Sciences elaborated:

> The modernisation of socialism in an independent and peaceful way requires strong national defence strength as a guarantee in coping with possible emergencies at all times ... the modernisation of national defence itself is ... an important guarantee for economic development in the coming decade.[11]

These modified priorities, and the resumed debate on military modernisation, have been reinforced following the U.S.-led counter-offensive against Iraq. PLA chief of the general staff Chi Haotian admitted: 'A higher defence consciousness is conducive not only to national unity and stronger combat will of the army, but also to the development of the economy'.[12] Higher defence consciousness, in professional rather than political terms, has now become more urgent not simply because of the threat of regional conflicts but, moreover, because of the inferiority of China's military system as implied by the Western intimidation of Iraq. On the one hand, the counter-offensive exposed the incompetence and backwardness of the Iraqi armed forces, equipped by weapons mostly originating in the socialist countries, including the P.R.C. On the other hand, Chinese generals and officials were reportedly 'astonished', 'amazed', and 'deeply frustrated', as they watched the performance of the superior Western military technology.[13]

These views were shared not only by current PLA commanders but also by a number of retired military leaders, such as former Chief of the General Staff Yang Dezhi, and former Defence Minister Zhang Aiping. All agreed that China's weapons and military equipment lag behind the West by twenty, even thirty years.[14] Their requests for additional investment in military research, development and production, cold-shouldered since Tiananmen if not before, have now been acknowledged – mainly because of the changes in the international situation. Some senior leaders, like Chen Yun, CCP Secretary General Jiang Zemin, and Premier Li Peng, who had rarely been involved in military reform debates, now supported these requests.[15] In his double capacity as chairman of the CMC of both the state and the party, Jiang reportedly instructed the Commission for National Defence Science, Technology and Industry, to 'concentrate its energy on developing sophisticated hi-tech weapons'.[16]

Such an effort required an increase in the defence budget. The CMC had already recommended such an increase in its January meeting. Now, another CMC enlarged meeting, held in early March, reportedly formulated the final decisions. President Yang Shangkun was quoted as saying that, following repeated discussions, the CCP politburo unanimously agreed that it was very necessary to increase military appropriations and decided to allocate an additional 30 billion yuan (some U.S.$6 billion), as special military expenditure over the next five years for military research and production.[17] This increase was officially approved during the Fourth Session of the National People's Congress (NPC), held in late March 1991. 'To handle unexpected changes in the increasingly complicated international arena', a total of 32.51 billion yuan has been earmarked for military spending in 1991, an addition of 3.48 billion yuan, or 12 per cent over the previous year's allocation. Falling far short of the U.S.$10 billion defence appropriation, hoped for by some PLA generals, this was the first increase, in real terms, for a number of years.[18] According to *Jiefangjun Bao*, Yang Shangkun promised PLA and NPC deputies: 'As compared with things ten years ago, national defence appropriations in the period of the Eighth Five Year Plan [1991-1995] will increase by a substantial margin'.[19]

Reassertion of Centrist Tendencies: Recent Modernisation

Having swung to the right, the military pendulum could not, under the existing political constellation, rest there. The following months, from the spring to the summer of 1991, indeed witnessed an all out offensive by those opposed to professional military reform to regain power. The 'swing to the left' is reflected in many articles, commentaries, speeches and conferences that emphasised, yet again, the predominance of political and ideological reform in the armed forces, of Party control over the military, and of Mao Zedong's military thought in general, and the People's War strategy in particular, as the fundamental PLA guidelines.[20] However, the pendulum has finally settled in the middle. Unlike in the post-Tiananmen period, these political-ideological orientations have been articulated not at the expense of professional modernisation.

Amid occasional reports on military technological achievements (particularly in the Air Force and the 2nd Artillery Corps), it was reported that a new syndicate, The China Electronics Industry Corporation, had been created in June, 1991, to provide the military with high-tech electronic devices whose necessity had been amply demonstrated by the Gulf War.[21] Indeed, professional military considerations reappeared during the 1991 August 1st PLA celebrations, yet in a more balanced way compared to 1990. This typically Confucian policy of 'laying an equal emphasis on two aspects' conformed to Jiang Zemin's July 1st speech marking the CCP 70th anniversary. 'Under the current conditions', he stated, 'further strengthening the army and national defence is of far-reaching strategic significance'. Still, while calling to 'constantly modernise the army's equipment', he insisted that 'the party must unswervingly exercise absolute leadership over the army' and that further efforts should be made to improve ideological and political work in the PLA, as well as military training, 'so that all our troops are politically qualified and militarily capable'.[22]

This combination was reiterated by a number of speakers during the Army Day receptions. Defence Minister Qin Jiwei said that 'the international situation is complicated and volatile, and destabilising factors still exist. The world is not yet safe. Under these circumstances, we should further strengthen our national defence and army building'. Yet his 'pledge to work hard to

modernise' the armed forces (in the words of *China Daily*) seemed
to be related to reaching a higher political and ideological level
under strict CCP control.[23] These combined tasks have become
even more urgent in view of the gradual disintegration of the
Soviet and East European socialist regimes and their ruling
communist parties and, particularly, following the abortive conservative coup against Gorbachov.

Shaking the foundations of Chinese politics, these events have
also affected Chinese security, both internal and external. In one
of the first reactions, a two-day enlarged meeting of the CMC was
reportedly opened on September 3, 1991. The keynote speech by
Yang Shangkun allegedly called on the Army to successfully fight
two important battles: The first, based on absolute ideological
unity, would ensure that the whole Army is ready to assemble at
the first call and be capable of fighting and winning. 'The second
battle', he said, 'is to get ourselves prepared for a war, a partial or
regional war, a modern three-dimensional war, or even a nuclear
war'.[24] If true, these unpublished remarks reflect P.R.C. defence
modernisation policy, namely, that the international situation
does not give cause for complacency; in fact, quite the contrary. As
CMC Vice Chairman Liu Huaqing put it: 'We should take advantage of the good opportunity of a relatively peaceful period to
promote the modernisation of national defence as well as the
revolutionised, modernised, and regularised building of our Army
in an all-around way'. And another senior officer was even more
specific, saying that 'the phase of international detente must now
be used for armaments. Weapons must be modernised, nuclear
strategies must be improved'.[25] Thus, while Moscow and Washington reach further agreements on arms reduction, both conventional and nuclear, China seems reluctant to join in and proceeds
with its plans to increase and upgrade its own arsenals.

Negative Trends Worrying China

This reluctance to disarm derives from growing anxieties about
the negative implications of the 'new' international situation on
China's regional and global role. To begin with, Beijing has become more sensitive to its territorial integrity, primarily in the
northwest and the southeast. Military parades and exercises were

held in the provinces of Guangdong and Fujian (including the cities Guangzhou, Nanjing, Fuzhou and Sanming), and in the Lanzhou Military Region, emphasising desert combat.[26] PLA units, local militia troops and People's Armed Police forces have been increasingly deployed along China's borders, especially in troublesome Tibet and even more so, in Xinjiang.[27] 'Separatism' and 'splittism' are now considered by the Chinese leadership as the most serious danger to stability in Xinjiang.

In recent years, usually between April and June (the period of Muslim Ramadan), Xinjiang was swept by unrest and uprising, stimulated by domestic grievances and external inspiration. Inhabited by nine million Muslims (60 per cent of its population), this region had been contested throughout history between the Chinese, the local tribes and foreign powers (which in the 1930s and 1940s created the short-lived East Turkestan Republic, now Beijing's nightmare). Following their incorporation in the P.R.C. in 1949, Xinjiang's Muslims, though split into ten different ethnic groups, have never ceased complaining about economic and educational neglect, the plundering of the region's natural resources, religious persecution, and suppression of national identity. In recent years, these complaints have been exacerbated by Beijing's 'open door' policy, the thaw in Sino-Soviet relations, the political reform in Mongolia, the revival of Islam and, last but not least, the autonomous tendencies among the neighbouring (formerly Soviet) republics of Kazakhstan, Kirghizia and Tajikistan (all of them Muslim). Concern about 'Pan Islam' and 'Pan Turkism' has already caused the Chinese to bolster their border defence:

> Under the current complex international situation, our border areas have become the forward position for combating infiltration, subversion, splittism, and peaceful evolution. In the future, border defence will be more complex. Therefore, strengthening the border defence has become more urgent and important.[28]

Taiwan

International developments, particularly the disintegration of the U.S.S.R. and the independence declarations of the Baltic and other republics, have also caused concern among P.R.C. leaders with regard to Taiwan.

These tendencies, producing a favourable atmosphere for the Taiwan independence movement, combined with the Iraqi invasion of Kuwait raised the possibility of the P.R.C. using force to 'liberate' Taiwan before it is too late. This possibility had occasionally been discussed by P.R.C. leaders even before the Iraqi invasion. Later, Jiang Zemin reportedly said that Beijing reserves the option to take Taiwan by force.[29] Indeed, the Republic of China (ROC), Taiwan, regarded the Iraqi invasion of Kuwait as a warning against a similar potential military threat from the P.R.C., and placed parts of its Army, including the Air Force, on full alert.[30] Another indication of the ROC anxiety is the establishment of a new Anti-submarine Command, as well as a new Air Force Command, and the acquisiton of new military equipment.[31]

These developments, for example, the sale of six frigate hulls to Taiwan by French companies, led to serious P.R.C. protests.[32] In early October, 1991, following talks among the top Chinese leaders (i.e. Deng Xiaoping, Chen Yun and Wang Zhen), a work conference on Taiwan affairs was allegedly held. A report submitted by the PLA's General Staff Department said that Taiwan-P.R.C. relations across the strait would become more tense in the next three to five years, so that if reunification is not realised within that time – it would become even more difficult to achieve later on and obstruct the progress toward Taiwan's independence. In addition to the changes in the international situation already mentioned, the report gave the following reasons for this prediction. First, the simultaneous entry of both South and North Korea into the United Nations would reinforce the feasibility of 'two Chinas' or, 'one China, one Taiwan' policy. Second, the political and, even more so, the economic collapse of Eastern Europe and the Soviet Union would provide Taiwan with more opportunities to apply their 'flexible diplomacy' to gain political support in return for financial aid. Third, dealing with Taiwan's pragmatic third generation leaders, who have no more than shallow ties with the mainland, and who lack the historical, ideolological, conceptual, and emotional basis for reunification – would be impossible. And, last but not least, according to PLA intelligence sources, Taiwan will be able to produce nuclear weapons within the next two years, an alarming development always considered a *casus belli* by Beijing.[33]

In view of its analysis, the report put forward three possible solutions to the Taiwan issue. The best one, to hold negotiations with Guomingdang (GMD) leaders who are determined to promote reunification, is now considered a remote possibility. A more realistic solution is to push the GMD leaders into negotiations by threatening to use force, and then settle the problem according to a generously modified 'one country, two systems' formula. As a last resort, the PLA would be used to resolve the issue once and for all. While battle plans have long been drafted, China expects that Washington would react with hostility, yet not with force: the United States itself, along with some 135 other governments, had already recognised the P.R.C. as the only legal government of China, implying that Taiwan is a domestic Chinese affair. Because of that, and also because the P.R.C. has a veto right in the UN Security Council, force cannot and will not be used against China under the auspices of the United Nations.

Hong Kong and Regional Issues

Indirectly related to Taiwan, and the international situation at large, is the Hong Kong issue. Recently, there has been growing Chinese sensitivity to the possibility of 'chaos' and 'turmoil' in Hong Kong. In an informal discussion held in late September, 1991, Ji Pengfei, former director of the P.R.C. Hong Kong and Macao Affairs Office, said that China would not interfere in Hong Kong or take it over before the due date – unless the British authorities of Hong Kong lose effective control in the face of sustained unrest, incited from inside or, more seriously, from outside, primarily by Taiwan. His message was clear: the P.R.C. is ready to use force in order to make sure that Hong Kong remains under P.R.C. sovereignty both before and after 1997 – notwithstanding the recent international manifestations of independence and greater autonomy.[34]

Beijing's ostensible readiness to use force when and where its perceived territorial integrity is at stake, is just one dimension of its regional policy to counter the challenges of the new international situation. Another dimension involves a Chinese effort to pacify the periphery and reduce regional tension. Included in this effort are the rapprochement between the P.R.C. and Vietnam, China's support for peace in Cambodia, Li Peng's recent visit to India, and an attempt to improve relations with Mongolia and South Korea and, at the same time, to restrain North Korea. None of these countries is considered a major threat to the P.R.C., now or in the future – something that cannot be said about Japan. The Chinese attitude toward Japan is more complicated.

While satisfied with bilateral relations in the short run, the Chinese hardly conceal their suspicions of Japan in the long run. These suspicions are fed by a number of developments that Beijing believes could gradually turn Japan from an economic giant into a political and military monster. These developments include the growing volume of Japanese military expenditure, now ranking third in the world, following the United States and the (disintegrated) Soviet Union; initial signs of changes in Japan's strategy from an emphasis on inland defence to an emphasis on ocean defence; an unprecedented increase in Japan's arms production which provides its troops with over 80 per cent of the best military equipment in the Asia Pacific region, next to the U.S. and the U.S.S.R.; the emergence of rightist groups, most of them militarist-minded that, though small in number (no more than 0.1 per cent of Japan's population), 'can by no means be underestimated in terms of their political capacity'.[35] Finally, what particularly exacerbated the latent Chinese anxieties was Japan's readiness and intention to send troops to participate in UN peace-keeping activities following the Gulf War.[36] In sum, the collapse of the Soviet Union on the one hand, and Washington's gradual military withdrawal from East Asia on the other, would leave Japan as the principal potential threat to Chinese security by the beginning of the 21st century, at least in regional terms. Globally, however, it is the United States that China will have to face.

Rejection of Single-Power Domination

This is probably the most significant outcome of the recent change in the international situation. 'In Beijing's judgement, a single-power domination of the world is emerging...and that is even worse than the previous two-superpower contention for hegemony.'[37] The loss of its bargaining card – and its inability to play (American) barbarians against (Soviet) barbarians – undoubtedly exposes China to growing international pressures, and affects its so-called 'comprehensive national strength', not only in terms of its economic, scientific, and technological systems but, also, in terms of its military modernisation.

Unless there is a significant change in China's stand on human rights and other civil liberties, the arms embargo imposed on the P.R.C. in retaliation to the Tiananmen massacre is bound to remain in force. Although alternative sources for military modernisation are available, they all have their limitations. Acquisition of Western defence equipment and technology by side-stepping the embargo will become more difficult since the consolidated European Community is now, following the lessons of the Gulf War, more sensitive to the issue of arms exports. Domestic military research, development, and design is a slow and expensive process, still handicapped by lower Chinese technology and a mentality of 'upgrading' existing models, and thereby duplicating backwardness, rather than creatively producing a new generation of high-tech weapons.[38] The last option, the Soviet one, emerged following Gorbachov's visit to Beijing in May 1989. Following the collapse of the Soviet Union, negotiations continued with the Commonwealth of Independent States (CIS), on the supply of aircraft and perhaps other weapons and technology, including T-72 tanks, air-defence and ground-based early warning systems. According to Taiwanese sources, Beijing's acquisition of 24 Su-27 high-performance fighters, some of which have already been supplied, would undoubtedly tip the military balance in the South China Sea, including Taiwan, in Beijing's favour.[39]

Still, with the fate of the Soviet Union sealed, China can by no means afford to depend, once again, on whatever remains of the Soviet empire. The new international situation leaves the P.R.C. with no one to rely on except itself in improving and strengthening its military system, as well as raising the necessary foreign exchange for this end from whatever sources – not least among which are arms sales. In both respects, Beijing now confronts the firm opposition of the United States – not so much as a direct threat to Chinese security, but more as an obstacle on the Chinese road to military modernisation, both conventional and nuclear.

Arms Sales

China began to sell arms on a massive scale in the late 1970s and early 1980s, taking advantage of the Iran-Iraq war. Primarily motivated by economic considerations, the Chinese have signed arms transfer agreements valued at more than U.S.$17 billion through 1990, approximately 90 per cent of which were with Middle Eastern governments.[40] The income from these sales has probably been channelled to supplement regular defence budgets, thus creating an invaluable and indispensable source of precious foreign exchange, essential for military modernisation. Beijing has been unable or unwilling to provide these resources from its regular budget. Largely overlooked until 1987, China's arms sales have become a target for Washington's opposition after ships carrying the U.S. flag were hit in the Persian Gulf by P.R.C.-made Silkworm missiles operated by Iran. Washington has become even more irritated following the reports, confirmed by Beijing and Riyadh, on the sale of Chinese CSS-2 (or DF-3) Intermediate Range Ballistic Missiles (IRBMs) to Saudi Arabia.

Since then Beijing has been under constant U.S. pressure to slow down its arms sales and, particularly, to withhold the sale of its short and medium-range missiles to countries such as Pakistan and Syria. Though not a member of the Missile Technology Control Regime (MTCR), China was urged to abide by its rules, as well as to sign the nuclear Non-Proliferation Treaty (NPT). Under these pressures, and their own willingness to play a greater role in settling outstanding international issues, the Chinese have gradually begun to give in. Thus, in August, 1991, Li Peng announced that the Chinese Government has agreed in principle to participate in the NPT. This decision was the easiest to reach, since China has always insisted that on no account would it ever engage in nuclear proliferation, nor would it be the first to use nuclear weapons. Nonetheless, the October 1991 NPC session failed to ratify the proposals submitted by the State Council and it was only on December 29 that the final decision to sign the NPT was reached.

China is even more reluctant to join the disarmament process, both conventional and nuclear. To justify their stand, the Chinese say:

The United States and the Soviet Union, which possess 97 per cent of the world's total nuclear warheads, have the unique responsibility to take the lead in deeply cutting their existing nuclear warheads of all types. Nevertheless, what concrete actions they are going to take to translate their plans into reality, and to what extent they will be carried out, remain to be seen. Moreover, even though they have cutback their nuclear weapons, the cutbacks will involve merely tactical nuclear weapons. The nuclear arsenals of the United States and the Soviet Union remain the largest in the world. Therefore, the nuclear threat facing the world is far from being eliminated.[41]

An identical argument applies to the issue of conventional arms transfers and the non-proliferation of chemical and biological weapons of mass destruction. The P.R.C. argues that its arms deliveries are much less significant, not only in terms of quantity (an average of 4.6 per cent of the entire arms transfers to the Third World from 1983 to 1990), but also in terms of quality. This is why the Chinese, who participated along with the other permanent members of the UN Security Council in the London Arms Talks in October 1991, are still 'studying' Japan's proposal to establish a system, under UN supervision, to register or record the flow of international arms trading.

Conclusion

It is perhaps too early to evaluate the implications of the recent changes in the international situation on P.R.C. defence and military modernisation. While the world is moving toward greater relaxation in international tension, the Chinese remain worried because of new kinds of threats and difficulties that they have never encountered before: domestically (primarily 'peaceful evolution', 'separatism' and 'splittism'); regionally (tension along the borders, independence tendencies in Taiwan, unrest in Hong Kong and, last but not least, the possible emergence of Japan as a military power); and globally (the rise of the United States as the only superpower with a freer hand to apply more pressure on China). To deal with these threats and difficulties Beijing has already taken steps to strengthen its defence and military system.

Notes

1. Joffe, E., (1967), *Party and Army, Professionalism and Political Control in the Chinese Officer Corps, 1949-1964*, Cambridge, Mass.: Harvard East Asian Monographs. Gittings, John, (1967), *The Role of the Chinese Army*, London: Oxford University Press.
2. Shichor, Y., 'Defence Policy Reform', in: Segal, G., (ed.), (1990), *Chinese Politics and Foreign Policy Reform*, London: Kegan Paul International, pp. 77-99. See also: Joffe, E., (1987), *The Chinese Army After Mao*, London: Weidenfeld and Nicolson.
3. On the PLA after Tiananmen see: Jencks, H.W., (May-June 1991), 'Civil-Military Relations in China: Tiananmen and After', *Problems of Communism* , pp. 14-29. Yang, R.H. (ed.), (October 1989), *The PLA and the Tiananmen Crisis*, SCPS Papers, No. 1, Kaohsiung: Sun Yat-sen Centre for Policy Studies, National Sun Yat-sen University. Gregor, A. James, (April 1991), *The Military in Post-Tiananmen China*, SCPS Papers, No. 3.
4. The following section is partly based on: Shichor, Y., (November-December 1991), 'China and the Gulf Crisis: Escape from Predicament', *Problems of Communism*, pp. 80-90.
5. Lo, Ping (August 15, 1990), 'Defence Minister has Courageously Defeated Generals of the Yang's Family', *Kai Fang*, Hong Kong, pp. 7-8, trans. in Foreign Broadcast Information Service, Daily Report: China (Washington, DC – hereafter FBIS-CHI), (August 23, 1990), p. 36.
6. Chen, Xiangong (September 7, 1990), 'World Military Situation in the 1990s', *Jiefangjun Bao*, (Beijing – hereafter *JFJB*), p. 3, trans. in *FBIS-CHI*, (September 7, 1990), p. 8.
7. Lo, Ping (September 1, 1990), 'The CCP Guiding Principles for the Middle East Crisis', *Cheng Ming*, Hong Kong, p. 15, in *FBIS-CHI*, (September 5, 1990), p. 15.
8. Chen, Shao-pin (February 10, 1991), 'Yang Shangkun on the Middle East War and the Tasks of the Three Armed Services', *Ching Pao*, Hong Kong, pp. 36-37, trans. in *FBIS-CHI*, (February 13, 1991), pp. 31-32. See also: Lam, Willy Wo-lap, (February 6, 1991), 'Army Told to Strengthen Combat Capabilities', *South China Morning Post*, Hong Kong, (hereafter *SCMP*), p. 8, also 'Army to Receive More Funds, Technology', (March 7, 1991), *SCMP*, p. 1.
9. Chen, Xiangong (see note 6), pp. 4-8.
10. Excerpts from a *JFJB* article by Sa, Benwang on the implications of

the Gulf Crisis on the world military situation, *XINHUA*, (January 11, 1991), in *FBIS-CHI*, (January 11, 1991), pp. 1-2.

11 Lu, Xiaobing (February 6, 1991), 'Strengthening National Defence Building is Important Guarantee for Economic Development', *JFJB*, p. 3, trans. in *FBIS-CHI*, (March 1, 1991), pp. 33-35. Since the 5th session of the 7th NPC (March 1992), the PLA has been ordered to 'escort' the reform. Yet, 'it is impossible for an army with weak combat ability to fulfil its historical 'escort' mission'. Lu, Tianyi and Yang, Xuequan (March 30, 1992), 'Chinese soldiers and Tide of Reform', *JFJB*, pp. 1, 4, trans. in *FBIS-CHI*, (April 16, 1992), p. 37.

12. Nip, A., (March 29, 1991), 'PLA Backs Proposed Defence Budget Increase', *Hongkong Standard*, p. 10. For similar views on the need to reinforce China's defence capabilities, see: *XINHUA*, (March 27, 1991), in *FBIS-CHI*, (March 28, 1991), p. 19.

13. For example: 'U.S.'s Warfare Gives Chinese Military an Inferiority Complex', (March 21, 1991), *International Herald Tribune*, p. 8. See also; Li, Tiran (September 1, 1991), 'Reconnaissance and Counter-reconnaissance in the Gulf War', *Xiandai Bingqui*, Beijing, no. 9, pp. 30-34, 16, trans. in Joint Publication Research Service, (December 12, 1991), *China Report*, Washington, D.C., pp. 43-47.

14. Lo, Ping (May 1, 1991), 'Old Generals Complain About Deng Delaying Improvement of Weapons Equipment', *Cheng Ming*, pp. 6-9, trans. in *FBIS-CHI*, (May 7, 1991), pp. 51-55.

15. Chen, Wei-chun (February 16, 1991), 'Army Generals Request Big Increase of Military Expenditures; Jiang Zemin and Li Peng Endorse the Demand', *Kuang-Chiao Ching*, Hong Kong, pp. 11-12, trans. in *FBIS-CHI*, (February 15, 1991), pp. 21-23.

16. *Ching Pao*, (March 10, 1991), p. 28, trans. in *FBIS-CHI*, (March 11, 1991), p. 26.

17. Chen, Shao-pin (April 10, 1991), 'Inside Story of CPC Increasing Military Spending', *Ching Pao*, p.42, trans. in *FBIS-CHI*, (April 12, 1991), pp. 31-32.

18. For details: 'Seventh National People's Congress, Fourth Session', (June 1, 1991), in *FRIS-CHI Supplement*, especially pp. 12, 29, 38, 64, 66, 68. See also *Beijing Review*, (hereafter-*BR*), (April 15-21, 1991), p. xiii; 'Increased Military Spending,' (March 25, 1991), *SCMP*, pp. 1, 11.

19. *JFJB*, (March 31, 1991), p. 1, trans. in *FBIS-CHI*, (April 11, 1991), pp. 19-20. Indeed, while China's 1991 defence expenses were up 13.8 per cent (instead of the allocated increase of 11.98 per cent), the 1992 defence budget was further increased by 13.9 per cent, reaching 37 billion yuan up 50.0 per cent over 1989, according to ROC sources. See; *Hongkong Standard*, (March 20, 1992), and *SCMP*, (March 21, 1992, *Far Eastern Economic Review* (hereafter - *FEER*), (April 2, 1992), p. 64

and China Broadcasting Corporation, (Taipei), (April 9, 1992), in *FBIS-CHI*, (April 15, 1992, p. 69.

20. For the re-emergence of political considerations in defence reform, see, for example: An, Sishan and Wang, Zhi (April 17, 1991), 'Upholding Absolute Party Leadership Over Armed Forces Fundamental Principle of Armed Forces', *JFJB*, trans. in *FBIS-CHI*, (May 9, 1991), pp.36-39; Kuo, Chien (May 15, 1991), 'PLA General Political Department Issues New Brainwashing Document; The CPC is Tightening Control Over the Army', *Tangtai*, trans. in *FBIS-CHI*, (May 21, 1991), pp. 52-55; Jiang, Siyi (July 3, 1991), 'Conscientiously Study Mao Zedong's Military Thinking', in *FBIS-CHI*, trans. in *FBIS-CHI*, (August 1, 1991), pp. 37-41; Hu, Nianqu (July 26, 1991), 'Seminar on Mao Zedong's Military Thinking Held by PLA Headquarters Organs Ends Satisfactorily,' *XINHUA*, in *Ibid.*, pp. 41-42.

21. Wu, Yunhe (August 9, 1991), 'Military To Acquire Modern Electronics', *China Daily*, p. 2; 'PLA's 2nd Artillery Corps Succeeds in Renovation Missiles, Equipment', (July 26, 1991), *JFJB*, p. 1, trans. in *FBIS-CHI*, (August 12, 1991), p. 38; Sun, Minqiang (August 7, 1991), 'China's Guided Missile Industry Develops Rapidly', *JFJB*, p. 1, trans. in *FBIS-CHI*, (August 26, 1991), pp. 37-38; 'China's 'Flying Fish' Missiles Greatly Boost Its Defence Capabilities', (August 11, 1991), *Zhongguo Xinwen She*, trans. in *FBIS-CHI*, (August 16, 1991), p. 23; Li, Wenyu (August 30, 1991), 'Modernisation Level of China's Artillery Weapons Remarkably Enhanced', *Zhongguo Xinwen She*, trans. in *FBIS-CHI*, (September 4, 1991), pp. 23-24.

22. 'Building Socialism the Chinese Way', (July 8-14, 1991), *BR*, p. 26. See also; Hua, Chen (August 15, 1991), 'Developments in Military Before and After Army Day on 1 August', *Tangtai*, Hong Kong, no. 5, trans. in *FBIS-CHI*, (August 23, 1991), pp.30-32.

23. *China Daily*, (August 1, 1991), p.1; *XINHUA*, (July 31, 1991), trans. in *FBIS-CHI*, (August 19, 1991), pp. 28-29.

24. He, Shao-ming and Yueh, Shan (October 1, 1991), 'CPC Claims To Be Prepared for War', *Cheng Ming*, pp. 16-17, trans. in *FBIS-CHI*, (October 29, 1991), pp. 37-39.

25. *XINHUA*, (November 5, 1991), trans, in *FBIS-CHI*, (November 7, 1991), pp. 30-31. See also interview in *Kurier*, (October 7, 1991), Vienna, p. 5, trans. in *FBIS-CHI*, (October 11, 1991), pp. 25-26.

26. Shih, Hua (November 1, 1991), 'Various Actions Taken by CPC to Guard Against Peaceful Evolution', *Chiushih Nientai*, Hong Kong, pp. 36-37, trans. in *FBIS-CHI*, (November 20, 1991), pp. 24-26. On the Lanzhou exercises, see; *JFJB*, (October 29, 1991), pp. 1, 2, trans. in *FBIS-CHI*, November 22, 1991, pp. 30-32. See also; 'The Entire Armed Forces Are Launching an Upsurge of Military Training', (March 19,

1991), *Renmin Ribao,* Beijing, trans. in *FBIS-CHI,* (March 21, 1991), p. 25; 'Chinese Troops Recently Carry Out Coordinated Air-Ground War Exercise', (June 6, 1991), *Zhongguo Tongxun She,* Hong Kong, trans. in *FBIS-CHI,* June 24, 1991, pp. 56-57.

27. Yin, Jun (August 16, 1991), 'Step Up Comprehensive Public Security Control for the Sake of Stability, Development in Border Areas', *Qiushi,* Beijing, no. 16, pp. 27-29, trans. in FBIS-CHI, (September 30, 1991), pp. 35-38.

28. Inner Mongolia People's Radio, (December 28, 1991), trans. in *FBIS-CHI,* (January 9, 1992), p. 42, and 'Amudun Niyaz Visits Border Defence Armed Police Corps', (August 13, 1991), *Xinjiang Ribao,* p. 1, trans. in FBIS-CHI, (August 16, 1991), pp. 23-24. This section is based on Shichor, Y., (December 2, 1991), 'Islam in Contemporary Chinese Politics', unpublished paper delivered at the 16th annual meeting of the Israel Oriental Society on 'Islam in the International System', Jerusalem. See also: Harris, L.C., (July 6, 1990), 'China; the Choice between Marx and Allah', *Middle East International,* London, no. 379, pp. 19-20.

29. 'CPC Assesses Taiwan's Military Strength – Chen Yun Favours Military Actions against Taiwan, but Deng Xiaoping Prefers Waiting for Another Year', (September 1, 1990), *Pai Hsing,* Hong Kong, p. 3, trans. in *FBIS-CHI,* (September 5, 1990), pp. 23-24.

30. *Central New Agency,* (Taipei - hereafter *CNA*), (August 10, 1990), in *FBIS-CHI,* (August 13, 1990), p. 66. See also: *Taipei International Service,* (January 26, 1991), in *FBIS-CHI,* (January 29, 1991), p. 60.

31. 'Taiwan Navy Sets Up Antisubmarine Command', (September 12, 1991), *Wen Wei Po,* Hong Kong, p. 6, trans. in *FBIS-CHI,* (September 20, 1991), p. 78.

32. *XINHUA,* (September 28, 1991) trans. in *FBIS-CHI,* (September 30, 1991), pp. 22-23.

33. These paragraphs are based on: 'CPC Discusses Use of Force Against Taiwan', (November 15, 1991), *Tanqtai,* no. 8, pp. 12-13, trans. in *FBIS-CHI,* (November 20, 1991), pp. 67-68, and Fang, Kang (December 1, 1991), 'CPC Sets Deadline for Taiwan', *Cheng Ming,* No. 170, pp. 20-22, trans. in *FBIS-CHI,* (December 4, 1991), pp. 24-26. See also: *Cheng Ming,* (November 1, 1991), no. 169, pp. 13-15, trans. in *FBIS-CHI,* (November 15, 1991), p. 26, and; 'If the Chinese Communists Blockade Taiwan', (November 16, 1991), *Kuang-chiao Ching,* Hong Kong, no. 230, pp. 18-21, trans. in *FBIS-CHI,* (March 11, 1992), pp. 44-46. According to the ROC Government Information Office, Beijing has threatened to take Taiwan by force 17 times during the seven months from March to October 1991: *CNA,* (December 5, 1991), Taipei, trans. in *FBIS-CHI,* (December 5, 1991, p. 62.

34. Lo, Ping, 'Possible Takeover of Hong Kong by Communist China Before Due Date', (November 1, 1991), *Cheng Ming*, no. 169, pp. 6-8, trans. in *FBIS-CHI*, (November 15, 1991), pp. 88-90. Such concern was also shown by Deng Xiaoping. He was quoted saying; 'A warning should be given to some people in Hong Kong. They must not always try to create turmoil in China. If there is turmoil in China, Hong Kong will be the first to suffer its consequences'. *Wen Wei Po*, (February 21, 1992), Hong Kong, p. 2, trans. in *FBIS-CHI*, (February 21, 1992), p. 17.

35. Guo, Simian (1991), *China's Peripheral Situation in the 1990s*, Berichte des Bundesinstituts fur ostwissenschaftliche und internationale Studien, No. 37, Koln, pp. 19-22.

36. For China's reactions to Japan's involvement in the Gulf see, for example: Zhi, Ai, (October 10, 1990), 'The Japanese Prime Minister Visits the Middle East; Intentions to Dispatch Troops While Giving Economic Aid', *Zhongguo Quingnian Bao*, p. 2, trans. in *FBIS-CHI*, (November 5, 1990), pp. 2-3. See also; Daling, Zhand, (October 13, 1991), 'Japan's UN Diplomacy', *Guoji Wenti Yanjiu*, Beijing, no. 42, pp. 25-32, trans. in *FBIS-CHI*, (December 31, 1991), pp. 10-15.

37. Hua, Di (August 1991), 'One Superpower Worse Than Two', *Asia-Pacific Defence Reporter*, pp. 14-16.

38. Lo, Ping (October 1, 1991), 'Deng Xiaoping Inspects New Fighter in Sicbuan', *Cheng Ming*, no. 168, pp. 14-15, trans. in *FBIS-CHI*, (October 3, 1991), pp. 27-29.

39. For example: *SCMP*, (August 7, 1991), p. 12; *China Post*, Taipei, (August 7, 1991), p. 16. See also: Jencks, H.W., (April 1991), *Some Political and Military Implications of Soviet Warplane Sales to the P.R.C.*, SCPS Papers, no. 6. See also: FEER, (August 26, 1991), p. 6, (September 5, 1991), p. 9., (March 19, 1992), p. 13, (March 26, 1992), p. 7, and *KYODD*, (May 3, 1992), Tokyo, trans. in *FBIS-CHI*, (May 5, 1992), p. 5.

40. For data on Chinese arms sales, see: Grimmett, R.F., (August 2, 1991) *Conventional Arms Transfers to the Third World, 1983-1990*, CRS Report for Congress, 91-578 F, Washington; Congressional Research Service. See also Shichor, Y., (1984), 'The Middle East', in Segal, G. and Tow, W.T. (eds), *Chinese Defence Policy*, London: Macmillan, pp. 263-278; *The Pacific Review*, (October 1988), vol. 1, no. 3, pp. 320-330; *East Wind Over Arabia: Origins and Implications of the Sino-Saudi Missile Deal*, (1989), China Research Monographs, no. 35, Centre for Chinese Studies, Institute of East Asian Studies, University of California, Berkeley.

41. Chen, Xiong, 'United States, Soviet Union Put Forth New Disarmament Plans', (October 16, 1991), *JFJB*, p. 4, trans. in *FBIS-CHI*, (October 31, 1991), p. 11.

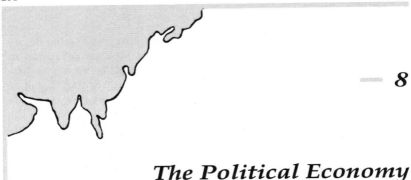

8

The Political Economy of Japan's Defence Production

Wayne Robinson

Introduction

In 1990 Japan became the world's third largest military spender, the defence budget reaching Y4.159 trillion or a little under $30 billion U.S.[1] The 1991-92 defence budget, the first year of the new five-year defence plan buildup will rise a further 5.4 per cent from Y4.159 trillion to Y4.386 trillion in contrast to the general decline evident among NATO states.[2] For some this development is indicative of a new realism by Tokyo towards Japan's responsibility for upholding the 'new world order'. Given reduced global tensions however, domestic and foreign critics wonder whether Japan's military capabilities may now be outstripping its defence needs. By world standards Japan's armed forces are modest in size, numbering 156,000 for the army, 46,400 for the navy and 46,400 for the air force – virtually unchanged from a decade ago.[3] The major part of Japan's defence budget is consumed not by personnel expenses but by domestically produced weapons systems, logistics support and heavy debt payments. High unit costs flow from a ban on the export of weapons and poor economies of scale associated with limited production runs. This has meant that effective purchasing power of the defence yen cannot easily be compared to that of the pound, the franc or the dollar. Major items may cost between three and five times the world price.[4] In addition, Japan's method of funding military research and development has contributed in a major way to cost inflation.

Despite these problems, Japan today produces small arms, tanks, armoured personnel carriers, artillery, naval gas turbines and ships, including submarines, advanced trainer and fighter aircraft, helicopters, transport planes and guided missiles. Considerable effort is also going into civilian aerospace technology including rocketry, satellites, and space shuttles which, while not militarily funded, could serve military as well as civilian purposes. In reply to critics of this military-industrial effort Japan has argued that Article 9 of the Constitution banning war preparation does not contradict the right of self defence, acknowledged under Article 51 of the UN Charter. Given Japan's enormous economic strength, and its military-industrial base, its current refusal to export weapons or to deploy combat troops abroad, suggests that its claim to be acting in a strictly defensive way is credible. Nevertheless, Japan's defence posture demonstrates a rather grudging acknowledgement of the dramatic changes in the world system. Clearly military doctrine and geostrategic factors alone are not able to account for the level and nature of Japan's military effort.

Argument

This chapter asserts that it is Japan's military production system which is beginning to exercise a dominant influence over the country's security calculations and the Japanese state (executive and bureaucracy) is not only having difficulty containing these pressures but may also be generating them.

Luckham, in a recent paper on the dynamics of the U.S. military industrial complex, also argues that rises and falls in military spending are only weakly connected with military threat assessments. Citing the American case he sees military budgeting today as:

...driven by military product cycles and technological change; the inter-connections between military spending, deficits and industrial decline; and the changing role of [U.S.] capital in the international division of labour.[5]

Japan today faces neither deficits nor industrial decline, yet its defence production dynamics are driven internally by the demands of Japanese producers and government ministries. Their decisions in turn are influenced by what is happening politically and militarily in the U.S.

Framework

The theoretical literature dealing with military expenditure has tended to view the state as a rational actor balancing effort, cost, and security benefits to maximise national interest. This perspective, however, obscures important political functions served by military spending in the generation of collective identity, prestige, and sovereignty, and it has diverted attention from the role of private interest. The framework of this chapter uses Kaldor's explanations to account for military-technical change in peacetime.[6]

Kaldor's starting point is whether pressure for weapons production in peacetime arises principally from external threat or domestic supply-side institutional interests. The core problem in locating the ultimate determinants of military spending is the absence of a rational test of utility for weapons, short of war. Unlike other collective goods such as health or education, there is no easy way of determining the public utility of weapons. No mechanism exists for reconciling quantities of military resources to a set of attainable objectives and any plausible peacetime rationale for military spending. Production and pricing therefore reflect the attitudes, beliefs, and interests of political and military élites. In peacetime Kaldor sees the emergence of a proxy mechanism to regulate the struggle over resources among those committed to the furtherance of weapons production. The demand side of this mechanism comprises the armed forces – the final users of armaments – and the state. They assume '...no distinction between use and acquisition, as though requirements defined by some external situation could be immediately translated into resources through the agency of some "rational" decision maker.[7] The potential requirement for weapons which is defined by the international situation, is called the systemic aspect of demand.[8]

The state is the major actor on the demand side. Because war is discontinuous, the act of purchase is separated in time from the use of a weapon. Decisions concerning what weapons to buy and in what quantities must therefore be made by the state on the basis of the existing situation, rather than on the basis of some imagined future military scenario. It is because of this that Kaldor introduces the cautious incrementalism of bureaucratic politics into her model. The armed forces, government ministries and politicians are the institutional embodiment of demand.[9]

Historical Background

The roots of Japan's post-war defence policy lie in the Yoshida doctrine. This doctrine was designed to overcome inconsistency between the Peace and Security treaties signed with the U.S. in September 1951 and the pacifist provisions of the 1947 Constitution.[10]

The comparatively small size of Japan's armed forces today continues to reflect the deal struck in 1951 whereby military potential was restricted to archipelago defence, providing the United States with the permanent rationale it needed to project its military power into the Far East. With its security underwritten, weapons production was, from the viewpoint of Japan's fiscal guardians, a low investment priority. During the 1950s and 1960s emphasis fell on maximising the advantages of acquiring defence production technology by producing American equipment for the Self Defence Forces (SDF) under licence. Underlying this approach was the policy of *kokusanka*, i.e. seeking national autonomy in weapons production.[11] While access to U.S. weapons technology was considered vital, development of indigenous capacity was seen as essential to meet the special tactical and operational requirements of the SDF. In practice it meant that while American weapons were purchased directly, there was also a parallel, more costly road of prototype development that often replicated work already incorporated in weapons systems elsewhere. Never-

theless the *kokusanka* companies received strong support from
the Japan Defence Agency (JDA – Boei Cho), which saw autonomy
as insurance against overdependence on U.S. suppliers. The Ministry of International Trade and Industry (MITI) also a strong
backer of *kokusanka*, regarded defence production as an important means of broadening Japan's technology base. As Drifte notes
however, the old debate about national defence turned less on
what kinds of weapons were needed to promote Japanese self-
defence and counter the Soviet threat, than on what level of
military spending would satisfy the U.S.[12]

The military strategic environment in which Japanese defence
production had evolved up to the mid-1970s was decisively altered
by two crucial decisions in 1976 and 1978. The first, taken by the
Miki Cabinet, was the adoption of the National Defence Programme Outline, or *Taiko*. This crystallised the Japanese Government's attitude towards U.S. nuclear guarantees and resulted in a
fundamental decision by the Miki Cabinet to make the U.S.-Japan
security relationship the basis of Japan's defence. An underlying
motivation for the *Taiko* was the government's opposition to
further increases in defence spending at a time when international relations – particularly with China – appeared less threatening. The *Taiko* imposed a strictly limited, small-scale defensive
role on the Self Defence Forces (SDF) and proposed a series of five-
year defence plans *(Chugyo)* to regulate future build-up. The
defence budget was limited strictly to one per cent of GNP. These
measures turned the tide strongly against the *kokusanka* advocates who had already, during 1974-75, suffered a number of
major reversals.

The *Taiko* had not been envisaged by the Miki Government as
a step towards re-armament. Nevertheless, in the aftermath of
Vietnam its effect was to heighten U.S. expectations of stronger
defence cooperation. In November 1978 the Guidelines Agreement was entered into between the Fukuda government and the
U.S.[13] The Guidelines Agreement heightened Japan's military
coordination with the U.S. and widened the SDF's role beyond
archipelago defence, to one of explicit support for U.S. nuclear
contingency planning. It resulted also in a shift of weapons procurement priorities within the SDF from the Ground Self Defence
Force (GSDF) to air and naval power. Joint operational plans,

joint training, common communications and logistical support with the U.S. were given high priority. Most importantly the U.S. now put great stress on weapons interoperability. This led to a higher priority being given to U.S. weapons procurements over domestic, *kokusanka* suppliers. The re-orientation towards U.S. defence suppliers, though allowing continued production under licence, frustrated attempts by Japanese aircraft companies in particular, to gain experience with full systems integration. Their role was thereby restricted to the manufacture of sub-systems and parts. The effect however, was to bind the SDF - particularly the Air Self Defence Force (ASDF) and Maritime Self Defence Force (MSDF) – to the U.S. defence industry. A serving ASDF officer – Obata Takeshi – has suggested that the Guidelines Agreement was really designed to prevent Japan's military independence.[14] Whether correct or not, a longer term effect on Japanese military aviation appeared to be a reduced ability to exploit technological spin-offs in the civil aviation field, thereby increasing the industry's reliance on state military contracts.[15]

In response to the changed Cold War security situation and the termination of clear U.S. military and economic supremacy, Japan moved to redefine its security interests in 1980-81. A study commissioned by the Japanese Prime Minister, Ohira Masayoshi, the Report on Comprehensive National Security, noted fundamental changes to the systemic environment that made it no longer possible for the U.S. to provide its allies and friends with 'nearly full security'.[16] The Report proposed overall integration of all security policies into a single framework resting on three pillars: diplomacy, military defence, and economic strategy. Omnidirectional diplomacy was to give way to a more strategically focused approach. There were to be efforts at greater self-reliance in meeting external threats, and closer cooperation with allies. Drifte argues that the underlying rationale for the adoption of Comprehensive Security was to free Japan's national security from 'the straitjacket of the Security Treaty'.[17] While military security now ranked as only one of three pillars of security, the move '... made it easier to elevate military efforts to more or less equal rank beside diplomacy and economic measures'.[18]

Overall Comprehensive Security did not result in greater independence from the U.S., but a first step towards alliance burden sharing. In operational terms it led to the announcement by the Suzuki government in 1981 that the MSDF would assume responsibility for securing Japan's sea lines of communication to a distance of 1,000 nautical miles from Honshu. At the level of geostrategic doctrine, Comprehensive Security appeared increasingly to reflect acceptance of the American view that Japan's security depended on the global balance of forces. Although the new course did not see a sudden rise in the overall defence budget, it led to a rapid increase in the procurement of advanced weapons systems. This was vigorously promoted by the new Nakasone government which took power in 1982.

The bleak prospects for *kokusanka* by 1979 led to a tactical shift by the Japan Defence Agency (JDA) from autonomy in production to autonomy in research and development (R & D).[19] (*Kenkyukaihatsu Ni kan Suru Shin Hoshin.*) Implicit in the new policy was a determination to achieve technological independence from the U.S. This coincided with American scientists claiming that the U.S. was giving more than it was receiving in the area of advanced weapons research. This criticism strengthened the determination among Japanese contractors to rely less on advanced U.S. military technology.

Since 1982-83 the issue of military technology has gone to the heart of the Security Treaty. From the U.S. military perspective it was only with American assistance that Japan's military industries were resuscitated after the war. Inter-operability was vital in operational terms due to joint exercises, and high level (nuclear) contingency planning. Most importantly the willingness to share advanced technology raised the question of trust between the two sides. By 1985-86, for a growing coalition of right-wing members of the U.S. Congress, techno-nationalists in the Pentagon and in the Commerce Department, technology transfer became the real test of Japan's political loyalty. This broad grouping, whatever its internal differences, saw Japan's reluctance to cooperate fully in military technology transfer as ingratitude for the grossly disproportionate burden the U.S. was carrying to defend Japan.[20] From about 1986, therefore, there was a clear tendency for U.S. security initiatives towards Japan to slip from the Pentagon's grasp into the hands of an amorphous anti-Japan coalition.

The close ideological affinity between the Nakasone and Reagan governments and Japanese fears of a serious rift in the alliance, resulted in concessions in the military security sphere to avert U.S. reprisals over wider economic issues. The risks of this were considerable as it cleared the way for open-ended supply-side pressures. The first gesture made in accordance with the new policy was the 1986 decision to exceed the one per cent ceiling on military spending, imposed by the Miki cabinet in 1976, closely followed by participation in the U.S. Strategic Defence Initiative (SDI). In 1987 the most important concession came when the Japanese government decided, against bitter opposition from Mitsubishi Heavy Industries (MHI) and the Air Self Defence Force (ASDF), to opt for co-development of a new fighter aircraft with the American company General Dynamics. The Japanese bureaucracy was itself severely divided on the issue of whether the new fighter, known as FS-X (Fighter Support Experimental), should be a *kokusanka* project. The final user, the ASDF, based its support for Mitsubishi on growing dissatisfaction with the delays and the quality of servicing of equipment supplied directly by the U.S. Ministry of International Trade and Industry (MITI), and also saw the merits of allowing Mitsubishi to demonstrate its capacity to go it alone, but it was persuaded by cost arguments and the delicate trade issue not to support the project.

Challenges to the U.S.-Japan Security Relationship

Japan's further retreat from independent defence production occurred against the background of three trends highly disadvantageous to the United States in Northeast Asia. First, the Intermediate Nuclear Force Agreement of December 1987 (which saw the removal of land-based SS.20 missiles from East Asia) altered Japanese public perceptions towards the Soviet threat. The subsequent lowering of troop levels in the Soviet Far East, Vietnam's withdrawal from Cambodia, and arms control developments in Europe raised new questions about the necessity for the U.S. nuclear security guarantee and the wisdom of participating in the denuclearisation taking place in other parts of the world. Within the Japanese Defence Agency (JDA) the rapidly changing international security environment during 1989-90, resulting from

Soviet initiatives, threatened to wreck planning for the next five-year defence plan build-up *(Chukibo)* due to begin in 1991. The belief in a credible Soviet threat had been of central political importance in maintaining national support for the Self Defence Forces (SDF) and the need for *kokusanka* in addition to the Security Treaty. Socialist gains in the Upper House of the Diet during 1989 further threatened the JDA's plans for continued budget growth in the 1991-95 plan.

The decline in the U.S. economy (1987-88), also resulted in more pressure on Japan's military budget. The presence of U.S. ground troops in the Asia Pacific region, particularly in South Korea, had been a 'constant' built into Japan's fundamental security calculations. In the course of 1988-89, statements by senior U.S. officials made it increasingly clear, however, that the U.S. was no longer able to sustain its existing level of military commitment in the Asia Pacific region. These statements, seen in the context of the new burden-sharing commitments, posed the question of the future extent of Japan's obligations to the U.S. for a security Japan would itself largely be responsible for providing, financially as well as operationally. The cost of maintaining U.S. bases in Japan therefore assumed growing political significance.[21] In September 1990 the anti-Japanese coalition in the U.S. House of Representatives, impatient with Japan's apparent reluctance to pay the full cost of U.S. bases in Japan, threatened to withdraw 5,000 troops annually from Japan.[22] The Kaifu Cabinet, continuing the Nakasone policy, responded in early October by indicating that an additional Y90 billion would be found for bases maintenance in 1991.[23] The effect of the additional funds was to bring forward by a year increases already scheduled for 1992, raising the amount borne by Japan to Y530.5 billion or about half the total cost of stationing U.S. forces.[24] Ishikawa Yozo, the Director-General (Minister) of the Defence Agency, reacted sharply to the U.S. threat:

> The U.S. Congress lacks common sense. Japan did not ask for the stationing of the U.S. forces. We will have to say to them 'Please return the forces home'.[25]

The third and potentially most damaging trend for the security relationship was friction over cooperation in military technology,

and direct weapons procurements. The root problem is the continued strengthening of Japanese research and development (R & D)
applicable to the military sector; relative to that of the United
States, Japanese military R & D has derived its vigour from its
close integration with commercial R & D, the flow being predominantly from the latter to the former. This process, termed 'spin-
on', stands in sharp contrast to the reverse process of 'spin-off'
witnessed in the U.S. and European defence industries. A much
greater part of Japan's entire R & D effort is thus potentially
available to the military sector than is true for the U.S., where R
& D has been sealed off and rendered heavily dependent on direct
Pentagon support. In the latter half of 1988 some of Japan's major
contractors, frustrated at the government's policy towards
kokusanka, abandoned their usual reticence and called for the ban
on weapons exporting to be lifted.[26] While unsuccessful, the move
reflected the seriousness of the supply-side pressures that had
accumulated.

By the late 1980s Japan's weapons sector had reached a new
level of technical maturity. As Japan became less dependent on
American military technology, however, U.S. contractors, faced
with a rapidly shrinking Pentagon budget, exhibited a steeply
rising need for procurements from, and technological cooperation
with, Japan.[27]

During 1989 and 1990 there was intense U.S. pressure on
Japan to purchase12 Boeing E-3A AWAC aircraft, the AEGIS
naval air defence system, the multiple launch rocket, McDonnell
Douglas KC-10A refuelling tankers, F-15 fighters, and additional
(Raytheon) Patriot missiles.[28] Until June of 1990 the Japanese
government appeared ready to proceed with the procurements.
However, at the end of July, the Prime Minister, Mr Kaifu, made
it clear there would be no new weapons systems allowed for, at
least in the 1991-92 budget.[29] The impression given in Tokyo was
that this decision had been taken in view of changed world
circumstances, and Socialist gains in the Upper House of the
Diet.[30] What was not made public was that the cancellations were
basically intended to release resources urgently needed to deal
with deficiencies in the SDF that were causing serious morale
problems.[31] The Kaifu cabinet's change of policy was not without
cost in alliance terms. Behind the scenes the Bush administration

demanded that, since $4 billions in badly needed procurements had been postponed, Tokyo should make a compensatory gesture towards burden sharing.[32] It was this that led to Kaifu's prompt offer in early October, of an additional Y90 billion for the maintenance of U.S. bases, a gesture that clearly angered the JDA.[33] Increased U.S. efforts to maintain its military supremacy by closer links with Japanese R & D in 1989-90 posed a major challenge to the strategic core of the *kokusanka* constituency.[34]

Keidanren Interests

The institutional apex of Japan's supply-side defence constituency is the Defence Production Committee of Keidanren,[35] representing some 200 companies.[36] Affiliated to the Committee are the Society of Japanese Aerospace Companies Inc. (SJAC), the Shipbuilders Association of Japan, and the Japan Association of Defence Industry (JADI).[37] These interests have to compete for resources within what is an extremely small sector of Japan's economy. Compared to the total value of industrial output in Japan in 1987, defence production accounted for 0.58 per cent.[38] By sector, 8.26 per cent (by value) of all ships under construction in Japanese yards in 1987 were for military orders. Military vehicles comprised a miniscule 0.09 per cent of industry sales, electric communications equipment 0.67 per cent, and petroleum products 0.68 per cent. Ninety eight per cent of arms and ammunition production was for military orders. Perhaps most significantly, 79.56 per cent of total aircraft output was for military orders.[39]

The concentration of market shares is very high by international standards. If the top ten Japanese contractors are considered, their collective share of total JDA contracts in 1989 was 60 per cent.[40] By comparison the top ten U.S. military contractors monopolised 30 per cent of total Pentagon contracts.[41] The extreme concentration of market shares in the defence sector suggests a high level of dependence on the state. Competition however, is highly self-regulated. An implicit order of ranking exists among the larger companies in which specialised spheres of competence or control are recognised. This gives the bidding process a stability not seen in the West.[42]

Mitsubishi Heavy Industries totally dominates defence contracting, receiving 24.2 per cent of all defence contracts let by the JDA in fiscal year 1989. What is important however, is the relatively low ratio of defence contracts to total business sales of MHI and other corporations. In 1989 military business constituted only 17.4 per cent of MHI's turnover, 21.5 per cent of Kawasaki Heavy Industries (KHI) turnover, 4.7 per cent in the case of Mitsubishi Electric Corporation (MELCO), and 0.8 per cent of Fuji Heavy Industry's (FHI) turnover.[43] This low ratio is evident in the case of other major defence contractors also, such as NEC Corporation, Toshiba, Hitachi, Oki, Fujitsu, and Nissan.[44] Since Japan's defence budget is not reflected proportionately in the economic activity of the largest Japanese producers, it is reasonable to assume that the JDA is spreading its expenditure and purchasing into the future through deferred payments. (See the overall growth of Japan's defence budget since 1980 in Table I below.)

Table I
Budgetary Profile 1980-1990

Year	Total Defence Budget Bill (Yen)	Per cent change from previous year	Total Defence Budget as % of GNP
1980	2,230.2	6.5	0.9
1981	2,400.0	7.6	0.9
1982	2,586.1	7.8	0.9
1983	2,754.2	6.5	1.0
1984	2,934.6	6.5	1.0
1985	3,137.1	6.9	1.0
1986	3,343.5	6.6	1.0
1987	3,517.4	5.2	1.004
1988	3,700.3	5.2	1.013
1989	3,919.8	5.9	1.006
1990	4,159.3	6.1	0.997

Source: Holland, H.M. *Managing Defence: Japan's Dilemma*. University Press of America, 1988, p. 30, and Outline of Japan's Defence Budget for Fiscal 1990, p. 2, JDA.

Table II
Japan's Military Budget 1990 Breakdown of Expenses
(Unit: Y100 million)

CATEGORY	FY 1986	FY 1988	FY 1990
Defence Budget	33,435	37,003	41,593
Growth rate from			
previous year	6.58%	5.2%	8.8%
Personnel and provisions			
expenses	15,086	15,789	16,680
Growth rate	6.7%	2.3%	3.4%
Equipment and Material			
Expenses	18,350	21,215	24,913
Growth rate	6.5%	7.5%	8.0%
Obligational outlay expenses	11,699	13,510	15,829
Growth rate	9.0%	6.8%	7.8%
Current-year material			
expenses	6,651	7,705	9,084
Growth rate	2.4%	8.7%	8.4%
Frontline equipment	7,733	9,292	9,576
Growth rate	7.0%	8.6%	0.7%
Logistics support	10,617	11,923	15,337
Growth rate	6.1%	6.6%	13.2%

Source: *Japan Defence Budget for Fiscal 1990.*

The above figures show that while the total defence budget grew 24.40 per cent over the plan period, personnel and provisions fell considerably behind, increasing by a modest 10.6 per cent. Looking at weaponry, i.e. the frontline equipment category, between 1986 and 1990 growth, at 23.8 per cent, was virtually the same as for the overall defence budget. Also, this component remained virtually unchanged as a proportion of the total annual defence budget (i.e. 23.13 per cent in 1986 compared with 23.02 per cent in 1990).

Turning from use to outlay the picture changes significantly. The budget data on obligational expenses show that these rose 35.3 per cent between 1986 and 1990, 15 per cent faster than the growth of the defence budget overall. These expenses are interest payments on loans for weapons ordered but not paid for. As a proportion of Japan's total defence expenditure, obligational payment – already consuming 35.0 per cent in 1986 – rose further to 38.76 per cent in 1990. This erosion of the annual defence budget, resulting in the acquisition of advanced weapons systems for which funds would otherwise not have been available, is directly attributable to the declining deposits required.

It seems fair to conclude therefore, that while bureaucratic containment of domestic supply-side pressures is being achieved, it has been made possible only by the administrative expedient of deferred payment equipment acquisitions which have obscured the true level of Japan's military spending.

To understand the vigour of the supply-side push in Japan it is necessary to account for why bureaucratic support for *kokusanka* production has been so sustained. Military research and development funding to private Japanese companies helps explain the budget blow-out. From a bureaucratic standpoint the extinction of *kokusanka* weapons production capability would deny Japan an important alternative source of supply should access to U.S. equipment be disrupted. Further, autonomous defence production has served as an important means of drawing on advanced technology from the international economy for use by industry. In systemic supply-side terms this has entailed upholding the international credibility of domestic military R & D to induce reciprocity, particularly with the U.S.

Companies engage in considerable investigative work into new weapons projects. These are often expensive and extend over several years. From what evidence there is it would appear that implicit undertakings are given by the JDA allowing major companies to recover pre-contract R & D costs at the production stage. These undertakings, once reached, would seem to lock the JDA into proceeding with significant defence projects if large scale commercial failure is to be avoided. This administrative practice exerts a powerful front-end 'pull' effect on military prototype development which continues to operate independently of oscillations in the overall level of military spending.

The arrangement appears to represent state subsidisation of basic high-risk research which may also have considerable spin-offs for commercial product lines. Finally, once the decision has been taken to award a contract to a company for prototype development, all R & D costs are automatically borne by the JDA.[45] It is here, then, where extremely expensive corporate research can be state-funded and perhaps in the case of failure, written off, outside the discipline of the market, that a major attraction of military contracting lies buried.

Conclusions

Japan's military production system is beginning to exercise an increasingly important influence over the country's security calculations as demonstrated by the striking unimportance of threat assessments in shaping weapons procurement decisions. Despite acknowledgement by the Self Defence Forces (SDF) that the Russian threat to Japan has considerably diminished, purchase of advanced systems and forward ordering have continued their gradual upward trend in the 1990s.[46] Until now this upward trend has reflected less the views of the SDF or *kokusanka* interests, than considerations of what U.S. military planners deemed important. In effect political criteria relating to the preservation of the alliance rather than purely military considerations have provided the major ideological justification for arms purchases. The SDF has exploited the zone of ambiguity existing between U.S. strategic doctrine and the more circumscribed roles and missions laid down by the *Taiko* in 1976. This can be seen in the re-equipping of the Maritime Self Defence Force (MSDF) and Air Self Defence Force (ASDF) to fulfil Japan's pledge in 1981 to police its sea lines of communication to a distance of 1000 nautical miles. The pledge inaugurated a buildup of naval tonnage which is still continuing. The emphasis by the Ground Self Defence Force (GSDF) on the defence of Hokkaido similarly has justified a substantial re-equipping of the Army's tank and missile capability. Until 1990 the GSDF continued officially to link its upgrading to a potential Soviet threat and the 'Northern Territories'. For the 1990s the GSDF appears set to continue what it sees as defensive preparations to block the Sugaru and Soya Straits in the event of an increasingly improbable Russian-U.S. conflict. As with the MSDF and the ASDF a decade earlier, the rationale for the current GSDF build-up has thus to be seen as firmly embedded within high level U.S.-Pacific naval doctrine rather than the *Taiko*.

Paradoxically, however, the rise to world supremacy of Japan's industrial giants has not been reflected in a disproportionate increase in the size of Japan's military-industrial sector. Weapons manufacture as of 1987 still remained a very small part of total sales turnover for most contractors. What stands out, though, is the critically supportive role key ministries (notably the MOF, MITI, and the JDA itself) have played towards *kokusanka* interests. While bureaucratic influence over military-strategic relations with the U.S. has been restricted, its influence over the new weapons development process has been profound. There is a consistent pattern of state-backed measures to acquire advanced weapons production technology. This does not mean state agencies have not sometimes opposed the more grandiose schemes put forward by business. Yet, the deferred payments scheme, R & D cost recovery arrangements, the virtually closed system of contract bidding, the absence of any Diet standing committee on defence,[47] the early decommissioning of equipment and export of 'dual-use' weapons technology have an inner consistency that bears the stamp of bureaucratic power.

Sustaining bureaucratic support for *kokusanka* has been a convergence of view, not on military strategy, but on those wider industrial values. These include the free flow of technological innovation between a country's civilian and military sectors, the preservation of state bureaucratic perogatives in guiding research, and defence of that research from foreign exploitation. This suggests that techno-bureaucratic nationalism lies at the heart of Japan's military overspending.

How does defence production dominate Japan's security affairs? The answer arises from the threat that political bartering of weapons technology poses to those systemic supply-side values noted above. The weakening of transatlantic defence cooperation has brought greater pressure on Japan to ensure the continued superiority of the U.S. weapons sector. Close integration with the U.S. at this level, however, blocks Japan's attempts to gain wider global access to technology. Further, the 'free flow' principle is seriously jeopardised by secrecy rules insisted on by the Pentagon. Most basically, closer military technology exchange requires that the Japanese state compel corporate cooperation with the U.S. The continuing option for the state, therefore, of sacrificing *kokusanka* interests to alliance norms, seems unsustainable, as the trade-offs involved now directly threaten the most basic elements of the protective bureaucratic mantle built over defence supply since the 1960s. Bureaucratic defence of this framework gains added political cogency from the imminent likelihood of U.S. military retrenchment in Asia. This latter development will undermine the link between the American willingness to protect and Japan's obligation to conform to the 1951 Security Treaty. Within the Japanese state the threat to systemic supply-side values thus points to a sharp decline in the willingness of the National Defence Council to mediate Japanese-U.S. supplier conflicts in a manner acceptable to Washington.

Appendix A
Japan's Military Strength 1990

Total personnel on active duty	249,000
Army (Five regional commands)	
Personnel	156,200
Main battle tanks	1,222
(Type 61 and type 74)	
SAM	
Stinger 48	180
Type 81 Tan	48
Improved Hawk	200

Air Force	
Personnel	46,400
Combat aircraft	387
Missiles	Not supplied
ASM:ASM-1	
AAM:AAM-1	
AIM-7 Sparrow	
AIM-9 Sidewinder	
SAM:6 air defence groups with 180 Nike J.	
(Patriot replacing)	

Navy

Personnel	46,400
Submarines	15
DDG Destroyers (armed with area SAM)	6
Frigates	58
Patrol and Coastal Combatant	14
Mine warfare	49
Mine Countermeasures	48

Para-Military

Maritime Safety Agency Personnel	12,000
Patrol vessels	335

Source: *The Military Balance 1990-91, pp.164-166. The International Institute for Strategic Studies (London), Brassey.*

Notes

1. Outline of Japan's Defence Budget 1990. Japan Defence Agency. See also Drifte, R., (1990), *Japan's Rise to International Responsibility: The Case of Arms Control*, Athlone Press. According to Drifte, if the NATO yardstick is used Japan's real spending had reached $41 billion U.S. by 1988. p. 14.
2. Source. Defence Agency.
3. *The Military Balance* (1990-91). The Ground Self Defence Force is thus considerably below its authorised ceiling of 180,000 troops. In June 1991 the Japan Defence Agency began a drastic reorganisation of the GSDF that will put the weight of its strength in Hokkaido facing the sea of Okhotsk and the (former) Soviet Far East military district. See *Asia Pacific Defence Reporter*, (August 1991), 'Defence Planners Uneasy'.
4. This is the view of Bruce Roscoe, an analyst with Goldman Sachs in Tokyo who has made a study of profitability in Japan's defence production sector. *The Economist*, (2 February, 1991). See also *The Economist*, (4 August, 1990).
5. Luckham, R., (1990), 'American Militarism and the Third World: The End of the Cold War?', Working Paper No. 94, Peace Research Centre, Research School of Pacific Studies, ANU. See Abstract.
6. Kaldor, M. , (1986), 'The Weapons Succession Process', *World Politics*, vol. xxxviii no. 4, pp. 577-595.

7. Kaldor, M., (see note 6), p. 580.
8. Kaldor notes that '...a more complete analysis of the systemic aspect would require an assessment of theories of international conflict and the current global order...' *Ibid*. p. 580. This is a complex requirement which is not fully addressed in this chapter.
9. *Ibid*. p. 580.
10. See Umegaki, M., (1988), 'The Politics of Japanese Defence', ch 4, pp. 53-74 in Gibert, S.P. (ed), *Security in Northeast Asia - Approaching the Pacific Century,* Westview Press.
11. Green, M.J., (May 1990), 'Kokusanka: FS-X and Japan's search for autonomous defence production', Centre for International Studies, Massachusetts Institute of Technology. Green notes, 'Based on receipts on income alone, defence contracting is not profitable. With *kokusanka,* however, there are often other advantages in the form of expanded resource utilisation, experimentation with spin-on applications of technology, systems integration experience, and momentum in technology development', p. 7.
12. See Drifte, R., (1990), *Japan's Foreign Policy,* Chatham House Paper, Routledge, p. 32.
13. 'Guidelines for Japan-U.S. Defence Cooperation', (November 1978), See *Defence of Japan,* (1989), JDA, pp. 97-99.
14. *See Far Eastern Economic Review (FEER),* (30 November, 1989), p. 25.
15. According to *FEER,* (22 February, 1990), Japanese aviation today is dependent on the state for 70 per cent of its orders and if repair work is included, 92.5 per cent.
16. Drifte, R., (see note 12), p. 29.
17. *Ibid.,* p. 31.
18. *Ibid.,* p. 31.
19. See Green , M.J., (see note 11), pp. 38-40.
20. For the extent of U.S. dependency on foreign military technology in 1986, see Awanohara, S., (28 February, 1991), 'On the Defensive', *FEER.*
21. In 1988 the budget allocation covered 37 per cent of the reported $7.1 billion U.S. cost of maintaining U.S. military bases. *The Daily Yomiuri,* (10 October, 1990). The most recent indications (late 1991) are that the U.S. prefers to base troops pulled out of South Korea in Japan rather than Guam, Hawaii or the continental U.S. because of host nation support.
22. *Japan Times,* (early October 1990).
23. There was more to Tokyo's prompt response than met the eye. This will be explained at a later point.

24. *The Daily Yomiuri*, (3 October, 1990). It was indicated that the Government was to focus its efforts on covering all yen-based expenses for U.S. forces in the new 1991-1995 defence build-up. These expenses would appear to run to more than half the total cost of maintaining the U.S. bases.

25. *Japan Times*, (early October, 1990).

26. Ishikawajima Harima was controlled by Doko Toshio, the Chairman of the Administrative Reform Council which had imposed strict fiscal discipline on the Japanese economy in the early and mid-80s. Defence, however, had been exempted from budget cuts. In 1988 Ishikawajima Harima changed its articles of incorporation to make weapons production a prime purpose. Source: *Tokyo Insider*, (May 1988).

27. *The Economist*, (2 February, 1990), reported that between 1990 and 1991 Pentagon procurements were to fall from $82.6 billion to $77.9 billion, i.e. nearly $5 billion.

28. *The Daily Yomiuri*, (17 November, 1989).

29. In recent years there has been considerable pressure from the MSDF for a light aircraft carrier, and from the ASDF for air refuelling tankers. Authority for these power projection items has, however, been consistently denied by the Diet.

30. The latter point had undoubtedly caused the JDA to modify its equipment demands as a defensive measure, but it remained publicly committed to acquiring most of the items the U.S. wished to sell to Japan in the longer term.

31. Source: Foreign Defence Attaché based in Tokyo.

32. Source: as above.

33. The additional funds constituted just over 2 per cent of the 1991 budget of Y=4.4 trillion.

34. In February 1990 Richard Cheney the U.S. Defence Secretary, arrived in Tokyo with a list of militarily critical technologies. Among the new technologies the U.S. was interested in were semi-conductors and gallium arsenide, a material that considerably enhances semi-conductor performance, carbon fibre, pre-impregnated composite materials derived from civilian synthetic fibre technology, electro-optics, optical fibres, 'third generation' tank armour, advanced guidance systems (e.g. the charge coupler device CCD) for missiles, carbon dioxide lasers to 'blind' enemy aircraft and satellites, technology to mask the magnetic fields of submarines and engine research on ultra high speed (2,000 mph +) aircraft. Source: *Business Tokyo*, (June 1990).

35. Japan Federation of Economic Organisations.

36. *Business Tokyo*, (June 1990), p. 23.

37. Source: Defence Production Committee, Keidanren, Tokyo.
38. *Defence Production in Japan*, (September 1990). Issued by the Defence Production Committee, p. 1.
39. *Ibid*. p. 1.
40. Calculated from figures provided by Keidanren.
41. Figures provided by Keidanren.
42. See Samuels, R.J. and Whipple, B.C., (1989), *Defence Production and Industrial Development: The Case of Japanese Aircraft*, MIT Japan Science and Technology Programme, pp. 13-14.
43. Source: Figures supplied by Keidanren. The comparison with U.S. companies is striking. If the top five U.S. contractors in 1988 are considered, McDonnell Douglas, with a market share of 5.83 per cent, had a dependency ratio of 53.1 per cent. General Dynamics, receiving 4.75 per cent of Pentagon contracts, had a dependency ratio of 68.29 per cent.
44. For example NEC received 4.7 per cent of JDA contracts in 1989; however military business amounted to only 2.8 per cent of total sales turnover.
45. Interview with Mr Tsutsui Ryozo, Director-General of TRDI. Tokyo, 9 October, 1990.
46. There has in fact been a marked levelling off in nominal weapons procurements since 1988. This however, appears more related to temporary problems within the SDF than to any long-term intention to cut back on the level of hardware spending.
47. Japan has no equivalent of the U.S. Congressional Office of Management and Budget, or the Defence Select Committee in the U.K.

9

Business Patterns in Nuclear Commerce and Nuclear Non-proliferation

Daniel W. Skubik

Introduction

The continuing export of nuclear energy generating technologies for energy generation carries a continuing risk of horizontal weapons proliferation.[1] This is of special concern when nuclear technologies are transferred to or between developing countries. As Professor William Potter has noted:

> Few popular and misleading ideas have proved more resilient than the belief that there are good 'atoms for peace' and bad 'atoms for war'. In fact, U.S. nuclear policy for much of the first three decades after Hiroshima nurtured this misconception by actively promoting the development of civilian, and presumably safe, nuclear technologies with little regard for their military or dangerous implications. Nevertheless, the raw materials and technology for the production of nuclear weapons and civilian nuclear power are essentially the same.[2]

Similarly misleading is the notion that the nuclear Non-Proliferation Treaty (NPT), commonly understood to be the cornerstone of any viable non-proliferation regime, places a significant check on the transfer of nuclear technologies between states. Opened for signature in July 1968, the NPT actually provides a counterproductive trade-off: the state parties are committed not to transfer or receive 'nuclear weapons or other nuclear explosive devices' (Articles I and II); but this pledge comes at the price of formal recognition that 'research, production and use of nuclear energy for peaceful purposes' is an 'inalienable right' of all parties, accompanied by an explicit undertaking by Nuclear Weapons States (NWS) to assiduously pursue 'the fullest possible exchange of equipment, materials and scientific and technological information for the peaceful uses of nuclear energy' with Non-Nuclear Weapons States (NNWS) as well as share 'potential benefits from any peaceful applications of nuclear explosions' (Articles IV and V). Paul Leventhal, of the Nuclear Control Institute in Washington, D.C., suggests that 'the non-proliferation system is really a proliferation system, ... the very treaty and safeguard regime helps promote the spread' of nuclear weapons.[3]

The developing world has not been entirely pleased with the advances made during the 20 plus years of the NPT regime. Discontent has been registered on two levels. The more publicised concerns have been over the reluctance of Nuclear Weapons States (NWS) to move towards eliminating their nuclear weapon stockpiles, a commitment they undertook in Article VI of the NPT. Such public statements are often accompanied by the threat that the NPT regime is 'endangered' (diplomatic language for 'you disarm or we'll arm, anyway'). Less publicised but more important, is the Non-Nuclear Weapons States' (NNWS) concern that NWS are withholding useful nuclear technologies from the developing world. The suspicion that technology transfers have not been readily forthcoming was expressed by Malaysia's Prime Minister, Dr Mahathir. When Malaysia signed a nuclear cooperation agreement with Pakistan in 1984, Dr Mahathir declared that, 'Western countries who control nuclear technology will not give it to us on a golden plate and, therefore, the developing countries must cooperate in this field to help each other'.[4]

A great many studies have addressed important political and

technical issues concerning technology transfers and proliferation controls. From the 1980s, for example, Professor Potter's seminal work *Nuclear Power and Nonproliferation,*[5] Snyder and Wells' edited collection entitled *Limiting Nuclear Proliferation,*[6] and Lewis Dunn's *The Emerging Nuclear Suppliers*[7] have all probed nation-states' policies and the activities of governmental actors concerning nuclear energy and proliferation regimes.

No published study to date however, has surveyed the global *business* patterns or the international and national legal impacts of such commercial transfers to developing states. This missing data is crucial to understanding the generation of nuclear expectations amongst the various actors, discerning proliferation implications and formulating viable policies for managing better political and economic relations between developed and developing states. This chapter identifies nuclear commerce and nuclear law as two core variables in the proliferation equation.[8]

Nuclear Commerce Database

As expected, a lot of useful information is classified. Nevertheless, a surprising amount of information on nuclear commerce is available in the public domain. Unfortunately, much of it is expensive, widely scattered, and difficult or tedious to correlate once gathered. For example, specialist industry trade journals carry significant coverage of nuclear deals, but subscription prices hover around U.S.$1000/year. Even universities with significant nuclear physics programmes find such costs daunting, and a knowledge of nuclear physics is essential to understanding the scientific information contained within them.

Much the same can be said of the available legal literature. Primary and secondary legal sources are also expensive and require considerable legal knowledge as well. Thus, the difficulties associated with access to nuclear commercial and legal information (what economists call the transaction costs of research) make research into this subject difficult.

User-friendly computerised databases however, provide an opportunity to collect and manipulate such data. The creation of this sort of database is the purpose of Professor William Potter's *Emerging Nuclear Suppliers Project* (ENSP) at the Monterey

Institute of International Studies in California. The *Project* is funded by a variety of governmental and non-governmental bodies. The researchers who are sensitive to the scientific and political issues of nuclear proliferation code, enter data according to a strict set of *Project* protocols. The resultant records can easily be searched and manipulated by social scientists without much specialist nuclear knowledge.

The ENSP database comprises three integrated data files: the interactive data file; the country attribute data file; and the bibliographic data file. Together they provide a portfolio of details covering transactions in nuclear technologies, information or commodities; associated structures for these transactions, such as licensing procedures for import/export/transit of sensitive items, indigenous capabilities of NNWS to develop or export nuclear commodities or services and the norms which cover these transactions, international treaties, domestic laws or public policies.

The power of the ENPS system lies in the steady accumulation of data by the *Project* staff, and the ability to search the database for various combinations of the nuclear transaction states and firms. In sum, the ENSP database represents a powerful tool for collecting data otherwise virtually unavailable to non-proliferation researchers.[9]

Nuclear Commerce in the Asia Pacific Region

In order to illustrate the utility and power of the ENSP database, the rest of this chapter will focus on nuclear commerce in the Asia Pacific region with special reference to ASEAN.

Nuclear Technology in ASEAN

The transfer of nuclear technologies to ASEAN countries over the past 20 years has been marked by one very well publicised failure – the Bataan Nuclear Power Plant (BNPP) in the Philippines, but also by less well publicised yet significant successes in Thailand, Malaysia, Indonesia, and also the Philippines. The now-mothballed nuclear power plant at Bataan in the Philippines provides a good negative example of the expansion of nuclear technology.

After extensive negotiations during 1973-74, General Electric (U.S.) was in an excellent position to land a contract to build the Philippines', and Southeast Asia's, first nuclear power plant. The Philippine decision to go nuclear for electricity generation was a response to the colossal rise in oil prices by OPEC, and General Electric's proposal seemed to provide the Marcos government a means of maintaining some control over energy costs while providing additional electricity generating capacity for industrial growth. Plans for a 600MWe PWR plant[10] were drawn-up in late 1974, a formal contract being signed in February 1976 after detailed location, design and price negotiations during 1975, but the contract was won by Westinghouse Electric – G.E.'s principal U.S. competitor. Construction of the plant was finally completed in early 1985, although it has never yet produced a single watt of electricity. It remains a U.S.$2.2 billion white elephant, costing Manila some U.S.$350,000 per day in loan interest charges alone.

Just why and how Westinghouse was able to secure the contract remains unclear. Whether the plant is capable of safely coming on-line is likewise uncertain. Indeed, these matters were recent subjects of litigation in the U.S. federal courts: the Aquino government filed several law suits against the firm, alleging *inter alia* defective construction, inflated pricing, fraud, and the bribery of Marcos himself to secure the original deal.[11]

While it remains unlikely that nuclear power will become an important source of electricity for the Philippines, it may relatively soon provide a stop-gap supply. Aquino came to power on the political promise that the Bataan Nuclear Power Plant would *never* be put into service, but some leaders in the local business community strongly argue that it should come on-line to eliminate the regular blackouts and spur economic growth,[12] at least until substitute plants (e.g. coal-powered) can be built. The recent out-of-court settlement the Aquino government reached with Westinghouse provides for future operations covering just that purpose, and President Ramos has pledged to get the settlement approved by the legislature. Despite this negative example, other nuclear facilities in the ASEAN states do play a positive role in nuclear research.

Nuclear research facilities are varied in size and use, but are normally small reactor units, useful for training university students and power authority staff in the basics of nuclear physics and engineering, as well as supporting medical and agricultural projects (e.g. production of isotopes for diagnostic imaging of patients in hospital, and irradiation of food or sterilisation of insect pests).[13] The Philippines, Malaysia and Thailand each operate one such facility within their respective borders, while Indonesia boasts three separate sites. While not every state with a research reactor has plans to go nuclear (e.g. Australia, which currently operates two research reactors but has no plans for nuclear generation), every country which has gone nuclear began its nuclear programme with expansion of research facilities to gain the necessary experience.[14] This is the case with Thailand, which had (pre-coup) announced its desire to mount a nuclear energy programme to meet growing power demands, and held preliminary talks with Taiwan about construction and financing of plants which might come on-line about 2010. The clearest example of this step-by-step expansion is Indonesia, where plans are well advanced to have the first of between seven and twelve plants[15] generating electricity by the turn of the century (current projections being 2002-03 for the first plant).

Indonesian authorities toyed with the idea of going nuclear in the early 1970s, participating in the International Atomic Energy Agency's (IAEA) 1973 nuclear marketing survey, a subsequent nuclear power planning study in 1975,[16] followed by pre-feasibility studies conducted in 1976. Although plans for a nuclear power plant were deferred, expansion of research facilities did move forward, along with training of specialised personnel. By the mid-1980s, Indonesia had signed agreements for major research facilities with companies from Canada, France, Germany, Italy, and the United States. The most recent facility at Serpong, opened by President Suharto in December 1989, is one of the largest and most sophisticated sites in Asia[17] and has been said to be 'the third largest of its kind in the world'.[18] The agreements also included training of staff in various locales: 68 BATAN personnel in Canada,[19] 25 engineers and operators in Germany, and 50 local engineers are receiving on-site training at Serpong, and a new agreement will permit electricity company staff to travel to South Korea for training in the management of nuclear energy facilities.

The 1976 pre-feasibility study was updated in 1987 at Indonesia's invitation by Nuclear Power International (NPI) a joint venture of Framatome (France) and Kraftwerk Union (KWU) a German firm which is now a subsidiary of Siemens AG, a German multinational corporation, Atomic Energy of Canada Limited (A.E.C.L.), and a consortium consisting of Mitsubishi Heavy Industries Limited (Japan), Westinghouse Electric (U.S.), and Ansaldo (Italy). A Swiss consulting firm, Motor Columbus, was chosen to evaluate Build Operate Transfer (BOT) construction options[20] in the bids put by the pre-feasibility study parties.

Bids for full feasibility studies were called in 1989, with the award of a U.S.$11 million contract to New Japan Engineering Consultants Inc., a unit of Kansai Electric Company Limited (Japan), in May 1991. The consultants are to spend the next two years evaluating prospective sites on Java (including one on the Muria Peninsula) and a range of designs.[21] After discussion and evaluation of that document, an additional two years will be given to finalising designs and bids so that a determination can be made as to who will build what, where and for how much.

Proliferation Implications

Japanese companies – like Mitsui and Mitsubishi – have made clear to Ministry of International Trade and Industry (MITI) and other government officials that the best way for Japan to maintain competence and profitability in the nuclear energy sector at home is to expand into export markets abroad. Such suggested moves are not of themselves unusual, in this or any other sector of an industrial economy, as evidenced by the export activities of most U.S., European, and Japanese firms. What gives pause is that Japan has explicitly targeted Southeast Asia as a viable market to ensure Japanese dominance in the transfer of nuclear technologies.[22] Rather than competing directly with larger, better established exporters from the U.S. and Europe, Japanese companies have sought and concluded joint venture agreements with those firms in order to develop their export capabilities in this market. (Conversely, U.S. firms are able to use Japanese partners to help overcome the very poor public relations generated by Westinghouse's problematic foray in the Philippines.) Thus, of the four sets of bids originally tendered to BATAN for nuclear energy plants, two involved consortia combining leading Japanese and U.S. firms.

The process of who is invited or permitted to bid and who survives the first evaluative rounds is strongly influenced by a recognition of Japanese negotiating strength in the region. Although the Japanese government has consistently refused Official Development Assistance (ODA) for nuclear power studies,[23] they remain the largest aid donor and investor in the area. Thus, it is not surprising a Japanese firm was awarded the feasibility study contract, and it is highly likely the Mitsubishi consortium (which has strong ties to Kansai) will be awarded the Build Operate Transfer (BOT) contract after the final feasibility study is filed with BATAN in 1995-96.[24] The dangers which may flow from this export transfer trend, are as follows. The least likely are:

1. *Terrorism.* Nuclear plants make attractive potential terrorist targets, both for theft and destruction. Theft of sensitive or toxic materials could pose a danger to the region – imagine Fretilin with a radioactive waste bomb capable of threatening Jakarta's water supplies. (Conventional or guerilla attacks against an operating installation also seriously threaten release of radioactive vapours with consequences potentially greater than Chernobyl.)

2 *Indonesia gets the bomb.* Some Australian academic and military analysts are privately worried about whether President Suharto or his military leaders are surreptitiously planning to expand indigenous nuclear capabilities to eventually produce nuclear weapons, posing a threat to Australia and the wider region. While the Iraq experience demonstrated that a determined leader can beat the current IAEA inspection and accounting safeguards system, there appears little reason to suspect Indonesian authorities are playing that game. While it is clear that the linkage between civilian and military nuclear capabilities is close, it is not simple. Other motivating factors – perceived military threats from within the region, prestige and need of foreign policy clout, abiding desire for territorial expansion, etc. – must combine with scientific and economic capabilities before a serious weapons programme could be

launched. Indonesia is not a likely proliferator on these crite-ria, now or in the near future, and is much more likely to take seriously its regional and international normative commit-ments to safeguards and the peaceful development of energy resources.[25]

A more problematic and likely scenario is that Indonesia may become an independent conduit or export source of nuclear energy expertise and equipment. In this regard, attention should be drawn to an analysis of this trans-shipping/re-export capability. These capabilities are principally of two types. The first type, namely technology transfer, between 'third world' states is much less a proliferation problem, than the second. This first is effectively a transfer between 'first world' subsidiaries located in developing countries: a recent transfer between Brazil and Argentina, for example, is evidence of this multinational *intra-company* transfer (from a KWU subsidiary in Brazil to its sister KWU subsidiary in Argentina). No new capabilities of expertise or sensitive nuclear related items, clearly flow from such movements.

A second type of transfer is more worrying, and represents the potential proliferation problem in the Southeast Asian context. Indonesia has nuclear cooperation links with Malaysia, and through Malaysia with Pakistan, and is discussing nuclear links with Iran.[26] The point is not that the world needs fear some sort of 'Islamic bomb'. But Argentina's transfer of technology to Algeria indicates careful notice should be taken of transfers between indigenous atomic energy authorities where the importing coun-tries cannot or will not undertake international obligations to use nuclear technologies for peaceful purposes only. Thus, one can imagine Pakistan continuing its nuclear weapons programme with the aid of developing Indonesian expertise early next century since it faces bans from North America and European exporters.[27] Indonesian incentives, to assist such proliferation, like that of Argentina, are economic as well as political: such cooperation would promise some level of prestige and independence from 'first world' suppliers, as well as supplying opportunities to earn over-seas dollars from ready, friendly purchasers.

Whether these more worrisome sorts of transfers occur de-pends on a variety of factors. But one important set of factors commonly overlooked is the quality of the relationship between developed countries' firms and developing countries' governments. That is, like Japan's qualitative negotiation leverage in securing initial contracts, the quality of the consortium's relationship with BATAN will affect the creation and strength of any incentives for Indonesia to re-export its growing expertise to gain additional experience and income.

Just how to measure and judge the quality of these nuclear relationships is the subject of current research utilising the database described above. Hypotheses for consideration based on a preliminary analysis of the data available are:

1. Proliferation behaviours are inversely correlated with:
   (a) Marginal nuclear energy production due to failure of direct transfer ventures to establish plants in developing countries.
   (b) Legal actions which lessen business confidence between firms and states.
   (c) Developed countries' training policies being inconsistent with their general equipment and services export policies.
2. The absence of, or a decrease in, proliferation behaviours is directly correlated with:
   (a) Successful production of electricity fulfilling contractual obligations and parties' expectations.
   (b) Use of mediation or arbitration to resolve disputes which arise between firms and states.
   (c) Developed countries' nuclear training policies being as generous as their equipment and services export policies.

In brief, how the consortium conducts its business over the short term, and how well the power plants meet the parties' expectations, will give a good indication of what proliferation concerns will materialise in the Asia Pacific region over the longer term.

Notes

1. 'Horizontal' proliferation being the construction and deployment of nuclear weapons by previously non-nuclear weapons states; to be

distinguished from 'vertical' proliferation, which constitutes the modernisation or enhancement of weapons by states already possessing nuclear arms.

2. Potter, W.C., (September 1987), 'Creating a Database on International Nuclear Commerce', CISA, UCLA Centre for International and Strategic Affairs, Working Paper No. 59, p. 1.

3. Rufford, N. and Leppard, D., (7-8 December 1991), 'How the West Gave Saddam the Bomb', *The Weekend Australian,* Review Section, p. 2.

4. *Nucleonics Week,* (5 April 1984), p. 7. This agreement quickly took substantive form with the report that Pakistani scientists were to assist Malaysia with a new nuclear research centre. *Nuclear Engineering International,* (June 1984), p. 13.

5. Potter, W.C., (1982), *Nuclear Power and Non-proliferation: An Interdisciplinary Perspective,* Oelgeschlager, Gunn and Hain.

6. Snyder, J.C., and Wells, S.F. Jr., (1985), *Limiting Nuclear Proliferation,* Ballinger Publishing.

7. Dunn, L.A., (February 1988), *The Emerging Nuclear Suppliers: Some Guidelines for Policy*, CISA, UCLA Centre for International and Strategic Affairs, Working Paper No. 61.

8. This assertion is not meant to slight some valuable recent work which is beginning to take commercial-cum-legal considerations seriously, e.g. the collection of conceptual analyses and country case studies in Potter, William C. (ed.), (1990), *International Nuclear Trade and Non-proliferation: The Challenge of the Emerging Suppliers,* Lexington Books. But more detailed and focused work is yet to be produced.

9. A full copy of this database is operating at Griffith University as well as Monterey.

10. MWe = Megawatt electric, i.e. 600 million watts of usable electricity would be generated by the plant. The PWR = Pressurised Water Reactor, one of a variety of reactor designs for heating water to generate steam to turn turbine generators to produce electricity. PWRs (and their modified modern varieties) are the most common reactors in use today.

11. For details *see* Dumaine, B., (September 1986), 'The $2.2 Billion Nuclear Fiasco', *Fortune,* 1 , pp. 15-22; Patanne, E.P., (February 1989), 'A Tangled Web' in Wrestling Over Nuclear Power', *Asian Business,* pp. 30-31; and Blum, A., (Monday, 23 September 1991), 'Groups Challenge Seal on Bribe-Suit Papers', *The National Law Journal,* p. 9. To be fair to Westinghouse, it should be noted that an arbitration panel of the International Chamber of Commerce in Geneva recently concluded that neither Westinghouse nor Burns and Roe Enterprises (a major subcontractor on the project) actually bribed Marcos: while the Tribunal

accepted there existed a 'fair amount of evidence' that Westinghouse intended to bribe him or at least were not overly concerned with where some money was going, there was 'no direct evidence' that Westinghouse succeeded in winning the contract because of such payments to/through national sales representatives like Herminio Disini, a first cousin of Imelda Marcos. (See Jim Strader's news item to the Associated Press on 30 December 1991.) On the basis of this arbitration decision, Westinghouse will ask the U.S. Federal Court to dismiss the Philippine's civil case against it.

12. Hydropower output on Mindanao, for example, is producing less than half the demand, forcing brown and black-outs of over 10 hours/day. Manila, too, is suffering power outages, though less severely. See Clift, J., news item to Reuters, (14 January 1992), 'Oil Find May Ease Bleak Philippines' Energy Outlook'.

13. That ASEAN states are fully involved in these activities, one might note that the Fifth Asia and Oceania Congress of Nuclear Medicine and Biology scheduled for 25-30 October 1992 will be organised by and held in Indonesia (Jakarta and Bali).

14. Indeed, in terms of horizontal proliferation of nuclear weapons, re-search reactors are more dangerous than civil nuclear power plants in that weapons-grade material can more easily be created, diverted and converted to military uses from the former. Recall that the Israelis bombed Iraq's French-built research reactor, Ossirac, in June 1981 just before it became operational because of their now well-estab-lished fears that nuclear weapons were Hussein's purpose.

15. The first two expected to be 600MWe and 1000MWe, with all eventu-ally fueled by Indonesia's own uranium.

16. See *Nuclear Power Planning Study for Indonesia,* (1976), Java Island, Vienna: IAEA.

17. The site includes a 30MWt reactor, radio-metallurgical laboratory and radioisotope production plant. Nine different firms from five countries, representing Canada, France, Germany, Italy and the United States, participated in financing, supplying and constructing major portions of this facility.

18. Richardson, M., (8 September 1988), 'Fossil Fuels Pollutants Prompting Indonesia to Press for Nuclear Power', *International Herald Tribune.*

19. BATAN is the acronym for Baden Tenaga Atom Nasional, the Indone-sian Atomic Energy Agency. Top posts are currently held by Djali Ahimsa, who is BATAN's Director General, and Iiyos R. Subki, the Deputy Director General. Other officials involved in Indonesia's nu-clear decision making include Bacharuddin Jusuf Habibie, Minister of Research and Technology, and Mursid Jokolelono, Head of the

Nuclear Study Centre.

20. Indonesia is seeking to transfer the lion's share of contract risks to builders by calling for a Build-Operate-Transfer package. An increasingly utilised foreign direct investment option, such a package is similar to turnkey projects but includes the mandate for the builder to operate the plant for some specified number of years in order to recover most of its construction costs. Only then is the plant turned over to the purchaser.

21. A fourth bidder, a second consortium comprising Mitsui, Toshiba, Hitachi (all of Japan), with General Electric (U.S.) never represented a serious challenge to the other three bids and was relatively quickly dropped from consideration. NPI is having second thoughts about BOT guarantees, a similar deal having recently fallen through with Turkey, and so the viable bids are AECL versus the Japan-U.S. consortium.

22. Northeast Asia also represents possible market opportunities, but Taiwan and South Korea are as much potential competitors as they are buyers for Japanese export sales.

23. During the 'First International Conference for Nuclear Cooperation in Asia', promoted and hosted by Japan in March 1990, Indonesia, for the third year running, asked for $10 million to fund a final feasibility study for a BOT plant; and for the third time the request was denied. For all that, Japanese officials of the Science and Technology Agency recognise that regional cooperation programmes will require financial assistance including ODA. Participating countries at this conference included Indonesia, Malaysia, the Philippines, Peoples Republic of China, South Korea, and Thailand.

24. It might also be noted in passing that Japan has made some inroads to supplying Malaysia's nuclear research centre. An agreement covering 1988/89 saw the transfer of an electron beam accelerator along with six technical experts for training purposes.

25. E.g. Indonesia is a party to the NPT, and is a member in good standing of the IAEA. It likewise understands its commitment to a nuclear free ASEAN, and its general support of nuclear free zones like the South Pacific Nuclear Free Zone Treaty (SPNFZ), as consistent with the development of peaceful uses of nuclear power.

26. Pakistani scientists assisted in the establishment of Malaysia's nuclear research centre from June 1984; President Zia publicly called for nuclear cooperation between Muslim countries and this call has been reiterated by Sharif; Indonesia and Malaysia have discussed nuclear cooperation at highest levels, including a meeting between President Suharto and Prime Minister Mahathir in August 1989 (discussions having so far touched upon Malaysia tapping into Indonesia's electricity

grid to purchase any extra capacity generation, and sharing technical expertise between the nuclear research centres); and Reza Amrollahi, President of Iran's Atomic Energy Organisation, visited Jakarta in March 1990 to discuss nuclear cooperation, and invited Indonesian Vice President Sudharmono to visit Iran, an invitation which was accepted.

27. Pakistan, of course, will now look to China, which recently agreed to help finance and build a 600MWe PWR, for as long as OECD exporters are unavailable. But the Chinese are not as technologically advanced as Pakistan would like. Direct experience with more modern, Western plants is a perceived advantage.

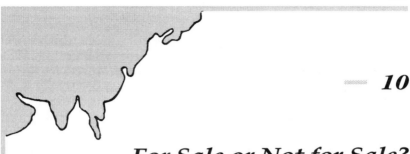

10

For Sale or Not for Sale? Attitudes of the North West to the South East on Arms Proliferation and Security

Scilla Elworthy

It is hard to overstate the enormity of the tide of change that has overwhelmed Europe in the past five years, leaving once-solid organisations (like NATO and the European Community) spluttering and scrambling to regain their foothold. For example:

* The Ukraine has asked for U.S. expert help in dismantling its nuclear weapons.
* Poland, Hungary, and the Czech and Slovak Federal Republics have applied to join both the European Community and NATO;[1] the Russian Republic wants to join NATO.[2]
* NATO troops are ready to distribute food in the former Soviet Union.[3]
* The U.S. administration has approved arms sales to Hungary, Poland and the Czech and Slovak Federal Republics.[4]
* A nuclear reactor has turned up for sale at the Moscow International Commodity Exchange![5]

There are four organisations vying for dominance in defence and security decision-making in Europe. This chapter will examine their attitudes to the Asia Pacific region, and the implications of the changes in Europe in two key security fields which affect the region namely, arms sales, and nuclear proliferation. The chapter will conclude with an analysis of the prospects for future security in the Asia Pacific region.

The Four Organisations

There are principally four institutions which now have a strong interest in decision-making on security and defence in the new Europe:

1. The Western European Union (WEU), set up in 1948, which now has nine members.
2. The North Atlantic Treaty Organisation (NATO), set up in 1949, with 16 members.
3. The European Community (EC), established in 1958, now with 12 members.
4. The Conference on Security and Cooperation in Europe (CSCE), which began its first session in 1973, and now has 52 members.

The overlapping membership of these organisation, plus the Council of Europe and the European Free Trade Association (EFTA), are shown in the diagram on the next page.[6]

The Western European Union (WEU) is the oldest, and the least known of the four. It has simply been a talking shop, in the view of many, with occasional forays into the world of reality, for example, to (nominally) oversee military operations in the Gulf, in which NATO could not formally participate. It has no command structure of its own and no forces, but would: (a) be a convenient 'hat' under which NATO forces could operate outside the NATO area, and (b) be an ideal partner for the European Community to develop its own defence policy.

The North Atlantic Treaty Organisation (NATO) is an alliance for collective defence linking 14 European nations to the U.S. and Canada, who declare that an armed attack on one or more of them shall be regarded as an attack on all, and that each member country will assist any member so attacked. It is at present the only multi-national organisation with a well-established integrated military command structure. Critics say that NATO is so desperately in search of a reason to survive that it has reversed the classic rules of military planning – it has decided on the force structure needed for the future, without first either having a strategy or having identified an enemy. They also say that NATO has no developed political structure or experience to enable it to meet the wider security needs of Europe in the future, which will include dealing with massive economic inequalities between East and West, with migration, pollution and ethnic rivalry.

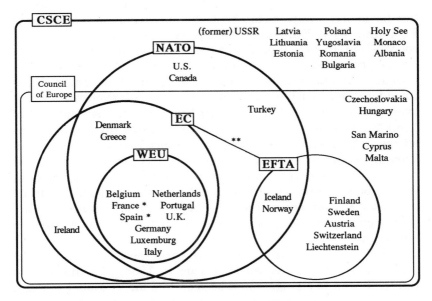

* Not part of the integrated military structure of NATO.
** There are strong economic links between the EC and EFTA, and there are fewer barriers to EFTA countries joining the EC.

The European Community (EC) comprises the Council (government representatives), the Commission (the executive civil servants), and the Parliament (518 directly elected members). The Parliament has very limited powers, and part of the December 1991 argument over the Maastricht Treaty on European

Union concerned additional powers for the Parliament. The Community has now decided to define and implement a common foreign and security policy, and the Western European Union (WEU) will be developed as the 'defence component' of the Twelve. This is significant, because the WEU's policy, unchanged since 1987, is one of nuclear deterrence.[7] The question therefore, is whether the European Community will become a nuclear power? The spotlight falls inevitably on the British and French nuclear forces, which would be the nucleus of a European nuclear superpower.

The Conference on Security and Cooperation in Europe (CSCE) has for nearly twenty years been the only forum for countries of East and West Europe to discuss arms control, security and cooperation. In 1975 it produced the Helsinki Final Act, which set out 10 principles to guide relations between states, and which is recognised as having been vital in promoting the human rights considerations which underpinned the peaceful revolutions which overturned Soviet rule in Eastern Europe in the second half of 1989. Since November 1990 the CSCE has had three permanent offices, a Secretariat in Prague, a Conflict Prevention centre in Vienna, and an Office for Free and Fair Elections in Warsaw. The biggest problem perceived in Europe is that of vast inequality in wealth between the countries of East Europe and West Europe and the CSCE is seen as having a key role to play, since it is the only organisation with all nations of East and West Europe as members.

All the changes that we have witnessed since the word *perestroika* entered the world lexicon in 1985, and the map of Europe began to change, must be seen in a larger global context. The number of sovereign states in the world has more than tripled since 1945, and the UN now has 166 members. There is both a strong sense of nationalism and, more importantly, a growing sense of regionalism, so that many communities which are bound by ethnic, religious or cultural ties wish to be governed as such. And yet 'international regionalism, particularly on security matters, still has to be invented'.[8] This question will be returned to in the last section.

In many ways, Europe is now facing challenges in the field of security which New Zealand and Australia understand rather well. These threats are less military ones than those born of economic inequality in the region, and fast-growing populations in some areas, resulting in economic migration, minority conflicts and tides of refugees. Let us hope Europe can learn from Australasian mistakes!

Attitudes to the Asia Pacific Region

The attitudes of these four organisations to the Asia Pacific region are lamentably inadequate. *NATO* refers to the Asia Pacific region in part of a document entitled *Broader Challenges*. It points out 'risks of a wider nature, including proliferation of weapons of mass destruction, disruption of the flow of vital resources, and actions of terrorism and sabotage, which can affect Alliance security interests'.[9] The prominence given to preventing proliferation and guarding resource availability aptly reflects the priorities of many Western nations, when it comes to the Southeast.

The attitude of the European Community depends on which institution is under analysis. The attitude of the European Parliament is to 're-iterate its request to the Commission and the Council to programme development aid multinationally by responding to specific needs ..... such aid should be concentrated on the poorest countries of Southeast Asia', and covers a host of detailed issues, including environmental protection, the indigenous population of West Papua, arms sales to rebel groups in the Philippines, and so on.[10] But the European Parliament has little power. The Council and Commission are more taken up with what has come to be called the 'East-South competition'.[11] There is now evident a marked preoccupation, where aid is concerned, in trying to solve the problems of Eastern Europe, probably at the expense of the South. 'The wells of international aid are gradually drying up for South Asia, as more interesting demands emerge from Eastern Europe, the Soviet Union, and perhaps China.'[12]

John Roper of *The Western European Union* expressed the general European attitude in a frank statement to the Oxford Research Group:

> I have to confess that usually when people in Western Europe think about implications for the South, they tend to think about implications for the Mediterranean rather than the

other side of the Equator. As far as I know, nothing in the discussions to date has in any way affected either French commitments to Polynesian defence and security or the residual British commitments under the five-power treaty of Manila... . There has been general discussion of the way in which a European Union might be able to contribute peace-keeping forces collectively to the United Nations as and when situations arose, but most of the contingencies contemplated have been north rather than south of the Equator.[13]

This general indifference to the security problems of the South is in stark contrast to a lively trading interest in Southeast Asia as the fastest growing economic region of the world. And the most significant trading items are armaments. Producing and selling weapons is the world's second biggest industry, after oil. Of the weapons produced annually by the world's weapons industries, about $60,000,000,000 worth are traded in the global arms market.

Arms Sales and Transfers

Here the first two words of the chapter title are the operative ones: FOR SALE. The region is becoming an ever more active arms bazaar, acting as magnet to salesmen from Europe and North America, whose home markets have shrunk dramatically as a result of the end of the Cold War. *The International Herald Tribune* ran an article in January 'An Arms Rush in South Asia', 'where merchants from around the world peddle Cold War left-overs, second-grade equipment and parts to buyers short on cash but eager to deal'. South Asia accounts for 24 per cent of all major weapons transferred to the developing world. (*The Times of Singapore* ran a conference in February 1992 entitled 'Meet the Emerging Military Powers of Asia', which had workshops on mine countermeasures and precision guided weapons, which was addressed by the Commander-in-Chief of the U.S. Pacific Command and the directors of the International Institute for Strategic Studies from London.)[14]

The biggest importers in the region are India, Japan, North Korea, Australia, Pakistan, Taiwan, Thailand and Indonesia, and the biggest exporters to the region are the U.S., the (former) Soviet

Union, France, the U.K., China, the Netherlands, Sweden, Italy and Germany.[15] The British government has a publicly-funded Defence Export Services Organisation with a budget of £8.4 million per annum to assist British companies to sell arms, with offices in India, Kuala Lumpur, Canberra, and South Korea. In addition, virtually every embassy has at least one military service attaché whose major responsibilities include assisting companies wishing to export to the area.

Perhaps the most significant power in this area is China, whose exports account for a significant proportion of the military imports of many Third World countries.

China's Exports of Major Conventional Weapons Systems to Selected Countries as % of their Total Imports of Such Systems

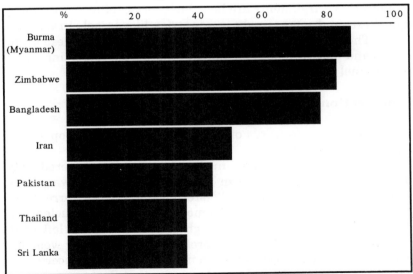

Source: SIPRI Yearbook 1991

Australia and New Zealand are by no means bit players in this market. For example, a team of U.S. and New Zealand companies is to offer modernised McDonnell Douglas A-4 Skyhawk aircraft for export. Some versions of the A-4 are nuclear capable. The Allied Aircraft Co. has been formed to manage the programme, and the aircraft will be based on the A-4K Kahu aircraft upgrade, developed by Smiths Industries in the U.S. for the Royal New Zealand Air Force, who will help with logistics and emergency services. The New Zealand company Safe Air will install new avionics.[16] The Australian Labor Party's relaxation of controls over arms exports was explained as follows by Defence Minister Robert Ray in advance of the AIDEX '92' exhibition:

> The benefits of the export market will serve to directly benefit the Australian people. If we cannot export we would be forced into the situation of having to import defence goods and, as a result, compromise self-reliance...[Defence exports are] vital for the survival of the country's defence industrial base.[17]

Both these arguments are heard in every capital in the North and West, and increasingly in countries like Israel, Brazil and Chile. The diagram on the next page illustrates how these arguments and motivations complement others from importing countries to fuel the arms trade.

Proliferation

Here the last three words of the chapter title are the operative ones: NOT FOR SALE.

The discoveries of Iraq's nuclear potential, uncovered only with the greatest difficulty in the months since the war, have jolted politicians in all the Western capitals into torrents of rhetoric, accusation and self-defence. North Korea's nuclear capacity has fallen under the spotlight, with the French left wing talking of the 'problem of chain proliferation of nuclear weapons from North Korea giving birth to a nightmare which concerns the whole of Asia',[18] and Washington's worries that Pyongyang 'is fast becoming Asia's Baghdad'.[19] Britain's newspapers have been full of horror at the idea that Soviet nuclear scientists might be bought by small countries wanting to develop nuclear weapons. In

January/February 1991, Western fears over chemical weapons
proliferation reached fever pitch during the Gulf War, but a
chemical weapons treaty has still not been signed.

If the tone of this argument sounds cynical, it is because these
two totally opposed attitudes – the promotion and encouragement
of sales of conventional weapons on the one hand, and the horri-
fied efforts to forbid and prevent the sales of nuclear weapons on
the other – constitute a double standard. Something is not being
said. Why should Western countries enthusiastically arm almost
every country in the world with certain weapons (the British
Foreign Office attitude is 'grant an export licence unless there is a
reason not to', not the other way round), while denying them the
weapon that it is maintained has kept the peace in Europe for
forty years?

The Main Factors Influencing the Arms Trade and their Inter-relationships

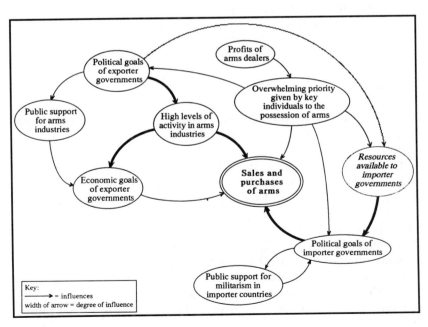

Scratch the surface of any argument in favour of (our) having nuclear weapons, however complex it may seem and underneath, if you go on long enough, you will find one simple statement, 'without nuclear weapons you cannot be a great power'. This is confirmed in interviews with nuclear weapons decision-makers in Britain.[20] Indeed, a very senior one of them told the Oxford Research Group recently that in his view about two thirds of all those 'in the business' had this visceral feeling for nuclear weapons, and that this number was not diminishing (as he would have expected) as the world gets further away in time from World War II. Bill Arkin puts it in another way:

> NATO is claiming for itself what it is trying to deny to Iraq and others – a nuclear deterrent. By insisting that nuclear bombs are needed in Europe as 'the ultimate [security] guarantee', despite the disappearance of the Soviet threat, NATO is admitting that it has no strategy for their use but wants them for another reason – prestige and influence.
>
> Similarly, the United States is now promoting a nuclear-free zone in the Middle East and considering one in South Asia, while a nuclear-free Europe remains beyond the pale.[21]

Conclusion

Until this double standard is resolved, it is doubtful if there can be any real prospect of peace and security in the Asia Pacific region.

On President Bush's 1992 Southeast Asia tour, much was heard of how the U.S. 'must maintain a military presence in Asia to discourage Japan and China'. Japan is indeed moving to reshape and expand its intelligence capabilities and military security. There are fears that Japan might develop nuclear weapons; this would oblige the U.S. either to keep pace in an economically ruinous nuclear arms race with Japan, or to accept the position of second-rate power. Neither alternative is desirable for the U.S., especially from a domestic political point of view. These are good reasons why it is in the U.S. interest to negotiate a test ban now, and to give pledges not only of vertical non-proliferation, but of building down nuclear weapons of all types.

The U.S. must also stop supplying reactor fuel to Japan. Three years ago, Washington gave Tokyo *carte blanche* to acquire all the plutonium it wanted from U.S.-supplied nuclear fuel. Britain and France will re-process Japan's spent reactor fuel and ship the plutonium back to Japan. Now South Korea, with its own large U.S.-built and fueled nuclear power programme, is seeking similar treatment. The United States, France and Britain cannot reasonably hope to divide the world into plutonium 'haves' and 'have nots'. Nor can they expect, to coin a phrase, to have their yellow-cake and eat it too.

This must happen in tandem with international agreements to control arms transfers. The UN Register of Arms Transfers, which will come into operation in 1993, will be a step forward in providing better information on arms sales. But much more is needed and fast. (The Oxford Research Group is shortly to publish a report, with contributions from experts and defence ministries throughout the world, on how the obstacles to international controls might be overcome.)

The five permanent members of the Security Council account for 80 per cent of the world's arms sales. Given political will, it is perfectly possible for them to reach agreement for stage by stage cuts in arms sales, and to provide financial incentives to their domestic industries for conversion. The first cut must be in the supply of plant and equipment for production in other countries – for example the sale to Chile by British Royal Ordnance of an entire plant to manufacture the Multiple Launch Rocket System.

A number of reputable commentators, people not normally given to hyperbole, are talking about the beginning of the Pacific century. It takes no more than common sense to realise that the Pacific – so unimaginably immense, so teeming with religious and cultural heritages that stress such laudable concepts as duty and devotion and asceticism – was inevitably going to assume global primacy one day.

The best vehicle for increased peace and security in the region may be a regional security system. Approaching security as a *system* has a great advantage – it involves economic, political, environmental and social issues as well as military ones. It would work from the principle of prevention of conflict, rather than cure, and it would do this by processes of confidence building and mediation, rather than by offering arms to this country or that, attempting to 'balance' military power and thus play God.

This solution is a great deal cheaper than a military solution. Europe's mistakes are clear. Before there is any talk of arms, equipment, soldiers, it is important we remember the members of NATO contribute $2,000,000,000[22] to NATO's infrastructure. The entire CSCE budget, by contrast, is $2,900,000.[23] If Southeast Asia continues to arm itself as it is doing, it will merely be subsidising cheaper weapons for the North. If it goes down the track of seeking security in rival blocs or military alliances, the costs will be astronomical, both in money and human lives. There are more cost-effective ways to build security. The peoples of this region have deep spiritual roots – traditions and values that have disappeared elsewhere. If they can re-assert them now, and use them, there is no doubt that they will build a security system in the Pacific which will make the whole world a safer place.

Notes

1. *Arms Control Reporter*, (7.9.91).
2. *Janes Defence Weekly*, (7.1.92).
3. Agreed at NATO Foreign Ministers' Meeting, Brussels, (19.12.91).
4. *Janes Defence Weekly,* (12.12.91).
5. *Financial Times*, London, (10.12.91).
6. For detailed descriptions of these organisations and their present roles, see *Defence and Security in the New Europe: who will decide?*, Current decisions report No. 7, Oxford Research Group, November (1991).
7. As set out in 'The Hague Platform on European Security Interests', (1987).
8. Sur, S., (1991), *The United Nations, Disarmament and Security*, United Nations Institute for Disarmament Research, New York.
9. *Rome Declaration on Peace and Cooperation,* Issued by the heads of state and governments participating in the meeting of the North Atlantic Council in Rome, 7/8 November 1991.
10. Resolution on the situation in Southeast Asia, (12.9.91).
11. Bonvicini, G., (June 1991), 'The Broader Political Framework' in *The Community and the Emerging European Democracies,* a joint policy of six security policy institutions.

12. Ghoshal, Baladas, Professor of International Relations, Jadavpur University Calcutta, *South Asia Security Dynamics: Problems and Prospects,* Occasional Paper, University of Illinois, Urbana-Champaign, August 1991.

13. Letter from John Roper, director WEU Institute for Security Studies, 8.1.92.

14. *Janes Defence Weekly*, (11.1.92).

15. Source: *SIPRI Yearbook*, (1991).

16. *Janes Defence Weekly,* (30.11.91).

17. *Janes Defence Weekly*, (23.11.91).

18. *Liberation*, 17 (17.12.9)1.

19. *Independent*, (21.11.91).

20. Hamwee, J. et. al., 'The Attitudes of British Nuclear Weapons Decision-Makers' in *Journal of Peace Research,* vol. 27, no. 4, November 1990.

21. *Bulletin of the Atomic Scientists,* December 1991.

22. NATO Sources, 19.11.91.

23. Budgets for the year 1992 for the CSCE secretariat, the Conflict Prevention Centre, the Office of Free Elections. 'Fourth Capital Meeting of the Committee of Senior Officials', Prague, 1991.

Part Three

The Prospects for Peace:
New Solutions to Old Problems

11

Multinational Maritime Peace-keeping – Should the UN Put to Sea?

*Mike Pugh **

In the new international environment it is vital that peace and security specialists start thinking creatively about peace-keeping and related activities. There are two major reasons for doing this. The first is that the concept of peace-keeping has been frozen in a mould which is now insufficient for the needs of the international system, and the second is that there is a need to explore peace-keeping in a broader security framework especially in the area of multinational maritime activities.[1]

Cold War Orthodoxies

Although world politics have changed dramatically, some concepts have changed little. Nuclear deterrence maintains its grip among strategists and defence policy-makers. It has been justified as an insurance against proliferation *and* urged as a universal security panacea.[2] Nuclear deterrence is the great security religion of our age, credible to the credulous because, like religious faith, it cannot be easily falsified. Nor can it be proven to have worked. More so than in the past, there is a case for changing the term 'nuclear deterrence' to 'unclear deference'.

Likewise, the peace-keeping role of the UN from 1945-1988 was not so much a vision of international security as a limited instrument manipulated by permanent members of the Security Council. The minimalism was set in concrete by Dag Hammarskjöld in his reports of 1958 and 1960, after the experience of setting up UN Emergency Force I (UNEF). He developed a framework partly dictated by the limitations of the international system and partly by the exigencies of the Cold War. The Hammarskjöld vision resulted in a consensus that peace-keeping was not peace-making, and activities such as non-military observer missions were often excluded.[3] Moreover, the Korean and Congo operations gave peace enforcement a bad name. The maxims, drawn here mainly from Alan James, are well known:

1. Peace-keeping is an activity which relies on policies of sovereign states, particularly those in the Security Council, and is therefore a dependent and secondary activity deriving essentially from the provisional measures allowed under Article 40.
2. It requires the cooperation of parties through a competent authority, and the provision of finance, personnel, transport and logistic support. The mandate and provisions are decided on an ad hoc basis, though Nordic states and Canada earmark forces for UN roles.
3. It requires the consent of hosts and disputants – which can be withdrawn as it was for UNEF in 1967.
4. The forces are based on sovereign territory and the host's sovereignty is not limited.
5. Peace-keepers need the trust of all sides and their impartiality is essential.
6. The forces are supplied by national armed forces but are lightly armed for self-defence, adopting non-threatening, highly visible postures.
7. The roles can include: 'defusion' (interposition of peace-keepers in crisis prevention situations), 'stabilisation' (to maintain calm after a situation has been defused, to affect the context for negotiations, reducing anxieties and incidents), and the 'supervision' of agreed settlements (such as the monitoring of demilitarisation).[4]

These orthodoxies reflect the practical limits of universal security activities in the Westphalian system, and they overshadow, if
not replace, the original intentions of the UN Charter and the
widely debated plans in the 1930s for international policing.[5]
Soviet proposals for the United Nations included a permanent
centralised force, whilst Britain and the United States preferred
contingency forces for ad hoc coalitions. The UN Charter, itself,
allowed the powers to 'take effective collective measures' for the
prevention and removal of threats to peace and for the suppression of acts of aggression or other breaches of the peace. The
concepts of enforcement and deterrence (in the sense of military
demonstrations to influence an aggressor) were enshrined in
Chapter VII. The Military Staff Committee (MSC) would coordinate the contingency forces of the Security Council's permanent
members. Article 42 enabled the Council to 'take such action by
air, sea or land forces as may be necessary to maintain or restore
international peace. Such action may include demonstrations,
blockade, and other operations by air, sea, or land forces of
members of the United Nations'. These sections were a casualty of
post-war rivalries and the exercise of the veto in the Security
Council. As early as April 1947, the Military Staff Committee
reported to the Security Council that it had failed to get agreement on the forces to be made available. The MSC soon lan-
guished and the envisaged police power failed to supplant traditional, unilateral and alliance war powers.[6]

Security Without Frontiers

There is now an opportunity to review measures for maintaining
international security, not simply because this is a post-Cold War
world but also because it is a post-Westphalian one, and there are
many processes which weaken traditional statist thinking about
security. These include the expansion of inter-firm trade; changes
in the hierarchy of states; regional integration and shared sovereignty; the demise of military security in relations between 'liberal' communities; the politicisation of global issues which lie
beyond the competence of nation states; the advent of non-state
actors, some of which (such as Greenpeace, Amnesty Interna-

tional and *Médecins sans frontières*) promote universal principles.[7] In Eastern Europe and the former U.S.S.R., the state was so closely identified with communist parties that its legitimacy has been affected by the discrediting of communism. Ethnic intrastate conflict has been the negative consequence. More positively, anti-statism has manifested itself in the success of 'people power' in Eastern Europe; creeping international law which has affected sovereign immunity (including the immunity of warships) and the weakening of distinctions between domestic and foreign policies. In Europe, the 38 CSCE states agreed in October 1991 that violations of human and minority rights in the 'value community' (*Weltgemeinschaft*) are a collective interest which permits external pressures to be applied against offending regimes.[8] In December 1991, the United Nations also adopted a resolution creating a humanitarian coordinator responsible to the Secretary General, and giving the UN rights to intervene physically for humanitarian assistance, in principle, but not necessarily in practice, by invitation of the country concerned.[9] The willingness to accept such assaults on state sovereignty has not been uniform throughout the world, and some transnational processes have increased the danger of North/South conflicts.

However, both positive and negative developments have led seasoned observers of the international system to remark that the UN has entered its second youth. Indeed a special UN committee reported in 1988 on measures to strengthen the role of the UN in crisis prevention. Reformers, such as Brian Urquhart, have also called for consensus-building on global issues and procedural reforms to facilitate Security Council authorisation of sanctions and deployment of trip-wire crisis prevention forces.[10] There is, in brief, a climate of opinion for exploring means which break down barriers to cooperation for international security.[11] Maritime cooperation can play a part in this by building on the 'brotherhood of the sea' – though to date the UN's naval activities have been ancillary to land operations, notably in West Irian in 1962 and the Bay of Fonseca since 1990.

The peace-keeping model was devised for the land. According to Alan James, naval analogies are difficult to envisage because most disputes at sea are unlikely to involve interposition by UN-flagged ships. Other maritime operations, such as keeping order on the high seas, fall outside the strict definition of peace-keeping, either because the situations do not threaten peace or because activities such as mine clearing during a conflict would be partisan.[12] For these reasons it might be better to retain 'peace-keeping' as a sub-category of multinational security operations. James further argues that there is no half-way house between traditional peace-keeping and peace enforcement, and that tougher measures risk making peace-keeping less acceptable.[13]

Against these arguments, maritime forces have advantages which would facilitate more extensive implementation of the UN's security role. In short, orthodox peace-keeping rules might not apply. Ships are politically valuable instruments for a whole range of measures, being relatively self-sufficient, tightly controlled, often operating in international waters and easily withdrawn from difficult situations. Nor do they merely fight. As New Zealanders are well aware, navies can have a political impact out of proportion to their actual presence. Fewer than a quarter of the world's navies have been engaged in war since 1945. Remarkably, the Soviet Navy rarely fired a shot in anger after the Second World War.[14]

It is also true that the world's oceans are a focus of potential insecurity. A study by the British Ministry of Defence of coastal security concerns in 1990 found that the greatest perceived threat was the illicit narcotics trade and its potential to corrupt coastal communities. A second concern was to protect fish stocks. The people of some 40 countries in the developing world rely heavily on fish protein for their diet. Third, protection of offshore oil and mining resources may become important. At present, there are economic but no technical obstacles to the exploitation of sea-bed resources in any depth of ocean. Finally, jurisdictional claims lead to disputes over straits and waters, such as that outstanding between Venezuela and Colombia.[15] Traditional concepts of freedom of the seas are under increasing pressure, and it is a 'safe bet' that attempts to police straits will 'lead to disputes, perhaps even conflicts', at a time when a strong body of legal opinion argues that the law of armed conflict at sea is in urgent need of overhaul.[16]

About 36 per cent of the world's ocean area can be claimed by states under the United Nations Convention on the Law of the Sea (UNCLOS) (which looks increasingly like coming into effect). But this bounty brings with it the need for maritime policing. European waters are generally well policed. Indeed, the Royal Navy was first involved in fishery protection in 1575, although the Fishery Protection Squadron was not formed until 1881. Throughout the world 43 states have separate sea-going forces for Exclusive Economic Zone (EEZ) protection, assisted in many cases by coastguards. But maritime policing is a burden for developing countries which lack the means to ensure compliance with their EEZ management policies.

In sum, many maritime issues are beyond the jurisdiction, competence or perceived legitimacy of any single naval power to deal with. For example, coping with refugees can place national military personnel in ethically difficult situations for which they are untrained. So is there scope for deep-blue berets operating directly under the UN mandates or competent regional authorities? Evidently there is because the major naval powers have been investigating multinational maritime cooperation, partly as a reaction to the Gulf War.

Ripples from the Gulf

In terms of coping with displaced refugees, lost overseas remittances, a short-term increase in oil prices and redirected OECD aid, the Third World in general was the clear loser in the Gulf War. By stark contrast, the United States made gains in terms of long-term oil access, post-war reconstruction contracts and arms sales, and offset war subsidies. But even for the United States, the Gulf conflict may yet prove to have been the zenith of its hegemony.

America's resort to the United Nations and the arguments over burden-sharing may in fact have been a function of relative decline. In spite of the war, the U.S. Navy and Marine Corps, which account for about 55 per cent of the Pentagon's budget, will reduce by between a half and a third in strength in the next five years. For all President Bush's bravado about the American naval presence in the Pacific, there is little doubt that the Navy's ability to project force unilaterally has been affected.

Some navy experts assess that for political as well as economic reasons, it is now less likely the United States will undertake major military operations which do not have UN approval. For example, Vice-Admiral S. F. Loftus has said:

We should act jointly, perhaps through the United Nations, to develop an identifiable pool of sealift assets to be available in event of contingencies. These assets would be used *only* [his emphasis] for a UN-sanctioned intervention, and would of course be subject to the approval of the country supplying those assets at the time they were needed.[17]

Loftus was not giving up the hegemonic veto or Article 51, and the U.S. Navy clearly had problems with sealift, but there is a mood in the Pentagon not only for ending the Navy's domestic autonomy but for cooperation in multinational humanitarian operations.

Similarly, the Royal Navy is more likely to operate as part of a multinational force in the future than on its own.

There are other new developments in international policing. Swedes are wearing EC badges in Yugoslavia, German helicopters and planes are in Baghdad as part of the International Atomic Energy Agency (IAEA) inspection regime and Japan has undertaken 'humanitarian' minesweeping in the Gulf. Other countries do not necessarily welcome the signs of German or Japanese involvement, but might tolerate it if firmly subordinated to the United Nations in non-coercive roles. The proposals for deep-blue berets canvassed by the Commonwealth of Independent States are thus of particular interest.

Proposals for Deep-blue Berets

It is doubtful whether the Commonwealth of Independent States is in a position to do anything creative internationally at present. Nevertheless, assuming that the Ukraine and Russia will divide ownership and command of the Black Sea fleet to their mutual satisfaction, there would be obvious merit in integrating the former Soviet Navy into an international security system. The scheme currently circulating in the Russian Foreign and Defence Ministries seems to have grown out of a proposal by Eduard Shevardnadze in September 1987 for a UN taskforce in the Persian Gulf to convoy merchant ships and ensure freedom of navigation. At a UN seminar in August 1989, Vladimir F. Petrovsky argued for an extension of UN activities to maritime operations. In its October 1990 Memorandum to the Security Council on strengthening the UN, the Soviet government urged analysis of joint actions, reserve forces and appropriate contingencies to be indicated in advance by the permanent members of the Security Council. Subsequent developments in the Gulf and the collapse of Soviet operational capabilities have given additional impetus to the idea, though it is not yet official policy.[18]

The assumption is that consensus in the Security Council has created an opportunity for implementing Chapter VII of the UN Charter. It would involve reviving the Military Staff Committee (MSC) to work out in advance options and procedures for joint actions. The forces of any members could be put at the Security Council's disposal. For particular situations there would be a joint force under a UN command reouiring additional expenditure for members according to their force contributions and economic power. In addition there would be Standing Joint Task Forces in each of the Atlantic and Pacific Oceans, with ships regularly rotated. These would provide the basis for UN forces in case of regional conflicts. Joint training to coordinate fleet operations would be required, and perhaps a large exercise once every two or three years under UN auspices. Regional military/naval structures authorised by the United Nations might be developed. Their functions would include:

* Showing the UN flag, including visits to foreign ports.
* Deployment to regions of tension for deterrence purposes.
* Reconnaissance and verification to detect violations of international law.
* Policing actions.

Similar proposals have been put forward by non-government organisations (NGOs).[19]

Potential Functions

The potential functions can be discussed under three main headings: peace enforcement, maritime policing and humanitarian measures.

Peace enforcement

This would include deterrent functions and blockades with the purpose of upholding international law, enforcing UN rulings or defending shipping in war zones. During the Iran/Iraq War there was a degree of confusion about whose navy was protecting which tankers from attack. An international force to protect Gulf shipping would have been a more effective deterrent.[20] In 1990, the naval blockade of Iraq to enforce Security Council sanctions after the invasion of Kuwait also focused world attention on the problems and possibilities of naval operations in maintaining international law. The war highlighted important features of the 'legal landscape' and led to legal and maritime precedents.[21]

Not that it can be considered a model UN operation. Legally it rested on collective self-defence under Article 51 of the Charter, though Resolution 678 authorising force was also implicitly consistent with Article 42. Moreover, the situation was probably unique because Iraq's aggression was clear cut, the Coalition had over five months to prepare for war and had no submarines to contend with. The UN may yet prove to be a poor peace-maker. Iraq has been subjected to unprecedented UN surveillance and on-site inspection and there is a risk that in the Middle East the UN will be viewed increasingly as having intervened to sustain undemocratic monarchies and impose demilitarisation selectively. If UN enforcement is a viable proposition in the future, there should be no illusions. Missions regarded as peace enforcement by the international community will be interpreted as acts of war by the victims.

Maritime policing

This could involve a range of ocean management and safety measures, including mine clearing, dealing with smuggling (of arms, drugs, animals and artifacts) and combating pollution (from oil fires to raising toxic drums from the ocean floor). Although incidents of piracy have declined since about 1983, pirates have adapted to modern technical, economic and social developments and will require new means of suppression.[22] The policing of

fishing grounds to enforce Exclusive Economic Zone (EEZ) juris-
dictions may be further functions appropriate for multinational
forces.

Humanitarian measures

Navies have commonly been involved in search-and-rescue and
disaster relief. Clearly there are risks that intervention to rescue
nationals will be resented or will disguise less worthy goals. The
United States intervened, unasked, in the Dominican Republic in
1965 to rescue nationals from civil unrest. After a week there
were 19,000 U.S. troops, including marines, trying to prevent a
left-wing faction taking power.[23]

Indeed, it is essential to acknowledge the obstacles which
would confront multinational naval operations.

Problems and Requirements: Sailing into Trouble?

The most significant problems are political rather than technical.
First, operations by deep-blue berets could become a cloak for the
interests of the strongest naval power, or perceived as such. The
main areas of conflict and potential intervention are likely to be in
the developing world, and perhaps reconstructed Cold War warri-
ors are promoting reform of alliance security to keep themselves
in business and the developing world in check. The developing
world is bound to resent the rich countries sailing gunboats to
impose their vision of a world order on the rest, especially if
conducted under UN auspices. Yet no action to uphold international law or to deal with global security problems will ever be
entirely impartial; no intervention policy is ever entirely fair.
Even orthodox peace-keeping is partial in the sense that no state
with a say in the matter is completely disinterested. Quite apart
from the veto power in the Security Council, reliance on ad hoc
financial, logistical and personnel support allows states to refuse
support for peace-keeping if it is not in their interests to lend it.

Second, the economic and political roots of unrest in the developing world are not easily resolved by military intervention.
Indeed some operations, such as coping with refugees, could also

place national military personnel in ethical predicaments. Yet tackling the deep-seated ills is problematic. For example, the facile notion of a bargain involving redistribution of wealth from the rich North in return for implementation of human rights in the South,[24] overlooks the prospect that the South will dismiss it as blackmail. All the same, once unrest or a threat to peace occurs an emergency response may be difficult to avoid.

Third, even if an intervention were acceptable on legal and ethical grounds, it would not necessarily be a politically wise undertaking. As the United Nations appreciated in regard to Yugoslavia, civil wars and ethnic and intrastate disputes are not likely to be rewarding engagements for outside powers until cease-fires are secured. However, there was certainly scope for a full-scale UN naval relief operation to Dubrovnik in lieu of the motley squadron (including a vessel chartered by UNICEF) which risked the blockade in October 1991.

What might be the relevance of UN maritime forces for the Asia Pacific region?

Pacific Relevance

The notion that the Pacific is somehow immune from post-Cold War or post-Westphalian change is ludicrous. The process has differed from that in Europe, but the military security outlook has changed significantly for the better and there is a high probability that nations in the Asia Pacific region will negotiate more confidence-building measures in the future. There has already been multilateral confidence building on the Korean peninsula. In the maritime sphere, the Five Power Defence Arrangements continue to form a basis for some multinational naval cooperation. In the South Pacific there is exemplary maritime cooperation on non-military security problems, directly or indirectly supporting the Forum Fisheries Agency and the 1986 Convention for the Protection of Natural Resources and the Environment.[25]

Despite these and other examples of security cooperation, the Pacific is regionally fractured and encompasses several security complexes. States do not share threat perceptions and there are outstanding disputes over sovereignty. In the predominantly maritime environment, the U.S. Navy probably retains a casting vote, or thinks it does.[26] Most Asian states do not have blue-water forces; their green/brown-water navies are not therefore conducive to cooperation on the high seas.

If there is less scope for fixed security menus in the Pacific than in European-Atlantic waters, is there room for cooperation *à la carte*?[27] Two environments, the South China Sea and the South Pacific, might be considered.

The Spratlys and Paracels

Significant for strategic, navigational and resource reasons, the EEZs in the South China Sea have not been properly charted but might yield energy resources. The Spratlys and Paracels should not be underestimated as a potential maritime flashpoint. The Spratlys have long been contested by China, Taiwan, Vietnam, Malaysia, Brunei and the Philippines. Some islands are occupied already by China, Vietnam and Taiwan. Patrols by Chinese naval vessels culminated in an armed clash with Vietnam in March 1988, and Malaysia has seized fishing vessels registered in Taiwan and the Philippines.[28]

Although the hope of controlling resources stiffens national claims, none of the disputants has the economic clout to exploit them fully. Nor do they have the power to protect them. China may be extending its air cover, but Vietnam has no blue-water capability and can no longer turn to a Soviet Union for assistance. It is an opportune time for the parties taking part in the Indonesian-facilitated talks on the joint development of the Spratlys to explore the prospect for an International Court of Justice (ICJ) boundary delimitation, a partition agreement or a condominium backed by multinational policing. Although there are no precise rules for equitable delimitation of maritime boundaries, there is now a significant record of ICJ success and a body of delimitation case law.[29] In any event there would have to be a ruling on the sovereignty of the base points before the EEZs could be arbitrated. Nevertheless, the possibility of multinational supervision of delimitation and resource protection in the Spratly and Paracel Islands would be worth considering to monitor any future agreement covering these islands.

Pacific Forum

In the South Pacific, there are tensions and instabilities which arise from economic, social and environmental problems. Further, the issues of sovereignty and interventionism are particularly acute because the small states rely on sovereignty to survive in the international system and because they are particularly vulnerable to multinational corporations and external interference.[30] This extends of course to perceived interference by Australia and New Zealand – as was demonstrated in 1991 when Papua New Guinea complained about Australian Signals Intelligence (SIGINT) operations at Cape York. To some extent, perhaps, there should be a political asymmetry which enables the voices of islanders to offset any hegemonic inclinations and capabilities of Australia and New Zealand. Although there is debate about the extent to which Australia's policy of 'Constructive Commitment' is enlightened, Australia bowed to the exclusion of non-Forum fishing states from the Forum Fisheries Agreement (FFA) and has accepted flexible use of funds. Appreciation of regional sensitivities is also reflected in the recommendation of the New Zealand South Pacific Policy Review Group of 1990:

> That the guiding principle underlying New Zealand government consideration of a request from a Pacific Island government for direct military assistance should be, except in cases where New Zealand lives are threatened, a commitment to regional consultation and, if appropriate, regional involvement in the assistance provided.[31]

However, Australia and New Zealand might not live easily with a particular Forum decision, and the prospect for consensus on issues of relative sovereignty seems slight. Not only does sovereignty shore up small states in the international system, but the associated doctrine of non-intervention enables governments to establish domestic regimes which flout norms relating to human, ethnic, political and civil rights. The existence of mixed 'indigenous' and settler populations would create difficulties in defining a Forum Human Rights Charter. Indeed the issues of racism and indigenous rights have divided the progressive Nuclear Free and Independent Pacific movement. At its Conference in Manila in November 1987, the New Zealand and Hawaiian delegations rallied behind the Rabuka regime in spite of objections by a native Fijian.[32]

Without consensus about various forms of rights and obligations, there will be people who have more to fear from the depredations of their own government than from external threats. External intervention will be difficult to legitimise, unless arising from appeals to a professional Conflict Resolution Centre as suggested by Peter King.[33] The success of maritime cooperation is highly significant in the Forum's resource management and development programmes, but it must not be assumed that the FFA is the South Pacific's answer to the European Coal and Steel Community of 1951 as the first step to political integration.

Conclusion

The political and practical problems of reviving the UN Military Staff Committee in order to establish fully-fledged standing UN naval forces which might engage in peace enforcement may prove intractable. Yet the new internationalism, with its emphasis on relative sovereignty, interventions to uphold fundamental human rights and sanctions for clear breaches of international law, invites states and people to consider ways of enhancing global and regional security. Also, it is quite simply anachronistic for the UN to avoid going to sea.

The use of maritime forces to extend the global security functions of the United Nations, or competent regional authorities, implies a break from the traditional concept of peace-keeping. This represents an opportunity which should be explored in the light of evolving maritime issues and an emerging consensus for upholding international law and humanitarian intervention. However, without an awareness of the political difficulties, and unless there is a determined effort to find a wide consensus about the legitimating principles, the break would be counter-productive.

The Pacific presents difficulties for proponents of security schemes; and advocates have to be particularly discreet about the packaging. Whereas a small, permanent multinational naval unit might be feasible in European or Latin American waters to develop modalities, the Soviet/Russian proposals would be difficult to realise in the Pacific. Even here, however, the deepening and broadening of existing maritime cooperation should be encouraged and the temporary reflagging of ships under the UN for non-military security purposes should not be ruled out.

Notes

1. The current Secretary General of the United Nations made a significant contribution to both of these questions in the report he tabled to the Security Council (17 June 1992), *An Agenda for Peace.*
2. See, e.g., Martin, L., (July 1991), 'Dismantling Deterrence?', *Review of International Studies,* vol. 17, no. 3, pp. 215-224; Quinlan, M., (April 1991), 'Nuclear weapons and the abolition of war', *International Affairs,* vol. 67, no. 2, pp. 293-301.
3. Alan James makes an exception for forceful initiatives to maintain order in internal conflicts on behalf of a government generally accepted within the jurisdiction in question as above politics, and where use of force is impartial. *Peacekeeping in International Politics,* London, IISS, 1990, pp. 3-4.
4. *Ibid.,* pp. 1-12.
5. For example, the British PM, Neville Chamberlain, circulated a plan for an international air force, Pugh, M.C., (November 1988), 'An International Police Force; Lord Davies and the British debate in the 1930s', *International Relations,* vol. 9, no. 4, , pp. 335-351.
6. Franck, T. M. and Patel, F., (January 1991), 'UN police action in lieu of war: "the old order changeth", *American Journal of International Law,* vol. 85, no. 1, p. 64. The MSC's papers are classified, but a dispute may have arisen because the U.S. wanted to supply aircraft carriers which China could not match. The idea of a permanent UN force resurfaced after UNEF was created in 1956, see, Johnson, E., (July 1991), 'A permanent UN force: British thinking after Suez', *Review of International Studies,* vol. 17, no. 3, pp. 251-266.
7. It should be noted that there were 13 peace-keeping operations between 1945-1988 and 13 since then. Which means that the UN has mounted as many peace-keeping operations in the last four years as it did in the previous 43. This new emphasis on peace-keeping, and the new document associated with their operations underlines the significance of the UN in the maintenance of international peace and security.

8. In government torts the practice has increasingly restricted state
    immunity, contributing to the 'demystification of the State as a su-
    preme being'. Crawford, J., (1983), 'International law and foreign
    sovereigns: distinguishing immune transactions', *British Yearbook of
    International Law*, vol. 54, n. 23, p. 77. See also, Luard, E., (1990), *The
    Globalisation of World Politics. The Changed Focus of Political Action
    in the Modern World*, London: Macmillan, pp. 33-45; Booth, K., (Octo-
    ber 1991), 'Security and emancipation', *Review of International Stud-
    ies*, vol. 17, no. 4, pp. 313-326; Greene, O., (1992), 'Transnational
    processes in European security', in Pugh (ed.), *European Security
    Towards 2000*, Manchester: Manchester University Press, pp. 140-
    162; Moskos, C., (ed.), *The Warless Society* (to be published in 1993).
9. Doyle, L., (18 December 1991), 'UN gives itself the power to inter-
    vene', *The Independent*, p.8.
10. See e.g., Gott, R., (27 December 1991), 'Mr Fixit seeks a new role', *The
    Guardian*, p. 19; Freedman, L., (January 1991), 'Escalators and quag-
    mires: expectations and the use of force', *International Affairs*, vol.
    67, no. 1, pp. 15-31. Note, however, that China and Cuba blocked UN
    involvement in Haiti where a legitimate government was overthrown
    in 1991, Pick, H., (9 October 1991), 'Fighting on to keep the peace, *The
    Guardian*, p. 23.
11. Highlighted by Boutros Ghali, B., (June 1992), *Agenda for Peace,*
    which outlines a much more pro-active role for the UN in peace-
    keeping than what was possible during the 1950s and 1960s.
12. James, A., (see note 3), pp. 80-83, 177-178.
13. *Ibid.*, p. 368.
14. Cable, J.,(1989), *Navies in Violent Peace,* London: Macmillan, p. 39.
15. Study by the Defence Export Services Organisation cited by Steven
    Haines, 'The maritime domain – jurisdictional profiles and opera-
    tional requirements in a developing market', paper at Naval Forecast
    conference, Advanced Technology International, London and Brus-
    sels, 20-24 May 1991.
16. Cable, J., *Navies in Violent Peace*, p. 88; Ronzitti, N., (1988)'The crisis of
    the traditional law regulating international armed conflicts at sea and
    the need for its revision', in Ronzitti (ed.), *The Law of Naval Warfare*,
    Dordrecht: Kluwer Academic, pp. 1-58. See also, Booth, K., (1985), *Law,
    Force and Diplomacy at Sea,* London: Allen and Unwin, *passim.*
17. Loftus, Vice-Admiral S.F., Deputy CNO (Logistics), (8 October 1991),
    'Logistics and sealift in multinational cooperation', paper at Seapower
    Symposium, U.S. Naval War College, Newport, RI.
18. See, U.S.S.R., 'The United Nations in the Post-Confrontation World,
    UN Doc a/S-15/AC.1/12,16; Petrovksy, V.F., (4 August 1989), speech

at Seminar on Problems of UN Peace-keeping Operations, Salzburg, official text; Kocheev, M.E., (Soviet Ministry of Foreign Affairs), (1990), 'Naval nuclear disarmament', in Lodgaard, S., (ed.), *Naval Arms Control,* Oslo: PRIO/Sage, pp. 198-205.

19. World Association for World Federation, (1989), *A Proposal for United Nations Security Forces (UNSF),* Amsterdam. See also: Prins, G., (June 1991), 'The United Nations and peace keeping in the post-Cold War world: the case of naval power', *Bulletin of Peace Proposals,* vol. 22, no. 2, pp. 135-155; Meconis, C.A. and Wallace, M., 'A modest proposal for a UN Naval Peace-keeping Force', in Wallace and Meconis (eds), (1991), *Halting the Arms Race at Sea: Naval Arms Control and Maritime Strategy in the 21st Century,* Boulder, Col.: Lynne Reiner, ch. 6.

20. Swire, Sir Adrian, (1987), 'Merchant shipping and the Gulf War', *Naval Forces,* vol. 8, no. 3.

21. See, Schachter, O., (1991), 'United Nations Law in the Gulf Conflict', *American Journal of International Law,* vol. 85, no. 3, pp. 452-73.

22. Birnie, P.W., (1989), 'Piracy past, present and future', in Ellen, E. (ed.), *Piracy at Sea,* Paris: ICC Publishing, p. 132.

23. James, A., (see note 3) pp. 50-59.

24. Booth, K., (September 1991), 'Security in the New Europe: ten debates about "Whose Security?" and "Which Europe?"', paper at Conference on *Sicherheit Im Neuen Europa,* SAS Evangelische Akademie Loccum, Germany, pp. 27-29.

25. Doulman, D.J., (1990),'An assessment of Australia's role in the South Pacific Forum Fisheries Agency', in Bateman, W.S.G. and Ward, M.W., (eds), *Australia's Maritime Interests – Views From Overseas,* Canberra: Australian Centre for Maritime Studies, pp. 90-101; Bateman, (12-13 December 1991), 'Multinational naval cooperation – a Pacific view', paper at Conference on Multinational Naval Cooperation, RN College, Greenwich.

26. Findlay, T., (1990), 'Stockholm on the Mekong? CBMs for Asia/Pacific', *Pacific Review,* vol. 3, no. 1, pp. 55-64; Polomka, P., (March/April 1991), 'Towards a "Pacific House"', *Survival,* vol. 33, no. 2, pp. 173-182.

27. Segal, G., (1991), 'North-East Asia: common security or *à la carte'*, *International Affairs,* vol. 67, no. 4, pp. 755-767.

28. Kien-hong Yu, P., (1990), 'Protecting the Spratlys', *Pacific Review,* vol. 3, no. 1, pp. 78-83; Milivojevic, M., (January/February 1989), 'The Spratly and Paracel Islands Conflict', *Survival,* vol. 31, no. 1, pp. 70-78.

29. Evans, M.D., (1989), *Relevant Circumstances and Maritime Delimitation,* Oxford: Clarendon, pp. 190-197; Churchill, R.R., and Lowe, A.V., (1988), *The Law of the Sea,* Manchester: Manchester University Press, rev. ed., pp. 153-161.

30. King, P., (1991), 'Redefining South Pacific security', in Thakur, R., *The South Pacific: Problems, Issues and Prospects*, London: Macmillan, pp. 55-57.
31. Report of the South Pacific Policy Review Group, (31 May 1990), *Towards a Pacific Island Community*, Wellington.
32. Statement by Fiji Anti-Nuclear Group, NFIP Conference Report, 1987.
33. King, P., (see note 30), p. 62.

*   The author acknowledges the help of the E.S.R.C. Award R 000.23.2856 in the production of this chapter.

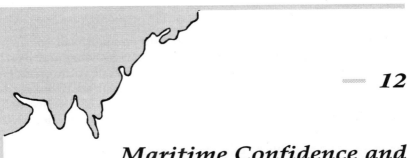

12

Maritime Confidence and Security-Building Measures in the Asia Pacific Area

Sam Bateman

The Royal Australian Navy (RAN) Maritime Studies Program was established in the Department of Defence (Navy Office) in Canberra nearly two years ago with a view towards,

> ... developing a greater level of knowledge within the RAN of maritime issues in general and maritime strategy in particular; and promoting greater public awareness of the need for sea power in the defence of Australia and her sovereign interests.[1]

In pursuance of these broad objectives, the programme has included:

* The study of developments in maritime strategy worldwide.
* The development of a liaison on maritime strategic topics with allied and friendly navies (especially the navies of South and Southeast Asia).

In many ways, the Royal Australian Navy Maritime Studies Program is a maritime confidence- and security-building measure

(MCSBM) in its own right. In the last fifteen months or so, there have been extensive exchanges or visits in Southeast and South Asia between the RAN and regional navies on maritime strategic topics. This has been a very real and practical contribution to regional security cooperation and transparency of defence policies. It is of course one of the characteristics of navies that, perhaps because of the nature of the environment in which they operate, they are able to talk frankly and easily with each other.

This chapter draws heavily on the experience so far with the Maritime Studies Program, particularly in regional activities. It brings together thoughts on some major issues of contemporary maritime strategic interest. Issues which are especially important for the Asia Pacific region include:

* The importance of maritime developments in the region, particularly insofar as they affect regional stability.
* Maritime Confidence and Security-Building Measures (MCSBM).
* Multinational naval cooperation.

These issues will be discussed through an operational perspective rather than a political one. While maritime issues play a major role in international relations in the Asia Pacific area, they are also becoming more complex. Regional conflict is much more likely to have a maritime dimension now than it may have had in the past. All these considerations, which will be argued in more detail later in this chapter, point to the importance of MCSBM in the region. However, first the scene will be set by discussing some of the more important maritime developments in the region.

Regional Maritime Developments

The geo-strategic environment of the Asia Pacific region is distinctly maritime. The sea is a major source of food for both the South Pacific and Southeast Asia and an important means of communication. Regional peoples are traditional seafarers. It is not surprising that maritime issues, such as offshore resources, sea-borne trade, fishing rights, illegal migration, piracy, marine pollution, the law of the sea and maritime boundaries loom very large on the political agenda of regional countries. Inevitably, a risk of conflict with these issues arises when the interests of different states run against each other.

This situation, coupled with the concern of Southeast Asian nations over possible instability following the drawdown in U.S. forces in Southeast Asia and the potential flexing of improved power projection capabilities by the Chinese, Indian and Japanese navies, has tended to shift the strategic attention of regional countries towards maritime security. In the words of one observer, there has been 'the re-emergence of the importance of seapower, until recent years a neglected dimension in the defence calculations of regional states'.[2] This is reflected in the priority now accorded regional countries to developing the maritime capabilities (ships, aircraft and submarines) of their armed forces. These developments will be discussed at greater length shortly.

As far as the region is concerned, the navies of the erstwhile superpowers have declined both in their relative importance and in their ability to influence maritime developments. Although the U.S. will remain strategically involved in the region, budgetary pressures mean that some drawdown in actual forces is inevitable. What is likely in Southeast Asia is a token presence (e.g., the USAF F16s in Singapore) rather than a real maritime presence in the South China Sea such as the U.S. bases in the Philippines. Paradoxically however, the establishment of logistic support facilities for the United States Navy in Southeast Asian waters may mean a more active engagement of the United States Navy there now than in the 1980s when the focus of United States Navy Western Pacific deployments was very much in Northeast Asia.

In the short term, a decline in naval activity in the Asia Pacific area seems unlikely. In fact this activity may well increase as the force development aspirations of regional navies are realised. China, India and Japan continue to expand their already significant naval power, while Korea and Taiwan are also acquiring more powerful naval forces.

All the ASEAN countries, with the exception of the Philippines, are according greater priority to maritime capabilities in the force structure of their defence forces. With the resources available from sustaining high rates of economic growth over a number of years, the ASEAN countries will acquire a greater range of equipment for high technology maritime warfare, including submarines, maritime strike aircraft, surveillance aircraft, and more advanced surface combatants with longer range, over-the-horizon missile systems. Some idea of the growth in surface fleets of regional navies is revealed by Table I which shows changes in numbers of major surface combatants (i.e., including corvettes, frigates and destroyers) between 1981 and 1991. Of course this table only shows quantitative changes – the qualitative changes have also been significant.

Table I
Major Surface Combatants in Asian Navies, 1981-1991

	1981	1991
CHINA	27	52
INDIA	30	41
INDONESIA	11	17
JAPAN	48	61
KOREA	20	38
MALAYSIA	2	4
PHILIPPINES	21	13
THAILAND	6	12
SINGAPORE	-	6
TAIWAN	35	37
TOTAL	200	281

Source: Janes Fighting Ships 1980-81 and 1991-92.

Similar growth has been evident in the submarine fleets of Japan, China, India, Taiwan and Korea, with Malaysia and Thailand also planning to acquire submarines.

However, it should be acknowledged that there is no naval arms race in the region *per se*. It seems more an example of what Barry Buzan has called an 'arms dynamic'.[3] The naval force structural developments are more a consequence of increased economic strength and national self-confidence than acts of competition between potential adversaries. There is nevertheless an atmosphere of uncertainty and some lack of trust regarding the maritime force structural developments of India, China and Japan, particularly while there is little transparency with regard to the motivations and intentions of individual countries.

The other point here is that as much as some people might lament these maritime force structural developments, there is little prospect of any change at least in the short term. The countries concerned think they have strong strategic justification for their enhanced maritime capabilities and they are not going to be put off by any rhetoric of naval arms control, or for that matter any other concepts of security and strategic wisdom, passed on from the other side of the world. They have won their independence, in some instances at a price, and resent outside interference in their national policy-making, particularly in the field of defence and national security.

On 'the commercial maritime scene, and in line with the general pace of economic growth, the merchant fleets of ASEAN countries have grown significantly in recent years with the total ASEAN merchant fleet growing in numbers from 3105 in 1980-81 to 4863 in 1991-92, with total tonnage almost doubling.[4]

Thus protection of shipping is now a consideration in the naval planning of ASEAN countries. Off-shore resources and measures for their protection are another concern, particularly as the area is rich in reserves of oil and gas beneath the seabed.

The 1982 UN Convention on the Law of the Sea is of particular importance in both Southeast Asia and the South Pacific. All regional countries (except Kiribati) have signed the Convention, but it has only been ratified by the major archipelagic states – Indonesia, Philippines and Fiji. These clearly have the most to gain by the Convention because of the recognition it provides for the archipelagic regime.

The archipelagic regime is a significant factor in the geostrategic make-up of the region. To the north of Australia and New Zealand there is a whole chain of states which have claimed archipelagic status – Indonesia, Papua New Guinea, the Solomon Islands, Vanuatu and Fiji. An independent New Caledonia would also be able to claim archipelagic status.

Indonesia and the Philippines are the world's two most significant archipelagic states and both fought strongly for international
acceptance of the archipelagic regime. They argue that the sea
and ocean spaces enclosed within their archipelagos were an
integral part of the nation state and a national asset to be defended in its own right rather than merely an adjunct to land
territory and as a barrier to external attack. Some aspects of the
archipelagic regime and the associated freedoms of navigation
remain unresolved and are a potential source of friction between
the archipelagic states and other countries.

In terms of maritime boundaries, the major area of difficulty
in Asia Pacific waters is in the South China Sea where there are
conflicting claims over the Spratly Islands.[5] These claims over
small remote islands, which in some cases are barely above sea
level, and previously seen as valueless, relate to their importance
for the demarcation of national sea zones. The area is strategically significant and potentially rich in undersea resources.

As Brigadier General Lee of Singapore said in 1990, 'if one day
oil is actually found, the scramble for ownership may spark off a
fierce and probably bloody struggle, especially if by then the U.S.
no longer has a military presence in the region'.[6] Limited military
clashes have already occurred and the claimant countries occupy-
ing islands have improved their garrisoning arrangements including the establishment of military outposts on islands which
were previously uninhabited. The claims of China over the Spratly
Islands are of the greatest concern to regional nations, particularly those which are themselves claimants to the islands.

The upshot of these developments on the regional maritime
scene is that potential causes of maritime conflict exist. The
waters of the Northeast Indian Ocean, the China Sea and the
Western Pacific are becoming a more complex operating area for
maritime forces than they have been in the past. There will be
more navies of consequence on the maritime scene and there will
be greater numbers of surface combatants, submarines and aircraft.

While there is this degree of uncertainty (and some lack of
transparency) in the maritime environment, and potential sources
of conflict exist, particularly in the South China Sea, there is a

real risk of misunderstanding between maritime forces of so many different nations all operating in similar areas. The risk is heightened by the presence of submarines and long-range missile systems which require well developed procedures and effective command and control systems if errors and miscalculations are to be avoided. All of this suggests the desirability of pursuing MCSBMs in this part of the world.

Maritime Confidence and Security Building

Maritime confidence and security building is a new area of maritime strategic interest. Just a few years ago it was not on the agenda at all – certainly not at the regional level. Discussion of MCSBM so far has occurred largely at the global level. There have been sweeping initiatives by the U.S. to remove all tactical nuclear weapons, including cruise missiles, from its surface ships and attack submarines. These are classic maritime confidence- and security-building developments.

At the regional level, however, Senator Evans noted in 1991:

> With growing prosperity, overall stability and regional cooperation, several countries have begun to look more broadly at their notions of security, especially the importance of maritime areas. What is important about the changes of force structures that flow from this, such as Indonesia's improvement of its naval capabilities, is that they are appropriate and expected, and no more than what Australia has put in place, adjusting capabilities to circumstances.[7]

In other words, Senator Evans was saying that:

* Maritime security is becoming more important to regional countries.
* Hence they are allocating more resources to capabilities for maritime defence.
* That these developments are an understandable response to perceived national requirements (and in no way, constitute a naval arms race).

The Foreign Minister went on to note that the Asia Pacific region has 'its share of major neuralgic trouble spots'.[8] These, coupled with the maritime capability developments mentioned above, mean that we have the environment in which some ideas on regional MCSBM could be worth thinking about – as opposed to global MCSBM which have been the main concern of strategic analysts so far.

In a major speech in May 1991 on 'Australia's Security in Asia', the then Australian Prime Minister spoke of how enhanced regional security cooperation could emerge through a gradual process of bilateral and multilateral informal discussion of relevant security issues.[9] Because of the predominantly maritime nature of the region, maritime capabilities and issues will be a central feature of regional security cooperation.

The Prime Minister went on to say that this regional dialogue could lead to 'confidence-building measures such as procedures among regional states for handling naval incidents at sea' and increased cooperation in maritime surveillance.[10] Senator Evans also noted subsequently that 'There are a number of specific Confidence-Building Measures (CBMs) which might, even at this early stage of the regional security dialogue process, be considered feasible and desirable in our region'.[11] He then referred specifically to both incidents-at-sea agreements and 'a cooperative approach to security of sealanes and sealines of communication, with the enhancement of capabilities and maritime surveillance, safety and search and rescue operations'.[12]

A joint paper was presented to a workshop in Kuala Lumpur on 'Naval Confidence and Security-building regimes for the Asia Pacific Region' in July 1991 (Ball and Bateman).[13] This paper gave an Australian perspective of MCSBM in this region. It assessed the regional security environment, particularly the maritime aspects, including the prospects for increased regional cooperation. It went on to discuss the two particular MCSBM mentioned by Prime Minister Hawke – a regional maritime surveillance and safety regime, and a regional 'avoidance of incidents at sea' regime. The beauty of these regimes lies in their clear foundation in operations being routinely conducted by regional navies or covered in their basic contingency planning. They also

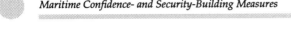

fit well within the general 'building block' approach to regional security.

Maritime Surveillance and Safety

Maritime surveillance and safety covers a spectrum of related activities ranging in the most narrow sense from contingency planning for the protection of shipping in a conflict situation to a comprehensive regime for maritime safety in the region applicable to both peacetime and periods of conflict. The range of tasks which could be covered by a comprehensive regime include:

* Maritime surveillance, including the compilation of a shipping plot of all vessels within the area at any one time.
* Planning for the naval control and protection of shipping transiting the area.
* Monitoring illegal activities, including smuggling, unauthorised population movement and unlicensed fishing.
* Combating piracy, which has further increased in the region in recent years, particularly in the Singapore and Malacca Straits.[14]
* Enhancing maritime safety along the busy shipping routes in the area.
* Controlling and monitoring marine pollution, and taking remedial action as required.
* Generally sharing maritime information and intelligence.

These involve a great range of activities and, at least in the first instance, countries are unlikely to subscribe to all of them. Planning for operations in time of conflict, and the actual conduct of such operations, require that there be an 'enemy' to pose the threat. Since there are many sensitivities involved in going too far down the threat path, it may be preferable to restrict the regime to peacetime activities. By doing so, the MCSBM benefits of the regime would not be reduced.

There will also be problems in dealing with activities which are not covered by some commonality of interest. Illegal fishing and migration are two areas where there may be some divergence of interest. The whole question of delineating the area to be covered by the regime will also be difficult due to unresolved maritime boundaries and different views on aspects of the law of the sea.

Despite these difficulties, there are clear benefits to be gained in endeavouring to establish a regional surveillance and safety regime covering at least some of the activities identified above. In operational terms, it would markedly improve maritime surveillance of areas under some degree of sovereignty (including in the approaches to such areas), in a manner which is cost-effective, given that no regional country in the foreseeable future is likely to be able to afford such comprehensive surveillance on its own. Establishing and maintaining the regime would provide a good catalyst for dialogue between regional maritime forces.

In a broader strategic sense, the establishment of such a regime would be a clear demonstration of the preparedness of regional countries to act together to ensure the security of the region and to prevent threats arising. It might also contribute to fulfilling the perceived need to establish a strong regional influence to avoid the notion that a vacuum could develop following any drawdown in the region in United States maritime forces.

Avoidance of Incidents at Sea

The 1972 agreement between the United States and the former Soviet Union to prevent incidents on and over the high seas is an excellent example of a practical maritime CBM which has stood the test of lengthy and demanding operational experience.[15] Bilateral incident-at-sea agreements were also negotiated between the Soviet Union and several other Western European navies and the United States and and the Soviet Union also signed an agreement on the uniform interpretation of the rules of international law governing innocent passage.

There are several provisions of the existing incident-at-sea agreements which are particularly relevant to this chapter. These are that the agreements:

*   Cover incidents involving warships, military aircraft and
         naval auxiliaries.

*   Exclude operations by submerged submarines as they are
     not operating *on* the high seas.
*   Relate only to activities on the high seas, reflecting the
     significance attached by all parties to the agreements on the
     freedom of the *high seas.*

The success of these agreements has led to suggestions of
multilateral arrangements. These were first put forward in the
UN report on the naval arms race[16] and more recently, Sweden
has drawn up a draft multilateral treaty on incidents at sea.[17] On
first glance, such a treaty looks attractive for possible application
within the Asia Pacific region but there are some qualifications
and possible impediments which should be noted.

First, the existing agreements are not necessarily a good model
for this part of the world. They relate to the activities of navies
which routinely conducted close surveillance of each other's exercises and operations. That is not the case with regional navies
which are unlikely to be involved in the types of close-quarter
activities which led to the NATO/Soviet agreements although this
is not to say that such situations may not arise in the future.

Second, the agreements are limited to high seas activities only,
whereas the waters any regional incident-at-sea agreement should
apply to are largely not high seas. Thus the agreement could be
seen as a restriction both on the rights of the coastal state involved and on the freedom of navigation exercised by other nations in such waters. Undesirable precedents could arise such as
restrictions on certain naval operations in Exclusive Economic
Zones (EEZ), or the inclusion in the agreement of provisions
which appear to require the prior notification of straits transit or
archipelagic sealanes passage.

Third, much of the success of the current agreements can be
attributed to the fact that they are all bilateral. The interest of
different countries in the range of maritime operations is so
diverse that not only would the negotiation of multilateral agreements be very difficult, but also the investigation of particular
incidents which may or may not have contravened the agreement
would become more complicated if third parties had to be con-
sulted. The third parties could well perceive that their interests

were affected in ways which were perhaps different to those of the countries directly involved in the incident.

Lastly, submerged submarine operations are excluded from the current incident-at-sea agreements involving the former Soviet Navy but, in view of the probable growing numbers of submarines in the region, their inclusion will need to be considered in any regional agreement for the avoidance of incidents at sea. The safety of submerged submarine operations will be a particular concern and it may be necessary to consider the establishment of a regional submarine Movement Advisory Authority along the lines of the procedures currently followed by NATO and other Western navies. The current such authority for United States and allied submarines in the Asia Pacific region is located at Yokosuka in Japan.

In the interests of submarine safety, Australia currently designates the entire 200 mile Australian Fishing Zone as a permanently established submarine exercise area.[18] This means that foreign submarines wishing to operate into this area, under their right of high seas freedom of navigation applicable to the EEZ, should either transit on the surface or advise their movements, if the risk of submarine collision is to be removed. However, given that virtually the entire area covered by any regional agreement is likely to be part of the Economic Enforcement Zone of one country or another, such an arrangement would not be viable for the region generally.

The Way Ahead with MCSBM

The debate on MCSBM has a long way to go and inevitably many of the questions can only have a political answer. The issues involved are so complex and there are potentially so many conflicting interests involved that a purely legal answer is unlikely to be satisfactory. Operational, strategic and political factors will all have to be considered.

However, this does not mean that we should do nothing. There is a growing need for regional MCSBM and it is important to get the debate going. One of the ways in which we can do this is to do adopt a 'bottom-up' approach with some discussion between regional navies on the operational aspects of MCSBM – incidents-at-sea avoidance procedures, cooperative maritime surveillance, cooperative protection of shipping, etc., along the lines suggested by the then Prime Minister, Hawke, and Foreign Minister, Evans.

Discussion of operational aspects of MCSBM, primarily conducted between professional naval officers, either on a bilateral or multilateral basis, would be both a sound, practical MCSBM in its own right and a way of avoiding the political stumbling blocks. As one commentator on the role of naval CBM has noted, 'Small steps in which States could find some common ground can help modify doctrinal thinking in a manner that might later make far-reaching measures possible.'[19]

Multinational Naval Cooperation

The issue of multinational naval cooperation has been raised as a maritime confidence- and security-building dimension in its own right and is going to become much more important in the future. Much interest is being shown in the concept. This is particularly so in Europe and North America following the manifest success of multinational naval cooperation during the Gulf War and the demise of the Soviet threat to NATO.

It is important to develop specific regional perspectives on multinational naval cooperation in order to avoid applying inappropriate concepts from other parts of the world.[20]

Much depends on what is meant by 'multinational'. If it means naval peace-keeping under the auspices of the United Nations, then there is not a problem. If it means the navies of like-minded, neighbouring countries operating together when there is some common objective to be served, then there is also not a problem. But if it means so-called 'out of area' combined operations by extra-regional navies, then there may be problems.

These problems could be particularly acute in the Asia Pacific region where the sensitivity to external interference is high. Needless to say, this sensitivity would be even higher if the former European colonial powers in Asia were to be involved; the possible exception being the U.K. which still has entrée to Southeast Asia under the Five Power Defence Arrangement (FPDA).

There is a need for circumspection in relation to multinational cooperation, and the deployment of multinational naval forces. Grand global terminology suggestive of the international naval policemen 'on the beat' should be avoided lest alarm bells be rung in regions of the world which aspire to the resilience of looking after themselves. Even if there is increased use of multinational forces at sea by the NATO alliance or some other association such as the Western European Union, it is doubtful whether there would be a move towards multinationality in an operational sense in the Pacific at least in the foreseeable future. The contrary pressures at present are simply too great. Bilateral, rather than multilateral cooperation, will remain the norm for the time being.

Before multinational naval cooperation can exist the countries involved must have some common sense of purpose and see some potential mutual benefits in having such cooperation. Possibly the way to achieve this in the Pacific is not so much by seeking some higher level strategic or security framework but by a 'bottom-up' approach with better dialogue between regional navies on issues of common concern. This is the approach of the Western Pacific Naval Symposium which meets biennially and has a membership comprised of the ASEAN states, China, Japan, South Korea, the United States, Australia, New Zealand and Papua New Guinea. The last Western Pacific Naval Symposium held in Bangkok in November 1990 agreed that a technical working committee should be established with representatives of regional navies to develop ideas about enhanced naval cooperation in relevant areas. Special mention was made of protection of shipping and the need for procedures which allow for the exchange of information on maritime activities of common concern. Action is in hand to hold the first meeting of this committee, which is now described as a 'workshop' to get away from any suggestion of a standing multinational committee. Establishment of this activity can also be seen as a reflection of the general desire in the region for a 'bottom-up' approach to multinational cooperation rather than a 'top-down' one with the inevitable distraction of the political sensitivities which are still rife in the Asia Pacific region. This type of potential cooperation is rather different to the more operationally focused cooperation being discussed in the NATO context.

Rather than multinational naval cooperation, there seems to be good scope in the Pacific for the introduction of some MCSBM. Basically the problem is one of the region 'walking' before it can 'run'. The problem with multinational naval cooperation, if it primarily encompasses combined operations by naval forces of different countries in actual or potential conflict against some common threat, is that the participating nations must share some view about the threat. But at present, there is no such thing as a common Asia Pacific threat perception.

Conclusion

It seems certain that in the short term maritime competition will increase in the Asia Pacific region. But there is also increased potential for cooperation in maritime affairs. Southeast Asian waters are going to be a more complex operating area in the future, particularly the South China Sea and the Bay of Bengal. There will be more players in the maritime scene and they will have available some fairly sophisticated maritime capabilities. There will need to be good dialogue between regional and extra-regional navies operating in the area if incidents and misunderstandings are to be avoided. This suggests the importance of some MCSBM.

The maritime environment and associated issues will continue to figure prominently in regional affairs. In Southeast Asia, the strategic concerns of regional nations have tended to move offshore while in the South Pacific maritime matters are uppermost in the minds of Pacific Islanders who will strongly pursue activities to preserve the maritime environment and to protect their marine resources.

On the credit side, the problems with the maritime environment are amenable to solution, given goodwill and cooperation from the states involved. The South Pacific has a good record in this regard and perhaps is an example to Southeast Asia where a cooperative approach to maritime affairs is less well developed. Whatever the outcome, vital security interests are involved for both Australia and New Zealand and these would be best served by active participation in the dialogue on MCSBM.

Notes

1. Chief of Naval Staff Directive to RAN Studies Program, April 1991.
2. Cheung, Tai Ming, (July, 1989), 'Command of the Seas', *Far Eastern Economic Review*, 27 p. 16.
3. Buzan, B., (1987), *An Introduction to Strategic Studies; Military Technology and International Relations*, Basingstoke: MacMillan, p. 131.
4. Data from *Janes Fighting Ships*, 1980-1981 and 1991-1992.
5. For a review of the background to these claims see Milivojenic, M., (Jan/Feb 1989), 'The Spratly and Paracel Island Conflict', Survival, vol. 31, no. 1, pp. 70-78.
6. Loong, Brigadier General Lee Hsien, (2/90), 'The FPDA and Regional Security', *Asian Defence Journal*, pp. 28-32.
7. Evans, Senator Gareth, (31 July 1991), 'Australia's Regional Security Environment', Address to the Conference on Strategic Studies in a Changing World, Australian National University, p. 6.
8. Ibid., p. 11.
9. Hawke, The Hon. R.J., Prime Minister, (24 May, 1991), 'Australia's Security in Asia', (*The Asia Lecture*, The Asia – Australia Institute, University of New South Wales, Sydney).
10. Ibid., p. 7.
11. Evans, Senator, (see note 7), p. 13.
12. Ibid.
13. Ball, D., and Bateman, W.S.G., (8-10 July, 1991), 'An Australian Perspective on Maritime C.S.B.M.s in the Asia Pacific Region'. Working Paper No. 234, Strategic and Defence Studies Centre, Australian National University Canberra, August 1991.
14. The Singapore National Shipping association has advised, for example, that there were 29 reported cases of piracy in the vicinity of Singapore in the first 11 months of 1990 as compared with only three incidents in 1989. Advice from that association to the Federation of ASEAN Shipowners' Associations, 27 November, 1990.
15. See Lynn-Jones, S.M., 'Applying and Extending the U.S.A.-U.S.S.R. Incidents at Sea Agreements', pp. 203-219, and Prawitz, J., (1990), 'A Multilateral Regime for Prevention of Incidents at Sea', pp. 220-225, in Fieldhouse, R., *Security at Sea: Naval Forces and Arms Control*, Oxford: Oxford University Press.
16. United Nations, (1986), *The Naval Arms Race*, Report of the Secretary General, UN Study Series No. 16, UN document A/40/535, p. 5, United Nations: New York.

17. Prawitz, J., (see note 15).
18. Australian Annual Notice to Mariners No. 8.
19. Deyanov, R., (1990), 'The Role and Security Objectives of Confidence-Building Measures at Sea' in UN, Department for Disarmament Affairs, 'Naval Confidence-Building Measures', Disarmament Topical Papers 4, p. 15, United Nations: New York.
20. Bateman, W.S.G., (12-13 December 1991), 'Multinational Naval Cooperation – A Pacific View', Paper for conference on 'Multinational Naval Cooperation in a Changing World', U.K.: RN Staff College Greenwich.

13

Asia Pacific Security Forums – Rationale and Options – Canadian Views

Peggy Mason

Introduction

Canada's interest in, and contributions to, Asia Pacific security have a long history, not least of all because geographically it is a Pacific country. Canadians participated in the Pacific War, and contributed to the United Nations forces operating in Korea. It was active in the various Indo-China control commissions, and is currently contributing to United Nations peace-keeping and observation missions in West, South and Southeast Asia. Throughout the post-war era, Canada has assisted the countries of Asia Pacific to maintain the security and stability necessary to stimulate and continue economic development.

In this regard it seems as if strategic thinkers are constantly breaking new ground. There is a virtual plethora of ideas, of 'options', on how to enhance security, but only a few – really very few – living or practical examples of how this can actually be done.

Canadian support for multilateralism or dialogue as a primary means of achieving security builds on existing institutions. For example: the Canadian International Development Agency (CIDA), through the University of British Columbia's Centre for

Asian Legal Studies, has provided support for Indonesia to host a series of meetings on conflict resolution in the South China Sea. These meetings have been credited with significantly advancing confidence-building measures among the interested parties.

The Canada-ASEAN Centre in Singapore has supported a series of initiatives put forward by individual scholars and institutions to examine various aspects of security in Southeast Asia. This support has been very broad in scope, reflecting an inclusive Canadian view of security incorporating economic and social, as well as political and military issues. Canadian support over the past decade, through CIDA, for a number of institutes and research organisations in ASEAN countries (the Institute of Strategic and International Studies, Malaysia, and the Thailand Development Research Institute are two examples) has contributed – if indirectly – to the sharing of ideas and improved communication throughout the region.

A forum, in its implicit sense, is an opportunity for dialogue, a coming together. Repeated, it establishes a practice, or what Canada calls a habit of dialogue. It is this habit of dialogue that is so important in the context of security, since those whose habit it is to talk when there is a problem have made a huge leap toward mutual understanding and a resolution of the problem.

The end of the Cold War has fundamentally changed the definitions of security, although it will take some time before this is fully understood by governments and appropriate policy responses are developed. There is cause for hope and despair. While there is substantial momentum for strengthening the capacity of the United Nations, especially in preventive diplomacy, the reduction of arms transfers, and in peace-making, recent events in Central and Eastern Europe have led to a recognition that traditional approaches to national and regional security are still needed.

Canada recognises that security is complex but indivisible, and that no one state can be secure either at the expense of, or in isolation from others. The Canadian approach to cooperative security is the development of working relationships and functional links (political, economic and social) at all levels of interaction, official and unofficial, and through regular and systematic dialogue to promote transparency, confidence, knowledge and reassurance. Put in its most simple terms, Canada's approach has been to contribute to the development of a habit of dialogue through discussion, negotiation, cooperation and compromise.

While it is possible to work towards global cooperative security within the context of the United Nations, it is more realistic to focus, in the first instance, on developing cooperative security at a regional level where there may be more similar interests, values, and experiences. Such frameworks, successfully established and implemented, can and should then interact to contribute to broader cooperative security frameworks. This is a building block approach to common security.

Multilateral arrangements often have a functional, as well as regional, common denominator. Cooperative mechanisms such as development banks, economic and environmental agreements, and dialogue arrangements (such as the GATT, the IMF, the UN) can secure their members' broader interests through cooperation and, perhaps more importantly, pre-empt tension and conflict. Success is dependent upon states acknowledging that participation in legally or politically binding arrangements flowing from such dialogue contributes in concrete ways to their national security.

The Canadian initiative to investigate the establishment of a North Pacific Cooperative Security Dialogue (NPCSD) was first introduced by the Secretary of State for External Affairs in speeches in Victoria, Tokyo, and Jakarta in July 1990. It has been the subject of much discussion, and some debate, ever since.

The NPCSD has had two tracks – a non-governmental and a governmental element – and is focused on the North Pacific countries of China, the Democratic Peoples Republic of Korea, Japan, the Soviet Union, the Republic of Korea, the United States, and Canada. This region has a significant concentration of conventional and nuclear forces, it is not fully represented in Asia Pacific Economic Cooperation (APEC), and if there is instability, e.g. on the Korean Peninsula, this would have an adverse effect on Canada's political, economic, social and environmental interests, yet there is *still* no multilateral forum to allow the timely discussion of policy.

The NGO track of the Canadian initiative, while encouraging an exchange of views by regional experts, was designed specifically to explore issues and prospects for dialogue and to focus knowledge and awareness on the North Pacific.

The official, or government, track of the Canadian initiative was an open-ended process intended to explore the merits of establishing a regional dialogue encompassing all relevant themes and issues. The Canadian view was that such a dialogue must not be the result of an attempt to transplant the Conference on Security and Cooperation in Europe (CSCE). The sources of tension and the nature of the regional challenges in the North Pacific still do not lend themselves to such an approach. Rather, stability will be enhanced by accommodating the specific traditions, history and geopolitical dynamics of the region. The continuing emphasis is on consultation, not negotiation, and on seeking consensus on how best to address the need for a North Pacific dialogue.

Why a *forum*? In a way, it is not the actual forum that is important; it is the mutual understanding and the sense of common or mutual interest that dialogue nurtures. Dialogue and the building of dialogue is crucial in the Asia Pacific because the region is vast and culturally diverse.

The end of the Cold War has ended confrontation but also old certainties. The emerging new world order has opened up new possibilities for cooperation as well as new complexities in regional relationships. The multipolarisation or diffusion of power has replaced the Cold War framework – the shared context all countries of the region understood and accepted (even while disputing it). The rise of non-superpower national interests is now an elemental factor in the global and regional power equations.

Collective security arrangements, if they are defensive in nature, are fully compatible with a cooperative security framework. Regional bilateral military arrangements have underpinned regional stability for decades. They remain an essential part of the regional security framework, but there is now room for other multilateral relationships which can complement these bilateral security pillars – on the basis of cooperative security.

What does this mean in practical terms? It means informal discussions among a mix of academic, officials and non-governmental specialists. At another level, it means a more regular dialogue among governments, if that is what the governments in the region want. It is important not to be overly ambitious nor too modest but there is a need for an open and flexible *framework* to facilitate such dialogue.

What will the future hold for viable regional security forums?

Russia

The first inkling of what would lead to a fundamental shift in strategic thinking in the Asia Pacific was President Gorbachev's 28 July 1986, Vladivostok speech, the first of a series of statements, interviews and initiatives which came to be known as the 'Vladivostok-Krasnoyarsk track',[1] and which called *inter alia* for a pan-Asian foreign ministers' meeting, to be held in Vladivostok in 1993 and followed by a pan-Asian summit; regional security consultations to be held on the margins of the United Nations General Assembly; and agreement on a multilateral convention on the conservation of biological resources, leading to a convention on environmental protection in the Pacific.

From 1986 until mid-1991, Soviet Asia Pacific regional security proposals were at best challenged and at worst dismissed by Western and most Asian governments, among the most resistant being the Japanese. The long-expected visit to Japan by Gorbachev in April 1991 did not produce the anticipated breakthrough in bilateral relations that might have led to Japanese agreement on the need for regional security discussions. Gorbachev's new security proposals (the establishment of a five nation forum – U.S.S.R., U.S.A., China, India and Japan – to discuss broad Asia Pacific issues; and U.S.S.R.-U.S.A.-Japan trilateral discussions on regional security) were described by the Japanese as premature.

Since the disintegration of the Soviet Union, there has been no authoritative statement from Moscow on Russian foreign policy towards the Asia Pacific, and there may not be for some time. While understandably pre-occupied with domestic economic and political issues, the reluctance of President Yeltsin to address Asia Pacific issues has led some observers in the region to question Russia's Asia Pacific vocation, and to challenge Russia to take the same bold steps East of the Urals that it took to the West. It is nonsensical for Russia to lose six years of diplomatic effort through an unwillingness or inability to follow up or participate actively in the region. Admittedly, the boundary dispute with Japan and the difficulties associated with force redeployments are mitigating circumstances, but Moscow should be urged to participate as actively as possible in all aspects of regional stability and well-being.

The Republic of Korea

During his October 1988 address to the United Nations General Assembly, President Roh Tae-Woo proposed a six nation (North and South Korea, Japan, China, U.S.A. and U.S.S.R.) Consultative Conference for Peace to '... deal with a broad range of ideas concerning peace, stability, progress, and prosperity within the area'. The initiative failed to receive support from North Korea and China, and was not pursued by Seoul.

President Roh referred to his proposal during an interview with TASS shortly before his December 1990 trip to the Soviet Union. Three months later, the Korean media reported the Government's moves to establish a six nation 'international security body' to study Peninsula security issues. In his 29 June 1991 speech to the Hoover Institution, President Roh stated:

> It is now time to design and frame a structure of cooperation which will ensure a higher dimension of peace, prosperity and happiness to people (of the Asia Pacific region).[2]

There was some speculation that President Roh might have used the occasion of the Republic of Korea's (ROK) entry into the United Nations as an opportunity to flesh out his proposal, but the initiative, having been bypassed by the advancements in Seoul-Pyongyang relations, is no longer being pursued. This is unfortunate because a conflict on the Korean Peninsula would have regional and perhaps global ramifications, and a multilateral approach (not necessarily limited to any number of participants) offers yet another avenue to pursue dialogue and dispute resolution.

Australia

Australian strategic thinkers have for some time been concerned with political, economic and social trends in the Asia Pacific, particularly about the potential for negative power vacuums. An additional concern was the increased sophistication of weapons being acquired by countries in the region and the emergence of new sub-regional power relationships. The latter development was seen largely incorrectly as a result of a reduced American security profile in the Asia Pacific. Under Foreign Minister Hayden, and later Evans, Australia has also embarked on a more activist foreign policy agenda designed to raise Canberra's profile in the region and to prove Australia's credentials as an Asia Pacific country. Both APEC and the 'Cambodia blueprint' are noteworthy products of this activism.

In his 12 August 1987 speech to the Conference on Security and Arms Control in the North Pacific, Hayden suggested the time was ripe for regional Confidence-Building Measures (CBMs). On 27 July 1990. Evans submitted to the *International Herald Tribune* an article which included the statement that, 'It is not unreasonable to expect that new Europe-style patterns of cooperation between old adversaries will find their echo in this part of the world'.

Senator Evans expanded on his 'Asia Pacific Security Dialogue' at the August 1990 ASEAN Post-Ministerial Conference. Japan, the United States and a number of ASEAN countries expressed concern with the 'Conference on Security and Cooperation in Asia' (CSCA) aspects of the Australian proposal, arguing that it granted the Soviet Union regional respectability without requiring it to reduce its forces in the Asia Pacific region, and that it ran the risk of providing the Soviets with greater leverage in advance of the planned visits to Japan by Shevardnadze and Gorbachev. Underlying the Japanese misgivings was the belief that the Soviets might seize on support for a regional security dialogue as an opportunity to multilateralise the unresolved U.S.S.R.-Japan border dispute. Washington saw no reason to replace the successful model of U.S.A.-directed bilateral military alliances with a multilateral forum where United States influence would necessarily be diluted. 'If it ain't broke, don't fix it' became a refrain of American policy-makers.

The Australian response was to expand on their initiative, to differentiate it from the Conference on Security and Cooperation in Europe (CSCE) and to distance it from earlier Soviet proposals.[3] This nuanced approach was further developed by Evans in the lead-up to the July 1991 ASEAN-PMC, with emphasis placed on canvassing ideas from other regional actors rather than proposing further initiatives. Evans lowered Australia's profile by deferring to ASEAN's views that the ASEAN-PMC be the preferred vehicle for regional security discussions. This seeming withdrawal was somewhat compensated for by more activist studies by Australian research institutes on traditional military Confidence- and Security-Building Measures (CSBMs), and through enhanced bilateral security discussions with several Asia Pacific countries, specifically in the area of maritime surveillance.

Australian and Canadian views on regional security are remarkably similar, and the differences relate more to process than to substance. In the past few months Canadian and Australian officials have held detailed discussions on this and other issues. Canada has benefited greatly from Australian expertise, both at the official and non-governmental levels, and this will affect their evolving approaches to a wide variety of regional issues.

Mongolia

Mongolia's emergence from the domination of the former Soviet Union coincided with an attempt to develop an independent diplomatic profile in Asia Pacific. This double evolution was evident in Ulan Bator's changing stance on regional security issues. At the time of the Second Vladivostok Conference in September 1990, Mongolia uncritically supported the Soviet Union's regional security agenda, an attitude which led many observers to discount Mongolia's own 1989 initiative to establish an eight country forum (Mongolia, U.S.S.R., U.S.A., China, North and South Korea, Japan and Canada) to create a 'mechanism of political dialogue among the countries of the region (and) cooperation in economy, science and technology, culture and education, ecology and humanitarian links'.[4]

After hosting a small regional security conference in Ulan Bator in the fall of 1990, and participating in the Second

Vladivostok Conference and the Canadian North Pacific Cooperative Security Dialogue (NPCSD) Colloquium in April 1991, Mongolia, preoccupied by domestic concerns, has placed emphasis on
being a consultative party rather than an initiator of policy.

ASEAN

The evolution of ASEAN serves as a stellar example of how
political cooperation among nations which do not aspire to great
power status can bring about peace, security and stability. The
often disparate views of ASEAN member countries have, however, made formal discussion of regional security with the Association problematic. ASEAN consideration of traditional security
matters was often left to research institutes, such as the Institute
of Strategic and International Studies (ISIS), which have held
regular, well-attended symposia, roundtables, and conferences to
discuss various aspects of regional security, at a 'semi-official'
level, with emphasis on traditional military security.[5] The role
ISIS played in stimulating careful consideration of security issues
within the ASEAN region should not be underestimated.

ASEAN as a group was not supportive of either the Soviet,
Australian, or Canadian forays into Asia Pacific security. (The
Mongolian and Korean initiatives were not seriously considered
by ASEAN.) While ostensibly discussing issues of regional scope,
ASEAN's focus was understandably on Southeast Asia, particularly Indo-China, the growing influence of Japan, and the necessity of maintaining a stabilising U.S.A. military presence in the
region.

The decline of the Soviet threat, the anticipated resolution of
the Cambodian conflict, and the reduced U.S.A. military presence
in the region, contributed to a growing sense that ASEAN should
adopt a more direct role in approaching regional security issues.[6]
A collective decision was reached at the ASEAN Ministerial Meeting in 1991 that serious re-thinking of ASEAN's approach to
regional security was needed and that the Association should
balance 'out-of-region' security initiatives with its own proposals.
The result was an increase in research by the major think-tanks,
paralleled by policy papers from several foreign ministries. This
contributed to the decision to invite the Soviet Union and China to

observe the 1991 ASEAN Ministerial Meeting in order to broaden the consultative process. In addition, Japan took advantage of the 1991 PMC to put forward its own proposal for an active discussion of security issues in the Post-Ministerial Conference (PMC) context.

Through these actions, the entire diplomatic equation in the Asia Pacific changed. At the ASEAN Summit in 1992, it was decided that the Association was now in favour of using ASEAN as the primary forum for discussing Asia Pacific security issues.

The 1992 Post-Ministerial Conference gives security issues a prominent place on the agenda. The first major grouping of items on the programme for the important Six Plus Seven closed sessions deals entirely with security questions. Under the general heading of 'Potential Sources of Tension in the Asia Pacific Region', the issues of the Korean Peninsula and the South China Sea will be reviewed. This will be followed by consideration of 'Trends in Regional Security'. Finally, 'Regional Problems' including Cambodia and Indo-Chinese Refugees will be reviewed.

This makes for a very full consideration of regional security topics in the PMC context and clearly underlines ASEAN's commitment to address these issues in an open manner with other interested nations. Indications are that the dialogue partners have responded positively to the proposed consideration of the security issues on the PMC agenda and are even prepared to take the lead in the debate of these items in certain circumstances, as in the case of Korea on the 'Situation of the Korean Peninsula'. Canada is pleased to see that not only are security issues present in the ASEAN-PMC agenda, but that the range of issues is broad. This indeed promises to be the beginning of a security dialogue firmly rooted in the realities of the region, and therefore of practical use to the participants.

In addition to the formal consideration of security issues on the agenda of the PMC, it is also worth noting that the ASEAN Ministerial Meeting will be attended by the Foreign Ministers of China, Russia, Vietnam and Laos as observers. Their presence at the 6th Asia Pacific Roundtable is also a positive sign. It showed the recognition by ASEAN of the interdependence of issues and relationships and the clear benefits of including, rather than excluding, potential partners in this emerging security dialogue.

Their presence will clearly have the effect of strengthening regional links, increasing confidence, and furthering security in the area in the widest sense. This broadened senior level interest in the ASEAN Ministerial Meeting and the emergence of a full-scale discussion of security issues at the PMC, means that an effective new mechanism has emerged at the Foreign Ministers level. This should contribute significantly to strengthening the debate in a wider regional context.

It cannot be doubted that the discussion of security in a formal, multilateral process will, in itself, be a major regional confidence-building mechanism. Identifying common concerns, discussing them, sharing problems and solutions is the essence of a security dialogue. Transparency, whether in military movements or economic policies, contributes to stability.

Japan

Since the end of the Pacific War, Japan has relied exclusively on the United States for its security. The Japanese economic miracle was a direct result of enlightened occupation policies and the economic benefits of supplying material and entrepôt facilities to UN forces in Korea. Japan was the essential component of United States security policy in Asia Pacific, and every aspect of Japanese Asia Pacific foreign policy is related to maintaining harmonious relations with the United States.

Japanese views of the various regional security proposals were almost uniform in their disapproval. Suggestions from Mongolia and Korea were commented on favourably but not pursued. Tokyo dismissed the Soviet proposals as self-serving and hollow, and criticised Australia and Canada for their naïveté in appearing to follow the Soviet's regional agenda (views which were echoed in a gentler way by Washington) or to impose European models on Asia.

The approach taken by ASEAN in the lead-up to the 1991 PMC obliged Japan to reconsider its attitude towards discussion of regional security arrangements. By the time news of ASEAN's intentions had reached Tokyo, much rethinking had already been done[7] and the decision taken to support calls for multilateral security discussions. To ensure that the Soviet Union would continue to be isolated from the process, it was decided to support

ASEAN's proposals with the proviso that the existing PMC be the preferred forum. This would allow discussions on 'regional reassurance' to take place among like-minded countries while deferring – probably for several years – participation by the Soviet Union.

Having launched the 'Nakayama initiative'[8] at the 1991 ASEAN-PMC, Japan has effectively committed itself to participation in a multilateral dialogue on regional security issues.

The United States

The U.S.A. has been steadfast in its preference for bilateral security arrangements over multilateral discussion. Yet, suggestions of broadening the concept of security to include non-traditional, non-military threats – which until recently were dismissed in Washington – are being re-evaluated in the light of belated recognition that cooperative security discussions in Asia Pacific are, in many respects, already occurring.

APEC

The emergence of the Asia Pacific Economic Cooperation (APEC) process has led some people, largely in non-governmental circles, to muse about the possibility of broadening this forum's economic agenda to include the discussion of regional security issues. Canada believes, as do most if not all APEC governments, that the hazards of such an approach, particularly the danger of rupturing the fragile consensus which has been painstakingly nurtured within APEC, far outweigh any incremental benefits that could realistically be expected from introducing contentious security issues in this forum.

Canada and others have no wish to put at risk the remarkable progress that has already been achieved in APEC in enhancing economic cooperation in the region. To jeopardise this would not only be a loss in its own right, but would also be counter-productive in view of the importance of economic development to the political stability of the region.

Furthermore, there remains within APEC a lingering trepidation on the part of some ASEAN members that the consolidation of APEC could undermine the relevance of ASEAN in the region. Broadening APEC's agenda into the political/security spheres at this time could fuel these concerns. At the same time, dialogue in APEC on economic issues helps establish a frame of mind conducive to the peaceful resolution of disputes. Limited to an economic agenda, it still has a contribution to make to what is called cooperative security.

Canada

The Canadian North Pacific security initiative initially received mixed reviews from Asia Pacific states. The Soviet Union and Mongolia supported it, claiming – unhelpfully and inaccurately – that is was an extension of their own regional security proposals. Australia and New Zealand supported the concepts, but argued that the geographic focus was skewed in that it excluded participation from important South Pacific actors. ASEAN initially viewed the Canadian proposal as an unwelcome, out-of-region initiative. The United States and Japan remained the last to be convinced of the utility of the Canadian approach.

The initiative, refined and with its emphasis firmly on the NGO track, has proven to be a useful process which has contributed to the development of a body of academic and policy knowledge in Canada and elsewhere on the benefits and costs of establishing a multilateral security dialogue, and on traditional and non-traditional threats to North Pacific stability.

The events of 1992 have altered the geopolitical landscape. The original NPCSD formula was designed for an earlier era, and Canadian approaches to Asia Pacific security have continued to evolve. While a primary focus for Canada on Asia Pacific security continues to be the North Pacific, the emergence of the ASEAN-PMC as a useful forum for multilateral discussions of security is fully supported.

Where all this leads will depend as much on the changing strategic environment in the region as on the energies of governments and academics. Recent trends in regional security thinking indicate that a regional or sub-regional dialogue is recognised by most countries as a stabilising and Confidence-Building Measure. While traditional security issues remain of central concern, they must neither be ignored nor over-emphasised by those involved in broadening the definition of cooperative security.

It appears that the Asia Pacific region (or at least Southeast Asia and the North Pacific) will soon be engaged in a formal multilateral dialogue which will consider both traditional and non-traditional security issues. No one country can take credit for this. The former Soviet Union, by its handling of relations with the United States more than its various Asia Pacific initiatives, made a signal contribution to the relaxation of tensions in the region. The initiatives by Mongolia and Korea show that countries often considered peripheral (the dangers of the DMZ notwithstanding) can play a catalyst's role in regional affairs. And Canberra and Ottawa can each claim authorship of many of the principles taken on board by ASEAN. Japan, while slow and appearing at times inflexible in the past, has accepted that open discussion of Japanese security concerns is, for its neighbours, a serious and far-reaching confidence building measure. The participation of the United States, still the paramount military, economic, and diplomatic power in Asia Pacific, will be essential to the success of the emerging regional cooperative security dialogue.

Canada is ready to assist in evaluating which areas of cooperative security offer the most promising avenues, which obstacles appear insurmountable (at least at present), and which existing institutions or organisations offer enhanced avenues for dialogue and consultation.

Notes

1. This term was applied by Western diplomats to describe the overall Soviet Asia Pacific security initiative. The term took its name form Gorbachev's speeches in Vladivostok (1986) and Krasnoyarsk (1988) and from Shevardnadze's speech at the Second Vladivostok Conference in September 1990. One major element of the Soviet initiative not reflected by this term was Gorbachev's widely-quoted interview in *Merdeka*, (July 21, 1987) when he stepped back from the parallel with Helsinki and offered more concrete suggestions for arms control and confidence-building in the Asia Pacific region.
2. 'Korea's Emerging Role in a New Pacific Order', (29 June, 1991), Palo Alto, California.

3. There were also attempts to disassociate Australia from the term 'CSCA' at times going so far as to repudiate the authenticity of the *International Herald Tribune* headline. A more convincing argument was that early references to the value of the guiding principles of the CSCE were misconstrued and misinterpreted as a suggestion to transfer, holus-bolus, the European experience to the Asia Pacific.

4. Speech by President Z.H. Batmunkh, (18 August, 1989).

5. These events have provided regional governments with an 'unofficial' forum for floating regional security initiatives. At the Malaysian ISIS-organised Fifth Asia Pacific Roundtable, Vietnam proposed the establishment of a new Southeast Asia security relationship which would focus initially on confidence-building.

6. Individual ASEAN members have offered suggestions to enhance regional security. In June 1989, Malaysian Prime Minister Mahathir, in addressing the Malaysian ISIS organised Third Asia Pacific Roundtable, called for modest regional CSBMs such as prior notification of military exercises and transparency. More recently, Malaysian Defence Minister Najib, in a speech given in Darwin, spoke of the utility of holding a regional security conference.

7. Much of this thinking was reflected in Yukio Satoh's paper, 'Asian Pacific Process for Stability and Security' presented at the Fifth Asia Pacific Roundtable: Confidence Building and Conflict Reduction in the Pacific, Kuala Lumpur, 10-14 June 1991.

8. The Japanese initiative consisted of two tiers: an enhanced political and security dialogue using all available fora; and an ASEAN senior officials' meeting on security, with participation by officials from Dialogue Partners.

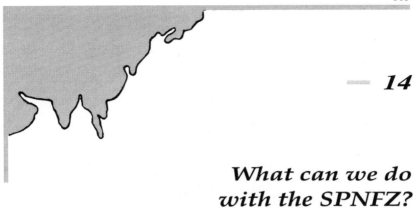

14

What can we do with the SPNFZ?

Llewelyn Richards

A Brief Description of the Zone

From the perspective of those living in the South Pacific half the world is water, with two large islands, Australia and Antarctica and a scattering of smaller islands. Some continental masses lie way out on the rim. Chart 1, centred on the international date line and level with Auckland (37 degrees S), shows the picture. The boundaries for the South Pacific Nuclear Free Zone[1] (Spinfiz, the diplomats call it) are shown in Chart 2. The Zone 'covers' that area, but not all states inside the boundaries are members of the Treaty. The colonial territories of French Polynesia, New Caledonia, Wallis and Futuna, American (Eastern) Samoa, are not members. Nor is the Kingdom of Tonga, nor the Republic of Vanuatu. For the states of the South Pacific see Chart 3. As most of the prohibitions of the Treaty apply only to land and territorial waters, the true extent of the zone is shown in Chart 4. This sequence of maps has given rise to the nickname 'The Disappearing Zone'. It seems rather irrelevant to have a 'picture-frame' zone with boundaries way out in the sea beyond even the 200 mile limit Exclusive Economic Zones. At a meeting called by the New

Chart 1
The Pacific Hemisphere
(Centred 37°S, 180°E/W)

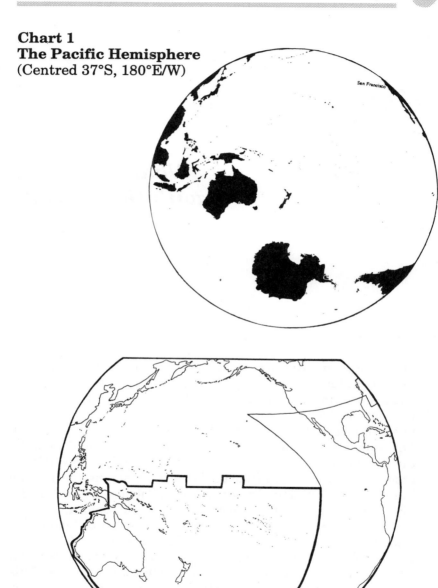

Chart 2
The Treaties

AS	American Samoa
CI	Cook Islands
FSM	Federated States of Micronesia
F	Fiji
FP	French Polynesia
GG	Guam
K	Kiribati
MI	Marshall Islands
Na	Nauru
NC	New Caledonia
Ni	Niue
NM	Northern Marianas
B	Palau
PNG	Papua New Guinea
Pt	Pitcairn
SI	Solomon Islands
TI	Tokelau Islands
To	Tonga
Tu	Tuvalu
V	Vanuatu
WF	Wallis and Futuna
WS	Western Samoa

Chart 3
The States

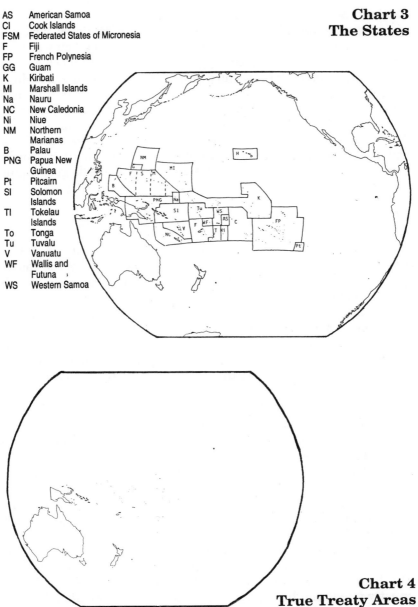

Chart 4
True Treaty Areas

Zealand Ministry of Foreign Affairs in 1985 to 'explain' to peace groups what the Treaty would contain, the Ministry was not interested in boundaries at all and the impression given was that there might well be none, possibly to make it absolutely clear that the Treaty would claim no jurisdiction over the high seas. However, in the event, boundaries were drawn, possibly in imitation of the Tlatelolco Treaty which has a Northern boundary cutting from Los Angeles to Cape Hatteras in North Carolina. Perhaps boundaries were drawn because they make it look like a zone, not splatter from a scratchy nib. However, the most likely reason is because the anti-testing and dumping sections needs geographic limits.

How it Came into Being

The Zone came into being entirely through pressure of public opinion in the South Pacific. There were no calls by the major powers nor by anyone else outside the region to have the South Pacific nuclear free. An early published call for a zone was by the N.Z. Campaign for Nuclear Disarmament in 1963 with the slogan 'No bombs south of the line'. In August 1964 the N.Z. Parliament debated the topic. By the time Bill Rowling introduced a resolution on the subject at the UN in 1975, the missile scare which drove the U.S.A. to accept and assist the birth of the Tlatelolco Treaty was well past.

For New Zealanders the continued bomb testing by France at Mururoa was a powerful reminder of the radiation hazards of nuclear war. A nuclear-free Pacific was a natural extension of the nuclear-free New Zealand people were looking for.

In Australia things were more complicated, particularly because uranium mining and the U.S. bases were good money earners. Public opinion was not nearly so clearly anti-nuclear. In the Pacific Islands public opinion and politics is a very difficult study for the outsider. Being small and inconsequential, international media reporting from these states is sporadic and superficial. For example, no New Zealand paper has its own reporter in the Islands. Academic study has been even less obvious. Being mostly tribal and hierarchical in structure (despite added democratic features) South Pacific public opinion and political decision-making are generally hidden from outsider analysis behind language and custom.

Nevertheless, in the Pacific Island states, fishing is a major part of everyone's livelihood, culture and recreation, so anything threatening fishing is understood as a direct threat to the people which cannot be brushed aside, ignored, or rushed through. The sea and its fish return again and again in Pacific Island negotiations, the subject is never dropped, assurances and promises about it must be repeated, reiterated, re-argued, re-made, recounted, till Palangi (Europeans) wonder if Polynesians think about anything else. Nuclear contamination of the sea, by dumping, testing, accident or fighting, is thus totally unacceptable. In July 1991, non-colonial delegates to the South Pacific Commission declared, 'Nuclear residue poses the greatest threat for the environment, present and future, in the oceanic countries'.

The states and territories of the South Pacific are loosely joined in two organisations: (i) The South Pacific Commission, which was set up by the old colonial powers and still includes the French and British; (ii) The South Pacific Forum, set up by the island States, which excludes the French. It has recently invited the U.S.-connected Republic of the Marshall Islands and the Federated States of Micronesia to join. It was at Forum meetings that the SPNFZ idea was introduced and agreed to. There are also less political but important bodies: (iii) The South Pacific Bureau for Economic Cooperation (SPBEC), the fore-runner of the Forum, now its executive arm, and the body that oversees compliance of the SPNFZ; (iv) The South Pacific Regional Environmental Programme (SPREP), recently moved out from under the thumb of the French in Noumea to Apia in Western Samoa; (v) the increasingly important Forum Fishing Agency (FFA) to control fishing by foreigners, especially of migratory species such as tuna; (vi) an agency, hardly begun but likely to be very important, to control mineral exploitation.

The Treaty resulted from the efforts of the anti-nuclear movements, but they did not get the treaty they had asked for. Clearly politicking, politicians, and power-block pressure all had an influence on the final outcome.

Michael Hamel-Green provides a very important account of evolution of the Treaty and the Zone.[2] He has been criticised for articulating a conspiratorial account of why politicians diluted its impact to suit the United States. But the important point is that the Treaty was passed, ten South Pacific states have signed it and two nuclear powers have signed the protocols. None of this was an accident.

There are good statements of the U.S.A.'s position to the Zone in U.S. Senate records. For example, Richard Perle states 'the Australian government for one, did work hard to deprive the resolution [the Treaty of Rarotonga] of all meaning'.[3] Other interesting accounts of the creation of the SPNFZ can be found in David Lange's, *Nuclear Free the New Zealand Way*, such as '... I went to the 1984 meeting of the South Pacific Forum to resurrect the idea of a South Pacific nuclear-free zone'.[4] In the New Zealand peace movement's magazine *Peacelink*, articles on the SPNFZ are surprisingly few, but the possible writers were busy producing alternative treaties and lobbying the government directly.

What does Nuclear-free Mean for the South Pacific?

It is clear from the maps that to keep the South Pacific free of nuclear war and preparations for nuclear war the seas, as well as the tiny land areas, must be kept free of nuclear weapons and their back-up facilities. A true Pacific Nuclear Free Zone needs to:

1. Keep nuclear weapons out of the whole region, not just the tiny land areas.
2. Keep out not only the warheads but their delivery vehicles, the ships, planes and missiles. This means denying passage through and over the seas (as well as ship visits to territorial waters).
3. Make the fighting of a nuclear war in the area impossible, or nearly impossible, by excluding targeting systems, control systems, navigation systems and surveillance systems.
4. Contribute to global disarmament and to global security by making war fighting from the region or into the region impossible. This can be done by excluding the same infrastructure, the C3I installations, the military satellite tracking stations, and the telecommunications spying network, such as at Tangimoana and Waihopai in New Zealand and Pine Gap in Australia.

5. Ban uranium mining and export – uranium is turned by power stations into plutonium for bombs.
6. Prohibit all nuclear waste dumping on land or sea.

The present Treaty fails to do all of these, even the first, since nuclear-armed ship visits are allowed. Michael Hamel-Green has a comparable list of 20 things a comprehensive Nuclear Free Zone Treaty should prohibit, of which the Rarotonga Treaty prohibits only five.[5] His list is longer than the one above because he carefully distinguishes aircraft from ships. This seems a somewhat artificial distinction so all comments about ships, port visits, in this chapter will include aircraft, aircraft landings, and so on.

What does the SPNFZ Ban?

1. No party will manufacture, acquire, or control nuclear weapons nor help any other state to do so.
2. No party will supply nuclear materials or technology outside the Non-Proliferation Treaty (NPT) and the International Atomic Energy Agency (IAEA) safeguards.
3. No party permits the stationing of nuclear weapons on its territory.
4. No party permits testing; none will encourage testing by anyone.
5. No party will dump radioactive waste at sea in the Zone; they will prevent anyone else dumping in their territorial waters; they will not assist or encourage anyone to dump at sea in the Zone.

What Nuclear Elements are Left Untouched by the SPNFZ?

1. The sea: 88 per cent of the Zone is sea and nuclear weapons, their vehicles, and their command and control systems, may move at will inside the Zone. Even dumping is not totally prohibited – states outside the Zone (or not party to the Treaty) will only 'lack assistance and encouragement' if they dump at sea, inside the Zone.
2. The territorial waters of the parties are still nuclear, if nuclear

powers desire to transport weapons through them. Only New Zealand has passed legislation banning nuclear weapons from its territorial waters, and even here it is only from its harbours. The Law of the Sea still allows 'innocent passage' through all other territorial waters.

3. The land is still available for nuclear waste dumping.
4. Uranium mining is not banned.
5. Communications, Command, Control and Intelligence facilities for nuclear weapons are not banned.
6. Flight testing of nuclear delivery vehicles, such as missiles, is not banned.

Historical Developments

The Treaty of Rarotonga was signed on Hiroshima Day, 1985. State parties then began a diplomatic round to get the protocols signed.

> PROTOCOL 1 asks the U.S.A., France and the U.K. to accept the Treaty on behalf of their dependent territories within the Zone.
> PROTOCOL 2 invites the nuclear-weapons powers not to test in or on the seas of the South Pacific.
> PROTOCOL 3 is a negative security guarantee to the Treaty parties from the nuclear weapons powers.

The Soviet Union and China signed the protocols. The U.S.A., for whom the Treaty was watered down, refused to sign. The United Kingdom followed the United States. As the only Soviet and Chinese nuclear presence in the South Pacific had been splash-downs from their ICBM missile tests, and the Royal Navy seldom enters the South Pacific, the Treaty was felt to be aimed fairly and squarely at France and the U.S.A. France was irate and said so, for example, in the UN 3rd Special Session on Disarmament, where they tried to block all mention of the zone. The U.S.A. got what it wanted – a land only, bombs only treaty – but still felt unable to sign due protocols.

The U.S.A. says that it 'abides by the provisions of the Treaty' but will not sign 'to maintain flexibility in the event of a crisis'.[6] Congress has passed a non-binding resolution recommending to the President that the Treaty be signed, but so far he has not.

Michael Hamel-Green has discussed the fact that the U.S.A. has been able to continue to develop its strategic use of the South Pacific, deploying cruise missiles and improving its C3I.[7] Moves to strengthen the nuclear freedom of the South Pacific have been stopped also.

The real achievement of the Zone has been that it applied pressure at the UN, on France, to stop its testing. Also, the U.S.S.R. and China have been able, since they signed the protocols, to get better access to the South Pacific, and have negotiated fishing agreements with Vanuatu and Kiribati.

The 'failures' of the Treaty are first, that it did not stop French testing till the year-long moratorium announced in May 1992. Whether the SPNFZ was a cause of that moratorium will be the subject of debate; economic pressures at home will no doubt be cited by the French military as more important. Second, it did not reduce the risk of nuclear weapons being fired into the area at U.S. ships and C3I targets; it was the collapse of the U.S.S.R. that did that.

Otherwise the failures are mainly the result of the U.S.A. not signing the protocols. This failure caused bitterness, often voiced by Melanesians, against the U.S.A. and its ally Australia. Signing would have brought much more pressure on France (there is some uncertainty as to whether the U.S.A.'s refusal was a trade-off for French participation in the Missile Technology Control Regime). Now, in 1992, there is the irony of France asking the U.S.A. to follow its lead with a test ban; and again the U.S.A. is isolated in world opinion. The U.S.A. has not signed the Law of the Sea either, and baulks at restraining its fishermen poaching tuna. The result is that the U.S.A. has lost mana (regard), and Japan, the EC, Russia and Asian countries are becoming more welcome.

Not signing has worked against the influence of the two-member ANZUS military alliance. Papua New Guinea has asked to join ASEAN, and if U.S. policy continues an outmoded containment policy, then the appeal of an internationally-sanctioned regional neutrality will grow.

Ways of Expanding the Treaty

It is clear that touting the protocols and encouraging island states to join the SPNFZ is insufficient to promote a more effective Zone. The Antarctic Treaty is a good example of how a treaty can be expanded in scope. It has carefully, with occasional hiccups, been extended from simply excluding things nuclear (in a trade-off for waiving territorial claims) to encouraging things scientific, to protecting things environmental and now, for 50 years, to excluding things minerally extractive.

The scope of the SPNFZ could be extended to:

1. Improve the bans already in place.
2. Add new nuclear bans.
3. Add non-nuclear bans.

For example, the SPNFZ could extend the dumping provisions: to ban waste dumping on land (an example of 1 above); with a protocol added, it could invite all states with nuclear power stations or research facilities to agree not to dump nuclear waste in the Zone, (an example of 2 above); an extension could be made for all toxic waste, chemical and biological as well as nuclear, (an example of 3 above).

These new bans, being closely related to fishing and the proper use of the tiny land areas of the Pacific Islands, should not be difficult to introduce, once Australia is convinced of their worth.

The best improvement to the bans already in place would be to extend the Treaty to ban the transit of nuclear weapons on the high seas. This is one of the things many of the island States dearly wanted, and it remains a sticking point for Vanuatu.

The most important type of new nuclear ban – would be to prohibit all nuclear C3I facilities on land. This would be a difficult ban for Australia because the U.S.A. relies on an Australian VLF transmitter at Northwest Cape to send launch orders to U.S. Trident submarines.

Another way of ensuring that the Zone really limits unhelpful military activity would be to expand the scope of the Treaty, to include non-nuclear topics. This would open the way for a host of useful security-enhancing clauses and protocols. There could be biological weapons prohibitions, chemical weapons prohibitions, seabed mining clauses, and even ecological and resource agreements, such as banning all drift-nets, whaling, purse-seining, or whatever is needed. Although some of these seem far from the original reason for the SPNFZ, they are all matters of great concern to a broad concept of security in the region. As nuclear weapons become less important (with the Bush initiative, and the moratorium on testing by the French), so security against exploitation and environmental degradation become much more urgent issues.

Hints that politicians and military people in the U.S.A. see the new role of the U.S. Navy as providing force to secure economic objectives – namely markets and raw materials to maintain the U.S.A.'s standard of living – are emerging. If such becomes its role, an expanded SPNFZ, including environmental protection clauses, is important. If the U.S.A. were to abide by the protocols, it would be a 'paper barrier' that most South Pacific states would be pleased to have against wholesale exploitation.

A possibility in the 1990s is expanding SPNFZ to include missiles. This is not entirely a nuclear issue since it would, presumably, aim to ban missiles with conventional warheads – banning the nuclear warheads alone, would be unworkable. The French, when announcing their intention to join the Non-Proliferation Treaty (NPT) revived (or invented) the idea of Ballistic Missile Free Zones, Chemical Weapons Free Zones, Biological Weapons Free Zones, and Weapons of Mass Destruction Free Zones.

One or more of these could easily be added to the SPNFZ. Ballistic missiles look the most hopeful for a first try since the U.S.A. is so keen on the idea. Despite France bringing the subject into discussion, a South Pacific Weapons-of-Mass-Destruction Free Zone looked the least likely whilst France continued testing at Mururoa. (Since the French threw out every attempted reference to the SPNFZ at the Third United Nations Special Session on Disarmament, it is intriguing to see them espousing zones free of all weapons of mass destruction, and announcing a halt to testing in 1992.)

Geographical / Political Enlargement

This is the easy one: more and more states should be persuaded to join the SPNFZ.

On the edges of the Zone to the North are island states which may well join, thus enlarging the boundaries and making the word 'South' a bit of a misnomer. The Federated States of Micronesia, the Marshall Islands, are obvious candidates, having just become Forum members. Belau, if it is ever allowed to become independent whilst its nuclear-free constitution is in place, will be most welcome. Further away, but possible members, are the Northern Marianas, and Guam. Although they opted to become territories of the U.S.A. they could still become Forum members in the same way as Niue, which is, to all intents and purposes, part of New Zealand. Similarly, Eastern (American) Samoa could join, first the Forum, then the SPNFZ.

To the West are Indonesia, Singapore, part of Malaysia (Sarawak) and Brunei. These countries would, no doubt, be more inclined to be part of a Southeast Asian Zone should one be adopted. A Zone of Peace, Freedom and Neutrality (ZOPFAN) was proposed by ASEAN in 1971 and, as a sub-set, the South East Asian Nuclear Weapons Free Zone (SEANWFZ) was designed in 1985. The key ideas seem to have been greater cooperation between regional states to cut down on dangerous incidents. However, protection from external threats was still assumed to be the responsibility of the U.S.A. Thus a SEANWFZ seems unlikely whilst the U.S.A., which opposes the idea, is seen as providing some sort of nuclear umbrella. ZOPFAN and SEANWFZ have so far come to nothing. Despite the end of the Cold War and the disappearance of the U.S.S.R.'s navy from the South China Sea, the U.S.A. is using Southeast Asian facilities such as Ta Kli airfield in Thailand and ship repair facilities in Singapore. There are still considerable difficulties for such a zone as long as there is a desire for a U.S. presence in Southeast Asia.

The Philippines, with its nuclear-free constitution, is perhaps the most likely candidate for membership of the SPNFZ. When the base at Subic Bay is removed and if no Southeast Asian nuclear-free zone is created, the Philippines may well think the South Pacific Zone worth joining. It gives a clear safeguard against nuclear attack and prohibits waste dumping in the sea. Near-neighbours China and Japan may be seen by the Filipinos as the most likely culprits in these matters. Certainly if the Philippines joined, the position of Australia as the major SPFNZ partner would be ended. However, the Pacific Islands states might be unhappy about inviting another large nation, with a possible eye on fishing rights, to become part of the Zone.

There are Pacific Islands states which have not joined. The Kingdom of Tonga is rather an anomaly in the world; it is ruled by a King, with some assistance from hereditary chiefs, supported by the strong conservative influence of the almost universal Methodist Church. There is a growing movement for a more democratic government, but until that materialises or the King loses his delight in military show, Tonga is unlikely to join the SPNFZ. Vanuatu, an early nuclear-free country under its first Prime Minister, the Rev. Fr. Walter Lini, found the SPNFZ document too weak. The seas were too important to be left nuclear in Vanuatu's eyes. It has not joined the land-only SPNFZ that Australia agreed to in Rarotonga. Its example has been an encouragement to activists to keep up the struggle for a better treaty. Vanuatu could join the SPNFZ and argue for tougher clauses, but it no doubt knows the obstacles to change. Recent political turmoil in Vanuatu is not likely to change its anti-nuclear sentiment but perhaps joining the weak SPNFZ may be an acceptably moderate move for its new Franco-phone Prime Minister.

France is, of course, the nation which the Treaty partners most wish to see join SPNFZ. The political position of its colonial territories – New Caledonia/Kanaky, Wallis and Futuna, and French Polynesia – differ, but the outlook for independence in them is not good. In New Caledonia/Kanaky immigration policies have upset the 50:50 balance of settlers to Kanaks, so the three-year lull in hostilities that was agreed may not work in the Kanaks' favour. Wallis and Futuna are tiny islands (population 11,000, but, Tuvalu, an independent state, is smaller at 8,000). French Polynesia has a strong independence movement but economic carrots held out by mainland France are attractive. Ending France's nuclear testing programme has always seemed more plausible than independence in these territories, and this has been demonstrated by recent events.

No one seems to have noticed that Kerguelen Island, once noted only for the native Kerguelen Cabbage on which shipwrecked sailors survived, is a French naval base. It lies in the Southern Indian Ocean but could, with a French change of heart, be added to the SPNFZ. This may seem very unlikely, but it looks just as likely as the creation of an Indian Ocean Zone of Peace, an idea often floated and just as often left to sink. Maybe the Zone could be pushed out to the Cocos/Keeling Islands as well since these are already part of Australia?

Linking Zones

This idea came from Mexico. The Latin American Nuclear Free Zone body (OPNAL) made a specific overture to New Zealand at the time when the New Zealand Foreign Minister, Russell Marshall, visited Mexico City after attending the UN General Assembly in December 1987. The New Zealand peace movement has encouraged the government to keep the idea afloat, but with the change of government in 1990 it appears to have been lost. The SPNFZ and the Tlatelolco Treaties could be linked by some form of words and exchanges between regulatory bodies.

In a more confrontational world such links between zones would have had a major effect in stimulating nations to think about nuclear free zones and re-assessing their success, especially in the light of reviews of the Non-Proliferation Treaty (NPT) and Partial Test Ban Treaty (PTBT). An early 1980s idea from the Nuclear Free and Independent Pacific (NFIP) movement was a Nuclear-free Southern Hemisphere, begun by linking zones. A new interest in the differences between Tlatelolco, Rarotonga and Antarctica might have sparked more consideration of the problem of keeping nuclear weapons off the seas.

Other Possibilities

Instead of trying to improve the Zone there are other possibilities. If nuclear weapons vanish, the need for a Nuclear-free zone may likewise vanish. However, until that consummation, there are other possibilities. Before the Treaty was given its final form and signed in Rarotonga in 1985 there had been other treaties proposed.

NFIP Charter

In 1983 the Nuclear Free and Independent Pacific Conference in Vanuatu revamped its previous Charter and after a preamble, made 16 statements. These include five Articles and two Protocols:

1. Outlines the Zone to include Micronesia, the Philippines, Japan, Hawaii, and Easter Island as well as the present Zone.
2. Bans all testing, test facilities, testing of delivery vehicles and systems, storage, transit and deployment bases, C3I facilities, nuclear reactors, waste dumping and uranium mining, etc.
3. Organises withdrawal from all defence alliances with nuclear weapons powers.
4. Promises to work for the withdrawal of the colonial powers.
5. Promises to meet every three years to try to extend the Zone and make it more comprehensive.

The Protocols are agreements to observe the prohibitions, to grant independence, to permit inspections and not to use or threaten nuclear war against the members.

One could hardly ask for a more comprehensive Zone. This Charter was urged on Forum members by the Conference and later by other bodies including the N.Z. International Year of Peace Committee.

Michael Hamel-Green's Proposal

In his 1985 NFIP submission to the Forum states Hamel-Green spelled out a very comprehensive treaty which banned the full 20 activities he saw as essential to get the South Pacific properly free of nuclear weapons and the means of nuclear war fighting.[8] Later, in his book, he got to grips with some of the problems (with, for example, the Law of the Sea) which such a treaty raises.[9]

The Perfectible Treaty

This was proposed by the Wellington Ad Hoc Committee on the Pacific Nuclear Free Zone, in 1985. It has strong clauses banning communications command and control facilities, missiles, missile testing, as well as the weapons themselves. It would ban uranium mining, and waste dumping. It aimed to be as comprehensive as possible and if anything was left out the designers said they would be happy to add it. However, it was to be introduced in a Fabian manner. It was designed with two levels of membership – full and part – so that upon two or more states becoming full members (bringing the Treaty into force) other states could be invited to become part members. Part members would sign and ratify only those parts of the Treaty they felt they could. They would then progress to full membership by signing and ratifying more and more of the clauses. The beauty of this procedure is that:

1. The states do not have to swallow the comprehensive treaty whole.
2. The states do not need to come together to change the membership, nor the content, nor re-submit protocols to the nuclear powers.
3. Progress to full membership is accomplished in simple stages, involving only internal government processes – the ratifying of further clauses – as the peoples convince their governments that it should be done.

The Perfectible Treaty dealt with the problem of the high seas and transit by:

1. Having a clause such that a country signing it agrees to treat the high seas between itself and all other Treaty members as territorial waters of one signatory or another, in the matter of nuclear weapons, delivery vehicles, facilities, etc.
2. Having a protocol in which nuclear weapons states agree to treat all high seas in the Zone as if they were territorial waters, in the matter of weapons, etc.

Treaties are like concrete once set in place, and fall by neglect and time rather than active attack. Therefore, the New Zealand peace movement, whilst endorsing the present SPNFZ, despair of it ever being improved. They would like to see a better parallel treaty launched, and had hoped that Vanuatu might give this some attention.

Changes to International Law

Changes to make the passage of nuclear weapons on or under the sea illegal, have been mentioned. More radical plans would either:

1. Have all nuclear weapons declared illegal at the World Court – such endeavours have been in progress for several years.
2. Have new or tightened clauses inserted into a United Nations Conference on the Law of the Sea (UNCLOS 4).

Banning the Movement of Nuclear Weapons

The Bush and Gorbachev initiatives to nuclear-disarm surface ships notwithstanding, seeking ways to ban nuclear weapons from the high seas in the South Pacific is not just an academic exercise. Nuclear-armed submarines are still important to the U.S.A., and although their main beat is up to Alaska and back, they could be sent to roam into the South Pacific. Also, the transit of nuclear weapons, or their C3I appendages, could be carried out by cargo vessels, on their way, presumably, to some non-member, or to a place outside the Zone.

The Treaty of Tlatelolco, like SPNFZ, covers a lot of sea. But it avoids the problem of how to ban nuclear weapons from the seas by ignoring it. Some theorists have declared that Tlatelolco bans the transit of nuclear weapons inside its zone since the transit has to be either by a member of the Treaty (members are not allowed to own nuclear weapons) or by a party to the protocols (all the nuclear powers of the time). According to this argument only Israel, which it must be admitted is a nuclear weapons state, could move nuclear weapons through the zone without contravening the Treaty. If this interpretation is valid it must be assumed also that the British contravened the Treaty if they took nuclear-armed warships to the Falklands/Malvinas war zone. This interpretation of the Tlatelolco Treaty is denied by the U.S.A. and U.K.

The SPNFZ, touted as 'stronger' than the Treaty of Tlatelolco, avoids the problem of transit by keeping its provisions to the land and territorial waters only. The peace movement in New Zealand was told in 1984 that lawyers were unable to produce a way of avoiding the Law of the Sea's 'right of innocent passage'. This was just an excuse. It was certainly not the reason for the Rarotonga Treaty rejecting transit bans. Papua New Guinea, the Solomons, and Vanuatu, sought a treaty which would stop transit. However, Australia signalled that it would not sign a treaty which attempted to restrict the U.S. navy's desire to sail its nuclear-armed warships all over the Pacific.

There are two main ways of tackling the problem of how to ban the transit of nuclear weapons: (i) look for legal loopholes and interpretations of the Law of the Sea, or even to contemplate changing it; (ii) have a treaty which invites nations, rather as the protocols do, to voluntarily keep nuclear weapons out, without disturbing the Law of the Sea.

In relation to innocent passage for example under United Nations Conference on the Law of the Sea (UNCLOS 3), some experts consider that:

> Since passage of nuclear-armed warships is 'non-innocent', meaning 'prejudicial to the peace, good order or security' of the state, the Nuclear Free Weapons Zone (NFWZ) could exclude nuclear weapons from the parties' *territorial* waters under UNCLOS 3. If possession and/or deployment is not an 'internationally lawful' use of the sea, and passage of nuclear-armed warships is non-innocent, then the NWFZ could be extended to the limits of the Exclusive Economic Zone (EEZ) of each party. If the term 'peaceful purposes' in Article 88 of UNCLOS 3 is construed to mean either 'non-military purposes', or 'purposes not involving the possession, deployment or testing of nuclear weapons' then the NWFZ could be extended to the high seas...[10]

Robert Philp Jr. thinks the last two would require inspired diplomacy! He also points out that there are interpretive difficulties: there is a strong argument that carrying combat-ready nuclear weapons at sea is illegal under international law, but common usage contradicts this.[11] A ruling from the World Court on the legality of all nuclear weapons would help clear this one up. This approach, which uses the intent of UNCLOS 3 (to keep the seas peaceful), has been attempted by others independently. For example, the author indicated at the United Nations Special Session on Disarmament 3

(UNSSOD 3) that as a rhetorical device one could declare that no warship can ever be said to be making an innocent passage. Vladamir F. Tsarev, a Russian marine lawyer suggests that UNCLOS 3, in binding states to carry out their activities on the high seas in such a way as to ensure peace and security, upholds the principle of international law, in particular the non-application of force or threat in international relations.[12]

Similarly, Mark J. Valencia of the East-West Centre in Hawai'i suggests a 'smorgasbord' of legal avenues which could be pursued.[13] His first suggests that states which have signed UNCLOS 3 could deny passage along sealanes, in archipelagos and through straits within their territorial seas to nations which have not signed – notably the U.S.A. – arguing that these rights are not customary law and do not accrue to non-signatories.

His second is that states could substitute the 'innocent passage' regime for 'transit passage and sealane passage'. Spain and Morocco have done this for the Straits of Gibraltar. It is useful because innocent passage may be suspended, for example, because the military vessel will not declare its cargo, or not guarantee not to discharge radioactive material. And so on with other legal niceties.

Mark Valencia also details important precedents created by states declaring 'closed seas' and 'maritime exclusion zones'. For example, this has been done for the Sea of Okhotsk by the U.S.S.R., and the British declared a 'no-go' zone around the Falklands/Malvinas during that war, by Canada closing the Northwest passage to the U.S.A., by France refusing the ship Greenpeace access to its harbours for repairs, by the U.S.A. declaring over 100 'defensive sea areas', 17 on the high seas, and blockading Cuba during the missile crisis. Most of these are not precedents one would like to see followed into respectability.[14]

Another possibility is to change the Law of the Sea, for since piracy is forbidden on the high seas, it should be possible to forbid the transit of nuclear weapons as well.

A treaty could circumvent the Law of the Sea by requiring member states, and (through protocols) non-member states, to keep the Zone completely free of nuclear weapons. This route to a South Pacific truly free of nuclear weapons was proposed in at least two forms to Forum states and one of these is discussed later.

The Atrophy of Nuclear Free Zones

Is all this agonising about transit of nuclear weapons on the high seas an example of the generals preparing to fight the last war again? President Bush has announced the removal of all nuclear weapons from surface warships and then President Gorbachev appears to have made the same unilateral decision about Soviet cruise missiles. The submarine-launched strategic missiles are not, however, affected. This leaves the South Pacific virtually weapons-free, since U.S. Trident and other submarines with ICBMs do not roam the world's oceans – in most cases they go up to Alaska and back.

If no U.S. nuclear weapons arrive in the South Pacific, then, what purpose has the Zone? Can it just wither away, or even be repealed? The following must be considered:

1. The French have not joined the Zone and until they do the Zone is a reminder of how other Pacific nations feel about nuclear issues.
2. Dumping is a worry, and will be for hundreds of years, even after the last nuclear power station is de-commissioned.
3. U.S. submarine commanders, looking for exercises to keep their men well trained, or even from sheer boredom in a peaceful world, may wish to exercise in the South Pacific.
4. Nuclear war fighting into or from the Zone must also be kept in mind and, whatever protection against either can be devised, should be devised – this means missile and C3I bans as soon as possible.

Whilst one nuclear weapon remains, peace activists will keep the Nuclear Free Zone idea alive. It may be harder now to develop new Zones elsewhere but scares, such as the revelations of Iraq's well advanced bomb programme, and Arab fear of Israel's nuclear weapons, certainly suggest the need for such a zone in the Middle East. If the U.S.A. flaunts its nuclear weapons in Southeast Asia, the increasingly scientifically sophisticated populations may react against them and insist on a Southeast Asia Nuclear Weapons Free Zone (SEANWFZ).

The Politics of Change

Changes in the U.S.A.

There have been major shifts of attitude to the Zone by the U.S.A.
At first the U.S.A. did not want such a Zone at all. Then, bowing to
the will of Pacific people it did not openly prevent it but made sure
its close ally, Australia, understood what sort of a Zone would be
acceptable. Even then it did not accept it, refusing to sign the
protocols. However, the House of Representatives, and recently the
Hawaiian State legislature, now both want the President to sign the
protocols, and the administration says it is 'abiding' by them.

However, the return of a National government in New Zealand,
has changed the situation. The National government has broken
many promises; it could break the promise not to repeal the N.Z.
Nuclear Free Zone Act. It has an American-educated Minister of
Foreign Affairs, Don McKinnon, who is keen to change New
Zealand's anti-nuclear legislation (which ratifies the SPNFZ, among
other things). So the U.S. navy sees a chance to cruise the Southern
Pacific unrestricted by any country.

If New Zealand changes the N.Z. Nuclear Free Zone Act to allow
nuclear-armed and propelled warships into New Zealand ports,
that will not change the SPNFZ at all. But it does highlight its
weaknesses.

Changes in New Zealand

New Zealand public opinion is being softened up for a change in the
Nuclear Free Zone Act. Peace and environmental activists are
busy with the struggle to maintain public opinion against a
change. Therefore the movement does not see this as the time to be
pushing for changes in the SPNFZ, nor for the introduction of a
parallel treaty. The public knows the U.S.A. is giving away its
nuclear weapons on ships and sees little need for tougher legislation or a strengthened SPNFZ. New Zealanders have for a long
time been unimpressed by talk of threats to the South Pacific from
the Soviet Union – its nearest base, Cam Ran Bay, was after all
closer to Moscow than to Wellington. With the Soviet Union no

longer even a vague threat, the need for a SPNFZ to protect South Pacific targets from Soviet strikes has vanished completely.

Another part of a less tense security situation is the one-year moratorium the French have imposed on their own testing. New Zealanders are very hopeful it will be extended indefinitely.

New Zealanders are aware they have no enemies, and Government Defence Reviews (White Papers) say so in so many words. So there is no political need for change to any stronger zone. However, Foreign Minister Don McKinnon's hoped-for change to something weaker for New Zealand (the SPNFZ on its own would suit him) needs addressing.

Changes in Australia

Australia is unlikely to change its official attitude to the U.S.A. and to the SPNFZ. Pressure to close the U.S. C3I bases, exclude nuclear arms carrying ships and planes, stop uranium mining, and strengthen the SPNFZ could only come about, if (a) the left wing of the Labor Party gained strong support (which is unlikely), or if (b) some nuclear accident had a direct effect on Australians. The only examples of the latter one can think of are:

1. An accident on a U.S. nuclear-propelled or armed ship whilst in an Australian port.
2. Radiation from a nuclear power-station accident arriving in Australia.
3. The rejection of Australian products which had passed through a radiated area.

Changes in the Pacific Islands

In the Pacific Islands states the tradition of government-by-chiefs has been modified in international contacts to government-by-chiefs-in-consensus. This is blithely called 'The Pacific Way' and when, for example, Australian Prime Minister Bob Hawke starts laying down the law at Pacific Forum meetings about what MUST be done he is upbraided by an equally white and irreligious New Zealand Prime Minister for 'not following the Pacific way'. One result of the Pacific Way of arriving at decisions is that any decision can take forever to get to the table, an age to get discussed, and even when it seems that a decision has been reached the whole topic can reappear at any time, pushed by any chief. The topic will then be negotiated in a circular way yet again. Problems do not go away, they merely take a nap. Because of this, changing the SPNFZ is not something any New Zealand diplomat wants to contemplate.

Conclusion

There are quite a few more PhDs waiting to be unpacked from the SPNFZ. The really tough ones will be those which dig deep into the Pacific Islands states' motives and internal politics. The easy ones will re-hash speculation about what the United States, Australia and New Zealand thought they were doing. Sorting out the U.S.A.'s internal, conflicting and self-subversive policies would be interesting since such a wealth of material is available in Congressional and other records – of which university academics seem surprisingly ignorant. However, for the peace advocates, who want to help make the world a better place there is a need to:

1. Nudge the South Pacific Forum, perhaps via its South Pacific Regional Environmental Commission, towards considering expansion of the SPNFZ to include clauses and protocols dealing with economic and environmental issues. In the Pacific Islands these are pretty synonymous, anyway. These should deal first with nuclear waste, then other toxic wastes, and if these are acceptable, other additions for environmental protection.
2. Consolidate the movement for a judgement from the World Court to declare nuclear weapons illegal. Much would flow from such a declaration, including clarification of the Law of the Sea.
3. Remind the public and politicians from time to time (10 years seems to be the limit of collective memory on such things) that the SPNFZ is worth preserving until all nuclear weapons have been destroyed.

Notes

1. The text of the South Pacific Nuclear Free Zone Treaty is most easily found attached to the *New Zealand Nuclear Free Zone, Disarmament, and Arms Control Act*, (1987), Wellington: Government Printer, as its first Schedule. Other (UNO) Disarmament Treaties are appended as the 2nd, 3rd, 4th and 5th Schedules.
2. Hamel-Green, M., (1990), *The South Pacific Nuclear Free Zone Treaty: a Critical Assessment*, Australian Peace Research Centre.
3. Committee on Foreign Affairs, (1987), 'The South Pacific Nuclear Free Zone, Hearings and Markup before the Committee on Foreign Affairs and its Subcommittee on Asian and Pacific Affairs', House of Representatives, One Hundredth Congress, First Session, on H. Con. Res. 158, June 9 and, July 15, 1987, Washington DC: U.S. Government Printing Office, p. 10.
4. Lange, D., (1990), *Nuclear Free the New Zealand Way*, Harmondsworth: Penguin Books, p. 168.
5. Hamel-Green, M., (1985), 'The Case for a Comprehensive Nuclear Free Zone in the South Pacific', Unpublished paper to the NFIP National Consultation, Canberra.
6. Letter to the (N.Z.) National Consultative Committee on Disarmament.
7. A very interesting discussion of the achievements and failures of the Zone. Hamel-Green, M., (Spring 1991), 'Regional Arms Control in the South Pacific: Island State Responses to Australia's Nuclear Free Zone Initiative', *The Contemporary Pacific*, vol. 2, no. 1, pp. 58-84.
8. Hamel-Green, M., (1985), (see note 5).
9. Hamel-Green, M., (1990), (see note 2).
10. Philp, P.R., Jr, (1986), 'The South Pacific Nuclear-Weapon-Free-Zone, the Law of the Sea, and the ANZUS Alliance: An Exploration of Conflicts, a Step Towards World Peace', *Californian Western International Law Journal*, vol. 16, no. 1, Winter 1986, pp. 138-177.
11. *Ibid.*
12. Tsarev, V.F., (April 1988), 'Peaceful Use of the Seas', *Marine Policy*, pp. 153-159.
13. Valencia, M.J., (1986), 'Beyond Independence: Legal/Political Avenues for Realising a Nuclear Free Pacific', Paper to the UN University Conference on Peace and Security in Oceania.
14. *Ibid.*

15

Rethinking the
Security Agenda in
the Asia Pacific Region*

Joseph A. Camilleri

In the last few years the accelerated improvement in Soviet-American relations, the tangible signs of progress in disarmament and arms control negotiations and the considerable steps taken towards the resolution of several regional conflicts have prompted scholars and policy-makers alike to rethink traditional notions of security. The same factors have made this an opportune time to move beyond the Cold War in the Asia Pacific region and think creatively about the prospects and process of regional security.

In this chapter the focus is primarily on geopolitical threats to security. Relevant here are the military interests and capabilities of the great powers and the transition of the international geopolitical system from rigid bipolarity to diffuse and complex multipolarity. Yet, these are by no means the only factors to be considered. International influences invariably interact with territorial disputes, ideological antagonisms and military competition between neighbouring states on the one hand, and with domestic, social, and economic inequalities, ethnic conflicts, and political instability on the other. This multi-dimensional interaction must inform any attempt to construct a comprehensive and durable framework of regional security.

Defining the Region

Defining the perimeter of any region is ultimately an arbitrary exercise, for boundaries and their significance are always time, space and function specific. There are, however, several grounds for considering the Asia Pacific as a relatively coherent security region by virtue of history, geography and the present pattern of economic and strategic interaction. This region comprises three sub-regions: the North Pacific (Japan, the two Koreas and China, but also Russia, the United States and Canada), Southeast Asia, and the South Pacific. By virtue of their reach, great powers (especially the United States) have a presence in two or even all three sub-regions.

The grounds for attributing coherence or cohesion to such a large and diverse region may be summarised as follows:

1. Containment policies pursued by the United States for the best part of forty years as a function of the Cold War resulted in the establishment of a ring of alliances and military power designed to encircle the two Communist giants and their respective clients and allies. The United States created a relatively integrated security system linking most of its allies (e.g. Canada, Japan, the Philippines, Thailand, Australia and even Indonesia) in order to enhance inter-operability, logistics and command, control and communications capabilities.
2. Japanese economic expansion in the region, both pre-war (in its 'co-prosperity sphere' phase) and post-war.
3. Increasing economic interdependence of the region associated with the rapid growth in trade as well as trans-national production, finance and aid flows.
4. Expanding diplomatic interaction stimulated by the great powers and their overlapping membership of the three sub-regions: the United States is politically and strategically omnipresent; Japan is beginning to complement its economic penetration of the region with a growing involvement in issues of regional security (e.g. Cambodian peace process); China has

important ties with Russia, North Korea and Vietnam and is developing a multifaceted relationship with ASEAN. It is a key player in the Cambodian conflict and an important protagonist in the Spratlys dispute; Australia is a bridge between the South Pacific (ANZUS, South Pacific Forum) and Southeast Asia (Five Power Defence Agreement, bilateral defence cooperation programmes).

5. The accelerating internationalisation of the region expressed in the growing participation of many countries in international organisations (e.g. China's membership of international governmental organisations rose from two in 1960 to 37 in 1989; its membership of international non-governmental organisations during the same period rose from 30 to 677;[1] similar trends are evident for Japan and many of the ASEAN countries).[2]

Thus with this economically, culturally and politically diverse region it is possible to discern patterns of interaction which force us to reconsider the assumed contrast between European homogeneity and Asian heterogeneity. The apparent divergence of interests and perceptions need not be an impediment to cooperation but can become an added incentive for increased communication flows. The fact that regional cooperation is unlikely to be swift or painless does not necessarily mean that both governmental and non-governmental organisations may not be disposed to encourage the process.

Reconceptualising Security

It is now understood that security cannot be viewed as a zero-sum game. Rather the aim must be common security in the sense that the security (or insecurity) of each contributes to the security (or insecurity) of all. The idea of common security is an advance on the notion of collective security because it is not premissed on the dangerous and ultimately artificial division between the aggressive and peace-loving states but rather on the proposition that any durable security framework must incorporate the legitimate interests of all its members. It is only when these interests are clearly recognised and institutionalised, when the interests of

weaker or less privileged societies are accorded the same consideration as those of stronger or more privileged ones that the
incentive for aggression will have been reduced.

But common security is unlikely to be realised if it is narrowly
defined to refer only to military security.[3] If insecurity is a state
of mind involving a mixture of fears and apprehensions about the
future well-being of one's group or society, then security policy
must somehow respond to all these concerns. For many situated
in the Asia Pacific region, damage to the global ecology (e.g.
global warming arising from greenhouse gas emissions) or the
harsh consequences of rising foreign debt, have a direct bearing
on their quality of life or even physical integrity. It is not merely
the case that security is a multi-faceted concept but that its
various elements are closely interdependent. An effective security framework must give effect to comprehensive security. It
must be sensitive to the way one type of threat (e.g. military
threat) may contribute to or reinforce another type (e.g. environmental threat). An appropriate response at one level should
facilitate positive action at another.

Comprehensiveness has another important dimension. What
happens within a state and in its relations with other states are
inextricably intertwined. Social and political arrangements within
a country (including internal conflict, state repression and revo-
lution) affect and are in turn affected by regional and international decisions, processes and institutions (including distribution of resources, environmental pollution and military intervention). Security factors are very much at the interface between the
domestic and the external. The need to rethink the traditional
notion of boundaries (both the physical boundaries between states
and the psychological boundaries between insider and outsider)[4]
has an obvious corollary: the need to rethink the boundaries
between official and unofficial channels, between governmental
and non-governmental institutions, between the state and civil
society. Any viable security system has to involve large numbers
of citizens and the various associations to which they belong.
There must be extensive and continuous public participation,
both within and across state boundaries, in formulating, institu-
tionalising and implementing security policy.

The question now confronting the peoples and governments of

the Asia Pacific region is whether the positive signs of the last few years can form the basis of a concerted effort to create a durable system of peace, and whether the undeniable cultural, political, ethnic and religious differences, can provide a stimulus for mutually reinforcing, cross-cultural bridge-building. As a guide for this process this chapter explores five strategic principles: dealignment, demilitarisation, economic security, democratisation and regionalisation.

Dealignment

If a key objective is to reduce the probability and intensity of military conflict then the dismantling of existing military alliances is likely to have a beneficial effect. At a time when Cold War rivalries are rapidly subsiding and a new framework for European cooperation is emerging, there is little argument for retaining security arrangements in this part of the world whose primary function has been to nurture the dynamic of Soviet-American rivalry. The interests of small and middle powers are likely to be better served to the extent that local and regional conflicts are insulated from great power rivalries.

Alliance termination is not, however, an all-or-nothing proposition. A strategy of dealignment may be seen as a gradual or phased approach in which the steps taken at a particular time will reflect both internal and external circumstances, not least the state of public opinion in the relevant countries. The aim, however, must be to hasten the process and bring it to its logical conclusion. This means creating the conditions whereby states can pursue foreign and defence policies which exclude military alliances with external powers or military involvement in conflicts that do not directly threaten their national security. Dealignment may be pursued by any number of unilateral, bilateral or multilateral initiatives.

In some instances, it may be possible for a security treaty to be formally abrogated or severely weakened by the unilateral withdrawal of one of its signatories. New Zealand's nuclear free policy, which resulted in the suspension of the tripartite security arrangements under ANZUS, is a recent example of a unilateral initiative which most closely approximates this scenario.

Steps towards military disengagement by senior or junior allies represent another option. Initiatives for the removal of foreign troops and military facilities (e.g. from Vietnam, the Philippines, South Korea) have in recent years moved much closer to fruition. Many of these military arrangements are increasingly viewed as the product of an anachronistic Cold War mentality; they are costly for the foreign power and are less and less likely to contribute to domestic or regional stability. The refusal of the Philippines Senate to approve the 10-year treaty that would have allowed the United States to retain Subic Bay suggests that the process of withdrawal is well advanced and probably irreversible. In the case of South Korea, the withdrawal of U.S. nuclear weapons may be conducive to the North's application of full non-proliferation safeguards and foster a diplomatic dialogue between Pyongyang and Washington, which may in turn enhance the prospects of Korean reunification.[5] Political and economic considerations may therefore combine – not just in the Philippines and Korea but in several other countries – to change the character and context of existing alliances by eliminating their most objectionable military features.

Multilateral approaches to military disengagement may also contribute to a policy of dealignment. A range of zoning arrangements may be particularly useful in this regard. The idea of zoning arrangements is not new and has already attracted the support of several governments. A useful first step would be the establishment of nuclear-free zones. The precedent has already been set with the South Pacific Nuclear Free Zone Treaty, although the provisions of this treaty have been specifically designed to protect American strategic interests in the region.[6]

Nevertheless, the establishment of nuclear-free zones also has relevance to various parts of Asia. In his Vladivostok speech of July 1986, Gorbachev specifically endorsed the creation of such zones on the Korean peninsula, in Southeast Asia and the Southern Indian Ocean.[7] A Northeast Asian nuclear-free zone might include the two Koreas – still one of the more dangerous powderkegs in Asia – but also Japan, Soviet and American nuclear forces deployed in, or targeted on the region. The denuclearisation of the region would obviously ease tensions between the two Koreas and reduce the likelihood of great power intervention. The draft accord between the two Korean Governments, signed in December 1991, is a useful step in this direction. The agreement bans the possession or development of nuclear weapons as well as nuclear reprocessing and uranium enrichment technologies. It also establishes a Joint Nuclear Control Commission to monitor the implementation of these commitments.[8] Pyongyang's acceptance of International Atomic Energy Agency (IAEA) safeguards in principle, in return for Washington's conditional suspension of the Team Spirit exercises, suggests useful spin-offs for the process of demilitarisation.

Zoning arrangements may also have considerable relevance for Southeast Asia. The proposal to establish a Zone of Peace, Freedom and Neutrality (ZOPFAN) in Southeast Asia has a long, if ambiguous, history. First endorsed by the ASEAN countries in their 1971 Kuala Lumpur Declaration, the idea was given further impetus by the reactivation of the ASEAN Working Group on ZOPFAN in 1984 and by the third ASEAN summit in 1987 which directed the Group to work towards the early realisation of ZOPFAN and the creation of a nuclear weapons-free zone in Southeast Asia.[9] The key objective is to establish a zone from which all foreign military bases would be excluded. Differences of emphasis between some member states (e.g. Malaysia, Indonesia) who are advocates of neutrality and others (e.g. Singapore, Thailand) who favour the balancing of power, has slowed down progress on the proposal. The initiative has thus far elicited strong Chinese and Soviet support, an ambivalent response from Japan and firm opposition from the United States. In time, however, the idea may become increasingly attractive, especially in the context of a possible settlement of the Cambodian conflict and renewed international efforts to arrest the dynamic of horizontal nuclear proliferation.

Demilitarisation

Yet dealignment is not enough. Insulating the region from great power conflict would be of limited value, if local powers chose instead to pursue the path of high and rising military expenditures, with all that this implies for regional arms races and the expanding role and power of military establishments. If demilitarisation is the objective, then new concepts of defence must aim at self-reliance and avoid international entanglements or dependence on external sources of supply, financial and strategic guidance; they must be non-provocative in character and designed to enhance self-defence without endangering the security of others.[10]

A first step would be to establish a regional framework to discuss and agree on the principles of non-provocative defence. A non-provocative defence policy would presumably place a priority on the peaceful settlement of disputes; exhaust all peaceful avenues, including international mediation, conciliation and arbitration, before entertaining the use of force, and then only in response to a direct threat to the security of the nation; concentrate the use of force within the territorial boundaries of the country under attack and its immediate maritime approaches; and resort to the use of force in strict compliance with the provisions of the law of war and international law generally. For the defence effort to be non-provocative it must be transparent (i.e. the defensive intention must be fully apparent to the would-be enemy). This requires not only that the choice of individual weapons should be non-offensive use, but that the entire combination of weapons, force structure, deployment and intelligence-gathering should be seen as non-provocative in intent and design.

The specific application of the principles outlined above would vary from country to country, depending on local geography, economic conditions and political culture. Its main impact on the region, however, would be to place severe limits on Japan's rearmament programme, establish a more favourable climate for negotiation between the two Korean regimes, and reduce the mutual suspicion which has recently dominated Sino-Vietnamese relations. It may also help to defuse an incipient arms race between Australia and its ASEAN neighbours.

The ethos and procedures of non-provocative defence would reinforce and neatly dovetail efforts to limit or reduce the present volume of arms deliveries in and out of the region. There is a need to formulate a set of generally acceptable guidelines governing the supply of arms, particularly to governments whose conduct is considered a threat to the peace and stability of the region. Support for such guidelines is likely to be more enthusiastic and widespread to the extent that zoning and other arms control arrangements have been introduced to reduce the intensity of conflict and facilitate the peaceful settlement of disputes. Ideally, a regional arms transfer regime would require the participation of both suppliers and recipients, encompass transfers associated with various forms of defence cooperation, and seek to regulate the production (possession) as well as the transfer of weapons in both producing and non-producing countries.[11]

Democratisation

There is unlikely to be much progress towards dealignment and demilitarisation without widespread public mobilisation. Democratisation of the decision-making process, which would encompass various forms of political pluralism and respect for human rights, is not only a desirable end in itself, but a necessary means for the achievement of the wider security objective. If access to information is a critical instrument of democratic politics, then it follows that executive decisions on foreign policy and questions of security should be placed under the scrutiny of legislatures, which should in turn be provided with greatly expanded access to information and a capacity for independent analysis. A related objective must be the dismantling of national security and intelligence agencies which violate the civil rights of their citizens, or do not fully respect international law and the independence and democratic processes of other countries.

Desirable though it may be, the democratisation of security policy, long regarded by national authorities as the exclusive preserve of military and political élites, will remain an elusive goal so long as the necessary conditions for democratic politics generally have not been established. This is likely to prove a difficult and protracted task given the recent record of political repression in the region. Yet, despite authoritarian tendencies in state formation there is much in Asian and Pacific cultural traditions which is sympathetic to the democratic imperative. Over the last few decades political and social movements in many of these countries have campaigned vigorously around issues of popular democracy, human rights, and self-determination. The application of ethical principles to political life is not a purely Judeo-Christian intellectual construct. It has significant roots in the religious and philosophical traditions of most Asian and Pacific cultures. The opportunities for developing standards by which to evaluate political processes and institutions are therefore considerably greater than is often supposed.

All the indications are that the political process in many parts of the Asia Pacific region will devote increasing attention to the achievement of human rights. Although universally applicable, certain core rights have particular relevance to Asia and the Pacific. They include the right to development, the right to political dissent, the rights of peoples to cultural and political self-determination, and the right to a healthy and sustainable environment. The unfolding situation in China, Burma, Korea, Indonesia (East Timor, West New Guinea), Cambodia, Philippines, Papua New Guinea, Fiji, to name the obvious examples, suggests the need for more effective regional mechanisms to monitor and institutionalise the observance of these rights. Placed in this context, human rights represent a meeting point between domestic social order and regional security. They provide the arena and the battleground for the various social and political movements struggling for self-determination, for land rights, for economic and political self-reliance, for denuclearisation and ecological balance.

Economic Security

The last twenty years have seen an increasing preoccupation by most governments in East and Southeast Asia with economic growth in what has become an increasingly competitive yet interdependent region. On the one hand, Japanese-American trade is still expanding, and despite its persistent trade deficit, America's exports to Japan have been rising at a faster rate than Japanese exports to the United States.[12] On the other hand, trade frictions have acquired renewed intensity and are now a normal feature of the relationship. Japan, for its part, has become the leading source of capital, aid and technology for much of the Asia Pacific region. More recently, South Korea and Taiwan have also become a source of investment, particularly in Southeast Asia. Within this growing and interdependent economic arena, Japan's financial and commercial influence has eclipsed America's economic presence, although the United States remains the paramount military power. It is not yet clear how and to what extent Japanese-American trade rivalry will affect the security relationship between the two countries.

Nor is economic growth an unmitigated blessing. For Japan, trade rivalries and financial instability will prove more difficult to manage in the 1990s than in the previous decade. In South Korea, rising inflation, itself the result of rising wage demands, is likely to place severe strains on future export performance. The competitive edge achieved by the newly industrialising countries owes a great deal to relatively low labour costs, a highly disciplined workforce and varying degrees of political repression. Sooner or later social tensions will give rise to a powerful dynamic for political change. The periodic waves of student and industrial unrest in South Korea are but the most conspicuous signs of this trend. Compounding these sources of instability is the considerable uncertainty that hangs over the future direction of the Chinese economy and China's incorporation of Hong Kong in 1997.

In addition to the uncertainty surrounding future rates of growth in Japan, Korea, Taiwan or any of the other industrialising economies, is the long-term impact of a model of development which depends so heavily on export-oriented industrialisation. This model has implications for trade rivalries, the disposal of toxic wastes and the management of other forms of environmental pollution, for widening economic inequalities within and between countries, and for the forward projection of military power as competing states seek to defend their markets, access to resources and exclusive economic zones. The proliferation risks associated with established or future nuclear power programmes reinforces the connection between economy and security.

To moderate these actual or potential conflicts within the region and at the same time enhance leverage *vis à vis* other major centres of economic power, various proposals have been advanced for greater regional economic cooperation and the creation of a Pacific trading forum. One such initiative is the Australian-inspired Asia Pacific Economic Cooperation (APEC) group which held its first ministerial meeting in November 1989. APEC's expansion to include China, Hong Kong and Taiwan will be an important step in the direction of greater inclusiveness, but several unanswered questions still cloud the future of the organisation. Will its function be primarily one of consultation, data gathering and forecasting, or will it have a major coordinating role? Will it include the interests of the region's poorer or less developed economies (e.g. Russia, Vietnam, Cambodia, South Pacific islands)? Will it provide an arena for resolving regional tensions and averting conflict between trading blocs?[13] Will it be able to balance and reconcile the objectives of industrial competitiveness, export performance, and economic growth with other important criteria of security, including distributive justice, political autonomy, democratisation, protection of the environment and demilitarisation? How will it handle the complex linkages between economy, environment and military security? How will it relate to other forums, let alone competing models, of regional or sub-regional cooperation (e.g. the East Asian Economic Group proposed by Malaysia)? All of these questions bring us face to face with the purpose, structure and content of regionalisation.

Regional Cooperation

The key question may be simply stated: What is the kind of regional framework most conducive to the requirements of common and comprehensive security in the Asia Pacific region and at the same time sensitive to the region's circumstances? Many proposals are already on the table offering a variety of answers to this question. In two major speeches made at Vladivostok in 1986 and Krasnoyarsk in 1988, in which he outlined the Soviet Union's new Asia policy, Gorbachev called for a forum modelled perhaps on the Conference for Security and Cooperation in Europe (CSCE) whose task would be to consider a number of proposals aimed at lessening tensions in the Asia Pacific region.[14] The idea was inspired in part by Moscow's desire to moderate the Soviet Union's strategic and diplomatic isolation in East Asia (a legacy of America's containment policy) but also by the hope of integrating Soviet Asia with the dynamic and rapidly expanding economies of East Asia. There was, however, more to the Soviet proposal than naked self-interest. It was an attempt to apply the notion of common security to the Asian Pacific theatre where it had so far made relatively little headway.

Though regional responses were not immediately enthusiastic, Gorbachev's proposal has since gained considerable currency, with similar suggestions emanating from a number of quarters. In May 1990, the Indonesian Defence Minister, Benny Murdani, floated the idea of a regional forum to discuss a post-cold war security order.[15] In September 1990, the Canadian Secretary of State for External Affairs, Joe Clark, proposed a dialogue on security in the North Pacific as a way of bringing the new East-West détente to Asia.[16] In similar vein, in July 1990, Australia's Foreign Minister, Gareth Evans, expressed the hope that 'new Europe-style patterns of cooperation between old adversaries (would) find their echo in this part of the world', and perhaps lead to a new institutional framework, a Conference for Security and Cooperation in Asia (CSCA), capable of 'addressing the apparently intractable security issues which exist in Asia'.[17] In subsequent statements Australian policy-makers, in response to Washington's negative reaction, sought to moderate the scope of the proposal (by all accounts a poorly articulated and ill-prepared proposal) and dispel any impression of inconsistency with existing security arrangements. A number of other contributions surfaced in 1990-1991 from both governmental and non-governmental sources, all proposing, despite widely diverging perspectives, improved or expanded consultative mechanisms on issues of regional security.[18]

As we have already noted, the United States has tended to view with considerable suspicion any attempt to establish a new multilateral framework for regional security. The U.S. Assistant Secretary of State for East Asian and Pacific Affairs, Richard Solomon, cast doubt on the utility of an all-Pacific security grouping, and echoed Secretary Baker's assessment that it was 'preferable to adapt existing, proven mechanisms to meet the challenges of changing circumstances before creating new ones'.[19] The United States could see little merit in any initiative which might disturb its strategic pre-eminence in the region, particularly any arms control measure which might restrict its navy's freedom of action.[20]

Washington's hostility to many of these proposals stemmed

from its marked preference for the existing security architecture based on the 'spoked-wheel' concept, that is on a network of bilateral security relationships with itself as the hub.[21] From the American vantage point, these arrangements, which have the U.S.-Japan security 'partnership' as their centrepiece, offer the United States considerable freedom of action and a useful degree of ambiguity in dealing with allies, China and Russia. The U.S.-centred unipolar security system, by taking advantage of America's global organisational outreach and cementing its role as ultimate guarantor of regional and sub-regional security, might also be used to maintain access to resources, markets and technology.

Attractive though it may be to U.S. policy-makers, the spoked-wheel concept is theoretically and practically flawed on several counts:

1. The relative decline of America's economic position.
2. Its steadily diminishing capacity to sustain the costs of its extensive military presence in the region.
3. The failure to deal constructively with the far-reaching consequences of economic decline and military withdrawal.
4. The failure to recognise that the United States can no longer perform the same stabilising function which it assumed at the height of the Cold War.
5. The fact that bilateral security relationships are poorly equipped to cope with increasing interdependence and the demands of common and comprehenisve security.
6. The risk that bilateral arrangements will fuel new suspicions and animosities.
7. The potential for mishandling U.S.-Japan relations and its far-reaching economic and strategic implications.
8. The inappropriateness of imposing an anachronistic Cold War security system on a region that is gradually acquiring greater self-confidence in the articulation of its interests and perceptions.
9. The need to integrate the substantial improvement in relations between Russia on the one hand and the United States, China and Japan on the other into a more permanent and predictable institutional arrangement.

Japan's initial response to the multilateral approach has also been negative. The Japanese Government presumably prefers the bilateral framework as the basis for resolving the Northern Territories dispute with Russia, and sees advantages in making visible progress in the resolution of the Korean conflict and further reduction of Russian forces in the Far East preconditions for a multilateral security dialogue. But this reasoning too, is seriously flawed:

1. The resolution of the Korean conflict (and the prospect of Korean reunification) will require significant input from all four neighbouring great powers.
2. Excessive emphasis on bilateralism by Japan may inflame Chinese, ASEAN and Australian suspicions.
3. Japanese acceptance in the region will presumably have to be grounded in the institutional webs of a regional multilateral framework that makes its economic dominance less abrasive and subject to a degree of oversight.
4. A multilateral framework may also hold the best prospects for handling the increasingly sensitive U.S.-Japan relationship.

Therefore the initial U.S. and Japanese reactions are more a reflection of habit than self-interest and will sooner or later have to take account of rapidly changing political realities. The unwillingness of the two most powerful states of the region to play a key role in shaping a new security framework is no reason, then, why the effort should be abandoned. It simply means that for some little time yet the initiative will lie elsewhere, primarily with the governments of smaller states and a range of national and regional non-governmental organisations.

This is an opportune moment to move towards a fully fledged multilateral framework which encompasses[22] the United States, the relevant republics of the former Soviet Union, all the countries of East and Southeast Asia, Australia, New Zealand and the Pacific Islands states. The task of this new security framework would be to respond effectively to the shift from East-West confrontation to East-West cooperation, phase out obsolete military alliances and agreements whose origins lie in the Cold War, and provide a vehicle for elaborating and applying notions of common and comprehensive security. This is not to say that the transition to such a framework will be swift or uniform across the region.

The proposed regional arrangements would run along two interconnected tracks:

1. *Agreement on Confidence and Security-Building Measures* (CSBMs). Some of these measures would apply specifically to Russian-American military deployments, others would have wider regional application. These measures could be expected to include notification of exercises and troop movements; restrictions on the scale of exercises and manoeuvres (here it may be easier to concentrate initially on one or two regions but gradually move towards a more universal regime); regular contacts among military chiefs and field commanders along or near disputed borders; thinning out of troops in areas of actual or potential conflict; agreements for handling piracy, smuggling, illegal migration, illegal fishing and environmentally damaging activities.

2. *Disarmament negotiations.* The aim here would be to initiate a process of substantial reductions of both nuclear and conventional forces, involving not only Russia and the United States, but all other regional powers which have acquired or are on the verge of acquiring significant military capabilities. Relevant here would be a number of the zoning and other disengagement proposals noted above. Consideration would need to be given to the possible regulation of the arms trade, which might include multilateral guidelines on the size of defence forces and even defence industries.

So far as the actual architecture of the security framework is concerned, there are two distinct but closely connected tiers:

1. *A roof or umbrella for the Pacific House.* This may take the form of a new organisation created specifically for the purpose. Alternatively it may take the form of an extension or refinement of the ASEAN Post-Ministerial Conference – an idea which was given considerable prominence in the lead-up to the 1992 ASEAN Summit.[23] Another, perhaps less feasible, option might be to

expand or reorganise APEC so as to give it a more explicit security focus. Whichever option is chosen – and there is no reason why in the early stages all avenues should not be explored – the aim must be to establish a widely representative forum which embraces all the countries of the region and places on its agenda all the issues which have a direct bearing on regional security.

2. *A series of interlinked sub-regional forums.* These would parallel and give practical effect to the concerns and priorities of the regional structure. Some would be geographically based (i.e. covering a particular area or sub-region), while others would be functionally based (i.e. addressing a particular conflict or problem area). Several examples of such forums come to mind. Some are already functioning: the South Pacific Forum, ASEAN (particularly if its membership is expanded to include the Indo-Chinese states) and the Cambodian peace process (which has brought together all the parties to the dispute and a number of regional powers as well as the United Nations). Forums which should be expanded include: a North-Pacific dialogue (to concentrate on CSBMs and various forms of military disengagement); a multilateral mechanism for the South China Sea (helping to establish a regional Spratlys regime, beginning perhaps with the less contentious issues of resource management, maritime safety, environmental protection and moving to questions of transparency and mutual surveillance of military capabilities); a regional dialogue for Korean demilitarisation and eventual reunification.[24]

The design, of this new architecture should be based on the twin concepts of common and comprehensive security, thereby ensuring that both human rights and the environment are firmly integrated into the emerging security framework.

There is no compelling reason, for example, why the governments of the region should not take collective action to deal with the brutal suppression of political dissent by the Burmese military regime. There is no suggestion here that such action need involve the use of force, although it may require a carefully targeted programme of diplomatic and economic sanctions. The ASEAN policy of 'positive engagement' has yielded no tangible result. Similar inaction with respect to the genocidal practices of the Khmer Rouge simply exacerbated the conflict and increased the pressures for external intervention. China's increasing political, military and economic penetration of Myanmar is ominously pointing in the same direction.[25] If governments have thus far refrained from taking the initiative it is partly because they recognise that their own performance is not entirely blameless. To pass judgment on others is therefore likely to invite international criticism of one's own shortcomings. It is precisely because of this powerful disincentive to action that a collective approach is often preferable. A regional institution may be able to intervene in ways which are more sensitive to local circumstances, although such intervention would need to proceed cautiously and on the basis of widely accepted criteria applied uniformly and without bias. This is not to suggest that an Asia Pacific system of security should favour frequent regional intervention in domestic conflicts, but rather that it could, in unusual circumstances deemed prejudicial to regional security and stability, offer an effective avenue for communication, conciliation, mediation and even peace-keeping.

A comprehensive regional security framework, however, will have limited success unless it represents the aspirations not only of states but of civil society generally. After all, it is often governments that are resistant to local aspirations for self-determination, democratic change, observance of human rights or preservation of ecological values. It is here that social movements and non-governmental organisations (e.g. trade unions, professional associations, conservation groups, development agencies, peace movements, religious organisations) may have a vital part to play in setting political agendas, mobilising popular energies and creating more durable cross-national and cross-cultural links.

Non-governmental organisations are important because they reflect the fears and aspirations of large numbers of people, and because they empower those who have been marginalised by the state. But public involvement, however successful, cannot be confined to the national arena. The experience of local and national communities is that their security is indivisible, that their needs cut across national boundaries, and that a constructive response requires not only moral solidarity but practical regional and international coordination. More effective regional networking between local and national organisations may be an important contribution to a more habitable future for the peoples of Asia and the Pacific. A regional non-governmental forum bringing together social movements concerned with issues of development, ecology, peace, human rights, racial equality, democracy, ethnic autonomy and political independence would greatly assist the process. Indeed, there is a strong argument that regionalisation at the governmental level should be paralleled and nurtured by regionalisation at the non-governmental level. To this end, it may be useful to consider a range of institutional links between the two processes, although care should be taken to ensure that such links do not compromise the independence of community organisations.

Regional initiatives at the non-governmental level may, in fact, help to create a more favourable environment for action at the governmental level. A useful step in the direction of a multi-lateral security framework might be the convening of a major conference bringing together NGO representatives from all the countries of the region. Such a conference might also have strong academic participation and allow for substantial representation from a number of governments. Preceded by a series of confidence-building agenda-setting workshops, it could then set the stage for a major inter-governmental conference (with a number of NGOs having consultative status). Though the necessary practical steps cannot be identified, let alone timetabled in advance of extensive consultations, the process itself may generate a significant amount of good will and degree of momentum which could begin to bear fruit by the mid-1990s.

Notes

1. Kim, S.S., (1992), 'International Organisational Behavior', in Robinson, T. and Shambaugh, D., (eds), *Ideas and Interpretations in Chinese Foreign Policy*, New York: Oxford University Press.
2. Palmer, N.D., (1991), *The New Regionalism in Asia and the Pacific*, p. 128, Lexington, Mass.: Lexington Books.
3. I argue the case for a multi-dimensional approach to security in Camilleri, J.A., (1987), *ANZUS: Australia's Predicament in the Nuclear*

Age, pp. 206-210, Melbourne: Macmillan; also Camilleri, J.A., (1991), 'Australia's Regional Security': Old Wine in New Bottles', in Fry, G., (ed.), Australia's Regional Security, pp. 96-106, Sydney: Allen and Unwin.

4. Walker, R.B.J., (1988), One World, Many Worlds, pp. 81-114, Boulder, Co.: Lynne Rienner.

5. FEER, (9 May 1991), p. 15.

6. Hamel-Green, M., (May 1989), 'The Not-So-Nuclear-Free-Zone: Australia's Arms Control Policy in the South Pacific Region', Interdisciplinary Peace Research, vol. 1, no. 1, pp. 46-52.

7. The Current Digest of the Soviet Press, (27 August 1986), vol. xxxviii, no. 30, pp. 1-8, 32.

8. FEER, (9 January, 1992), p. 10.

9. For a history and evaluation of the proposal, see Alagappa, Muthiah, (March 1991), 'Regional Arrangements and International Security in Southeast Asia: Going Beyond ZOPFAN', Contemporary Southeast Asia, vol. 12, no. 4, pp. 269-305.

10. For a succinct outline of the rationale for defensive strategies and force postures, see Mack, A., 'Reassurance Versus Deterrence Strategies for the Asia Pacific Region', pp. 22-23.

11. The implications of regulating the arms trade in the Indian Ocean context are discussed in Camilleri, J., (1987), 'Arms Control and the Indian Ocean' in Ball, D. and Mack, A., The Future of Arms Control, pp. 174-176, Sydney: Australian National University Press.

12. Gordon, B., (Fall 1991), 'The Asian-Pacific Rim', Foreign Affairs, vol. 70, no. 1, p. 154.

13. Elek, A., (1991), 'The Challenge of Asian Pacific Economic Cooperation', The Pacific Review, vol. 4, no. 4, pp. 322-332.

14. The Current Digest of the Soviet Press, (27 August, 1986), vol. xxxviii, no. 30, p. 8.

15. International Herald Tribune, (13 September 1990), p. 2.

16. 'The Canadian Initiative for a North Pacific Cooperative Security Dialogue', (3 December 1990), a Position Paper of External Affairs and International Trade Canada; see also Job, B.L., (August 1991), 'Canadian Defence Policy in the Pacific: Relevance, Commitments, and Capabilities', Canadian Defence Quarterly, vol. 21, no. 1, pp. 32-39.

17. The Monthly Record, (July 1990), vol. 61, no. 7, p. 425.

18. Henderson, S., (1992), 'Canada and Asia Pacific Security: The North Pacific Cooperative Security Dialogue Recent Trends', University of York, Center for International and Strategic Studies, NPCSD Working Paper No. 1, pp. 6-15.

19. Solomon, R.H., (30 October 1990), 'Asian Security in the 1990's: Integration in Economics: Diversity in Defence', Address to the University of California at San Diego, Graduate School of International Relations and Pacific Studies, pp. 5-6.

20. For a brief survey of the American response and its impact on the subsequent Australian formulation of the proposal, see *Pacific Research*, (May 1991), vol. 4, no. 2, p. 9.

21. Polomka, P., (March/April 1991), 'Towards a Pacific House', *Survival*, vol. xxxiii, pp. 173-174.

22. *Ibid.*, pp. 179-182.

23. Henderson, S., 'Canada and Asia Pacific Security', pp. 12-14.

24. Mason, P., 'Asia Pacific Security Forums', Chapter 14.

25. *FEER*, (28 November 1991), p. 28.

*   An earlier and longer version of this chapter appeared in Gary Smith and St John Kettle, *Threats Without Enemies*, Plato Press, Sydney, 1992.

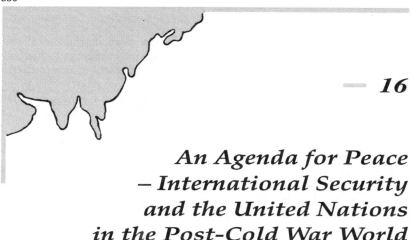

16

An Agenda for Peace – International Security and the United Nations in the Post-Cold War World

Kennedy Graham

Introduction

The early years of the post-Cold War era are proving to be a critical period of transition in which new political relationships and norms are being developed to underpin international peace and security into the 21st century. The transition is by no means completed, so it is difficult to foresee the precise structural outlines of the security system under which the world will strive to govern itself in the future. The process is a volatile one, however, answering not to a central consciously formulated design but rather to a set of unpredictable and largely unrelated factors. It is in response to this disorder that the United Nations is increasingly being called upon to try to generate some order and to help develop new rules to govern international relations.

Security during the Cold War rested not on the rule of law but on the threat of force. A balance of power prevailed, not among many nations of equal strength as in the century before, but between two undisputed superpowers, with less powerful allies grouped around them in a global bloc alignment of strict formality. The bottom line of global security was nuclear deterrence to avert major conflict between two ideological opponents. Competition for influence in the non-aligned world was intense, wars were fought between the superpowers by proxy, and unilateral intervention by them was frequent, often with scant regard to the niceties of international law. Collective security through the United Nations was dormant, with the UN unable to intervene to end wars such as the bitter ten-year struggle between Iran and Iraq, and the war in Vietnam. Global strategic stability rested on nuclear weaponry held by the major powers but outside the effective control of the United Nations. Regional and local peace was maintained, inadequately, through various means of non-nuclear deterrence, with UN peace-keeping providing some assistance on the periphery.

The challenge of the post-Cold War era is whether the United Nations can take centre-stage in the development of a global strategy for peace. It will need to do more than pass resolutions on disarmament; it will need to participate in central decisions over the deployment of weapons and the use of force to direct the lawful conduct of nations.

The fundamental features of the post-Cold War era will be different from those of the past four decades. Cultural and political values will remain diverse, but the world of power and political leadership will become increasingly regional with multilateral challenges to unipolar hegemons. Although strategic nuclear weapons will remain in large numbers during the 1990s, strategic doctrines will change in order to reflect the more benign world that already exists. Bloc alignment and nuclear alliance diplomacy no longer make sense, and nuclear weapons are increasingly seen as instruments 'of truly last resort'. NATO will seek, and probably find, a broader regulatory role in European security through cooperation with the Conference on Security and Cooperation in Europe (CSCE) and the new North Atlantic Cooperation Council (NACC). The principal role of nuclear deterrence will slowly, but almost inevitably, change from the prevention of major power conflict to preventing the spread of nuclear weapons themselves. Fewer numbers will be needed – perhaps as few as 300 to 1,000 each, but discrimination will remain a feature of the non-proliferation debate. There will be less competition and more alignment of policy among the major powers in promoting values and pursuing interests in the Third World. Conflict is more likely to fall within rather than outside the purview of the United Nations, and there will be fewer unilateral interventions by the major powers in future.

New Roles for the United Nations

In seeking to take a more central role in maintaining global peace and stability, the UN needs to re-appropriate or 're-invent' collective security as a central task of the organisation. The military success of the enforcement operation against Iraqi aggression provides many political lessons for the future, while the sheer complexity of the peace-keeping operation in Yugoslavia shows the continuing difficulties of maintaining the peace in a world of lingering grievances and unresolved tensions.

Because the post-Cold War world has produced a rather violent peace, there is a need for a more assertive United Nations, capable of intervening more frequently in disputes of many kinds. The emerging 'doctrine of humanitarian intervention' propounded by France would accord primacy, in some instances, to international moral concern and intervention in situations of humanitarian plight. Such intervention would transcend traditional notions of exclusive national sovereignty, something anticipated by former Secretary General Perez De Cuellar in his valedictory address to the United Nations in 1991. Three cases of humanitarian intervention have been undertaken by the UN in the past two years: in Kurdistan (under UN Security Council Resolution 688 of 5 April 1991), in Somalia (UNSC Resolution 751 of 24 April 1992), and Sarajevo (UNSC Resolution 770 of 13 August 1992). Each operation has been undertaken in complex and difficult circumstances, and the manner in which the UN handles these will largely determine the propensity of member states to act upon this doctrine in future.

A second new area of UN authority in the early 1990s concerns inspection rights. The decision of the Security Council in April 1991 (UNSC Resolution 687), that Iraq shall forfeit any right it may have to possess weapons of mass destruction, is unprecedented, both in its severity as a penal measure and in expanding the authority of the UN. It is one thing to take enforcement action to repel aggression back to the border of the liberated state. But to have the Council proceed, under enforcement authority, from the military realm into the political realm by divesting Iraq of certain rights possessed by other member states, is controversial indeed. As of mid-1992, for example, New Zealand has the right in international law to possess chemical weapons and also to withdraw from the Non-Proliferation Treaty at three months' notice and proceed to manufacture nuclear weapons if it so desired. Iraq does not have these rights anymore. The distinction draws simply on a political judgement by the Security Council and reflects the new-found power accorded to the UN by member states.

Less controversial is the enforcement authority of the United Nations, (also contained in Security Council Resolution 687), concerning Iraqi liability for damages and the new demarcation lines between Kuwait and Iraq to be determined by a UN survey team.

A major new area of activity for the UN involves acting as a 'transition authority' for countries attaining independence or undergoing a return to democracy after a period of autocracy, violence and trauma. Assistance of this kind was extended to new states in the decolonisation process in the 1950s and 1960s. More recent undertakings, however, such as Namibia (in 1989-90) and Cambodia (1991-92) are enormous undertakings with far reaching responsibilities for territorial administration for a specified period of time. The United Nations Transitional Authority in Cambodia (UNTAC) was established in February 1992 (UNSC Resolution 745) following an advance mission in 1991, and is going to cost the international community some $1.9 billion, which is about twice the regular budget of the UN.

A related service is the 'civil assistance' the United Nations is extending to member states in the form of electoral observation and verification. The undertaking which the UN mounted in Nicaragua in 1990 included technical assistance, in cooperation with the Organisation of American States (OAS), and the certification to the General Assembly that the elections, which ousted the incumbent regime after an intensive civil war, were free and fair. The unprecedented action of certifying an election in a member state was justified on the grounds that it was part of the regional peace package for Central America emerging from the Esquipulas Accords. This process was so successful that the UN was asked to do the same for Haiti a year later. This request also included providing 'security officers' for its first election.

The decision of the General Assembly in 1990 to provide such assistance shows the extent to which nation-states are prepared to facilitate UN intervention in domestic affairs when national authorities are incapable of achieving key political or economic objectives. It is one thing for the UN to provide assistance during a national election, which to some extent is simply the political reflection of economic assistance provided by UN agencies such as the United Nations Development Programme (UNDP). It is quite another to have the Secretary General report to the Assembly, verifying that a member state's election was free and fair. That is a highly political judgement, notwithstanding the care taken to keep to the technicalities of what constitutes 'free and fair'. It raises the possibility of various forms of political conditionality of a kind the IMF requires for extending financial and economic assistance, in which a state may be obliged to pursue a particular structural adjustment programme for economic reform. The military overthrow of President Aristide of Haiti after the election offered a poignant challenge to the international community in terms of the election results that the United Nations had verified. The acceptance of Aristide's delegation-in-exile at Rio for the United Nations Conference on Environment and Development (UNCED) Conference and the continuing pressure applied by the UN and the OAS against the military-backed regime, shows the potency of having the UN involved in basic election processes.

Electoral verification is closely related to the peace process in a number of instances. The experience of Nicaragua, in which UN assistance with elections was seen as an integral part of a peace settlement, has been followed also in Africa. In the case of the Western Sahara, the UN Security Council approved the efforts of the Secretary General towards a referendum for self-determination, and called upon the two parties involved in the long-standing dispute to cooperate with the Settlement Plan (UNSC Resolution 725 of 31 December 1991). In Angola, the Council decided to establish, and subsequently enlarge, its electoral mission known as the United Nations Angola Verification Mission (UNAVEM). It urged the demobilisation of the combatants, the creation of a unified armed force and called for free and fair elections to be held on schedule (September 1992). It urged the parties involved in the conflict to comply with the provisions of the 'Acordos de Paz' and its deadlines (UNSC Resolution 747 of 24 March 1992). Even South Africa is now turning to the UN to assist in its political evolution. Following the Boipatong massacre in June 1992, the Security Council expressed concern that continuing violence could 'seriously jeopardise peace and security in the region' and urged the South African authorities to take stronger measures to end the violence. It called for the implementation of the National Peace Accord, and invited the Secretary General to appoint a Special Representative to consult with the parties and recommend new measures (UNSC Resolution 765 of 16 July 1992).

One of the more dramatic interventions of the UN in recent times has been its involvement in the termination of the internal conflict in El Salvador. An Observer Mission, the United Nations Observer Mission in El Salvador (ONUSAL), has been established to verify and monitor the various agreements signed in Mexico in early 1992 between the government and the Faribundi Marti Front for National Liberation (FMFLN), especially the termination of the conflict and the establishment of a national police force (UNSC Resolution 729 of 14 January 1992). The UN has also assisted in a *Comision de la Veridad*, a fact-finding enquiry set up as part of the peace package negotiated between the combatant parties, and intended to defuse much of the animosity and grievances resulting from the war. In addition, it has been involved in supervising land reform and other efforts to reconstitute political legitimacy in El Salvador.

New Demands

These peace processes have resulted in a ferment of activity in the United Nations in new areas of work, imposing new stresses and strains on the organisation in both financial and human terms. A three-person unit for electoral assistance has recently been established within the Secretariat, but the UN will be hard-pressed to respond to all the requests for electoral assistance that it is now receiving. Requests to keep the peace now have the UN involved in Mozambique, Moldova and Afghanistan in addition to the operations already described. And requests for electoral assistance are being received from many developing countries, especially in Africa.

With so many requests to venture into new and untried areas, some envisaged in the Charter, some not, the United Nations is being called upon to make critical judgements about its areas of competence, legitimacy, authority and power. As in the Cold War period, the UN is effectively the product of decision-making, not by the Secretariat, but by political leaders in the international community. These decisions determine which initiatives it can take and the lengths to which it can go. Some of these decisions, taken by the leaders of the major powers, will set the tone for UN credibility and action for some time to come. Two problem areas can already be discerned.

The first concerns enforcement powers. Acting under its enforcement mandate to expel Iraq from Kuwait, the UN authorised a coalition of nations to cooperate militarily to achieve this goal. Strategic command of the operation was left entirely to the nations concerned. With so little control by the UN (that is to say the Secretary General) over the military operation, problems over the political objectives and the military means were bound to arise. Questions concerning limitations of powers in the enforcement action itself (when and where the military action should cease), proportionality of military response and related humanitarian obligations, and reporting responsibilities (from the coalition nations to the Security Council) have all been raised by the Secretary General. The lessons of the Gulf conflict will require considerable thought and reflection if they are to result in better UN enforcement actions in future.

The second problem concerns a particularly difficult area of judgement: the extent of authority of the Security Council in matters of dispute settlement. The decision of the Council to apply binding sanctions against Libya for failure to provide information or hand over the agents alleged to have been responsible for two terrorist actions (UNSC Resolution 748 of 31 March 1992) raise very difficult questions for the UN. In taking its decision, the Council determined that Libya's failure to respond constituted a 'threat to international peace and security', and then applied sanctions under Chapter VII of the Charter. Such action is seen by many as controversial, since the decision was initiated by the parties involved in the dispute. It had less to do with outright aggression than allegations of criminal activity, and it blurs the distinction, never clear at the international level, between political and legal authority. The International Court of Justice, at the request of Libya, deliberated on the powers of the Council in this respect, concluding that the Council's resolution prevailed over a State Party's treaty right (such as those under the Montreal Convention, 1971). The court declined to make a judicial decision when a matter was actually under the Council's purview. The Libyan case raises some profound questions about political and legal authority which will not be clarified and resolved for a long time to come.

The new challenges and opportunities before the United Nations in the post-Cold War world will require unprecedented attention by the political leaders of the 179 member states, particularly the members of the Security Council. Meetings of the Council are replacing Soviet-American summits as the critical determinant of world affairs. Mindful of these trends, the United Kingdom proposed the first UN Security Council Summit, which was convened on 31 January 1992, at the start of the new Secretary General's tenure. The Summit requested the Secretary General to report to member states on ways of strengthening the capacity of the UN for preventive diplomacy, peace-making and peace-keeping.

Boutros Ghali's *Agenda for Peace*

The report, *Agenda for Peace* (UN doc. A/47/277 of 17 June 1992), is an important and far-reaching document. The Secretary General has combined vision with realism and produced a list of proposals which go beyond the expectations, and perhaps the preferences, of at least some of the major powers. The report seeks to offer, perhaps for the first time in UN thinking, a coherent theory of peace, with four interrelated components. These are as follows.

1. Preventive diplomacy is action to prevent disputes from arising between parties, to prevent existing disputes from escalating into conflicts, and to limit the spread of the latter when they occur.

2. Peace-making is action to bring hostile parties to agreement, essentially through such peaceful means as those foreseen in Chapter VI of the Charter of the UN.
3. Peace-keeping is the deployment of a UN presence in the field, hitherto with the consent of all the parties concerned, normally involving UN military and/or police personnel and frequently civilians as well. Peace-keeping is a technique that expands the possibilities for both the prevention of conflict and the making of peace.[1]
4. Post-conflict peace-building actions identify and support structures which will tend to strengthen and solidify peace in order to avoid a relapse into conflict.[2]

These four dimensions of UN work are intended to comprise a fabric of peace. 'Preventive diplomacy', says the Secretary General, 'seeks to resolve disputes before violence breaks out; peace-making and peace-keeping are required to halt conflicts and preserve peace once it is attained. If successful, they strengthen the opportunity for post-conflict peace-building, which can prevent the recurrence of violence among nations and peoples... . These four areas for action, taken together, and carried out with the backing of all members, offer a coherent contribution towards securing peace in the spirit of the Charter'.[3]

The Security Council's mandate specifically confined the Secretary General to proposals 'within the framework and provisions of the Charter'. There is therefore no direct reference in the report to any matter that might involve amendment or alteration of the Charter. Nevertheless, the report goes beyond urging implementation of under-used charter provisions, to include some imaginative innovations.

Preventive diplomacy is interpreted broadly to cover not only confidence-building measures, fact-finding and early warning, but also 'preventive deployment' by the UN which could include a military component – perhaps the single most important new proposal in the report.

Confidence-Building Measures that are recommended include military exchanges, risk reduction centres, and arrangements for the free flow of information including the monitoring of regional arms agreements. The Secretary General has requested all regional organisations to consider what further measures might be applied in their region and inform the UN of the results.[4]

Better fact finding, in the opinion of the Secretary General, is needed to enable him to act more effectively under Article 99 of the Charter. No far-reaching new proposals, however, are advanced to this end, or with 'early warning'. The UN already has a valuable network of systems that can forewarn of environmental threats, nuclear accidents, natural disasters, population movements, famine and disease. But there is a need, it is held, to synthesise this information with appropriate political indicators in order to assess whether a threat to the peace of the world exists. To this end, the Economic and Social Council (ECOSOC) is asked to report to the Security Council, under Article 65, on any trends within its purview that could threaten the peace. All regional organisations also are asked to establish links with the security mechanisms of the UN.[5]

The concept of preventive deployment is new and innovative, and must be seen as qualitatively different from traditional peace-keeping. The latter is employed after conflict has occurred, is dependent on the continuing consent of both belligerent parties, and is confined to passive military measures such as truce and disengagement monitoring, with UN troops firing only in self-defence. Preventive deployment, by contrast, is designed to prevent hostilities from occurring. It could be employed in three situations. Within a member state, during a time of national crisis, there could be a UN preventive deployment at the request of the government of all parties concerned, or with their consent.[6] Between member states, preventive deployment could occur when both countries feel a UN presence on both sides of their common border could discourage hostilities. And in absence of such a joint view, preventive deployment could take place where a country feels threatened and requests the deployment of an appropriate UN presence along its side of the border alone. In addition to maintaining the peace, preventive deployment could be used to provide humanitarian assistance in situations of human suffering.[7]

Demilitarised zones, hitherto used as a post-conflict measure to build confidence between belligerents, could also be tried as a form of preventive deployment, either on both sides or only on one side of a border.[8]

The recommendations on peace-making encompass a number of issues, including some not commonly associated with the term 'peace-making', which is usually taken to mean the peaceful resolution of conflict under Chapter VI of the Charter. Also raised is greater use of the World Court,[9] 'amelioration through assistance', use of sanctions, military enforcement (under Chapter VII), and an innovation called 'peace-enforcement units'. This last proposal would appear to represent a third form of UN military action, distinct from enforcement and peace-keeping.

The Secretary General recommends that he be authorised, under Article 96(2), to refer situations of dispute to the International Court for an advisory opinion. He also recommends that all member states accept, by the year 2000, the compulsory jurisdiction of the Court, without reservations. Use of the Chambers jurisdiction should be used where necessary, and greater support given to the Trust Fund for developing countries to utilise the Court more readily.[10]

When peace-making requires the imposition of sanctions under Article 41, some states will always be economically affected more than others. The Secretary General recommends that the Security Council devise a set of measures to insulate states from such difficulties.[11] The use of military force under Chapter VII is seen as part of peace-making. The Secretary General draws a critical distinction between the Security Council undertaking enforcement action, and authorising member states to do it on the Council's behalf.

The Security Council has not so far made use of the most coercive of these measures - the action by military force foreseen in Article 42. In the situation between Iraq and Kuwait, the Council chose to authorise member states to take measures on its behalf. The Charter, however, provides a detailed approach which now merits the attention of all member states.[12]

The implication is that 'farming out' enforcement action to member states should be a thing of the past. To this end, the

Secretary General recommends the negotiation of Article 43 agreements whereby member states undertake to make available armed forces, assistance and facilities to the Security Council, 'not only on an ad hoc basis but a permanent basis'.[13] This would deter breaches of the peace, since a potential aggressor would know that the Council always had at its disposal a means of response. The Military Staff Committee should be seen in the context of Chapter VII only, not for peace-keeping operations.

In a further innovation, the Secretary General identifies a new task for UN forces, to cover situations between peace-keeping and enforcement action. Cease-fires, he observes, have often been agreed to but not complied with, and the UN has sometimes been called upon to send forces to restore and maintain them. This task can exceed the mission of peace-keeping forces. The Secretary General therefore recommends 'peace enforcement units' in clearly defined circumstances, more heavily armed than peace-keeping forces and with extensive preparatory training.[14] Peace enforcement units would be seen as part of the provisional measures under Article 40. They should not be confused with either the forces that may eventually be constituted under Article 43 to deal with aggression, or with military personnel kept by member states on stand-by for peace-keeping.

The recommendations on peace-keeping focus essentially on the increased demands on the UN for such operations and on the issue of adequate resources. The Secretary General makes clear his impatience with those member states in financial arrears on their peace-keeping dues, and the absence of adequate mechanisms for covering the logistical phase of the operations. His principal proposal is for member states to finance their share of peace-keeping costs from national defence, rather than foreign affairs budgets. He urges the General Assembly to encourage this approach. He also requests member states to identify military personnel, especially logistics units, that they can make available for UN peace-keeping, and suggests that supply depots with pre-positioned stocks of peace-keeping equipment should be established.[15]

The theoretical innovation introduced in the report is post-conflict *peace-building*. Preventive diplomacy is to avoid a crisis; post-conflict peace-building is to prevent a recurrence.[16] This may take the form of concrete cooperative projects (between countries) to develop agriculture, improve transportation or utilise resources such as water or electricity that they need to share, or joint programmes through which barriers between nations are brought down by means of free travel, cultural exchange and mutually beneficial and educational projects.[17]

The report addresses two further issues – safety of UN personnel and UN financing. UN personnel, notes the Secretary General, must expect to go in harm's way at times; 'Duty in areas of danger can never be risk-free'...but the courage, commitment and idealism shown by UN personnel should be respected by the entire international community...the Security Council should, (in advance of an operation), 'gravely consider what action should be taken towards those who put UN personnel in danger'.[18]

The financial problems of the United Nations must be solved. 'Our vision cannot really extend to the prospect opening before us as long as our financing remains myopic.'[19] He recommends:

1. Establishment of a revolving peace-keeping reserve fund of $50 million.
2. Agreement that one third of the estimated cost of each new peace-keeping operation be appropriated by the General Assembly as soon as the Security Council decides to establish it.
3. The placing of contracts without competitive bidding in exceptional circumstances.
4. A select group of qualified persons of high international repute to examine the question of financing.[20]

An item of special interest to those concerned with regional peace and security is the section of the report dealing with the decentralisation and delegation of peace-making operation from the UN to regional organisations. The Secretary General urges a harmonisation of such initiatives to enhance regional and global cooperation and cites recent joint initiatives in Africa in relation to Somalia, in Asia with ASEAN on the Cambodian settlement and for El Salvador the development of a new group called 'Friends of the Secretary General'.[21]

Agenda for Peace should prompt the most profound evaluation of the role of the United Nations in the maintenance of international peace and security since the start of the Cold War, perhaps since the organisation was first established. As the Secretary General puts it:

> The nations and peoples of the United Nations are fortunate in a way that those of the League of Nations were not. We have been given a second chance to create the world of our Charter that they were denied.... There is a need to ensure that the lessons of the past four decades are learned...for there may not be a third opportunity for our planet....[22]

It is still too early to judge whether the nations of the world will make the United Nations workable as the mainstay of peace in the 21st century. The end of the Cold War does not solve the world's problems; it simply makes their effective resolution possible. Many challenges to wisdom and statecraft lie ahead. But the resurgence of activity and respect which the UN has already enjoyed in the early years of the post-Cold War era augur well for the organisation and the international community, and it may well be that this time, global stability and peace will finally be secured for all nations and peoples.

Notes

1. Boutros Ghali, (1992), *An Agenda for Peace*, UN Doc. A/47/277, 17 June 1992, pp. 10-11.
2. *Ibid.*, p. 11.
3. *Ibid.*
4. *Ibid.*, pp. 12-13.
5. *Ibid.*, pp. 15-16.
6. *Ibid.*, p. 17.
7. *Ibid.*, p. 18.
8. *Ibid.*, p. 19.
9. *Ibid.*, p. 22.
10. *Ibid.*, p. 23.

11. *Ibid.*, p. 25.
12. *Ibid.*, p. 26.
13. *Ibid.*, p. 26.
14. *Ibid.*, p. 27.
15. *Ibid.*, p. 33.
16. *Ibid.*, p. 35.
17. *Ibid.*, p. 34.
18. *Ibid.*, pp. 41-42.
19. *Ibid.*, p. 42.
20. *Ibid.*, pp. 45-46.
21. *Ibid.*, p. 38.
22. *Ibid.*, p. 47.

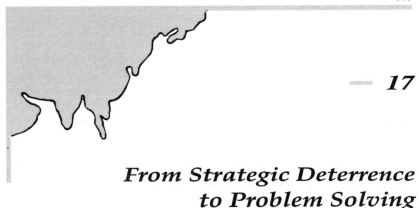

17

From Strategic Deterrence to Problem Solving

John Burton

The Problem: Universal Violence

This moment in history is characterised by uncontrollable violence and conflict on the streets of cities, among communities, and between nation-states. There is violence at all social levels. People have acquired a sense of resignation because they accept that there is little they can do to eliminate what is assumed to be its source, namely human nature.

Traditional power political philosophies rest on the assumption that 'Man is aggressive, therefore the state is aggressive', implying the need for social control of behaviours, nationally and internationally, by power and coercion. Breakdowns in law and order, such as revolutions and wars, become the accepted and inevitable means of change. They are the price that has to be paid for periods of continuing national and international stability. In this view the best that can be hoped for in human relations is improved means of control by power, for example, improved policing, and community and international peace-keeping forces. The use of power as the dominant means of control in social and political organisation has been termed 'political realism'.

A great deal of law and order and strategic thinking has rested, and still rests, on these traditional power theories and philosophies. Most members of the world society have institutionalised the traditional power and adversarial means of settling disputes, such as legal processes, arbitration, and forms of power bargaining. 'Peace-keeping' exercises are designed to separate warring factions.

The new reality is, however, that the general availability of means of violence, and communications between like-minded groups, are making defiance of political and military power possible. So-called 'political realism' becomes wholly unrealistic in contemporary conditions of universal communications and possession of the means of violent protest.

The world is currently faced with many situations, domestic and international, in which neither threat nor force can achieve deterrence, no matter how overwhelming it may be. At the domestic level protracted ethnic conflict is now almost universal, and police are being defeated in the streets of major cities in many developed and developing countries. The U.S. threat of overwhelming force did not coerce Iraq into submission.

But why should there be defiance of law, and of those who wield power, because the means of violence are now widely available? Why do individuals, communities and nations employ such violent means?

Human behaviour seems to be more complicated than the power-political realists thought. Modern communications are making possible expression of long-standing personal, social and international grievances. It is not just to use available means of violence that street gangs emerge, that the IRA have been active in opposing Westminster rule, that the Tamils are in revolt. Throughout history human aspirations have been largely repressed within this power frame, and civilisations have entered a new phase in which the individual, the ethnic identity group, the community, the nation, are seeking opportunities for development, and will no longer be socialised into the norms and behaviours set down by the more powerful. The empirical evidence suggests, in short, that aggression is not for its own sake. It is not a part of human nature, as has been assumed. The possibility is that violence is not the preferred means by which to remedy unacceptable conditions, but is the only one available within social institutions based on power.

Despite these altered realities, however, the élites of nation-states, and the United Nations through which they sometimes operate, continue to try to preserve a world order based on coercion by the more powerful.

Conflict Avoidance and Resolution

If military and economic power is no longer effective as a means of control, the world society has no rational option but deliberately to move from deterrence strategies, from the goal of 'control', to solving problems by getting at their roots. There can be few if any societal goals more pressing than substituting interactive problem-solving decision making for adversarial confrontation.

Peace researchers need to adopt a positive orientation and place conflict resolution high on their agenda. This is particularly so in relation to the peoples and nations of the Asia Pacific region. There is an urgent need to take some first steps in establishing a suitable institution to help parties in conflicts analyse their problems and find options that satisfy their needs, thus avoiding adversarial confrontations, and dysfunctional deterrent and defensive measures.

Studies are emerging now that challenge traditional power philosophies, and seek to identify the real sources of conflict so that they can be foreseen and prevented, or resolved to the satisfaction of all parties, even though this means questioning traditional beliefs and institutional frames.

There is a problem of communication when talking about conflict resolution. It still means to many a form of deterrence, arms control or police intervention, because most of us have no conceptual frame other than the traditional deterrence frame in which to deal with conflict. Furthermore, when conflict resolution is put forward as an alternative to deterrence, there is for many, an impractical and idealistic connotation.

Conflict resolution is a subject now widely researched and taught in many universities. It is not about strategic deterrence, nor is it the product of idealism and personal values. It is about solving problems that will lead to conflict. It is about using predictive decision making to avoid conflict. 'Conflict resolution' as the term is now being used, should be defined as 'analytical problem-solving decision making'.

False Assumptions

In order to predict accurately, a holistic and realistic theory of human behaviour is required. The 'man is aggressive' theory has misled us. The theories of separate disciplines, and their constructs such as 'economic man', do not provide an adequate alternative. Traditional sociologists seemed to assume that the person and groups were wholly malleable, or could be socialised into required behaviours. The premise of conflict resolution is that there are certain fundamental human aspirations and needs that will be pursued, and which cannot be contained in the longer term by socialisation processes and the use of power. It is the pursuit of needs of recognition and group identity that explain police defeats in the street, and military defeats in Vietnam, Korea and elsewhere. This has been captured in the title of a book by Jerel Rosati and Roger Coates, *The Power of Human Needs,*[1] implying a human power greater than any possible coercive power.

In trying to determine what kind of regional arrangement should be sought and what avoided, there is a need to rethink basic philosophies and assumptions.

Most people have inherited, and maintain, an authoritative political environment in which, to use Lord Lloyd's terms, 'there are those who have a right to expect obedience, and those who have an obligation to obey'.[2] This has been justified over the ages by power élites. These authoritarian institutions are supposed to be imperative for purposes of law and order. But when there is enforced law and little order it is time to start questioning. Why are prisons full, why is it not safe to walk the streets of a city, why do we adopt more and more security measures, why do we not solve problems such as have emerged in South Africa, Sri Lanka, Cyprus, Northern Ireland, Fiji, Yugoslavia and elsewhere? Maybe these outmoded authoritative institutions do not promote the needs of peoples?

These inherited coercive institutions are not just the police and military. They include the power-structured adversarial institutions that are an integral part of 'democracy'. There can be nothing more destructive of harmonious and fruitful relationships than we-they relations of any kind, including party parliamentary systems, adversarial legal systems, exploitive industrial systems and others, which seek short-term interests within a power bargaining frame and lead societies away from solving their longer-term problems.

Unfortunately, the newly independent nations of Asia and the Pacific have inherited the power political institutions of the former colonial powers. In many cases disagreements over territory, autonomy and ethnicity have led, not to attempts to get to the source of the problem, but to coercion and violent response.

It is important to rethink quite basic notions. Something basic such as 'democracy' or 'government by the people', for example may need to be rethought. In the past there were probably some societies in which the people formed a homogeneous group, and if all had a vote there could have been a democracy according to this definition. There are many other situations however, in which there is no such homogeneity. Imperialist intervention resulted in boundaries being drawn by the outcome of wars, not by natural population concentrations. In these circumstances, so-called 'democracy' becomes rule by one national ethnic or tribal group over others.

The world society is backing one-person-one-vote in South Africa as 'democratic', despite evidence that this form of franchise often generates majority rule over minorities which leads to violent and protracted conflict. Separate ethnic and tribal entities are required, which may require constitutional autonomies not yet considered by constitutionalism. Tamils as well as Singhalese in Sri Lanka, Turks as well as Greeks in Cyprus, Europeans as well as Blacks in South Africa, have needs to be fulfilled, and these needs are so basic that they must fight for them. There is a human need for identity and recognition, for its own sake and for reasons of security. Institutions must reflect these human needs if conflict is to be avoided. Human beings cannot be expected to adjust to institutions that frustrate their human needs.

Associated with the assumption that majority rule is democratic is a reluctance to accept separation as a desirable solution. It is assumed that 'integration' of peoples is the desirable goal.

Most states and peoples are loath to accept breakaways from the nation-state, or separate autonomies. The world was unable to accept a peacefully divided Cyprus as a desirable solution to the majority-minority problem there, and cannot accept a forced separation as the basis for a functional relationship. It is hard for the international community, and the great powers especially, to accept separation in Yugoslavia, together with readjustment of boundaries to satisfy basic ethnicity needs.

To deal with problems, to anticipate problems, it is important to have an adequate predictive capacity, which means an adequate theory of behaviour and sense of the future. It is now clear that the nation-state world order, of which the United Nations is part, has had its day. The future will be a world order comprising identity communities, separate autonomies, seemingly based on religion, ethnicity or tribes, but in practice based on the need for identity and recognition, a need that increases in intensity as living conditions become more threatening. The Soviet Union will not be the last major nation-state to break up into separate autonomies. In the Asia Pacific region there are demands for autonomy, too frequently resisted by existing nation-states.

The assumptions we must question include many that have been legitimised by special studies, such as economics, but which have no validity when applied outside the Western region in which economics was founded. Take, for example, the current issue of subsidies and tariffs. The great powers, the U.S. in particular, have become great economically as a result of subsidies, tariffs, and non-competitive opportunities provided by wars. Now they want underdeveloped countries to forego the processes by which they themselves became economically developed.

There are many such consensus assumptions that need to be challenged, and will be challenged as the coercive power of the industrialised nations declines in effectiveness.

Problem-solving Decision Making

Problems in human relationships require solution, not suppression. Creative solutions are possible when there is recognition by all concerned of the inherent human needs of peoples, and insight into the longer-term costs and consequences of frustrating these needs. The Asia Pacific region for example requires a fresh approach, in domestic politics and in international politics – an approach which avoids power politics and opts for new types of institutions that deal with problems at their source. Problems of cultural identity and its recognition are especially sensitive.

Such an approach challenges many preconceived notions. For example, right and wrong are irrelevant notions in a conflict situation: there are problems to be solved. Finding fault with the policies of some Asia Pacific country faced now with pressing domestic problems, is a superficial approach to the problems being experienced.

A no-fault approach is much more relevant to Asia Pacific concerns. Most regional problems are very much a carry-over from the past. It is vital therefore to understand the way in which the peoples and resources of Asia and the Pacific have been exploited by European colonial powers, and the long-term consequences of this. Forced migrations of cheap labour, and resource exploitation at the cost of denying local development, have left devastating consequences. Current conflicts in the region, both domestic and foreign, are a direct consequence of the past, for example, migrations that now threaten original autonomies, and colonial boundaries that may divide identity groups, or, on the other hand, enforce diversity.

Exploitation is, of course, what colonialism was and is all about. It has taken many forms in addition to direct resource exploitation. The depression policies of the European powers for example were to reserve colonies for their exclusive exploitation of resources and markets. This made Japan's entry into World War II on the side of Germany quite inevitable. It had to have access to markets and raw materials to survive. After World War II there was, on the part of colonial powers, intensive resistance to Asian and Pacific movements toward independence. There is little more concern today for the separate identity and welfare of the peoples of this heavily populated and extensive region. The harsh realities of market mechanisms and Western defence policies persist as though colonial conditions still remain.

This is not necessarily a condemnation of the former colonial powers and of the United States of America. The exploitation of others was and is part of the global system. The question now is, how the Asia Pacific countries, especially the smaller and less affluent ones, can promote their security, independence and development?

There are many approaches to dealing with conflicts, and conflict resolution is easily confused with mediation, negotiation and alternatives to courts. What has to be appreciated is that good will, including attentive listening and skilled mediation, is not likely to resolve deep-rooted conflict. The answers are not in the heads of the parties concerned. The answers usually are not within the traditional knowledge frame of a third party. Ethnicity problems cannot be resolved, even with good will, if demands for autonomy challenge the traditional right of states to preserve territorial boundaries, and to exercise control of inhabitants within those boundaries. Without a profound understanding of ethnicity, which means an understanding of human needs and motivations, it is unlikely that dominant groups will be able to assess the longer-term costs of their coercive policies. It is the same with male-female relations, work-place relations, and any relationships where recognition and identity become key issues.

The role of the third party in conflict resolution must be, therefore, a positive one, drawing attention to human aspirations, questioning the assumptions made by the parties, inducing consideration of issues that do not emerge in mediation and bargaining situations. Such a third party must be informed by intensive studies in human behaviour and relationships, that is, holistic studies that go beyond the fields covered by specialists such as psychologists, and by social scientists generally.

Conflict resolution, therefore, means changed notions about the nature of conflict, greater understanding of attitudes, and, furthermore, the availability of persons with special skills that go beyond those associated with diplomacy and negotiation.

International and Domestic Levels of Analysis

In making this analysis it is important to note a movement away from the international as a special case, toward perspectives that treat conflict as generic. Separating international from domestic, which is still usual in universities and in scholarship generally, has had serious consequences. Relations between states are essentially no different from relations between groups and persons. Conflict and violence are no less of a problem at these levels, and have the same fundamental sources.

Furthermore, the separation of international and domestic, implying international causes of international conflicts, has diverted attention from the reality that international conflict is usually if not always, a carry-over from domestic, that is, nation-state problems. U.S. intervention in Vietnam was occasioned by a special American definition of the situation there, influenced by current ideological conflicts within the U.S. Vietnam was not analysed in the context of post-colonial independence movements. As previously mentioned, war with Japan, a Western ally in World War I, was brought about directly as a result of U.K. domestic unemployment policies which shut off colonial markets in Asia from this island country which for survival required access to resources and markets. Many current ethnic conflicts are due to national boundaries being drawn as the result of colonial conquest which ignored population distributions. National attempts to maintain such boundaries are a major source of international conflict.

Whether we refer to nation-states, to community groups, to industrial relations or to personal relationships, we are referring to the same phenomena when we deal with the sources of conflicts.

The United Nations

The United Nations draws an arbitrary distinction between domestic and international affairs.

The domestic jurisdiction clause in the UN Charter totally ignores the link between domestic and international conflict, and thus excludes the United Nations from tackling the sources of international conflict.

This is not to suggest that the UN, or a regional body, should have an automatic right to intervene in the domestic affairs of a nation. But such interventions are not so problematic if there is a desire to move from coercive treatment of problems to attempts to resolve them. Nations should welcome multilateral help in resolving their problems through interactive and consultative means.

Furthermore, the basic assumptions of the Western-sponsored United Nations should be questioned, for they remain within the power-political frame and rarely adopt approaches that challenge Western nation-state norms. Peace-keeping forces, for example, do not solve problems, and diplomatic representatives of nation-states do not reflect the frustrations and needs of ethnic and cultural minorities within them.

The United Nations was founded on the domestic law-and-order model, it being assumed at the time that this was closest to the ideal conflict-free model: namely a central authority with coercive powers by which to control deviants. This élitist power model is now revealed as a prime source of global violence. The most industrially developed, prosperous and so-called democratic states are among the most violent as measured by murders and other forms of internal violence. A central coercive authority is not, therefore the answer to serious conflict. Fortunately, the United Nations has not had at its disposal a standing international force as was intended.

A state-centric United Nations is becoming an irrelevant institution. The future is a global society that comprises autonomies, and it is these autonomies that member states try to suppress within their own boundaries. Conflict in Yugoslavia, therefore, will be repeated in many African and European states.

The United Nations has limited potential for problem-solving conflict resolution. It operates within the traditional power frame, and peace-keeping is its doubtful contribution. The concept of conflict resolution does not come into the Charter. At a conference held in Singapore on the changing role of the United Nations, there was one session on conflict resolution. It was defined as having three aspects: prevention and persuasion; non-coercive pressure 'otherwise known as sanction'; and the use of collective force.[3] A new start that reflects experience and increased knowledge since 1945 seems to be required.

A Regional Organisation

A new approach to regional conflict suggests the need for an organisation designed to promote policies that would avoid conflict, and to deal with conflicts in a problem-solving mode if they occur.

Such a regional organisation would necessarily be non-governmental, for governments generally do not take a longer-term perspective, and are too involved in a particular situation to be able to analyse it. They can respond to an invitation to meet with others to discuss in an informal atmosphere and off the record, but it is difficult for them to take an initiative and invite the opposing party, or to respond to an initiative by an opposing party.

It would be desirable to have centres throughout the region that provided relevant training in conflict resolution, so that there are trained persons available to deal with problems within countries and between them. There are now available at various universities many conflict resolution courses that could become a shared asset. To begin, there is a need for a centre that would train persons from the region so that they could train others in their own countries.

An even earlier step might be some particular cases of facilitated conflict resolution that could be assessed quietly at some later stage.

A Region in the Global Society

Such an independent approach by the countries of Asia and the Pacific is not a simple matter of policy. When the independence movement of the post-war period commenced, the tendency was for newly independent states to be non-aligned, that is, free to pursue their own foreign policies outside the power alliance. Nehru took the lead, and was backed by Tito of Yugoslavia and Nasser of Egypt. The Bandung Conference was a significant attempt by newly independent states to remain independent. But in due course many nations in the region had no option but to seek financial and commercial support from former colonial powers. They did not, and still do not, feel that they have freedom of choice in determining their domestic and foreign policies.

So whether a regional organisation, outside the power-political frame, can achieve what was once sought within the wider global system is an interesting question. Perhaps regional cooperation could lead to greater regional independence, and opportunities to resolve problems in more constructive and problem-solving ways than have been attempted in the past. Indeed, the Asia Pacific region could become an experimental model for other regions and for the global society.

There are many pressing relational problems in the region, but these should not be dealt with within the coercive frame of great power political interests, or by applying feudal assumptions. Enforced integration is not a practical response. Peoples whose identity and traditional role are submerged as a consequence of past colonial migrations cannot be coerced into peaceable behaviours.

Fiji, for example, raises important questions about the limits of majority rule in multi-ethnic communities. The traditional one-person-one-vote, relevant in a homogeneous society, is not the answer to this now almost universal ethnicity problem. Multi-ethnic conflict is deep-rooted. Repression of minorities always generates long-term problems. So-called democratic majorities have a tendency to threaten the future security and development of minority cultures and identities. A solution to this problem calls for innovative responses which satisfy the legitimate needs of everyone. Such resolutions can emerge only if there is movement out of the traditional Western power frame, and an elevation of the human need for recognition shared by both majorities and minorities.

Fiji is but one country requiring new problem-solving approaches to its political dilemmas. There are others in Sri Lanka, India, Cambodia, Papua-New Guinea, Indonesia and elsewhere.

Conclusion

There is a need to establish a new and questioning approach to the vital issues of human relationships in the global society, and in Asia and the Pacific in particular. By this is not meant an approach based on idealism, or humanitarianism, or on a set of ethnic values. Rather it requires an approach that is realistic and practical because it is holistic and takes into account, not just élite interests, economic, political and commercial interests, and the cultural values of dominant powers, but also the pursuit of basic human needs that have led to independence movements, that now promote ethnic conflicts, and that can now help explain why within even developed societies there is widespread deviance and violence beyond the capacities of authorities to control.

There are many approaches to security, peace, and conflict resolution, some of which are false and should be abandoned, some of which are justified only by selected empirical support and need to be critically re-examined, many of which have their own specific relevance. In determining what approach is relevant to a particular situation – threat and coercion, arbitration, mediation or some problem-solving intervention – there is a need to define the situation first. Having done this, analysts must be prepared to change the approach as more information comes to the surface. What at first appears to be some unconstitutional leadership challenge can turn out to be a major ethnic conflict.

It is vital that countries in the Asia Pacific region declare their independence from outmoded ways of solving problems. An Asia Pacific mode of problem-solving, detached from the Western 'realist' tradition and which takes advantage of existing indigenous knowledge, and non-confrontational ways of resolving problems, may make the Asia Pacific region a model for the future.

Notes

1. Coate, R., and Rosati, J., (1988), *The Power of Human Needs in World Society,* Reinner.
2. Lloyd, D., (1964), *The Idea of Law,* Pelican.
3. UN Charter, Article 7.

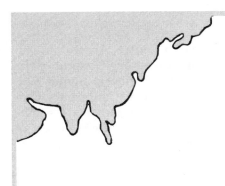

Notes on Contributors

Sam Bateman. Head Maritime Strategic Studies Project, Department of Defence (Navy Office) Australia, previously Director General Military Strategic Concepts, HQADF. Author/Editor of numerous articles and monographs on defence issues including most recently *Australia's Maritime Interests – Views from Overseas,* and with Desmond Ball, *An Australian Perspective on Maritime CSBM's in the Asia Pacific Region.*

John Burton. Author of 14 books on international relations and conflict resolution, most recently a four volume series on *Conflict Prevention; Needs Theory; Readings and Practices* (New York: St Martin's Press, and United Kingdom: MacMillan). Previously Professor at University College London, University of Kent, Maryland University and George Mason University. Now retired and living in NSW, Australia.

Joseph A. Camilleri. Reader in Politics at La Trobe University, has published several influential books including *The State and Nuclear Power; ANZUS* and most recently (with Jim Falk) *The End of Sovereignty?* He chairs the Editorial Committee of the journal *Interdisciplinary Peace Research.*

Kevin Clements. Head Peace Research Centre, Australian National University, Canberra Australia. Secretary General of the Asia Pacific Peace Research Association. Formerly Senior Lecturer Sociology and Coordinator Peace Studies, Canterbury University, New Zealand. Author of *Back from the Brink – The Creation of a Nuclear Free New Zealand; From Right to Left in Development Theory;* Co-editor, *Peace, Culture and Society: Transnational Research and Dialogue,* and numerous articles/ chapters on peace, development and security issues.

Scilla Elworthy. Director Oxford Research Group, formerly Research Director, Minority Rights Group (France), Consultant on Women's Issues to UNESCO and National Organiser, Kupugani. Author of *How Nuclear Weapons Decisions are Made; Who Decides? Accountability and Nuclear Weapon Decision Making in Britain,* and numerous articles,monographs on nuclear and conventional peace and security issues.

Elizabeth Ferris. Research Director, Life and Peace Institute, Uppsala Sweden. Previously Research Analyst on Refugee issues for the World Council of Churches. She has written extensively on refugee and foreign policy issues. Her books include *Beyond Borders; The Central American Refugees* and *Refugees and World Politics.*

Kennedy Graham. Secretary General, Parliamentarians for Global Action, New York. Former diplomat, New Zealand Ministry of Foreign Affairs, with postings to Canada, Thailand, and Geneva. Author of *National Security Concepts of New Zealand;* Co-author, *Towards a Strategy for New Zealand Agriculture,* and numerous articles on regional and global peace and security.

Govind Kelkar. Coordinator of the Gender and Development Studies Unit at the Asian Institute of Technology, Bangkok, Thailand. She is the author of various works on Chinese Development and Women's Studies. Her most recent co-authored book is *Gender and Tribe: Women, Land and Forest in Jharkand.*

Peter King. Senior Lecturer in Government and Director of Conflict and Peace Studies at Sydney University, Australia. Former Professor of Political and Administrative Studies at the University of Papua New Guinea, Author of *Australia and Nuclear Weapons; The Strategy of Total Withholding; Australia's Vietnam* and *From Rhetoric to Reality.* Co-editor, *Ethnicity and Conflict in a Post-Communist World: The Soviet Union, Eastern Europe and China.*

Stephanie Lawson. Post-Doctoral Fellow in the Department of Politics, University of New England, where she was previously a Lecturer. 1992 Poppleton Fellow at the Peace Research Centre, Australian National University. Author of many articles on politics in the Pacific. Her most recent book is *The Failure of Democratic Politics in Fiji.* Current research interests include ethnic nationalism, internal conflicts, democratic theory and the politics of tradition in the South Pacific.

J. Mohan Malik. Lecturer in Defence Studies, School of Australian and International Studies, Deakin University, Geelong, Australia. Author of *The Gulf War: Australia's Role and Asian-Pacific Responses; Chinese National Security and Nuclear Arms Control* and numerous articles on security issues in the Asia Pacific Region.

Peggy Mason. Canada's Ambassador for Disarmament. She represents Canada in a number of international forums dealing with arms control and disarmament issues including the First Committee of the United Nations and the UN Disarmament Commission. She is also mandated to engage in wide-ranging dialogue with interested members of the Canadian public and has chaired both national and regional consultations to this end. Based in Canada, she also participates in the development of Canadian Security policy, specialising on non-proliferation issues and the promotion of confidence-building measures in regional and sub-regional contexts.

Michael C. Pugh. Lecturer in International Relations, Department of Politics, University of Southampton and Director of the Mountbatten Centre's Naval Peacekeeping Project. He is the author of *The Anzus Crisis: Nuclear Visiting and Deterrence* and Editor of *European Security: Towards 2000,* plus numerous articles on defence and security issues. (He acknowledges the help of the ESRC Award R000.232.856 in the production of his chapter in this book.)

Llewelyn Richards. Editor for the New Zealand Council for Educational Research. Since 1980 Secretary to the National Consultative Committee on Disarmament – an NGO bringing major organisations such as the Combined Trade Unions, Churches and the National Council of Women together to lobby the government on peace, security and disarmament issues. In 1984 he won the print section of the Media Peace Prize with one of his many articles – that time on Peace Education

David Robie. Journalist and author writing on Asian and Pacific political and development issues. He is a former editor of the Melbourne *Sunday Observer* and has lived in several African countries and France. He is the coordinator of the Asia Pacific Network. Author of *UN Development Programme in the South Pacific; Eyes of Fire: The Last Voyage of the Rainbow Warrior; Blood on their Banner: Nationalist Struggles in the South Pacific* and Editor of *Tu Galala: Social Change in the Pacific.*

Daniel Skubik. Lecturer in International Business Relations at Griffith University, Brisbane, Australia and International Legal and Political Risk Analyst. His chapter on Nuclear Commerce in the Asia Pacific Region flows from a much larger data base project covering the transfer of nuclear technologies around the globe.

Wayne Robinson. Senior Lecturer in Politics, Waikato University, Hamilton, New Zealand. He has researched and written a number of articles on Asia Pacific political and economic themes with a particular focus on Japan and Indonesia. He is currently working exclusively on the Japanese political economy.

Yitzhak Shichor. Professor of Political Science the Hebrew University of Jerusalem and Dean of Students. He is a Specialist on Chinese Foreign Policy, and the Chinese Military. In addition to numerous articles/chapters on Chinese Foreign Policy, he is the author of *The Middle East in China's Foreign Policy* and *East Wind Over Arabia: Origins and Implications of the Sino-Saudi Missile Deal.*

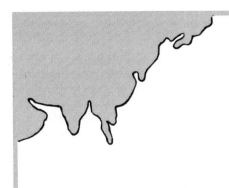

Index